"This innovative volume, which draws on a range of perspectives and case studies, demonstrates the synergy of bringing together heritage issues and development studies. The book reveals the myriad ways heritage and development are entangled and challenges the hegemonic practices and assumptions prevalent in each field. The concept of heritage is used to explore conceptualisations and experiences of 'progress' to challenge colonial practices in the Global South. I recommend this book to development and heritage studies scholars and practitioners interested in understanding how social and economic change is managed through appeals to the past that envisage productive and equitable futures."

Laurajane Smith, *Director, Centre for Heritage and Museum Studies, the Australian National University, Canberra*

CRITICAL APPROACHES TO HERITAGE FOR DEVELOPMENT

This book investigates the relationship between heritage and development from the global visions articulated by UNESCO and the Sustainable Development Goals (SDGs) to local activism, livelihood innovations and political strategies employed in diverse countries of the Global South.

In recent years, as culturally informed approaches to international development have become increasingly important, engaging with heritage has been seen as a way to draw on practices and meanings from the past to help build future development. This book gathers researchers and practitioners from across disciplines to address important themes such as health, the environment, sustainability, peace, security, tourism and economic growth. In doing so, the book asks us to consider whose past and whose future is ultimately at stake in efforts to use heritage for development. Key topics explored include histories and legacies of colonialism and calls for decolonisation, and related questions of expertise, ownership and agency.

Students, practitioners and researchers from across the broad areas of history, heritage, education, archaeology, geography and development studies will find this book an invaluable guide to dynamic and contested understandings of heritage and development and the relationship between them.

Charlotte Cross is a Senior Lecturer in International Development at The Open University, UK.

John D. Giblin is Keeper of Global Arts, Cultures and Design and Head of the Department of Global Arts, Cultures and Design at National Museums Scotland, UK.

RETHINKING DEVELOPMENT

Rethinking Development offers accessible and thought-provoking overviews of contemporary topics in international development and aid. Providing original empirical and analytical insights, the books in this series push thinking in new directions by challenging current conceptualizations and developing new ones.

This is a dynamic and inspiring series for all those engaged with today's debates surrounding development issues, whether they be students, scholars, policy makers and practitioners internationally. These interdisciplinary books provide an invaluable resource for discussion in advanced undergraduate and postgraduate courses in development studies as well as in anthropology, economics, politics, geography, media studies and sociology.

Arts and Culture in Global Development Practice
Expression, Identity and Empowerment
Edited by Ann Holt and Cindy Maguire

COVID-19 and Foreign Aid
Nationalism and Global Development in a New World Order
Edited by Viktor Jakupec, Max Kelly and Michael de Percy

Critical Approaches to Heritage for Development
Edited by Charlotte Cross and John D. Giblin

For more information about this series, please visit: www.routledge.com/Rethinking-Development/book-series/RDVPT

CRITICAL APPROACHES TO HERITAGE FOR DEVELOPMENT

Edited by Charlotte Cross and John D. Giblin

Routledge
Taylor & Francis Group
LONDON AND NEW YORK

Designed cover image: stellalevi

First published 2023
by Routledge
4 Park Square, Milton Park, Abingdon, Oxon OX14 4RN

and by Routledge
605 Third Avenue, New York, NY 10158

Routledge is an imprint of the Taylor & Francis Group, an informa business

British Library Cataloguing-in-Publication Data
A catalogue record for this book is available from the British Library

Library of Congress Cataloging-in-Publication Data
Names: Cross, Charlotte (Lecturer in international development), editor. |
Giblin, John D. (Curator), editor.
Title: Critical approaches to heritage for development / Charlotte Cross and John D. Giblin.
Description: Abingdon, Oxon ; New York, NY : Routledge, 2023. |
Series: Rethinking development | Includes bibliographical references and index.
Identifiers: LCCN 2022031032 (print) | LCCN 2022031033 (ebook) |
ISBN 9780367619756 (paperback) | ISBN 9780367619787 (hardback) |
ISBN 9781003107361 (ebook)
Subjects: LCSH: Sustainable development. | Economic development–Social aspects. |
Culture. | Cultural property.
Classification: LCC HC79.E5 .C7297 2023 (print) | LCC HC79.E5 (ebook) |
DDC 338.9/27–dc23/eng/20220818
LC record available at https://lccn.loc.gov/2022031032
LC ebook record available at https://lccn.loc.gov/2022031033

ISBN: 978-0-367-61978-7 (hbk)
ISBN: 978-0-367-61975-6 (pbk)
ISBN: 978-1-003-10736-1 (ebk)

DOI: 10.4324/9781003107361

Typeset in Bembo
by Newgen Publishing UK

CONTENTS

ILLUSTRATIONS

Figures

Table

CONTRIBUTORS

Abiti Nelson Adebo, National Museum of Uganda, Uganda.

Julian D. Bermeo, Deusto University, Spain.

Ananya Bhattacharya, Banglanatak Dot Com, India.

Robyn Bushell, Western Sydney University, Australia.

Arturo Charria, Comisión para el Esclarecimiento de la Verdad, la Convivencia y la No Repetición, Colombia.

Shadreck Chirikure, University of Cape Town, South Africa.

Charlotte Cross, The Open University, UK.

Harriet Deacon, University of Cape Town, South Africa and Coventry University, UK.

Tolulope Esther Fadeyi, University of Basel, Switzerland.

Nono Francis, National Memory and Peace Documentation Centre, Uganda.

John D. Giblin, National Museums Scotland and University College London, UK.

Rodney Harrison, University College London, UK.

Sandip Hazareesingh, The Open University, UK.

Pham Thi Thanh Huong, UNESCO, Viet Nam.

Ioanna Katapidi, University of Birmingham, UK.

Uma Kothari, University of Manchester, UK.

Sophia Labadi, University of Kent, UK.

Mark Lamont, The Open University, UK.

Paul J. Lane, University of Cambridge, UK.

Clare Melhuish, University College London, UK.

Lizzi O. Milligan, University of Bath, UK.

Kate Moles, Cardiff University, UK.

Maurice Mugabowagahunde, National Commission for the Fight Against Genocide, Rwanda.

Seggane Musisi, Makerere University, Uganda.

Rajat Nath, Banglanatak Dot Com, India.

André Ntagwabira, Rwanda Cultural Heritage Academy, Rwanda.

Anindita Patra, Banglanatak Dot Com, India.

Julia Paulson, University of Bristol, UK.

Yolana Pringle, University of Roehampton, UK.

Diego Rinallo, EM Lyon Business School, France.

Mike Robinson, Nottingham Trent University, UK.

Federica Sulas, University of Cambridge, UK.

June Taboroff, Independent Consultant.

Benedetta Ubertazzi, University of Milan-Bicocca, Italy.

Charlotte Waelde, University of Coventry, UK.

1

INTRODUCING HERITAGE FOR DEVELOPMENT

Practising the Past in the Pursuit of 'Progress'

Charlotte Cross and John D. Giblin

Introduction

Opened in 2016, the Kigali Convention Center, Rwanda, was reportedly the most expensive building in Africa at US $300 million. This hyper-modern, supposedly eco-friendly, building stands in part as a monument to Rwanda's aspirations, to its future, and its development on the road to that desired future. However, the design for the Convention Center, pictured on the front of this volume, is firmly rooted in Rwanda's precolonial heritage, with the central dome representing traditional royal residents and the outside walls of the Raddison Blu Hotel inspired by traditional Rwandan weaving (Briones, 2019). In this way, the Convention Center may be considered a visual statement about how Rwanda's development, its ideal future, is, officially at least, interwoven with dependent on the use of its past, a past which is being instrumentalised to steer and drive a future.

This is the theme of this volume and the focus of this introduction – the contemporary use of the inherited and constructed past, i.e., heritage, in myriad ways to contribute towards development in the so-called Global South.[1]

Relationships between culture and development have been widely recognised in scholarship and practice since at least the 1990s (Nederveen Pieterse, 1995; World Commission on Culture and Development, 1995; Rao and Walton, 2004; Radcliffe, 2006). Culture has been variously positioned as something to be understood in order to better implement development initiatives, as a property of the international development sector itself that shapes development outcomes, and as something that can be mobilised *for* development (Isar, 2014). As an aspect of the third type of relationship between culture and development, proponents of 'culture for development' have also identified a role for heritage, as an ostensibly past-looking aspect of culture, on which more sustainable and culturally appropriate futures may be built (World Commission on Culture and Development, 1995). This is reflected

DOI: 10.4324/9781003107361-1

in support for formalised heritage interventions and institutions (e.g., monuments, museums, architectural and archaeological sites, and memorial performances) as well as more general attempts to capitalise upon practices and meanings derived from the past as resources for more effective development (e.g., the institutionalisation of traditional and customary practices). For example: the United Nations Education Scientific and Cultural Organisation (UNESCO), has explicitly sought to align heritage practices with development agendas, such as the United Nations' (UN) Sustainable Development Goals (SDGs); the United Kingdom (UK) have promoted heritage approaches to development through government supported research opportunities, such as the Global Challenges Research Fund (GCRF) and the Newton Fund (NF); while countries such as Rwanda and Tanzania have incorporated precolonial institutions into postcolonial development policies (see Cross; Giblin, Mugabowagahunde and Ntagwabira, this volume).

Although large bodies of work within Heritage Studies and Development Studies demonstrate the diversity and complexity of what heritage and development might mean to different people in different places and times, and the extent to which such ideas are contested and contingent (e.g., Basu and Modest, 2014a; Labadi, 2020a), such critical understandings do not always inform attempts to instrumentalise heritage for development. For example, in terms of heritage projects that are driven by international development aims, there is a tendency to present heritage as something that is unproblematic, safe, static, and easily incorporated into existing strategies: just 'add heritage and stir' (Ashworth, 2014: 9). Similarly, heritage-led development initiatives often approach the idea of development as something that is self-evident, uncontested, and always desired. In response, this volume brings into conversation development and heritage practitioners and academics through chapters and opinion pieces in the broad areas of development studies, history, heritage, education, law, anthropology, and archaeology, that explore attempts to engender development in the Global South through engagement with the past. In so doing, the volume follows a broad definition of development as 'good change' (Chambers, 1997a), which accommodates dissonant understandings of what might be considered 'good', and a recognition that for some development can be destructive and undesirable. Our focus is largely on the pursuit of development as an 'intentional' practice (Cowen and Shenton, 1996), or an expression of the 'will to improve' (Li, 2007), although we recognise the connections between this 'big D' Development and broader 'small d' processes of social, political, and economic change (Hart, 2001; Lewis, 2019). We understand heritage as the use of the past in the present for contemporary and future needs as defined in diverse ways by different people (c.f. Harvey, 2001; Smith, 2006; Harrison, 2013; Ashworth, 2014; Schofield, 2014; Harrison et al., 2020; Holtorf and Högberg, 2020).

The volume introduces intersections between development and heritage across a range of thematic areas in which the past is increasingly being activated to provide 'better' futures. Rather than starting from different types of formalised heritage practices, or from specific development organisations or initiatives, the contributions to this volume are structured around related attributes that are typically valued as part of a good life: health (chapters by Fadeyi; Pringle and Musisi), education (Abiti, Milligan, Francis, and Moles; Bermeo, Paulson, and Charria), a sustainable environment (Hazareesingh; Lamont; Melhuish; Lane and Sulas), and peace and security (Cross; Giblin, Mugabowagahunde, and Ntagwabira), in addition to economic development and livelihoods (Huong and Bushell; Katapidi and Robinson; Waelde, Rinallo, Bhattacharya, Deacon, Patra, Nath, Taboroff, and Ubertazzi). The authors have reviewed scholarship and practice in their thematic field before drawing on their own research to interrogate contested ideas such as sustainability, inclusion, and participation, which animate appeals to heritage in the pursuit of development. Contributions for this volume were commissioned from a selection of speakers in a session of the same name as this chapter held at the 2019 Development Studies Association Conference, Open University, UK, and from non-participating authors who have filled thematic gaps not represented at that event. To offer more general critical reflections on the topic of heritage for development, leading scholars working in the fields of development and heritage and their intersections have produced shorter opinion-based contributions as an epilogue for the volume.

In this introduction, we distinguish this volume from other publications in the overlapping fields of culture, heritage, and development and describe how it builds on these existing publications, before summarising the recent and current state of heritage for development within international development. We then review critical perspectives on the formalised development and heritage 'industries', emphasising the extent to which authorised discourses of development and heritage often serve to depoliticise intensely contested processes, reproducing inequalities of power at different scales. This critique is then extended to consider their entanglements in heritage *for* development, and we suggest that articulations of heritage for development often fail to take into account the extent to which both heritage and development are dissonant processes, through which a range of actors pursue their own interests and ideas. The introduction concludes by summarising how heritage for development can productively be rethought as a common cultural production process, rather than as something easily amenable to instrumentalisation or to be achieved through the application of internationalised expertise.

Distinguishing heritage *for* development

This volume is distinct in its inclusive approach to what constitutes heritage for development. Other contributions to the discussion of development and heritage have focused on specific areas of the relationships between development and heritage, such as international aid (Labadi, 2020a) and related transnational mobilisations of heritage for transformative change (Lafrenz Samuels, 2018), the role of heritage in peacebuilding (Walters et al., 2017), or the potential for cultural institutions and heritage policies to drive development (Basu and Modest, 2014a). This volume builds on those publications by bringing into the discussion a range of actors and processes, at different scales, from UNESCO and the UN's SDGs to activism, livelihood strategies, and governance innovations at different scales in the Global South. These reflect diverse approaches to, and understandings of development and heritage, including 'big-H' heritage, such as museums, monuments and memorial performances, as well as other practices and interventions that may not be explicitly referred to as 'heritage' but nevertheless use the past as a development resource, such as the revival of precolonial traditions and customary practices. Similarly, contributions explore formalised initiatives and interventions associated with the professionalised international development sector and government development policy alongside the ways in which people think about, pursue, and negotiate development in their everyday lives. The aim of this volume is not to assess whether heritage can contribute to development, or to suggest how the past might better be mobilised for progress, but to explore how diverse actors are articulating and practising heritage for development and what the implications are.

Elsewhere, ideas of development and heritage have intersected in a variety of different ways in the separate, yet overlapping, disciplines of Heritage Studies, Cultural Studies, and Development Studies. For example, within Heritage Studies there have been regular discussions about the management and development of heritage sites and their potential to make economic contributions to societies and communities (Timothy and Nyaupane, 2009; Labadi and Logan, 2015; Larsen and Logan, 2018). However, while heritage tourism undoubtedly plays a dominant role in the way that the past is being activated for development, the focus on it obscures other ways in which the past is being mobilised within development practice. Similarly, Cultural Studies scholars have considered how the 'creative economy', through contemporary arts and art institutions, including museums, contributes to economic development (e.g., Clammer, 2015; Tan and Perleth, 2015; Stupples and Teaiwa, 2017; Cerisola, 2019). However, the 'creative economy' again focuses attention on economic contributions at the expense of other development issues and includes many institutions and actors that do not claim to draw on the past and thus does not engage specifically with the developmental potential of the past.

Within development studies, explicit engagement with heritage has also been limited, although heritage has been extensively discussed implicitly as an aspect of culture (Rao and Walton, 2004; Radcliffe, 2006) and as part of imagining 'alternatives to development' (Escobar, 1995). However, such analyses do not typically explore heritage in terms of the symbolic, political, or actual power of invoking the past in the present. Elsewhere, the importance of the past for international development practice has been considered in terms of critical reflections on the history of development as a discipline and practice, and how historical perspectives on development may illuminate contemporary development problems (Kothari, 2005a; Bayly et al., 2011). However, while the history of development, and indeed heritage informs this introduction and the chapters in the volume, here the focus is the more general, selective use of a sense of the past in the present for developmental aims.

Heritage *for* development drivers

Interest in the potential to use heritage for development in recent decades has been driven by recognition of the economic potential of heritage, the apparent compatibility of heritage with 'people-centred' and sustainable development, and through the co-option of heritage and development for foreign policy objectives. The adoption of the SDGs in 2015 also informs the context in which heritage is increasingly articulated as a potential contributor to development. Here we summarise those drivers and some key contemporary trends before reviewing more critical perspectives in the following section.

Economic development

The economic development potential of heritage has been the core driver of heritage for development for the past 40 years. Before the 1980s it was common for heritage to be viewed as an obstacle to development, something that needed to be negotiated to allow development to proceed, including traditions that were believed to be at odds with international development values, or remains that stood in the way of infrastructure projects (Wiktor-Mach, 2019). However, with the growth in popularity of heritage tourism from the 1980s onwards (see Wright, 1985; Hewison, 1987) the economic potential of heritage increasingly began to be recognised (Labadi, 2020b: 6). Today, as summarised by Ashworth (2014: 3, 9–11), there exist a 'rich variety of possibilities' for the instrumentalisation of the past for economic development, including: directly through the provision of 'resources for economic enterprises producing heritage products, often as part of a wider set of creative cultural industries producing heritage goods and services for sale' for example within heritage tourism; as well as indirectly contributing 'to the shaping of high amenity environments and place images and brands, promoted in internal or external markets in support of economic goals that are not directly concerned with the past.'

This shift is illustrated in the changing attitudes of the World Bank to heritage within its policy and programmes. Lafrenz Samuels (2020: 55–56; see also Lafrenz Samuels, 2018) has described how in the 1980s the World Bank initially took a 'do not harm the heritage' approach, influenced by their adoption of social and environmental safeguards drawn largely from cultural resource management laws in the USA. However, by the late 1990s, with the introduction of economically informed heritage significance assessments, economic value became the 'centrepiece of heritage at the World Bank' (Lafrenz Samuels, 2020: 56). Consequently, 'whereas cultural heritage was once seen as an *impediment to* the progress of development projects, during the late 1980s and 1990s cultural heritage underwent an important transformation at the World Bank and came to be seen as a *means for* development' (Lafrenz Samuels, 2020: 57; see also Labadi, 2020b; see Waelde et al., this volume for a discussion of heritage, economic development, and intellectual property).

Beyond development as economic growth

The economic potential of heritage remains the dominant way in which the past is instrumentalised for development. However, heritage-informed approaches have also received increased attention as part of shifts away from understanding and measuring development purely in terms of national economic growth, with growing interest in culturally-informed notions of 'well-being' and attempts to protect the environment and ways of living in it 'sustainably'. Heritage has also emerged both as a potential asset to be capitalised upon to make international development interventions more effective, and as representing alternatives to development as a Western-led and defined phenomenon.

Firstly, influenced by the work of Amartya Sen (1999) and others, dominant understandings of development have shifted from a focus on national economic indicators to more 'people-centred' ideas of development, encompassing a more holistic and diverse view of what constitutes a good life. In Sen's (1999) influential work, development is understood as a process of expanding people's substantive freedoms to live a life they value. Here economic growth might be a means to increase people's capabilities to be and do what they wish, but it is not the ultimate objective. The work of Sen and others on the 'capability approach' has informed attempts to encompass non-economic attributes in measuring development, such as access to education and health. The Human Development Index (HDI), produced each year by the United Nations Development Programme (UNDP), for example, considers a long and healthy life and the opportunity to be knowledgeable as important in shaping whether individuals can live a life they value, alongside their standard of living.

While indices like the HDI continue to rank countries based on national level statistical data against criteria set by UNDP, the expansion of development beyond economistic measures can also accommodate recognition of how cultural and historical diversity, and thus heritage, may shape ideas of what constitutes a good life. The 'cultural turn' (Nederveen Pieterse, 1995) in development since the 1990s thus reflects a recognition, if only rhetorical, of diversity in development trajectories and imaginings, contrary to the universalised trajectory towards 'Western' progress inherent to development as modernisation (Isar, 2014). Here culture, and cultural heritage, might be both a means to development, shaping how it is pursued, and an end, an integral part of what constitutes for many a valued life (Sen, 2004).

Attempts to measure 'well-being' as an alternative metric for evaluating development have incorporated subjective measures of quality of life, or 'happiness' alongside the 'objective' statistics considered in the HDI (e.g., Stiglitz, Sen and Fitoussi, 2009; Helliwell et al., 2021; Pringle and Musisi, this volume). While such approaches aggregate individual responses to extrapolate a picture of national well-being, qualitative understandings more fully recognise relational aspects of well-being, whereby relations with others, as well as broader normative frameworks and values about what a good life is and perceptions of material conditions and needs, inform assessments of whether one is doing and living well (White, 2010). Cultural heritage can thus be seen as important in shaping people's understandings of what well-being is and appraisals of their quality of life (Basu and Modest, 2014b).

Secondly, the idea of 'sustainable development' has become influential, if contested, since the 1980s, and is enshrined in the SDGs adopted by the UN General Assembly in 2015. Often defined, following a 1987 World Commission on Environment and Development (WCED) report, as 'development that meets the needs of the present, without compromising the ability of future generations to meet their own needs' (WCED, 1987: 43), sustainable development implies a concern with both intra- and intergenerational equity. The sustainability discourse thus has significant similarities to that of heritage preservation, whereby both natural and cultural resources are to be passed down to future generations (Throsby, 2003). Furthermore, the environment in which people live often has an important relationship to cultural heritage as well as livelihoods and well-being (Fadeyi; Lamont, this volume). The UN's *The Future We Want* resolution, for example, that informed the development of Agenda 2030 notes:

> We recognize that many people, especially the poor, depend directly on ecosystems for their livelihoods, their economic, social and physical well-being, and their cultural heritage. For this reason, it is essential to [...] promote sustainable livelihoods and practices and the sustainable use of natural resources and ecosystems.
>
> *United Nations General Assembly, 2012: 6*

Past ways of living have also been framed as potentially more sustainable and in sync with natural ecosystems, thus as offering a potential resource to learn from in contemporary adaptation and mitigation efforts in those locations and elsewhere (Hazareesingh; Lane and Sulas, this volume). In addition to environmental sustainability, taking greater account of culture has also been seen as a way to make development itself more sustainable as part of engagement with the context in which initiatives are implemented (Lafrenz Samuels, 2018: 68).

Thirdly, there has been an impetus towards 'localisation' of development since the 1980s, through increased support for various forms of 'community' involvement in development via participation and decentralisation, reflecting a response against 'top-down' development planning and a recognition, in principle, that people should shape their own development (Mansuri and Rao, 2013). In theory, supporting community-based development allows greater scope for diverse institutions that are based on locally appropriate ways of doing things and will generate more sustainable outcomes (Ostrom, 1990), while privileging the knowledge of 'communities' over that of 'experts' (Chambers, 1997b). Over the same period, community engagement and participation have become key aspects of contemporary heritage practice, perceived as an 'ethical obligation' for academics and practitioners in the field (Labadi and Gould, 2015: 202). The ubiquity of participation in heritage and development sectors individually is thus reflected in heritage for development initiatives (see Labadi and Gould, 2015; Lafrenz-Samuels, 2020: 63; Abiti et al.; Cross; Huong and Bushell; Katapidi and Robinson; Lamont, this volume). More broadly, incorporating heritage into development initiatives offered a means for large development organisations, such as international development banks, to demonstrate they were responding to criticism of existing models (Lafrenz Samuels, 2018). Incorporating reference to heritage offers a means to frame development as more locally rooted, attuned to context, and culturally appropriate. The British Council, for example, describe heritage as one of a set of 'powerful tools' with which to pursue 'alternative approaches to the applied, top-down solutions that are often seen in traditional international development practice' (British Council, 2021a).

Fourth, recognition of the limitations of the imposition of standardised templates for development based on Western models, and particularly the 'good governance' agenda, has also informed a growth in interest in attempts to 'go with the grain' (Booth and Cammack, 2013). This refers to the idea that development interventions should seek to harness existing practices, often described in terms of 'culture', 'custom', or 'tradition', to stimulate collective action for development. Such ideas inform work in a range of development sectors including governance and service delivery, management of natural resources, and post-conflict 'peacebuilding' (Cleaver et al., 2013; Mac Ginty and Richmond, 2013; Cross, this volume). Heritage is thus positioned as a means to render development more sustainable and legitimate, but also as a pragmatic way to address limited state capacity. Within the international development sector enthusiasm for such approaches has grown over the past decade, although it should be noted that attempts by colonial administrations and governments to instrumentalise heritage for development through the co-optation of customary institutions have a much longer history (Verweijen and Van Bockhaven, 2020).

Finally, greater impetus to consider heritage within understandings of what a good life might mean has come from post-development critiques of development itself. Post-development is premised upon the pursuit of 'alternatives to development', which are rooted in diverse local cultures and knowledges, rather than an assumed universal Western trajectory (Escobar, 1995: 215). The idea of a 'pluriverse', referring to a 'world in which many worlds fit' foregrounds such alternative perspectives and ideas of what a better life might look like and how it could be achieved (Kothari et al., 2019a: xxviii). Here, philosophies, values, and strategies informed by diverse cultures and histories are positioned alongside more recent social and political movements as holding transformative potential (Kothari et al., 2019b).

Securitisation and soft power

Heritage and international development aid have also converged in recent decades when heritage has been co-opted to support foreign policy objectives, as part of strategies aimed at bolstering 'soft power' and as part of the wider securitisation of development. The relationship between support for heritage preservation and diplomacy is well-established in the literature (Winter, 2015; Thiaw and Ly, 2020). Logan (2020: 165), for example, has described how patchy Australian funding for overseas heritage projects in the 1980s and 1990s largely resulted from the actions of individual Australian politicians following their visits to Asian historic city centres, or by Australian ambassadors posted to Asian countries, both 'motivated by the desire to strengthen bilateral relationships'. In heritage for development initiatives, such objectives are sometimes made explicit, for example, by the UK's National Commission for UNESCO, whereby the potential for heritage research and projects to contribute towards the UK's international development efforts is discussed as a means of maintaining the country's soft power, with projects envisaged as 'ambassadors for the UK's global aspirations' (UNESCO, 2019a: p. 34). The future of heritage for development funding will thus be shaped by the shifting geopolitics of foreign aid and investment, as well as negotiations of power within international organisations such as UNESCO (Winter, 2014; Wiktor-Mach, 2019).

Heritage has also become implicated in the securitisation of development over the past two decades, whereby 'underdevelopment' in the Global South is framed as generating insecurity, both in the country concerned and crucially in donor countries. In some cases, heritage has been leveraged in an attempt to more successfully implement security and development interventions. Following the terrorist attacks of September 11th 2001, for example, in contexts with majority Muslim populations, engagement with the 'right' kind of religious leaders became central to many externally-led development interventions with diverse objectives (Tadros and Sabates-Wheeler, 2020: 17–18). At the same time, development assistance aimed at protecting heritage 'at risk' has also grown, reflecting the foreign policy priorities and security concerns of donor states (Foradari, Giusti and Lamonica, 2018; Russo and Giusti, 2019). The UK's Official Development Assistance (ODA)-funded Cultural Protection Fund (CPF) exemplifies this trend, aiming to 'help to create sustainable opportunities for economic and social development through building capacity to foster, safeguard and promote cultural heritage' (British Council, 2021b), in conflict-affected countries in North Africa and the Middle East.

Sustainable Development Goals and challenge-led heritage

The emergence of people-centred, sustainable, local, and 'bottom-up' approaches to development, in addition to its utility in relation to diplomatic and security objectives, have provided the context for the adoption of heritage as a development option in addition to its economic potential. Aligned with this shift, the public discourse and practice of heritage for development can most clearly be seen in the work of UNESCO and recent attempts to position heritage as something that can be mobilised to address the UN SDGs (see Katapidi and Robinson; Lamont, this volume). UNESCO's promotion of heritage for development is unsurprising because it is the UN agency responsible for development through education, science, and culture (for summaries of UNESCO's history of promoting the importance of culture and development see Isar, 2014; Wiktor-Mach, 2019; De Beukelaer and Vlassis, 2020; Labadi, 2020c). It is also unsurprising that the UNESCO-led heritage for development discourse centres on the ambition that heritage should address aspects of the UN's 17 SDGs, which, having been ratified by 193 countries, have for many become *the* development agenda.

The uncritical acceptance of the SDGs as the sole way of conceptualising development will be discussed in more detail later in this chapter, but one consequence is that development agencies such as UNESCO have been forced to find synergies between their portfolios and the UN's targets as part of asserting the relevance of their portfolio and seeking to secure financial support (Wiktor-Mach, 2019). This is a challenge that UNESCO have negotiated by identifying and articulating for themselves implicit connections between heritage, culture, and the SDGs in the absence of a more explicit articulation within Agenda 2030. Indeed, heritage is only mentioned once under Goal 11 'Make cities and human settlements inclusive, safe, resilient and sustainable', Target 11.4 'Strengthen efforts to protect and safeguard the world's cultural and natural heritage'. In addition, culture, within which heritage might be considered implicit, is also only briefly mentioned in Targets 8.9 and 12.b in relation to 'sustainable tourism that creates jobs and promotes local culture and products'; and Target 4.7, through the educative 'promotion of a culture of peace and non-violence, global citizenship and appreciation of cultural diversity and of culture's contribution to sustainable development'. Thus, in the SDGs heritage has undefined value for human settlements, while culture is only understood to have the potential to provide economic benefits through sustainable tourism as well as being something people should be educated about to promote peaceful, diverse societies (for a discussion of the absence of culture and heritage in the SDGs and their precursor, the Millennium Development Goals, and the failure of UNESCO's campaigning to have them included, see Labadi, 2020c: 73, 80).

Organisations such as UNESCO, who have a vested interest in development and heritage, and moreover a belief that heritage as an aspect of culture has a role to play in development, have thus made considerable efforts to make the case for how heritage can address the SDGs. For example, in addition to the SDGs already cited, UNESCO have argued that culture addresses: SDG 3: Health and Wellbeing, because interventions will be more successful if they respond to cultural contexts; SDG 5: Gender Equality, because women are often employed in creative industries; SDG 10: Reducing Inequalities within and between countries by promoting locally-produced cultural goods; SDG 13: Climate Action by drawing on 'local knowledge of ecosystem management, natural resource extraction and local materials'; and SDG 16: Peace Justice and Strong institutions by promoting respect for cultural diversity (Hosagrahar, 2017; see also Giblin et al., this volume for a discussion of how UNESCO has articulated the relevance of post-conflict heritage to the SDGs). For UNESCO then, engagement with culture, and by extension heritage, is required to deliver development more effectively. In addition, the association of heritage with the SDGs has been enthusiastically taken up elsewhere in the heritage sector, for example, the International Council on Monuments and Sites (ICOMOS) (Labadi et al., 2021) have published policy guidance that sets out how heritage can contribute to all 17 SDGs.

An example of how the UNESCO-led discourse of heritage for the SDGs has been put into practice is the related research activities supported by the UK's GCRF and NF. The GCRF was a five year £1.5 billion grant programme administered by UK Research and Innovation (UKRI), which was set up in 2016 with the explicit aim of addressing the SDGs through research-led development as part of the UK's ODA. Although the £735 million NF was established before the SDGs, to provide match-funded development aid to specific countries, it is also a form of ODA and has increasingly been promoted in parallel with the GCRF. Most GCRF heritage research funding was provided by the UKRI's Arts and Humanities Research Council (AHRC) and the results of this funding programme have been summarised in a report reviewing AHRC-supported research projects funded through the GCRF and NF, *Heritage for Global Challenges* (Giliberto, 2021). This report, which also had the patronage of the UK National Commission for UNESCO, highlighted the relative absence of heritage in the SDGs and sought to address that by demonstrating how ODA money had supported international development through heritage research. The projects within the report can be largely characterised as heritage-led ones founded on the assumption that if you preserve and present formalised tangible and intangible heritage and educate the community about them then local and national benefits will follow. Of the 87 projects surveyed, covering 49 countries, and funded to £21 million, the report made links between individual projects and all 17 SDGs, grouped under 12 thematic headings, including: inclusive and sustainable cities (28 projects); digitisation, innovation, and technology (22); poverty alleviation and sustainable socio-economic development (25); balancing heritage and conservation and development (18); human rights, inequality reduction, and minorities' inclusion (17); adaptation to climate and environmental change (16); food security and sustainable agriculture (15); global health and well-being (13); inclusive equitable and quality education (13); disaster response and resilience (10); gender equality (10); and sustainable management of landscapes, ecosystems, and biodiversity (7).

Heritage for Global Challenges echoes many of the assumptions and findings of earlier UNESCO sponsored reports (e.g., UNESCO, 2019a), which reflect a concern to increase the profile and visibility of heritage within development debates. Indeed, bemoaning the absence of funding for heritage for development is a key element of these reports and the primary reason driving their publication as they aim to provide evidence to support future funding (see also Henderson, 2019: 22; Labadi, 2020d). One of the reasons given for the low profile, and thus limited funding, attributed to heritage within such debates is the difficulty in measuring the contribution heritage can make to development, necessitating attention to ways to better evidence impact (e.g., UNESCO, 2019a). Thus, UNESCO has produced Culture for Development Indicators to 'demonstrate through empirical data culture's role as both a driver and enabler of sustainable development processes' (UNESCO, 2014: 5). Subsequent Thematic Indicators for Culture in the 2030 Agenda (UNESCO, 2019b: 16) were intended partly to 'make visible culture's contribution to sustainable development', in order to strengthen advocacy efforts (see also Lamont, this volume).

Critical perspectives on development, heritage, and heritage *for* development

This section summarises some critical perspectives on the respective formalised practices of development, heritage, and heritage *for* development. In so doing, it highlights the shared roots and comparable trajectories of formalised international development and heritage, which have contributed to their cross-pollination as heritage for development in the late 20th and early 21st centuries. For example, the formalisation of both international development and heritage can be traced to European Enlightenment and colonial ideas of progress, rationality, racial, and moral superiority and responsibility to raise up those people and societies deemed to be lower in both race and class as part of a universalising modernity. This is an observation that has particular relevance for this volume, which is concerned with the postcolonial Global South. Furthermore, by the late 20th and early 21st centuries, powerful, globalised, authorised, or authorising, positivist discourses had come to dominate the respective industries of development and heritage based on the same universalising modernity spread in part through colonial and neocolonial polices. Finally, in response to the critique of universalism, alternatives emerged that promote local, culturally-contextual, community-based understandings of development and heritage, providing fertile, but no-less political nor necessarily less neocolonial, ground for their contemporary convergence.

Respective critiques of these parallel paths have highlighted how dominant discourses have operated to depoliticise and naturalise development and heritage when both are inherently political and contested practices and processes. A key observation of this section is that, despite widespread awareness of these well-established critiques, heritage for development continues to be presented as an apolitical option, rather than as implicated in complex and often unequal negotiations of the past and the future.

Development

The origins of international development are often located in the early post-Second World War period, with the establishment of the Bretton Woods institutions and US President Truman's 1949 inauguration speech, in which he called for a 'bold new program for making the benefits of our scientific advances and industrial progress available for the improvement and growth of underdeveloped areas' (Truman, 1949). While this 'rather shortened version of history' (Kothari, 2005b: 51) has remained influential within Development Studies teaching and scholarship, historical and postcolonial perspectives reveal longer genealogies of development as an idea and practice, and demonstrate the importance of histories and legacies of

European colonialism in generating the relationships and structures through which development takes place today.

The idea of development as a process of improvement over time can be traced back to the European Enlightenment in the 17th and 18th centuries, its emergence informed by associated notions of modernity and progress, as well as the superiority of European 'civilisation' (McEwan, 2018: 100–104). Cowen and Shenton (1996) outline how subsequently development came to be conceptualised as an intentional practice in 19th century Europe, where it was conceived as a means to impose order on the disruptive consequences of 'progress' realised through industrialisation, such as poverty, urbanisation, and unemployment. Fear of disorder associated with potentially destabilising change also provided an impetus for the pursuit of development in European colonial territories, where 'the extraction of resources and labour from the colonies required new forms of social control of subject populations in both metropolitan and colonial regions' (McEwan, 2018: 108). In Africa, for example, appeals to development intensified in the 1940s, after earlier resistance to articulation of development as an explicit policy aim, as colonial administrations hoped development might 'reinvigorate colonialism' in the face of challenges linked to labour unrest and demands for self-determination (Cooper, 1998: 64; Cooper, 2010). In colonies, as in early industrial Europe, development was to be achieved through forms of 'trusteeship', whereby those who viewed themselves as sufficiently 'developed' were to foster and direct the development of others (Cowen and Shenton, 1996).

The legacies of such ways of thinking about and practising development, and the power relations they imply, shaped the emergence of international development as a professionalised sector after the Second World War, over a period in which many former colonies gained independence, complicating attempts to neatly demarcate colonialism and development as distinct historical periods (Kothari, 2005b). Continuities were particularly explicit in some articulations of 'modernisation theory' from the 1950s (Cooper, 2010), which located European and North American countries at the pinnacle of a hierarchy of development, with less developed nations to be helped to replicate Western trajectories to modernity. Although such terminology is not typically used today, post-development critiques of development as an idea have identified the discursive continuities through which colonialism and development are legitimised, predicated upon 'the division of the world into a progressive, superior part, and a backward, inferior part' (Ziai, 2017: 33). While former colonial powers continue to dominate production of knowledge about 'development' and how it happens, those to be 'developed', in the Global South, are in contrast denied agency, positioned 'as if waiting for the (white) Western hand to help subjects along … not infrequently hungry, illiterate, needy and oppressed by its own stubbornness, lack of initiative, and traditions' (Escobar, 1995: 8). Importantly, the 'mythology' that underpins development as conceived in this way, as something that can and should be solved by 'the West' doing more, reflects a prevalent 'colonial amnesia' (Rutazibwa, 2019: 165), which occludes the historical role of today's aid donors in producing contemporary 'underdevelopment' (Rodney, 1972).

One of the ways through which colonial forms of power and knowledge are maintained is through depoliticising discourses that privilege the knowledge of development 'experts'. Ferguson (1990) argues that development operates as an 'anti-politics machine', whereby complex political issues, such as unemployment or distribution of land, are reframed as technical challenges amenable to technical solutions. Thus, historical and structural factors that appear outside of the remit of a planned intervention, including those associated with colonialism, are ignored. Through 'rendering technical' complex social problems, development interventions reassert boundaries between those who are to be developed and those with expertise to prescribe solutions (Li, 2007). With the emergence of a professionalised international development sector, such expertise became increasingly based not on knowledge of particular social and historical contexts, but on understanding of ideas about how to do development 'that masquerade as universal but are, in fact, particularly Western' (Kothari, 2005c: 437), and thus hierarchies of power and knowledge within development continue to be highly racialised (Kothari, 2006; Pailey, 2020).

While interventions based on depoliticised constructions of development problems often fail to achieve their stated goals, they do have political effects, increasing the authority of experts and enabling locally powerful actors, such as state authorities or political parties, to extend their influence (Ferguson, 1990). Postcolonial governments or political movements have also found apolitical constructions of development to be useful in delegitimising political opposition, evident within both 'developmental nationalisms' of the early post-independence period (Desai, 2008) and contemporary 'developmental authoritarianism' (Matfess, 2015). However, depoliticising discourses are not all-powerful and uncontested. While French and British colonial administrations, for example, sought to bolster their legitimacy through implementing technocratic development projects, the language of development was appropriated and reformulated by anti-colonial movements in making their own political demands (Cooper, 2010). Thus, development is also constituted by the 'practice of politics', whereby authorised formulations of problems and relationships of trusteeship are challenged (Li, 2007). Indeed, 'the meaning, direction, and control of development are at the heart of contentious politics, bound up with identity, place and belonging' (Mosse, 2013: 230). Thus, contemporary post-development work calls for a 'repoliticisation' of debates about social and economic transformation, referring to rejection of a universal Western-inspired path to 'progress' in favour of 'collaboration between dissenting voices over the kinds of alternative worlds we want to create' (Kothari et al., 2019a: xxi).

As outlined above, critiques of 'top-down' and expert-led models of development led to the emergence of participatory or community-based development in the 1980s, which aimed to privilege 'grassroots' knowledge and enable 'local' agency. Since then, participation has ascended to 'development orthodoxy' (Cornwall, 2006: 62), in part because of the elasticity and ambiguity of the concept, which enables it to attract support from diverse actors with very different objectives (Mosse, 2004). Although conceived as a counterpoint to technocratic development projects, participation has also been subject to the standardisation of sets of practices and institutional forms and the recognition of 'expertise' in how to implement them, in fact further privileging the dominance of the Western expert knowledge they were ostensibly intended to destabilise (Cooke and Kothari, 2001). Uncritical enthusiasm for participation is also vulnerable to neglecting power inequalities *within* 'communities' and between communities and the state, with important implications for how sustainable or inclusive participation can be (Gujit and Shah, 1998; Mohan and Stokke, 2000; Mansuri and Rao, 2013).

More recently recognition of the importance of politics and the limitations of technical approaches to development has grown within the international development sector, generating enthusiasm for 'thinking and working politically' (e.g., Menochal et al., 2018) or 'doing development differently' (e.g., Wild et al., 2016). This might entail incorporating analysis of political economy into programme design and a commitment to adaptive management of projects that is responsive to changing political context. However, even these efforts have to some extent been limited by attempts to apply standardised toolkits and continuing incentives for application of technical models, and there is limited evidence that they have improved development outcomes (Fisher and Marquette, 2014; Laws and Marquette, 2018; Whitty, 2019; McCulloch and Piron, 2019). More fundamentally, such initiatives tend to emphasise understanding political context in order to 'do development better', rather than a more fundamental reappraisal of development as a political process and the positioning of donors and 'experts' within that. This may be particularly pressing as in some contexts, such as the UK, international development policy has become more explicitly linked to supporting UK economic and strategic interests in recent years in ways that reproduce colonial policies and objectives (Noxolo, 2017; McEwan, 2018: 130–131).

Agenda 2030 and the SDGs represent to some extent a reframing of development away from international development and towards development as a global concern. The SDGs are goals for all countries to meet, rather than only 'poor' countries. Some of the goals recognise the impact of factors such as tax evasion on perpetuating inequality, rather than locating solutions only in overseas development aid. Southern actors were influential in shaping the norms embedded in the SDGs (Fukuda-Parr and Muchhala, 2020), and in ensuring the expectations placed on countries reflected their different resources and capacities (Muchhala, 2014). However, the SDGs have also been criticised on grounds similar to those outlined in this section, as legitimising extractive and exploitative neocolonial interventions, perpetuating the neoliberal model of development promoted by Western development organisations, and masking continued unequal power relations between development experts and 'beneficiaries' through the language of 'participation' (Enns, Bersaglio and Kepe, 2014; Kumi, Arhin and Yeboah, 2014; Langan, 2017; Ziai, 2017). By privileging technical and managerial knowledge and quantitative indicators, the goals perpetuate the separation of development challenges from their structural and systemic causes and strip important concepts and principles of their political meanings and implications (Belda-Miquel, Boni and Calabuig, 2019; Fukuda-Parr and McNeill, 2019).

Heritage

Formalised, official heritage can be characterised as various state-sanctioned practices that value, preserve, and present aspects of the past to promote selected historical narratives for political, economic, or social ends. This typically includes the preservation and promotion of sites, objects, and traditions, alongside the creation and commemoration, or celebration, of monuments and performances as memorials to past people or events. For example, Smith (2006) has shown how the idea of heritage as something from the past to be preserved by states, or state-sanctioned organisations, for the universal benefit of present and future generations, emerged in 19th century Europe. At that time, the results of the industrial revolution were destabilising traditional identities and new nationally unifying ones were being sought through selective recourse to the past. In parallel, Enlightenment ideas of European racial superiority, rationality, progress, and international moral duty underpinned a sense of a 'universalizing modernity', which was to be shared with the world through the expansion of European colonial empires. Thus, those things from the past that appeared to demonstrate European, i.e., white, superiority, and progress were to be valued and preserved. In addition, European nations jostled for individual superiority by comparing past cultural accomplishments, evidenced in national collections of things from the past, i.e., objects, buildings, and sites, around and through which celebratory national narratives were constructed (Smith, 2006: 17–18).

Across Europe and North America over the 19th century, a series of organisations emerged that campaigned for the preservation of archaeological and architectural sites and natural and cultural landscapes (Smith, 2006; Harrison, 2013). These organisations promoted the preservation of tangible things that encapsulated the values that the liberal elites who had established them believed were required by present societies in terms of national and moral education, unification, and celebration. Pressure from these organisations contributed to the proliferation of national heritage legislation across Europe in the 19th and early 20th centuries, which was then replicated and globalised through European colonial empires (see Basu and Damodaran, 2015). Colonial heritage legislation was subsequently maintained following the return to independence after the end of colonial rule and while postcolonial heritage legislation has been introduced in some countries, in many cases it is still based on formalised ideas of heritage introduced under colonial rule (Giblin, 2018).

The globalisation of formalised heritage was further advanced by the creation of UNESCO in 1946 and related international heritage legislation after the end of the Second World War. Of special relevance for the globalisation of European and North American heritage values was the creation of The International Council on

Monuments and Sites (ICOMOS) and their Venice Charter in 1964 and UNESCO's World Heritage Convention in 1972 and the consequent World Heritage List. ICOMOS' Venice Charter enshrined European conservation ideals for all its signatories by setting out what should be preserved and how, while the World Heritage List confirmed what was of global, universal heritage value. In terms of cultural criteria, the List quickly became dominated by tangible, monumental, archaeological, and architectural sites, largely located in Europe or sites located elsewhere that fulfilled a European aesthetic of civilisation. Criticism of the World Heritage List, largely led by heritage actors in the Global South whose heritage often did not meet UNESCO's criteria, has since led to the creation of UNESCO's List of Intangible Heritage and its predecessors. Nevertheless, there remains a sense that a global, universal heritage exists, which can be objectively assessed, owned, preserved, managed, and used (Smith, 2006; Harrison, 2013; Fredheim and Khalaf, 2016).

In parallel to the globalisation of European and North American heritage values, from the 1980s onwards heritage increasingly became commercialised through urban regeneration projects and heritage tourism. At the time, the critique of heritage for economic development centred on inauthentic, inaccurate representations of the past that were supposedly products of market-led dumbing down or 'Disneyfication', or were politically motivated, selective, and exclusionary with the aim of creating politically palatable national identities (for critiques of the commercialisation and politicisation of heritage in the UK in the 1980s see Wright, 1985; Hewison, 1987; see also Harrison, 2013: 98–101; see also Hall, 1999). For example, in terms of market forces, heritage tourism created an 'economically driven desire to maintain static stereotypical forms of "culture"' that tourists were interested in consuming (Harrison, 2013: 83; see also Huong and Bushell, this volume). However, as Harrison (2013: 84–88) has suggested, heritage tourism conservativism is being challenged by the rise in the experience economy, which demands a multiplicity of touristic experiences and thus heritages, if not necessarily historical accuracy within those experiences.

Smith (2006) has described how the nationalisation, globalisation, and commercialisation of European and North American heritage values contributed towards the emergence of a powerful Authorised Heritage Discourse (AHD). Through the privileging of a narrow set of bodies of heritage expertise (e.g., archaeologists, architects, historians), the AHD regulates, maintains, depoliticises, and naturalises elite, typically white, heritage values as an aspect of a universalising modernity (see also Hall, 1999; Harrison, 2013; Basu and Modest, 2014b; Högberg, 2015). This occurs at the expense of working class, diaspora and/or, Indigenous values. In addition, the AHD

> focuses attention on aesthetically pleasing material objects, sites, places and/or landscapes that current generations 'must' care for, protect and revere so that they may be passed to nebulous future generations for their 'education', and to forge a sense of common identity based on the past.
>
> *Smith, 2006: 29*

In so doing, by emphasising our moral duty to protect heritage for future generations through the application of expertise, the AHD distances contemporary populations from formalised heritage.

Increasingly heritage universality, objectivity, and positivism have been challenged by alternative ideas that highlight the agency, subjectivity, intangibility, fluidity, performativity, dissonance, locality, politics, and future-orientatedness of heritage as a common cultural production process (Ashworth, 1997, 2014; Graham, Ashworth and Tunbridge, 2000; Smith, 2006; Harrison, 2013). As explained by Harrison (2013: 2),

> [h]eritage is not a passive process of simply preserving things from the past that remain, but an active process of assembling a series of objects, places and practices that we choose to hold up as a mirror to the present, associated with a particular set of values that we wish to take with us into the future.

In this understanding, heritage is something that is performed actively, subjectively, and politically, both by individuals and collectives, as they shape the present for imagined futures. Furthermore, whether at local, national, or international scales, it will always be inclusionary for some and exclusionary for others. In addition, it may be 'authorised' or subversive, formal or informal, but it will always involve power and will be political, whether it is imposed from the top-down by governments or created from the bottom-up by local communities, as people attempt to control what should be remembered and what should be forgotten. At the time of writing, for example, postcolonial power relations are being renegotiated through highly politicised so-called 'culture wars', centred on the retention, removal, or reinterpretation of statuary celebrations of colonial era figures in places like South Africa, Ghana, the UK, Canada, Australia, and the USA (e.g., Shepherd, 2020). This is a political struggle over the right to remember that is being fought as much between different local communities of interest at the ground level as it is between governments and heritage institutions (e.g., see Giblin, Ramos and Grout, 2019; Wingfield, Giblin and King, 2020).

Nevertheless, despite the academic acceptance of a more comprehensive, critical and complex sense of heritage, many of the heritage perspectives and contradictions central to the AHD's universalising modernity persist in national legislation and international policies and practice. In addition, the reaction against the AHD has led to the uncritical promotion of bottom-up, grassroots, or local heritage as the panacea for all aspects of the AHD (for critical perspectives on community heritage see Crooke, 2010; Waterton and Smith, 2010; Waterton and Watson, 2011). In these models, community participation and capacity building are promoted within the context of support for more locally, culturally, and contextually appropriate and thus sustainable heritage initiatives (see Lafrenz Samuels, 2018; Labadi, 2020b). However, while these bottom-up initiatives present a challenge to the universalised, top-down heritage practices of the AHD, they can also be exclusionary and shaped by political interests, only at a different scale. Furthermore, bottom-up community approaches are typically entangled with top-down ones, for example through funding or training. Thus, just as the AHD depoliticises and naturalises top-down heritage practices, community, participatory, heritage responses often depoliticise bottom-up heritage practices, when heritage is inherently political and dissonant at all levels.

The identification of the AHD has provided a powerful explanation for how a certain set of official heritage values has come to be regulated and maintained at national and global scales, while its critique has highlighted the inequalities, contradictions and beneficiaries produced by the privileging of these values (Smith, 2006). In seeking to understand the parallel proliferation and popularity of heritage in recent decades, Harrison (2013: 1–3; see also Lowenthal, 1985 for an earlier discussion of the rise of heritage as a response to political and economic change occurring in the 1970s) has observed how the contemporary 'abundance of heritage' may be understood in terms of an equally abundant sense of uncertainty, crisis, and risk in our late-modern world. Harrison (2013: 3) has argued that this is the product of 'the sense of speed and rate of late-modern technological, social, and environmental change', 'the pervading sense of uncertainty that accompanies a series of social, economic, humanitarian, political and environmental emergencies', and 'the rise of the experience economy' amongst other factors. These observations are relevant for this discussion of the convergence of development and heritage for three reasons. Firstly, like development, heritage is a response to local, national and global crises, uncertainties, and risks. Secondly, the rise of the experience economy provides the primary economic basis for heritage for development through heritage tourism. Thirdly, these concerns converge with developmental questions of cultural and environmental instability that require responses from the supposedly more sustainable past.

In summary, formalised heritage may appear to be past looking but was founded upon the principle of preserving the past as evidence of, and a way of managing progress that maintained elite, white values and position in a constructed global, racial, and cultural hierarchy (see also Basu and Modest, 2014b: 2–4). Formalised heritage then became globalised through colonisation and postcolonial post-Second World War international agencies and today it is maintained and regulated through the existence of an AHD as an unquestionable, uncontested, depoliticised, natural, good thing to be identified and managed by experts for the benefit of the future. In addition, formalised heritage acts as an official, managed response to uncertainty, risk, crises, and, ultimately, rapid change in late-modernity, for which there is broad, popular support for different heritages within societies that are experiencing those changes. In these ways, formalised, authorised heritage has considerable parallels with international development. This includes: both being founded on elite, racial ideas of managing progress; comparable trajectories, timings and mechanisms of globalisation; shared contemporary concern with yet unrealised future generations; depoliticisation through technical expertise; and functioning both as drivers and responses to change, 'as both a product of Western [universalising] modernity and as a constituent part of that modernity' (Basu and Modest, 2014b: 6; Harrison, 2013).

In addition, the reaction against the universalising, top-down, exclusory practices of both development and heritage has led to the promotion of locally, culturally, and contextually specific alternatives based on participation and sustainability that are also exclusionary and political.

Heritage for development

In this subsection we draw on the foregoing respective discussions of development and heritage to highlight some critical questions emerging from their entanglements in heritage for development. We suggest that articulations of heritage for development can perpetuate the depoliticisation of these complex and contested ideas and processes, as outlined above, and that the emergence of recognised expertise and 'best practice' in using heritage to do development better may contradict the ostensible aims of localising and diversifying development. Furthermore, the political effects of heritage for development can be exclusionary and exacerbate inequalities, including those linked to colonial power relations.

Firstly, echoing Ferguson's (1990) 'anti-politics machine' of development or the AHD identified by Smith (2006), current formalisations of heritage for development often embed depoliticising narratives that obscure the extent to which both heritage and development are contested value-laden terms, whose realisation occurs through political processes shaped by unequal power relations. Recalling Li's (2007) discussion of 'rendering technical', heritage for development initiatives often present the act of using the past for a better future as an undertaking which can be best done by experts in accordance with universalised models derived from 'developed' countries with well-established formal heritage sectors and long experience of disbursing development aid. The UK National Commission for UNESCO, for example, in reviewing the opportunities for UK cultural heritage innovation to inform international development, presents recommendations for how to 'better deploy the UK's outstanding expertise in working with cultural heritage assets, to advance the economic and social welfare of ODA countries' (UNESCO, 2019a: 7). The instrumentalisation of heritage for development is ostensibly intended to recognise the diverse and culturally specific ways in which people practice the past and imagine the future. However, the imperative to identify 'best practice' policy models to be transplanted elsewhere (Lafrenz Samuels, 2009; Cross, this volume) and difficulties that arise when expressions of cultural diversity conflict with a framework of universalised ethics (Basu and Zetterstrom-Sharp, 2014) are indicative of a broader tension at the heart of heritage for development.

Heritage for development as a technical and neutral undertaking is further reinforced by its 'projectisation' (Nardella and Mallinson, 2014) and through attempts to increase policy impact and show effectiveness through adopting quantitative modes of measurement, such as UNESCO's Culture for Development Indicators (CDIS) (UNESCO, 2014) and Thematic Indicators for Culture in the 2030 Agenda (UNESCO, 2019b). Already widely used within both development and heritage fields, indicators have an aura of technical neutrality, obscuring the complex and contested nature of the ideas they purport to measure and privileging quantifiable value over impacts that are more difficult to evaluate (Basu and Modest, 2014b). While ostensibly apolitical, they nevertheless act as a 'technology of governance', reshaping incentives facing those whose performance is to be measured, and are informed by particular values and interests (Merry, 2011). Calls to better measure the impact of heritage on development are often justified not in terms of the need to evaluate the effects of policies and programmes on those affected, which are assumed to be positive, but as necessary to demonstrate the importance of recognising and funding heritage as part of development efforts (e.g., UNESCO, 2019a, 2019b).

Within such framings, heritage and development are positioned not as contested and dissonant, but as valued objectives about which there is consensus. Here, heritage is often equated to a form of capital, to be converted into economic gain, or comprising 'assets and sources of solutions' to development problems (Boege, Brown and Clements, 2009: 20; Katapidi and Robinson, this volume). Considering heritage ostensibly offers a means to make implementation of development plans easier, adding value to a project in terms of inclusivity, acceptability, and sustainability, but also, pragmatically, as a means to ensure 'fewer delays for developers' (Henderson, 2019: 5080) and to bolster the legitimacy of other actors by association (Clements, 2014). That preserving heritage is in itself desirable and will contribute to 'better' development is implied in the reference to heritage in Target 11.4 of the SDGs (Labadi, 2020c: 81), as well as in UNESCO's attempts to measure culture's contributions to development. The CDIS, for example, envisages heritage that is good for development as heritage that is 'sustainable', suggesting inherent value can be placed on heritage, however defined, and its protection (UNESCO, 2014).

Development, meanwhile, is often equated to the SDGs in articulations of heritage for development. Types of heritage, particular approaches or individual projects are thus assessed in terms of their potential contribution to achieving the Goals, with discussion often proceeding from the observation that there is insufficient reference to heritage within Agenda 2030 (e.g., ICOMOS, 2017; CPF, 2019; UNESCO, 2019a; British Council, 2020; Giliberto, 2021). Thus, part of the objective of such work, as noted above, is to raise the profile of heritage within formalised discourses and practices of development, or to increase its 'visibility' (Lamont, this volume), for example, through documenting the links between heritage and Overseas Development Assistance or finding better ways to demonstrate its 'impact' (UNESCO, 2019a), rather than considering how heritage might shape aspirations for development and ideas about ways to achieve it.

As observed above regarding both the professionalised heritage and development sectors individually, one response to criticism of 'top-down' and expert-led models of implementation has been a shift to 'community-based' or 'participatory' models. 'Communities' are thus positioned as the originators of both heritage and development, and the beneficiaries of efforts to produce them (Labadi and Gould, 2015). The emphasis placed on community in heritage for development initiatives, however, can reproduce the 'dangers of localism' (Mohan and Stokke, 2000) identified in participatory programmes more broadly, with 'communities' required to assume responsibility for the project outcomes and associated risks, obscuring the structural factors that contribute to the perceived need for such communities to be 'developed' (Lafrenz-Samuels, 2018: 78–80), or that put their heritage 'at risk'. Communities are typically not homogenous and harmonious entities with shared understandings of valued pasts and futures, and thus articulations of heritage for development within communities and between communities, the state, and other external actors, can be understood as political practices, which are shaped by inequalities of power. Interventions aimed at instrumentalising heritage for development may thus fail on their own terms or have unanticipated effects when taking insufficient account of local power relations (Labadi, 2020d: 247). Furthermore, the recognition of specialised professional expertise in using heritage for development has contributed to an emphasis on its achievement through 'capacity building' (Lafrenz Samuels, 2018) and its conceptualisation as something that should be promoted through 'outreach to communities, youth and civil society organisations to provide training and education on heritage and the SDGs, using publicity/guidance material' (ICOMOS, 2017: 9). Thus, ensuring the visibility of heritage in development is not targeted only at governments, policymakers, and funders, but also at 'communities' and heritage bearers who need to better recognise the value of their own heritage and their responsibilities as its custodians (Melhuish, this volume). The ways in which interventions aimed at stimulating heritage for development can reinforce existing inequalities, both within 'communities' and between communities and the state, businesses, or development organisations emerge clearly in this volume, both in formalised heritage projects aimed at producing development, and through the incorporation of 'traditional' institutions into development initiatives.

The often unequal distribution of costs and benefits that can result from attempts to generate development from heritage is clear from the well-established literature on the pursuit of economic gains through urban regeneration and heritage tourism (Huong and Bushell; Katapidi and Robinson; Melhuish, this volume). Clearly when heritage is successfully co-opted for these purposes there is the potential for it to make significant economic contributions. For example, as cited by Basu and Modest (2014b: 7), in 2010 the Global Heritage Fund estimated that 'revenue generated by heritage tourism in "developing and emerging countries and regions" [...] was likely to grow to US $152 billion by 2025'. However, problems persist at all scales in terms of the creation of 'more sustainable and socially-attuned foundations for economic development' (Lafrenz Samuels, 2020: 66). For example, as described by Lafrenz Samuels (2020: 66) in relation to the World Bank's heritage for development activities, '[u]rban regeneration slides too easily into gentrification, while tourism revenue tends to exacerbate rather than narrow existing social and economic inequalities' (see also Melhuish, this volume). In addition, heritage tourism presents a challenge to the ideas of sustainability at the heart of heritage for development, for example risking cultural sustainability by exacerbating social and economic inequalities and environmental sustainability through its carbon footprint. The commercialisation of heritage, whether from the top-down or the bottom-up, also raises questions around what is being included and what is being excluded from heritage representations. Typically, this will be defined by those who hold power and will reflect their political and economic interests, in many cases creating conservative and static heritage products invariably removed from the heterogeneous and dynamic communities the economic benefits of these products are intended to serve.

As outlined above, drawing on heritage in defining and pursuing alternatives to development can be understood as part of a pluriversal challenge to hegemonic discourses that privilege Western knowledge, and the value of cultural heritage for development is sometimes articulated in terms of its distinction from the colonial (Basu and Zetterstrom-Sharp, 2014; Giblin et al.; Melhuish; Pringle, and Musisi, this volume). However, the impact of colonial histories and legacies continues to be evident in some attempts to utilise heritage for development. Indeed, this is not surprising because as has been discussed, ideas of culture and 'tradition' were often closely implicated in and negotiated through colonial development endeavours (Dirks, 1992; Da Costa, 2010; Verweijen and Van Bockhaven, 2020) and today the institutions and actors through which developmental heritage is to be pursued often have their own association with colonialism. As Basu and Modest (2014b: 21) note, for example, 'the very idea of a museum carries a colonial baggage', as does the involvement of foreign 'experts'. Such continuities are made particularly stark, for example, in then UK Secretary of State for Digital, Culture, Media and Sport, Jeremy Wright's foreword to the annual report of the UK's CPF for 2018–2019, which noted the contribution of the UK in bringing 'hope, dignity and expertise to countries and communities affected by conflict and extremism' in the Middle East and North Africa, and concludes '[c]ivilisation will always triumph over barbarism, and [the UK] should continue to lead by example' (CPF, 2019: 3). Thus, the West is positioned as the location of authorised knowledge about how to 'do' heritage for development best. Sometimes, as discussed above, the objectives of such initiatives are explicitly articulated in terms of foreign policy agendas related to 'soft power' or security.

Institutional frameworks like the GCRF, which incentivised researchers to demonstrate their work's contribution to ODA and the SDGs and to identify 'partners' in the Global South, alongside funding models in development practice based on demonstrating 'impact' and 'value for money' risk entrenching a 'colonialist approach that [...] views knowledge as something to be extracted and applied' in order to address objectives consistent with Western interests (Noxolo, 2017: 343). And this danger has been explicitly recognized by some GCRF projects. For example, as Henderson (2019: 7) has reflected on his GCRF heritage for development project,

> [we] need to recognise this and avoid "sustainable development" being a stand-in for neo-colonialism with initiatives implemented by academics and scientists from the Global North with no involvement from local communities and limited knowledge of existing and past traditions.

Attempts to do heritage for development in a 'better' way, however, do not preclude the 'colonial amnesia' that Rutazibwa (2019) observes characterises international development more broadly, with 'more' action by the West positioned as the solution to development problems, without recognition of the extent to which countries like the UK are implicated in generating such problems and how they are maintained. A UK UNESCO report on the potential for UK heritage projects to contribute to overseas development aid, for example, praises UK organisations for the innovative approaches they are developing to 'contemporary challenges from climate change to repatriation issues' (UNESCO 2019a: 7), thus obscuring the role of the UK government and its heritage sector policies in causing and perpetuating such issues.

Rethinking heritage for development

By drawing on the respective critical perspectives on formalised development and heritage initiatives, the previous section has outlined how dominant framings of heritage for development can be similarly critiqued, noting: the presentation of heritage for development as something that is apolitical and that can be achieved through the application of technical expertise, despite the explicit and implicit political aims that inform such initiatives and their consequences; the positioning of both heritage and development as uncontested public goods about which there is consensus; a tension between privileging communities as heritage-bearers who should benefit from development and the requirement to educate and 'capacity build' in order for such communities to adequately assume their responsibilities; the assumption that the role of heritage in generating development can and should be measured, a position which privileges those aspects that can more readily be quantified at the expense of less tangible outcomes and reinforces the power of expertise, often located within international organisations, governments, and universities in the Global North; and relatedly, the extent to which heritage for development reflects and may perpetuate colonial power relations widely observed to be at work within each sector individually.

In contrast, here we understand development and heritage as related, common cultural production processes that are fluid and contested, within which authorised and formalised forms of development and heritage co-exist with other articulations of valued pasts in relation to the future. Contributions to this volume demonstrate that outside of formalised heritage and development organisations and explicit heritage for development initiatives, diverse actors are already grappling with questions about how the past can inform better futures, whether in the design of hospitals in Uganda (Pringle and Musisi), debates about history curriculum in Colombia (Bermeo, Paulson, and Charria), or in retaining and sharing gendered knowledge about agriculture, food preparation and nutrition in India (Hazareesingh). Thus, the objective of this volume is not to evaluate whether heritage for development works or to advance particular ways in which the past should be better instrumentalised for progress. Instead, we proceed from the starting point that heritage and development are often entangled and hope to understand the different ways in which these connections are articulated, to explore how particular visions of the past or the future become valued, and what the implications are.

Existing literature exploring the intersections between heritage and development as common cultural production processes has highlighted the role that heritage plays in negotiating ideas and aspirations of well-being and has proposed that heritage for development be reimagined as the attainment of culturally and contextually specific ideas of well-being through the negotiation of the past in the present (Basu and Modest, 2014b; Zetterstrom-Sharp, 2015; Labadi, 2020b). Similarly, Zetterstrom-Sharp (2015) has described how heritage can be understood as an articulation of aspirations for a common destiny and how heritage processes are implicated in instituting and shaping change for desired futures. Thus, rather than presenting heritage as a form of capital that can be invoked to make development more effective, heritage may better be understood as something that is contested and articulated as part of the dynamic process of working out what kind of development is desired to achieve subjective and relational forms of well-being. People frequently draw upon ideas and understandings drawn from the past in negotiating development and in deciding whether arrangements for pursuing it are acceptable and legitimate. This can be understood as 'bricolage' (Cleaver, 2002), whereby people consciously and unconsciously draw on established norms and expectations, existing forms of public authority, and generally accepted ways of doing things in responding to contemporary challenges. Whether articulated through reference to 'tradition', culture, or heritage, ideas about valued aspects of the past are often used to legitimise such arrangements. In this way, while development can be reimagined '*as* a cultural project, and particularly as a culturally context-specific project' (Basu and Modest, 2014b: 26), so can heritage be rethought as a culturally context-specific development project. Crucially, it is important to recognise such processes as political. Understanding who has the power to articulate authoritative visions of the past and the future and the relationship between them, and how these are contested and negotiated at different scales, is central to a better understanding of how development happens, or does not happen, and who benefits and who does not.

Recognising attempts to instrumentalise heritage for development as political undertakings that frequently reflect and generate inequalities, necessitates reflection on our own positionality as we seek to intervene in this debate (see also Basu and Modest, 2014b and Labadi, 2020b for comparable reflections). As white British scholars who work in a UK university Development Studies department (Cross) and a UK national museum (Giblin), we recognise the extent to which we have previously benefited from and continue to benefit from established hierarchies of knowledge production about both heritage and development in the Global South, which privilege Northern 'expertise' and experience. We have both received funding from the GCRF, discussed above, which has required articulation of research aims and outcomes in the ways critiqued in this introduction, for example in terms of contribution to the SDGs and UK ODA objectives, and has mostly resulted in projects led from the UK with a range of Southern partners.

Our aim here is not to propose 'better' ways to use heritage for development, but to explore the assumptions that shape such endeavours and how they are perceived and interpreted by those involved and affected. In considering both explicit 'heritage for development' initiatives that engage with the authoritative language and institutional forms of UNESCO and the SDGs, as well as alternative ways in which individuals, groups, organisations, and governments are looking to the past to reshape development, in this volume we hope to retain an open-minded approach to what can be considered a valued past or future, while acknowledging the extent to which our own judgements are shaped by the pervasive assumptions and incentive structures of the academic and professional contexts in which we work.

Conclusion

In this introduction we have set out an approach to understanding development and heritage as intimately entangled common cultural production processes that function as a means for people to negotiate their future well-being, albeit shaped by unequal power relations. The contributions to this volume explore diverse manifestations of these processes, connected to differing degrees to the authoritative articulations of heritage and development and the relationship between them reviewed in this introductory chapter. Our key concern is not to assess whether or to what extent heritage can or does contribute to development or how it might do so 'better', but to explore how the past is practised in the pursuit of very different understandings of 'progress', and what the implications are for how change does, or does not, happen and who benefits and who does not. Indeed, the wide range of actors and objectives surveyed in the remainder of this volume, implicated in different ways in negotiating the politics of the past for the future, demonstrates the extent to which heritage for development is often a dynamic and 'everyday' process, which cannot easily be captured in generalisable policy recommendations or quantifiable targets.

Note

1 While we recognise the term Global South is contested, we have used it here to refer to those regions that have historically been the principal subjects of 'international development', largely funded, conceptualised and directed from the Global North, and in which many countries have been subject to European and North American imperialism.

References

Ashworth, G. (1997) 'Conservation as preservation or as heritage: two paradigms and two answers', *Built Environment*, 23(2), pp. 92–102.

Ashworth, G. (2014) 'Heritage and economic development: selling the unsellable', *Heritage & Society*, 7(1), pp. 3–17.

Basu, P. and Damodaran, V. (2015) 'Colonial histories of heritage: legislative migrations and the politics of preservation', *Past & Present*, 226(10), pp. 240–271.

Basu, P. and Modest, M.(eds) (2014a) *Museums, heritage and international development.* New York: Routledge.
Basu, P. and Modest, W. (2014b) 'Museums, heritage and international development: a critical conversation', in Basu, P. and Modest, W. (eds) *Museums, heritage and international development.* New York: Routledge, pp. 1–32.
Basu, P. and Zetterstrom-Sharp, J. (2014) 'Complicating culture for development: negotiating 'dysfunctional heritage' in Sierra Leone', in Basu, P. and Modest, W. (eds) (2014a) *Museums, heritage and international development.* New York: Routledge, pp. 56–82.
Bayly, C.A., Rao, V., Szreter, S. and Woolcock, M. (2011) *History, historians and development policy.* Manchester: Manchester University Press.
Belda-Miquel, S., Boni, A. and Calabuig, C. (2019) 'SDG localisation and decentralised development aid: exploring opposing discourses and practices in Valencia's aid sector', *Journal of Human Development and Capabilities*, 20(4), pp. 386–402.
Boege, V., Brown, M.A. and Clements, K.P. (2009) 'Hybrid political orders, not fragile states', *Peace Review: A Journal of Social Justice*, 21(1), pp. 13–21.
Booth, D. and Cammack, D. (2013) *Governance for development in Africa: solving collective action problems.* London: Zed Books.
Briones, I. (2019) 'Everything that you need to know about Africa's most expensive building', *Architectural Digest.* Available at: www.architecturaldigest.com/story/everything-need-know-about-africa-most-expensive-building (Accessed 01 May 2022).
British Council (2021a) *Culture and development: about us.* Available at: www.britishcouncil.org/arts/culture-development/about-us (Accessed 19 April 2021).
British Council (2021b) *Cultural Protection Fund.* Available at: www.britishcouncil.org/arts/culture-development/cultural-protection-fund (Accessed 19 April 2021).
Cerisola, S. (2019) *Cultural heritage, creativity and economic development.* Cheltenham: Edward Elgar Publishing.
Chambers, R. (1997a) 'Responsible well-being—a personal agenda for development', *World Development*, 25(11), pp. 1743–1754.
Chambers, R. (1997b) *Whose reality counts? Putting the first last.* London: Intermediate Technology Publications.
Clammer, J. (2015) *Art, culture and international development: humanizing social transformation.* Abingdon: Routledge.
Cleaver, F. (2002) 'Reinventing institutions: Bricolage and the social embeddedness of natural resource management', *European Journal of Development Research*, 14(1), pp. 11–30.
Cleaver, F., Franks, T., Maganga, F. and Hall, K. (2013) 'Institutions, security, and pastoralism: exploring the limits of hybridity', *African Studies Review*, 56(3), pp. 165–189.
Clements, K.P. (2014) 'What is legitimacy and why does it matter for peace?' *Accord: An International Review of Peace Initiatives*, 25, pp. 12–16.
Cooke, B. and Kothari, U. (eds) (2001) *Participation: the new tyranny?* London: Zed Books.
Cooper, F. (1998) 'Modernizing bureaucrats, backward Africans, and the development concept', in Cooper, F. and Packard, R. (eds) *International development and the social sciences: essays on the history and politics of knowledge.* Oakland, CA: University of California Press, pp. 64–92.
Cooper, F. (2010) 'Writing the history of development', *Journal of Modern European History*, 8(1), pp. 5–23.
Cornwall, A. (2006) 'Historical perspectives on participation in development, *Commonwealth and Comparative Politics*, 44(1), pp. 62–83.
Cowen, M.P. and Shenton, R.W. (1996) *Doctrines of development.* London and New York: Routledge.

Crooke, E. (2010) 'The politics of community heritage: motivations, authority and control', *International Journal of Heritage Studies*, 16(1–2), pp. 16–29.

Cultural Protection Fund (2019) *Cultural Protection Fund annual report 2018–19*. London: British Council and Department for Culture, Media and Sport.

Da Costa, D. (2010) 'Introduction: relocating culture in development and development in culture', *Third World Quarterly*, 31(4), pp. 501–522.

De Beukelaer, C. and Vlassis, A. (2020) 'Creative economy and development: international institutions and policy synchronization', in Labadi, S. (ed.) (2020a) *The cultural turn in international aid: impacts and challenges for heritage and the creative industries*. Abingdon: Routledge, pp. 17–36.

Desai, R. (2008) 'Introduction: nationalisms and their understandings in historical perspective', *Third World Quarterly*, 29(3), pp. 397–428.

Dirks, N.B. (ed.) (1992) *Colonialism and culture*. Ann Arbor: University of Michigan Press.

Enns, C., Bersaglio, B. and Kepe, T. (2014) 'Indigenous voices and the making of the post-2015 development agenda: the recurring tyranny of participation', *Third World Quarterly*, 35(3), pp. 358–375.

Escobar, A. (1995) *Development: the making and unmaking of the Third World*. Princeton, NJ: Princeton University Press.

Ferguson, J. (1990) *The anti-politics machine: development, depoliticization, and bureaucratic power in Lesotho*. Cambridge: Cambridge University Press.

Fisher, J. and Marquette, H. (2014) 'Donors doing political economy analysis™: from process to product (and back again?)', Developmental Leadership Programme Research Paper 28. Available at: https://res.cloudinary.com/dlprog/image/upload/YMiWfSVCJsRHoBID8jtwrlJOPITIsVmjOLNx5vQx.pdf (Accessed 28 April 2022).

Foradori, P., Giusti, S. and Lamonica, A.G. (2018) 'Reshaping cultural heritage protection policies at a time of securitisation: France, Italy and the United Kingdom', *The International Spectator*, 53(3), pp. 86–101.

Fredheim, L.H. and Khalaf, M. (2016) 'The significance of values: heritage value typologies re-examined', *International Journal of Heritage Studies*, 22(6), pp. 466–481.

Fukuda-Parr, S. and McNeill, D. (2019) 'Knowledge and politics in setting and measuring the SDGs: introduction to special issue', *Global Policy*, 10(S1), pp. 5–15.

Fukuda-Parr, S. and Muchhala, B. (2020) 'The southern origins of sustainable development goals: ideas, actors, aspirations', *World Development*, 126, 104706.

Giblin, J.D. (2018) 'Heritage and the use of the past in East Africa', *Oxford Research Encyclopedia of African History*. doi: 10/1093/acrefore/9780190277734.013.135

Giblin, J.D., Ramos, I. and Grout, N. (2019) 'Dismantling the master's house: thoughts on representing empire and decolonising museums and public spaces in practice an introduction', *Third Text: Critical Perspectives on Contemporary Art and Culture*, 33(4–5), pp. 471–486.

Giliberto, F. (2021) *Heritage for global challenges: a research report by PRAXIS: arts and humanities for global development*. Leeds: University of Leeds.

Graham, B., Ashworth, G. and Tunbridge, J. (2000) *A geography of heritage: power, culture and economy*. Abingdon: Routledge.

Gujit, I. and Shah, M.K. (1998) *The myth of community: gender issues in participatory development*. Rugby: Practical Action Publishing.

Hall, S. (1999) 'Whose heritage? Un-settling 'the heritage', re-imagining the post-nation', *Third Text*, 13(49), pp. 3–13.

Harrison, R. (2013) *Heritage: critical approaches*. Abingdon: Routledge.

Harrison, R., Morgan, J., Penrose, S., DeSilvey, C., Holtorf, C., Macdonald, S., Bartolini, N., Breithoff, E., Fredheim, H. and Lyons, A. (2020) *Heritage futures: comparative approaches to natural and cultural heritage practices*. London: UCL Press.

Hart, G. (2001) 'Development critiques in the 1990s: culs de sac and promising paths', *Progress in Human Geography*, 25(4), pp. 649–658.

Harvey, D. (2001) 'Heritage pasts and heritage presents: temporality, meaning and the scope of heritage studies', *International Journal of Heritage Studies*, 7(4), pp. 319–338.

Helliwell, J.F., Layard, R., Sachs, J.D., De Neve, J-E., Aknin, L.B. and Wang, S. (2021) *World Happiness Report 2021*. Available at: https://worldhappiness.report/ed/2021/ (Accessed 28 April 2022).

Henderson, J. (2019) 'Oceans without history? marine cultural heritage and the sustainable development agenda', *Sustainability*, 11(8), 5080.

Hewison, R. (1987) *The heritage industry: Britain in a climate of decline*. York: Methuen Publishing.

Högberg, A. (2015) 'The heritage sector in a multicultural society: a discussion from a Swedish perspective', in Biehl, P.F., Comer, D.C., Prescott, C. and Soderland, H.A. (eds) *Identity and heritage: contemporary challenges in a globalized world*. Cham: Springer International Publishing, pp. 47–53.

Holtorf, C. and Högberg, A. (eds) (2020) *Cultural heritage and the future*. 1st edition. London and New York: Routledge.

Hosagrahar, J. (2017) 'Culture at the Heart of the SDGs', *The UNESCO Courier. Agenda 2030: challenges for us all*, April-June, pp. 12–14. Available at: https://unesdoc.unesco.org/ark:/48223/pf0000248106 (Accessed 28 April 2022).

ICOMOS (2017) *Action plan: cultural heritage and localizing the UN sustainable development goals (SDGs)*. Available at www.icomos.org/images/DOCUMENTS/Secretariat/2017/ICOMOS_Action_Plan_Cult_Heritage_and_Localizing_SDGs_20170721.pdf (Accessed 28 August 2022).

Isar, Y.R. (2014) 'UNESCO, museums and "development"', in Basu, P. and Modest, W. (eds) *Museums, heritage and international development*. New York: Routledge, pp. 33–55.

Kothari, U. (2005a) (ed.) *A radical history of development studies: individuals, institutions and ideologies*. London: Zed Books.

Kothari, U. (2005b) 'From colonial administration to development studies: a post-colonial critique of the history of development studies', in Kothari, U. (ed.) *A radical history of development studies: individuals, institutions and ideologies*. London: Zed Books, pp. 47–66.

Kothari, U. (2005c) 'Authority and expertise: the professionalisation of international development and the ordering of dissent', *Antipode*, 06(37), pp. 425–446.

Kothari, U. (2006) 'An agenda for thinking about "race" in development', *Progress in Development Studies*, 6(1), pp. 9–23.

Kothari, A., Salleh, A., Escobar, A., Demaria, F. and Acosta, A. (2019a) 'Introduction: finding pluriversal paths', in Kothari, A., Salleh, A., Escobar, A., Demaria, F. and Acosta, A. (eds) *Pluriverse: a post-development dictionary*. New Delhi: Tulika Books, pp. xxi–xl.

Kothari, A., Salleh, A., Escobar, A., Demaria, F. and Acosta, A. (eds) (2019b) *Pluriverse: a post-development dictionary*. New Delhi: Tulika Books.

Kumi, E., Arhin, A.A. and Yeboah, T. (2014) 'Can post-2015 sustainable development goals survive neoliberalism? A critical examination of the sustainable development-neoliberalism nexus in developing countries', *Environment, Development and Sustainability*, 16, pp. 539–554.

Labadi, S. (ed.) (2020a) *The cultural turn in international aid: impacts and challenges for heritage and the creative industries*. Abingdon: Routledge.

Labadi, S. (2020b) 'The cultural turn in international aid: setting the scene', in Labadi, S. (ed.) *The cultural turn in international aid: impacts and challenges for heritage and the creative industries.* Abingdon: Routledge, pp. 1–14.

Labadi, S. (2020c) 'UNESCO, culture, aid and development in the new millennium', in Labadi, S. (ed.) *The cultural turn in international aid: impacts and challenges for heritage and the creative industries.* Abingdon: Routledge, pp. 73–88.

Labadi, S. (2020d) 'The future of international aid for cultural projects', in Labadi, S. (ed.) *The cultural turn in international aid: impacts and challenges for heritage and the creative industries.* Abingdon: Routledge, pp. 243–252.

Labadi, S., Giliberto, F., Rosetti, I., Shetabi, L. and Yildrim, E. (2021) *Heritage and the Sustainable Development Goals: policy guidance for heritage and development actors.* Charenton-le-Pont: ICOMOS. Available at: http://openarchive.icomos.org/id/eprint/2453/ (Accessed 28 April 2022).

Labadi, S. and Gould, P. (2015) 'Sustainable development: heritage, community, economics', in Meskell, L. (ed.) *Global heritage: a reader.* Oxford: Wiley-Blackwell, pp. 196–216.

Labadi, S. and Logan, B. (eds) (2015) *Approaches to urban heritage, development and sustainability.* Abingdon: Routledge.

Lafrenz Samuels, K. (2009) 'Trajectories of development: international heritage management of archaeology in the Middle East and North Africa', *Archaeologies*, 5, pp. 68–91

Lafrenz Samuels, K. (2018) *Mobilising heritage: anthropological practice and transnational prospects.* Gainesville: University Press of Florida.

Lafrenz Samuels, K. (2020) 'Heritage development: culture and heritage at the World Bank', in Labadi, S. (ed.) *The cultural turn in international aid: impacts and challenges for heritage and the creative industries.* Abingdon: Routledge, pp. 55–72.

Langan, M. (2017) *Neo-colonialism and the poverty of 'development' in Africa.* London and New York: Palgrave Macmillan.

Larsen, P.B. and Logan, W. (eds) (2018) *World heritage and sustainable development: new directions in world heritage management.* Abingdon: Routledge.

Laws, E. and Marquette, H. (2018) *Thinking and working politically: reviewing the evidence on the integration of politics into development practice over the past decade.* Available at: https://twpcommunity.org/wp-content/uploads/2018/04/Thinking-and-working-politically-reviewing-the-evidence.pdf (Accessed 21 April 2021).

Lewis, D. (2019) ''Big D' and 'little d': two types of twenty-first century development?', *Third World Quarterly*, 40(11), pp. 1957–1975.

Li, T.M. (2007) *The will to improve: governmentality, development, and the practice of politics.* Durham, NC and London: Duke University Press.

Logan, W. (2020) 'Blowing hot and cold: culture-related activities in the deployment of Australia's soft power in Asia', in Labadi, S. (ed.) *The cultural turn in international aid: impacts and challenges for heritage and the creative industries.* Abingdon: Routledge, pp. 152–170

Lowenthal, D. (1985) *The past is a foreign country.* Cambridge: Cambridge University Press.

Mac Ginty, R. and Richmond, O.P. (2013) 'The local turn in peace building: a critical agenda for peace', *Third World Quarterly*, 34(5), pp. 763–783.

Mansuri, G. and Rao, V. (2013) *Localizing development: does participation work?* Washington DC: World Bank.

Matfess, H. (2015) 'Rwanda and Ethiopia: developmental authoritarianism and the new politics of African strong men', *African Studies Review*, 58(2), pp. 181–204.

McCulloch, N. and Piron, L-H. (2019) 'Thinking and working politically: learning from practice. Overview to special issue', *Development Policy Review*, 37(S1), pp. O1–O15.

McEwan, C. (2018) *Postcolonialism, decoloniality and development*. London and New York: Routledge.
Menochal, A.R., Cassidy, M., Swift, S., Jacobstein, D., Rothblum, C. and Tservil, I. (2018) *Thinking and working politically through applied political economy analysis: a guide for practitioners*. USAID Learning Lab. Available at: https://usaidlearninglab.org/sites/default/files/resource/files/pea_guide_final.pdf (Accessed 30 April 2021).
Merry, S. (2011) 'Measuring the world: indicators, human rights and global governance', *Current Anthropology*, 52(S3), pp. S83–S95.
Mohan, G. and Stokke, K. (2000) 'Participatory development and empowerment: the dangers of localism', *Third World Quarterly*, 21(2), pp. 247–268.
Mosse, D. (2004) 'Is good policy unimplementable? Reflections on the ethnography of aid policy and practice', *Development and Change*, 35(4), pp. 639–671.
Mosse, D. (2013) 'The anthropology of international development', *Annual Review of Anthropology*, 42, pp. 227–246.
Muchhala, B. (2014) 'North-South debate in the UN within context of sustainable development goals', *Third World Network Info Service on UN Sustainable Development Goals*, 14 March. Available at: www.twn.my/ title2/unsd/2014/unsd140303.htm (Accessed 29 April 2019).
Nardella, B.M. and Mallinson, M. (2014) '"Only foreigners can do it"? Technical assistance, advocacy and brokerage at Aksum, Ethiopia', in Basu, P. and Modest, W. (eds) *Museums, heritage and international development*. London: Routledge, pp. 188–210.
Nederveen Pieterse, J. (1995) 'The cultural turn in development: questions of power', *The European Journal of Development Research*, 7(1), pp. 176–192.
Noxolo, P. (2017) 'Decolonial theory in a time of the re-colonisation of UK research', *Transactions of the Institute of British Geographers*, 42(3), pp. 342–344.
Ostrom, E. (1990) *Governing the commons: the evolution of institutions for collective action*. Cambridge: Cambridge University Press.
Pailey, R.N. (2020) 'De-centring the "white gaze" of development', *Development and Change*, 51(3), pp. 729–745.
Radcliffe, A. (ed.) (2006) *Culture and development in a globalising world. Geographies, actors and paradigms*. London: Routledge.
Rao, V. and Walton, M. (eds) (2004) *Culture and public action*. Stanford: Stanford University Press.
Rodney, W. (1972) *How Europe underdeveloped Africa*. London: Bogle-L'Ouverture Publications.
Russo, A. and Giusti, S. (2019) 'The securitisation of cultural heritage', *International Journal of Cultural Policy*, 25(7), pp. 843–857.
Rutazibwa, O.U. (2019) 'On babies and bathwater: decolonizing international development studies', in de Jong, S., Icaza, R. and Rutazibwa, O.U. (eds) *Decolonization and feminisms in global teaching and learning*. London: Routledge, pp. 158–180.
Schofield, D.J. (2014) *Who needs experts? Counter-mapping cultural heritage*. Farnham: Ashgate.
Sen, A. (1999) *Development as freedom*. Oxford: Oxford University Press.
Sen, A. (2004) 'How Does Culture Matter?', in Rao, V. and Walton, M. (eds) *Culture and public action*. Stanford: Stanford University Press, pp. 37–58.
Shepherd, N. (2020) 'After the #fall: the shadow of Cecil Rhodes at the University of Cape Town', *City*, 24(3–4), pp. 565–579.
Smith, L. (2006) *Uses of heritage*. Abingdon: Routledge.
Stiglitz, J.E., Sen, A., Fitoussi, J-P. (2009) *Report by the commission on the measurement of economic performance and social progress*. Available at: https://ec.europa.eu/eurostat/documents/8131721/8131772/Stiglitz-Sen-Fitoussi-Commission-report.pdf (Accessed 4 May 2021).

Stupples, P. and Teaiwa, K. (eds) (2017) *Contemporary perspectives on art and international development*. Abingdon: Routledge.

Tadros, M. and Sabates-Wheeler, R. (2020) *Inclusive development: beyond need, not creed*. CREID Working Paper 1, Institute of Development Studies.

Tan, A.G., and Perleth, C. (eds) (2015) *Creativity, culture, and development*. Singapore: Springer.

Thiaw, I. and Ly, A. (2020) 'Behind the façade of the diplomacy of international culture aid', in Labadi, S. (ed.) *The cultural turn in international aid: impacts and challenges for heritage and the creative industries*. Abingdon: Routledge, pp. 109–122

Throsby, D. (2003) 'Cultural sustainability', in Towse, R. (ed.) *A handbook of cultural economics*. Cheltenham/Northampton, MA: Edward Elgar, pp. 183–186.

Timothy, D.J. and Nyaupane, G.P. (eds) (2009) *Cultural heritage and tourism in the developing world: a regional perspective*. Abingdon: Routledge.

Truman, H.S. (1949) 'Inaugural address of Harry S. Truman'. The Avalon Project: documents in law, history and diplomacy. Lillian Goldman Law Library. Available at: https://avalon.law.yale.edu/20th_century/truman.asp (Accessed 4 May 2021).

UNESCO (2014) *UNESCO culture for development indicators: methodology manual*. Paris: UNESCO.

UNESCO (2019a) *Cultural heritage innovation: opportunities for international development*. London: UK National Commission for UNESCO.

UNESCO (2019b) *Culture 2030 Indicators*. Paris: UNESCO.

United Nations General Assembly (2012) *Resolution adopted by the General Assembly on 27 July 2012. 66/288 The future we want*. Available at: www.un.org/ga/search/view_doc.asp?symbol=A/RES/66/288&Lang=E (Accessed 30 April 2022).

Verweijen, J. and Van Bockhaven, V. (2020) 'Revisiting colonial legacies in knowledge production on customary authority in Central and East Africa', *Journal of Eastern African Studies*, 14(1), pp. 1–23.

Walters, D., Laven, D. and Davis, P. (eds) (2017) *Heritage and peacebuilding*. Woodbridge: The Boyden Press.

Waterton, E and Smith. L. (2010) 'The recognition and misrecognition of community heritage', *International Journal of Heritage Studies*, 16(1–2), pp. 4–15.

Waterton, E. and Watson, S. (eds) (2011) *Heritage and community engagement: collaboration or contestation?* Abingdon: Routledge.

White, S.C. (2010) 'Analysing wellbeing: a framework for development practice', *Development in Practice*, 20(2), pp. 158–172.

Whitty, B.S. (2019) 'Practising politics: technical project templates and political practice in a DFID country office', *Development Policy Review*, 37(S2), pp. O293–O309.

Wild, L., Andrews, M., Pett, J. and Dempster, H. (2016) *Doing development differently: who we are, what we're doing, what we're learning*. Overseas Development Institute. Available at: https://cdn.odi.org/media/documents/11199.pdf (Accessed 8 May 2021).

Wiktor-Mach, D. (2019) 'Cultural heritage and development: UNESCO's new paradigm in a changing geopolitical context', *Third World Quarterly*, 40(9), pp. 1593–1612.

Wingfield, C., Giblin, J. and King, R. (2020) 'Introducing the pasts and presence of art in South Africa', in Wingfield, C., Giblin, J. and King, R. (eds) *The pasts and presence of art in South Africa: technologies, ontologies, and agents*. Cambridge: McDonald Institute for Archaeological Research, pp. 1–18.

Winter, T. (2014) 'Postconflict heritage in Asia: shifting geographies of aid', in Basu, P. and Modest, W. (eds) *Museums, heritage and international development*. New York: Routledge, pp. 295–309.

Winter, T. (2015) 'Heritage diplomacy', *International Journal of Heritage Studies*, 21(10), pp. 997–1015.

World Commission on Culture and Development (1995) *Our creative diversity: report of the World Commission on Culture and Development*. Available at: https://unesdoc.unesco.org/ark:/48223/pf0000101651 (Accessed 30 April 2022).

World Commission on Environment and Development (WCED) (1987) *Report of the World Commission on Environment and Development: our common future*. Available at https://sustainabledevelopment.un.org/content/documents/5987our-common-future.pdf (Accessed 28 August 2022).

Wright, P. (1985) *On living in an old country: the national past in contemporary Britain*. London: Verso Books.

Zetterstrom-Sharp, J. (2015) 'Heritage as future-making: aspiration and common destiny in Sierra Leone', *International Journal of Heritage Studies*, 21(6), pp. 609–627.

Ziai, A. (2017) *Development discourse and global history: from colonialism to the sustainable development goals*. London: Routledge.

PART 1

Heritage, Economic Development and Livelihoods

2

WORLD HERITAGE AND SUSTAINABLE DEVELOPMENT

Purpose, Practice and Possibilities

Ioanna Katapidi and Mike Robinson

Introduction

The concept of World Heritage as a way of attaching symbolic and transcendent value to both cultural and natural heritage sites/properties can be considered a tremendous success on many levels. For example, this can be evidenced by the number of state signatories to the UNESCO 1972 Convention, by the sheer number of sites inscribed on the World Heritage List (1,121 as at the time of writing) and by the huge latent demand for inscription from State Parties' Tentative Lists (currently listing 1,724 potential sites). The categorisation of heritage through a selective process of evaluation is now well embedded in a World Heritage system that is widely understood and engaged with across the globe.

At the same time, the achievements of the World Heritage Convention have consistently been scrutinised from a multitude of angles ranging from questions of process – the politics of inscription, the over-production of sites, a neglect of cultural relativism – to issues of outcome – capacities of management and the cost and benefits of designation to local communities. Despite inherent fractures in the system, World Heritage remains one of the more successful endeavours of global international engagement. The currency of World Heritage is strong with the label being imbued with a widely respected recognised kudos. However, it is argued that the powerful authority of sites with recognised global significance has largely remained under-utilised beyond instances of some with an ability to attract tourists and related development. Tourism aside, the World Heritage system can be characterised as being somewhat introspective and insular with attention almost solely directed to site conservation for the protection of Outstanding Universal Value. What is undoubtedly a system of production, manifests itself not as any coordinated, transnational, network of sites sharing the characteristics of 'World

DOI: 10.4324/9781003107361-3

Heritageness', but rather as a series of unconnected, nationally framed entities, whose focus has been (largely understandably) inward-looking and self-serving.

In recent years, foundations have been put in place for a reorientation of World Heritage. At the 2015 Bonn Meeting of the UNESCO World Heritage Committee (40 COM 5C), a new policy was adopted to recognise that a 'sustainable development perspective' should be integrated into the processes of the World Heritage Convention. This followed in the wake of the adoption of the Sustainable Development Goals (SDGs) by the United Nations, themselves a reworking of the previously set Millennium Development Goals in 2000. Far from being dismissed as institutional rhetoric, this still emergent policy opens up new challenges and possibilities for World Heritage Sites (WHSs) and marks a major philosophical shift from seeing World Heritage as an end in itself, rooted in notions of Eurocentric intrinsic value, towards a more pragmatic view of World Heritage designation as a means (or part of the means) to an end; addressing the SDGs. As the Policy states:

> In addition to protecting the OUV [Outstanding Universal Value] of World Heritage properties, States Parties should, therefore, recognise and promote the properties' inherent potential to contribute to all dimensions of sustainable development and work to harness the collective benefits for society, also by ensuring that their conservation and management strategies are aligned with broader sustainable development objectives. In this process, the properties' OUV [Outstanding Universal Value] should not be compromised.
>
> *UNESCO, 2015: 2*

The ambition of this new direction is extensive and goes beyond invoking tourism as the all too commonly cited instrument of WHS. Although tourism is critically important, this new policy of alignment with the sustainable development agenda recognises the potential that 'a well-protected World Heritage property may contribute directly to alleviating poverty and inequalities by providing basic goods and services, such as security and health, through shelter, access to clean air, water, food and other key resources' (UNESCO, 2021).

While within its own limited capacities UNESCO can but defer to the State Parties, such a statement is suggestive of a new way of integrating WHS into the interconnected global approach that is necessary for tackling the SDGs. There have indeed been several meetings to discuss the implementation of this major policy shift into national, regional and local action but what is important in this process is the communication of this explicit linking of WHS with sustainable development objectives, the ways in which this policy is interpreted by stakeholders and ultimately how it is articulated through local practices. As with all shifts in policy, structural change is intimately bound to cultural change with the latter often requiring longer to achieve. The ambitious 2030 target for meeting the 17 SDGs is already a major challenge for many States and within this WHS, their managers and their diverse range of stakeholders are being asked to consider how they help the wider world. It is a tall order, particularly within the context of the Covid-19 pandemic, which arguably has engendered entrenchment and introspection as WHS struggle for their own survival.

Within the context of such a shift in focus of the World Heritage concept, it is important to explore the extent to which this 'new' meta-level discourse filters down to Site level. As part of a larger Arts and Humanities Research Council project examining the interrelations between WHS and the SDGs, we examined the site of West Lake Cultural Landscape of Hangzhou in China to explore how the sustainable development imperative was permeating both management practices and community/stakeholder engagement.

West Lake Cultural Landscape

Since becoming a signatory to the World Heritage Convention in 1985, China has been actively engaged in nominating cultural, natural and mixed heritage sites for inscription on the World Heritage List with (at the time of writing) 55 designated sites and a further 60 on its Tentative List. This reflects China's position as a global superpower and the potential of its heritage as a valuable resource capable of contributing to the socio-economic development of the country (Ludwig and Walton, 2020). The proactive approach to safeguarding, developing and promoting Chinese heritage, through the high-profile international framework of the World Heritage Convention, is only part of a wider domestic 'heritage turn' (Denton, 2014; Madsen, 2014), which has witnessed an acceleration in concern to safeguard moveable and immoveable heritage against the realisation of its loss over a period of rapid economic growth and intensive urbanisation. As Huo (2015) points out, the expansion of the legislative framework to protect heritage in China remains problematic, not in its intention but rather in its implementation, enforcement and the administrative complexities of a decentralised system. All World Heritage is of course subject to extant heritage regulations of the State Party but the headline benefits of inscription and consequent global recognition, with attendant opportunities to harness economic development through tourism and the display of 'soft-power' are key priorities. China has indeed recognised these and has eagerly engaged in nominating sites (Yan, 2012, 2015) and with, as Zhang (2017) argues, a self-conscious willingness to engage with the Western values that underpin the World Heritage system, but which sit sometimes uneasily with deeply rooted Chinese values.

West Lake is located to the west of, and adjacent to, the vast urban centre of Hangzhou (population of nearly 11 million people), the capital city of Zhejiang Province in central-east China, covering around 6,5 km^2 and constituting one of the most famous attractions in China (Zhang and Taylor, 2019). For centuries, West Lake has been renowned for its idyllic landscape and cultural heritage, celebrated by poets and artists since the 9th century and well appreciated by the wider population, representing Chinese philosophies of harmony with nature (see Figure 2.1). Being surrounded on three sides by cloud-capped hills and on the fourth by the city of Hangzhou and including islands, causeways, pagodas, pavilions, gardens, temples and ornamental trees, which mingle with the farmed landscape of the surrounding tea plantations, West Lake is traditionally known as 'Heaven on Earth' (Giorgi et al., 2020; Zhang and Taylor, 2019).

In 1982, West Lake was one of the first National Scenic Areas placed under official heritage protection, while in 2011 it was listed as a WHS, making the first designated Cultural Landscape in China (Lu et al., 2019). This extensive site was inscribed against Criteria (iii), (iv), (v) and (vi) with its Outstanding Universal Value rooted in the harmonious blending of natural and man-made features to create a landscape redolent with meaning and symbolism (UNESCO, 2011). The associative values of the Site are powerful and pervasive and arguably are amongst the strongest attributes recognised by its millions of domestic visitors.

Significant is the proximity of Hangzhou City to the WHS. Hangzhou, the former capital of China during the Southern Song Dynasty, has long benefitted from the beauties and recreational assets of West Lake. The designation of West Lake as WHS has served to further enhance the attractiveness of the wider area (Wang and Bramwell, 2012) and has been instrumental for the city's imaging and its capacity to attract visitors. The expansion of Hangzhou's urban area from 177.18 km^2 in 2000 to 615.22 km^2 in 2018 (Fu and Jin, 2020), has undoubtedly impacted both West Lake's landscape and its living population. Given that Hangzhou is also home to two other WHS – a section of the Grand Canal and the archaeological ruins of

FIGURE 2.1 Angle of West Lake Hangzhou

Source: Photo taken by the authors.

Liangzhu City – and is also just over an hour away by bullet train to the 27 million population of Shanghai, one can understand why West Lake is rated as one of the most visited cultural heritage sites in China (Lu et al., 2019). The combination of proximity and popularity – enhanced by its UNESCO designation – means that West Lake continues to face issues and challenges regarding the sustainable development and management of the area and is illustrative of many World Heritage cases where notions of site protection and management cannot be viewed in isolation from the wider geographical and socio-economic context.

Given the high profile of West Lake, a significant number of studies have concerned themselves with the various dimensions of management relating to tourism, its impacts and wider development pressures (see for instance: Liu and Liu, 2011; Wang and Bramwell, 2012; Wu et al., 2014; Xu et al., 2017; Sun and Liu, 2020). These issues reach beyond West Lake as a WHS and indeed, a majority of studies pay more attention to the Site as a tourist destination as opposed to its status as World Heritage. This reflects a frequent ambiguity in the identity of WHS and illustrates at the very least, the complex overlaps between UNESCO designation and any pre-status as tourism attraction and at the most, a genuine unawareness of what a WHS means. What we are concerned with here specifically is the extent to which West Lake, as a WHS, is engaged with the emerging instrumentalist view of World Heritage as a tool for achieving the SDGs. This was explored during a site visit, with in-situ discussions with local businesses and attractions and through a two-day workshop, kindly coordinated by the Administrative Committee of West Lake Scenic Area (WLSA), which was attended by a variety of stakeholders.

Awareness of the Sustainable Development Goals

Similar to the World Heritage Convention, which in 2021 had 194 State Parties as signatories, the 2015 United Nations' 2030 Agenda for Sustainable Development with its 17 SDGs was signed by 193 States. In the latter case, as in the former, the open rhetoric of transnational acceptance defaults to the specifics of national action and the multitude of variables that feed into different systems of governance. The target date of 2030 for addressing the SDGs is without doubt a challenge for all nations complicated by a persistent issue, affecting all States, relating to the problems of translating public policy into action (Birkland, 2001). But, prior to programmes of implementation are general matters of communication and the extent to which policy imperatives are able to filter through layers of bureaucracy and wider civil society. This is undoubtedly a challenge for a country so vast as China, accentuated by the significant imbalances in social, economic and environmental conditions between its regions and what Wang et al. (2020) term the spatial variability of the SDGs.

Further issues for China and related to the above, are the complexities of managing across many different agencies, the changes amongst these agencies over a rapid period of heritage production, and the often-blurred boundaries of responsibility and points of friction, particularly between functional areas of conservation, planning, management, tourism development and finance (Zhang, 2017; Svensson and Maags, 2018). Notions of overlap and fragmentation are common in all arenas of heritage management and vary with the type of heritage. In the case of West Lake as a cultural landscape bordering a large urban area, site management has been particularly challenging but there is a healthy reflexivity amongst those engaged with the management of the West Lake WHS, born out of experience. Before West Lake was inscribed as World Heritage it was managed as a National Scenic Area (since 1982) and of course it has been a site for attracting visitors for a long time. The State Administration for Cultural Heritage has argued that Cultural Landscape is a category under cultural heritage. They are responsible for West Lake World Heritage Listing issues. However, according to Chinese policy and relevant law, cultural landscapes are not 'pure' cultural heritage and West Lake has rather been under the regulations pertaining to the management of Scenic and Historic Interest Areas.

Official approaches to heritage conservation and management in China are shaped through legislation at national, provincial and municipal level: National Administration Regulations that provide general directions for heritage conservation and Provincial and Municipal site regulations tailored specifically to each heritage site in order to address their needs (Huo, 2015). According to the Deputy Director of the Administrative Committee of WLSA there is an 'integration principle' in place which ensures the integration of WHSs in wider social and economic development plans. Hence, and irrespective of the knowledge of the SDGs and the related agenda, there is recognition that WHS are not merely sites of 'sterile' protection but potential active players in the socio-economic development of each respective area. However, the practice is somewhat different. Organisations, such as the Monitoring Centre at the Chinese Cultural Heritage Academy, organise symposia and conferences informing the relevant professionals about changes in UNESCO policies. But according to West Lake management this is a long process due to the research and processing of information that needs to be conducted prior to any dissemination. In relation to the SDGs, there usually remains a 'vagueness' as to how shifts in UNESCO thinking and direction can be translated to appropriate measures 'on the ground'. As a representative from the Department of Conservation of Relics pointed out, the World Heritage Convention itself and other relevant documents produced by UNESCO remain rather 'abstract' and their translation into rules and regulations, at both national and local level, is problematic. The language of UNESCO regarding World Heritage is not familiar to local officials and politicians. This issue of translating distant, transnational policies and guidelines formulated by UNESCO into measures that 'fit' with national laws of the state party is not of course unique to China. Furthermore, it goes beyond any form of 'filtering down' through the official heritage agencies but extends into wider civil society and the myriad of local organisations and businesses that are ultimately engaged in the delivery of WHS management. In the case of the SDGs, the focus is now on how World Heritage can contribute to sectors of society and the related wider economy and this entails prima facie communication networks that can reach out beyond the heritage sector as well as some common ground for policy interpretation and implementation. This need is recognised by the Management Committee of West Lake despite extant good practices and measures.

Broadly speaking, WHS can be said to have been programmed to deal with two dominant categories of activity: conservation and visitor management. Ongoing conservation issues at a site are officially supported through a Management Plan, the required State of Conservation Reports fed back to the World Heritage Committee and whatever ongoing monitoring work is undertaken by the site itself or related third parties. For sites that are particularly heavily visited by domestic and international tourists, the management of these visitors, in ways that prevents any negative impacts upon the defining Outstanding Universal Value of the site, is also a prime concern. Both activities are, in the main, reactive and resource/time-consuming. This is particularly the case for a cultural landscape site such as West Lake which works within a hierarchy of responsibilities shared amongst actors at the state/central level (including the Chinese Academy of Cultural Heritage) and local players such as the Planning and the Monitoring Department in Hangzhou. While monitoring of West Lake, evaluations and actions are highly developed around conservation and visitor management, they do not as yet feed into or involve any indicators relating to their contribution to the SDGs.

The broad sweep of the SDGs, paired with the fragmented interactions of administration with the local communities result in a limited awareness of sustainability and any associated guidelines or principles for operationalising by local actors. For instance, a local tea house owner from the West Lake area stated that the first time he heard about sustainable development was just five years ago when someone from the administration mentioned the term in the context of waste disposal. Similarly, a guest house owner said that although he understood the concept of sustainable development, this was through watching television programmes and he had heard nothing about this in relation to West Lake. Clearly China is not alone in facing the issues of communicating the SDGs with generally low levels of public and business awareness existing across the developed and developing world (GlobeScan, 2016). The processes of communication regarding the SDG goals tend to be informal and sporadic rather than official and organised. A tea house owner expressed the view that it is up to individual businesses to think about their contribution to sustainable development. However, there would seem to be a sectoral approach to communication that could be useful given that since 2014 there has been an expansion from around 100 tea houses in the West Lake area to almost 400 in 2019, but with no organised direction or guidance provided regarding the sustainable running of these businesses.

Emerging sustainable tourism development

While long popular with tourists before World Heritage designation in 2011, West Lakes' popularity has only increased since, as has the intensification of tourism related businesses within and just outside its boundaries. This intensification of tourism and its central role in economic development in the wider area was promoted by the local government in Hangzhou from the 1990s onwards. The responsibility for planning and management of West Lake tourism falls on West Lake Scenic District Management Committee which operates in collaboration with Hangzhou Tourism Committee (Hangzhou Municipal Government, 2006). In line with the entrepreneurial policy agenda of the local government, WLSA Master Plan and Protection Regulations, released in 2005, provided direction and restrictions concerning the urban development and the maintenance of the 'character' of West Lake to secure the continuous influx of tourism and investment (Wang and Bramwell, 2012). World Heritage status has been layered over municipal government's goal to increase the sites' popularity with West Lake receiving 28.14 million tourists in 2018 (Lu et al., 2019).

The vastly expanded patchwork of small tourism businesses ranging from souvenir sellers to accommodation providers entails a greater need but a more complicated pathway to communicate the sustainable development message. With a cultural landscape there are tourist pressure points, the main one being Duanqiao or 'broken bridge' at West Lake. In part to prevent exceeding carrying capacity at such sites and in part to spread the benefits of tourism, the Management Committee has sought to publicise lesser-known parts of the area and mobilise the World Heritage label and the cultural landscape concept. There are various initiatives in development that seek to build on a more coordinated and extensive role for tourism in the area with the objectives of adopting a more sustainable form of tourism. These involve attempts to encourage visitors outside of the main tourist season, exposing them to 'alternative' destinations within the WHS and drawing on local knowledge that can convey the diversity of heritage in the area. This is being supported by a West Lake ambassadors programme involving mainly young people who engage in a certified year-long training course and are involved in the promotion and implementation of a number of activities designed to showcase West Lake's identity as a WHS.

New business opportunities that can contribute to local economies are also vehicles for practising sustainable development. Despite the limited measures of the government to support community initiatives, the increase of tourism has 'stimulated the entrepreneurial spirit of local residents' (Lu et al., 2019: 9). Indeed, catering businesses, shops, teahouses and homestay operations have blossomed in the region, many exhibiting local creativity in interpreting heritage elements and generating new associated products. The owner of a recently established gift shop for instance, demonstrated an approach to business that cared for the craft and artisanship of the locale through the sales of goods that were locally produced (see Figure 2.2). Her souvenir store drew from the sense of place that was recognised in the 'World Heritageness' of West Lake and linked the intangible heritage of the area to offer alternatives to the mass-produced industrialised souvenirs that were once the norm for the area. Serving speciality teas from local producers to her customers in a purposely designed space further enhances visitor experience whilst creating a sustainable supply chain with local tea plantation owners.

FIGURE 2.2 Giftshop inspired by the craft and artisanship of the locale

Source: Photo taken by the authors.

One local guest house provider expressed the view that although there are almost no financial incentives for making small tourism businesses sustainable, he could nonetheless see the business benefits in demonstrating to visitors how he was part of a WHS. He was able to provide information as to the suppliers of the tea and food he served and was able to recommend quality goods and crafts particular to the area. He was also able to explain the World Heritage significance of West Lake; something that he recognised that other accommodation providers were slow to do. He wanted to make more of the UNESCO World Heritage 'brand' in his business and suggested that other small businesses wanted to do this too, though they were uncertain of how to approach this.

Marginal community engagement

The West Lake Cultural Landscape comprises nine communities with a total resident population in 2018 of 6,900 (Lu et al., 2019). Clearly these communities are swamped by the millions of tourists to the Site and some are better placed to capitalise on tourism than others. It appears that communities have been largely outside of the decision-making relating to tourism and related development in the WHS and yet they have been heavily impacted by the designation with some community

FIGURE 2.3 Areas with poor living conditions adjacent to the World Heritage Site

Source: Photo taken by the authors.

facilities moved outside of the area. In addition to a fall in community-oriented services, Lu et al. (2019) report old buildings demolished, a reduction of community buildings and restrictions placed upon building repairs to the extent that some 70% of the population expressed a wish to move out of the World Heritage protected area. Also reported by Lu et al. (2019) is that when tourist activity started to intensify in anticipation of the 2011 designation of West Lake, and particularly with the publication of the WLSA Master Plan (2005), some 1,037 households in the nine communities were forced to move out of the scenic area, due to the potential negative impacts of the decayed built environment on tourism and World Heritage status.

Regeneration and improvement schemes in the WHS, while focusing on improving the aesthetics of the site, have been less concerned with issues of social sustainability. The projects brought into play have focused more on servicing tourist needs (Shu, 2005; Han, 2006) and have largely been led by the management authorities. This has led to a clearly observable contrast between the beautified built environment within the boundaries of the WHS and poorer living conditions and structures within the buffer zone or just outside the Site's perimeters (see Figures 2.3, 2.4 and 2.5). Since 2011, the construction of basic support service facilities such as schools, healthcare facilities and infrastructure for water and power supplies have been heavily controlled. Indicatively, kindergartens and primary schools were relocated outside the Scenic Area and power and water outages in the area were reported by residents due to restrictions in upgrading the ageing infrastructure.

The priority given to the aesthetics of World Heritage is strong in China as it is across most countries. A pleasant, if somewhat sanitised and often lifeless environment is not at odds with the SDGs and is uncritically taken to be what tourists wish to experience. The social dimension of sustainable development is frequently overlooked in comparison and yet the well-being of local communities in terms of health, environment, water quality, education, employment etc. is deeply embedded across the SDGs and the socio-cultural vitality and uniqueness

FIGURE 2.4 Areas with poor living conditions adjacent to the World Heritage Site

Source: Photo taken by the authors.

FIGURE 2.5 Areas with poor living conditions adjacent to the World Heritage Site

Source: Photo taken by the authors.

of place is related to the satisfaction of these basic living factors. Sense of place, culture, social cohesion, diversity and the flourishing of local talent and craft are also increasingly desired by tourists. This is not something that is separate from World Heritage status, and its capacity to underpin related tourism development, but rather something that is the consequence of the policy adopted at the 2015 Bonn World Heritage Committee, which sought to position designation as an instrument in attaining the SDGs.

Connecting to the bigger picture

The case of West Lake Cultural Landscape reveals a set of disconnections, some of which are influenced by China's system of governance but are common to WHS across the globe. Disconnection between those responsible for the management of WHS, particularly living cultural sites and landscapes, and the local communities that live within these sites and predate designation, frequently occurs in the absence of community engagement and poor or multi-layered systems of communication. When policy changes push at the very purpose of the World Heritage system and direct it to addressing the SDGs, there is inevitably a lag-effect as new messages filter through administrative layers and across a multitude of stakeholders to local practitioners. It is not surprising that communities, small businesses and even part of the heritage sector itself, are not fully aware of the ways that World Heritage is linked to sustainable development and the possibilities it presents. What is interesting in the West Lake example, is that despite communication issues, local actors and businesses seem to have already started to act in line with sustainable development principles and are aware of the benefits it can have, both in terms of good business practice and an improved tourist experience. In a sense, they are ahead of the local authorities in implementing more 'bottom-up' practices that they have heard work in other places and which they can introduce as part of their own enterprise. The motivation for such actions arguably comes from a wider and growing awareness amongst Chinese small-to-medium-sized enterprises that the adoption of elements of the SDGs (elements that they feel they can implement and with limited investment), makes good business sense in their specific locale and stage of development, rather than from any grand and coordinated agenda to save the planet. The context of West Lake as a tourist 'hotspot', with or without the status of WHS, is relevant, as it entails tourism businesses directly dealing with, and meeting the needs of, increasingly environmentally aware consumers (He et al., 2018). Small economically inspired interventions that acknowledge local culture, local produce and craft appear to be contributing to an authentic tourist experience and to the sustainable development of the local communities. However, such uncoordinated local practices are not measured and are largely disconnected from any UNESCO or political framed local or national agenda towards the SDGs.

World Heritage managers are already preoccupied with required conservation practice and monitoring and, particularly in the case of West Lake, the management of large numbers of tourists. Asking management organisations to become more proactive in addressing the SDGs does not only require new ways of working but also new ways of thinking in which heritage is treated not only as a resource to be protected but also a catalyst for sustainability. The 'beautification' of the area through various projects introduced by the West Lake Management Committee points to an assumed priority of aesthetics, selective restoration of the built environment and the concomitant removal of poorly kept dwellings. There is a fine line between the presentation of WHS as necessarily well-protected, well-preserved places that can meet tourist expectations, and authentic, vital communities with distinctive histories and cultures that, at the same time, can meet contemporary needs.

The key to achieving balance – a concept that is central to sustainable development – and to reaching out into the wider arenas of society, economy and environment, is engagement with and participation of local communities, and particularly the communities of small tourism businesses. In the West Lake site there is a practice whereby suggested planning and development interventions in the area are published and open for public comment before implementation. This suggests that participation is limited to a form of information transfer that is still 'top-down', from the relevant authorities to the public. However, the West Lake Management Committee is aware of the need for increased community participation and its potential in co-managing and helping to conserve the Site in ways that can be of benefit for its heritage status, its tourism and the well-being of local communities and economies. Indeed, initiatives such as the young ambassadors programme denote a willingness to enhance public engagement by involving younger generations in the promotion of the site. But more active forms of engagement will require an open and trusting dialogue between the governing bodies, local communities and local businesses, based on a mutual understanding of what the WHS can be as a destination/attraction and also as a living place. A synergistic approach to site management implies effective communication channels with input from the various small tourism business stakeholders in a functional management plan that embraces the SDGs. The increased involvement of volunteers, together with the self-interested motivations of small businesses in adopting practices that fit with the sustainable development agenda combine to reach beyond the official, 'top-down' state-led measures and point to possibilities for increasing the ways in which the WHS of West Lake can better contribute to addressing the SDGs.

References

Birkland, T. A. (2001) *An introduction to the policy process: theories, concepts, and models of public policy making*. London: M E Sharpe.

Denton, K. (2014) *Exhibiting the past: historical memory and the politics of museums in postsocialist China*. Honolulu: University of Hawai'i Press.

Fu, S. and Jin, P. (2020) 'Formation of the modern scenic city of Hangzhou: towards conservation integrated urban planning, 1950s–1990s', *Built Heritage*, 4(16). doi:10.1186/s43238-020-00014-6

Giorgi E., Cattaneo, T., Ni, M. and Alatriste, R. E. (2020) 'Sustainability and effectiveness of Chinese Outline for National Tourism and Leisure', *Sustainability*, 12(3), pp. 1–30.

GlobeScan (2016) *Awareness of SDGs versus MDGs: how engaged are global citizens?* Presentation at the OECD DevCom Annual Meeting, 9th November. Available at: www.oecd.org/dev/pgd/Session4_Bouhana_GlobeScan_OECDTalk_MDGsvsSDGs_2016.pdf (Accessed 16 June 2017).

Han, Q. (2006) 'New image of Hangzhou', *City Express*, 10 September, p. 5.

Hangzhou Municipal Government (2006) Introduction to government departments in Hangzhou, Hangzhou, Hangzhou Municipal Government.

He. P., He, Y. and Xu, F. (2018) 'Evolutionary analysis of sustainable tourism', *Annals of Tourism Research*, 68, pp. 76–89.

Huo, Z. (2015) 'Legal protection of cultural heritage in China: a challenge to keep history alive', *International Journal of Cultural Policy*, 22(4), pp. 497–515.

Liu, S. and Liu, M. (2011) 'On the essence of free-admission model of West Lake scenic spots in Hangzhou and an analysis of duplication', *Tourism Tribune*, 26(10), pp. 50–57.

Lu, J., Luo, X., and Zhang, P. (2019) 'Rights–values–interests: the conflict between world cultural heritage and community: a case study of the West Lake Cultural Landscape heritage in China', *Sustainability*, 11(17), 4560. doi:10.3390/SU11174560

Ludwig, C. and Walton, L. (2020) 'Introduction' in Ludwig, C., Walton, L. and Wang Y. (eds) *The heritage turn in China: the reinvention, dissemination and consumption of heritage*. Amsterdam: Amsterdam University Press, pp. 15–39.

Madsen, R. (2014) 'From socialist ideology to cultural heritage: the changing basis of legitimacy in the People's Republic of China', *Anthropology and Medicine*, 21(1). doi: 10.1080/13648470.2014.880875

Shu, Y. (2005) 'Image of Mei Jia Wu', *Xinhua News2*, 27 September.

Sun, Q. and Liu, Z. (2020) 'Impact of tourism activities on water pollution in the West Lake Basin (Hangzhou, China)', *Open Geosciences*, 12, pp. 1302–1308.

Svensson, M. and Maags, C. (2018) 'Mapping the Chinese heritage regime', in Maags, C. and Svensson, M. (eds) *Chinese heritage in the making: experiences, negotiations, and contestations*. Amsterdam: Amsterdam University Press, pp. 11–37.

UNESCO (2011) *Decision 35 COM 8B.25. Cultural Properties – West Lake Cultural Landscape of Hangzhou (China)*. Available at: https://whc.unesco.org/en/decisions/4296 (Accessed 25 November 2019).

UNESCO (2015) *WHC-15/20.GA/INF.13. Policy for the integration of a sustainable development perspective into the processes of the World Heritage Convention*. Available at: https://whc.unesco.org/en/decisions/6578 (Accessed 20 October 2020).

UNESCO (2021) *The contribution of World Heritage to sustainable development*. Available at: https://whc.unesco.org/en/sustainabledevelopment (Accessed 10 June 2021).

Wang, Y. and Bramwell, B. (2012) 'Heritage protection and tourism development priorities in Hangzhou, China: a political economy and governance perspective', *Tourism Management*, 33(4), pp. 988–998.

Wang, Y., Lu, Y., He, G., Wang, C., Yuan, J. and Cao, X. (2020) 'Spatial variability of sustainable development goals in China: A provincial level evaluation', *Environmental Development*, 35. doi:10.1016/j.envdev.2019.100483

Wu, M.Y., Wall, G. and Zhou, L. (2014) 'A free pricing strategy at a major tourist attraction: The case of West Lake, China', *Journal of Destination Marketing and Management*, 3(2), pp. 96–104.

Xu, S., Liu, Y., Qian, Y. and Wang Q. (2017) 'The significance of the West Lake pattern and its heuristic implications for creating China's heritage tourism economics', *Tourism Management*, 58, pp. 286–292.

Yan, H. (2012) 'World Heritage in China: Universal Discourse and National Culture', PhD thesis, University of Virginia, Virginia.

Yan, H. (2015) 'World Heritage as discourse: knowledge, discipline and dissonance in Fujian Tulou sites', *International Journal of Heritage Studies*, 21(1), pp. 65–80.

Zhang, R. (2017) 'World heritage listing and changes of political values: a case study in West Lake cultural landscape in Hangzhou, China', *International Journal of Heritage Studies*, 23(3), pp. 215–233.

Zhang, R. and Taylor, K. (2019) 'Cultural landscape meanings. The case of West Lake, Hangzhou, China', *Landscape Research*, 45(5), pp. 1–15.

3

LEVERAGING HERITAGE, TOURISM AND PARTNERSHIPS IN DEVELOPMENT

Pham Thi Thanh Huong and Robyn Bushell

Introduction

Throughout the developing world, tourism has been one of the most dynamic, fastest growing economic sectors. Despite COVID disruption, tourism will presumably continue to be an important driver for inclusive socio-economic development. Tourism has significant capacity to stimulate enterprise and job creation, particularly for women and young people. It therefore has important potential in contributing to the achievement of the United Nations' (UN) Sustainable Development Goals (SDGs) (Kozel, 2014). Yet, despite this potential, employment and enterprise generation are often overlooked in tourism policies and planning strategies. Consequently, tourism can fail to achieve development goals and objectives, particularly those linked to poverty. In this chapter we examine heritage tourism as a very specific sector of tourism, one clearly focused on the past, that embraces the promise of a better future. This is of paramount importance in destinations where the SDGs count most, where communities are struggling. In many such developing countries, the partnership between heritage and tourism is often regarded as a crucial component in the shift toward improved standards of living. Many nations with weak or growing economies, that are rich in natural and cultural heritages have, for example, embraced World Heritage listing of their historic sites and landscapes, with a very strategic view to encouraging tourism investment as a direct means of supporting national economic agendas (ADB, 2017). We look critically at this intersection of heritage, tourism and development to consider if this is indeed a productive mechanism to achieve the promise of a better future. We also consider the role partnerships play.

Our focus, in the context of heritage-based tourism, is to assess if tourism through the provision of training and employment does assist with poverty alleviation. We will, however start with a broader perspective to demonstrate the

DOI: 10.4324/9781003107361-4

controversial relationship between development and tourism. And then explore how adding heritage into the various considerations, adds additional challenges, highlighting the need for specific policies to protect the people and places intended as beneficiaries. When the tourism attraction is the local heritage, the heritage may have state, national and international recognition such as World Heritage listing, but invariably the custodians, the stewards, those connected to the land, its history, built environment, tangible and intangible heritages, are local, which is also where tourism production and consumption occurs (Urry, 1995). In this context, where heritage is central to the tourism potential, the questions broaden to encompass whether tourism development is a reliable means of ensuring protection, or does it simply result in the exploitation of heritage? Does the 'community' benefit from a partnership between tourism and heritage? To explore some of the messiness and complexities, we draw on fieldwork in Viet Nam to illustrate some of the problems and some of the possibilities. This includes the crucial role partnerships can play, in both failures and success in poverty alleviation.

Tourism and development

To harness tourism in the service of providing life-changing opportunities and raising standards of living, while also protecting and celebrating heritage, is an attractive proposition. Many nations, UN bodies, aid and conservation agencies have embraced this concept (Mitchell, 2009). However, the relationship between heritage, development and tourism is in reality rather vexed. While not intending to overlook the many positives and great successes, it is also important to not neglect the numerous contentious and awkward aspects which relate to how the promised benefits are realized, and whether these benefits reach their intended target. Key is the question of who gains from the growth of tourism? Countless published reports extol the very positive relationship between tourism and job creation (Servoz, 2016). However, it is necessary to carefully determine whether the opportunity of training and employment results in meaningful work, and who is gaining the work. Are they locals, are they the unemployed and needy? It is not uncommon in destinations in poorer nations, where locals may lack the relevant experience, confidence and range of skills required, that expatriates fill many roles in tourism, especially the higher level and better paid. These things can, should and in some cases, are changing. But to be as productive as possible it is necessary to mandate the provision of 'local' opportunities for entry level employment, skills development as well as career advancement as a priority, or even as a condition of development approval, especially for non-local investment companies. Likewise, ample evidence demonstrates tourism can be a very significant contributor to Gross Domestic Product (GDP) (WTTC, 2017; WTO, 2021), especially in developing nations where there may be limited prospects and expertise to develop new industries. Tourism has flourished in locations with otherwise poor employment prospects. As tourism requires infrastructure, such as major transport and accommodation, the development is often provided by international investment and/or aid. Without appropriate and strategic planning, and development policies focused on local job creation, investors, business operators and management companies frequently bring with them their own skilled workforce and attract educated and experienced workers from major centres with language skills and other cultural awareness, resulting in fewer local opportunities than anticipated. Investors reap the financial benefits, and more so when salaries also leak out of the local economy (Hummel, 2015). Therefore, these two key benefits of employment and economic growth can readily evaporate at a local and regional level, even if at the national scale the data looks impressive.

Access to, and benefit from local resources is another point of contention. Does national economic growth from tourism equate to improved quality of life at the local level, and for those most in need, especially when jobs creation is somewhat tenuous as a key benefit. In many developing countries, the prospect of cheap holidays in attractive destinations has attracted tourism investment since the early 1980s. Idyllic sandy beaches and sunny skies also attracted hordes of visitors. And this of course should be a good thing because tourism marketing theory (Butcher, 2003) suggests the more visitors, the more jobs, and, the more jobs, the greater injection into the local as well as the national economy. Places like Phuket, Bali and Fiji come to mind. In Phuket, hillsides and farming land was removed to create airports and resorts, with farming communities and their local temples moved from the most desirable seaside locations to allow endless resorts to be built. In Bali, people left rice growing in favour of jobs in tourism. In Fiji, young couples left their villages to work in island resorts, leaving behind their children in the care of their older parents, ironically, often in order to care for other people's children holidaying with their families and sending remittances home to their villages while adopting a culturally disparate and more Western way of life. While tourism boomed in these places, the changes were not what many expected or hoped for when they swapped an agrarian lifestyle for a life in a tourist hotspot (Scheyvens, 2011). The very early work of sociologist Eduard De Kadt (1979) questioned the relationship between tourism and development even before the real mass tourism boom. In all tourism destinations, in all countries, the aspects of tourism that cause irritation to local people are highest for those living or working in close proximity to where most tourists spend their time. This is due to the effects of crowding, noise, changes in what is available in shops, increases in prices, increased traffic congestion and so on (Sofield, 2000). Research also shows, unsurprisingly, a strong correlation between people who make a living from tourism having much greater tolerance to the negative aspects, than people who receive few if any benefits – financial, social or cultural (Szromek et al., 2020).

The more recent work of Ashley et al., (2001), Harrison (2008), Mitchell and Ashley (2010), Scheyvens (2002) among others working on the conceptual development of pro-poor tourism, have examined more current practices. The realities and pitfalls are much better understood, and the need for poverty alleviation strategies is well recognized as an urgent priority, rather than seeing these places as just 'destinations', great for affordable and luxury holidays, with scant concern about the impacts on local lives of often profligate use of local resources for tourism. For example, excessive use of water in water scarce locations, for extravagant swimming pools, lush gardens, golf courses and endless quantities of washing, while locals can lack access to meagre supplies of safe water and struggle to survive (Honey, 1999). Much has been done to address this early style of tourism that had frequently turned a blind eye to many such social injustices, and pro-poor tourism is promoted by the various UN bodies including being championed by the World Tourism Organization (WTO, 2002) and various aid agencies, especially in South East Asia (Harrison and Schipani, 2009; Hummel, 2015). Has this twinning of poverty alleviation with tourism development been successful, or is it still a very sound concept in need of more thorough interrogation and policy formulation to improve the praxis and its outcomes?

There is also a sizable body of work examining many other social problems that tourism brings, with the often stark contrast between the lives of locals and the visitor, all part and parcel of modernization, economic growth and change. In brief, the social change associated with rapid tourism development is often also accompanied by attracting unwanted, opportunistic, illegal activity leading to undesirable behaviours, including gambling, excessive alcohol consumption, sale of illicit drugs, prostitution, including child sexual exploitation (Glotfelty and Miles, 2018), and a range of other criminal activities resulting from tourists bringing relaxed attitudes, higher spending capacity and a range of easily stolen items of value. Tourism in the midst of poor communities can also lead to begging, encourage families to leave traditional skilled work, create dietary issues with major health implications from either the loss of productive farming land for resort development, the sale of the best quality food for higher prices to tourism businesses, and/or losing farming practices in favour of working in tourism, among numerous other negative social impacts (Hitchcock et al., 1993).

In part, the problems are a result of tourism attracting the market to the resource, unlike most industries, where goods are exported to a market. This exposes the host community to a wide range of social, cultural and environment disruptors which change everyday life once an area becomes established as a popular tourism destination. While all are important, we don't delve into these aspects, apart from noting that tourism brings its share of issues as well as benefits. Nor do we unpack the numerous significant environmental costs of tourism development, other than acknowledging they are part of the compounding problems confronting those living in poverty. It is also important to note that very few locations are solely places of heritage tourism, so even if heritage conservation is successful, many other issues may remain. In addition, there are often questions about the integrity of heritage protection when exposed to the forces of commodification, when authenticity is compromised, and/or the sheer volume of visitors puts pressure on heritage sites (Edensor, 2001). Think of ritual becoming performance, such as alms giving becoming a morning circus/photographers' delight, or hordes climbing sacred sites or fragile structures to watch sunrise or sunset, or just to snap yet another Instagram pic; imported weavings mass produced by machine for sale to tourists as ethnic artefacts; cable cars and theme parks installed detracting from World Heritage values and so on. The list of issues is considerable, and so too the challenge to policy makers and practitioners.

National economic growth vs. improved quality of life for all

The UN mantra is to 'leave no-one behind' (World Bank, 2016). However, poverty is a multidimensional phenomenon, and the disadvantage extends beyond income (ESCAP, 2016). As tourism flourishes, those living in the greatest poverty can find themselves facing even harsher conditions with ever-increasing demands from tourism for resources, such as land, water, power; prices of everyday goods and services escalate; the loss of access to traditional markets for goods as living standards of others rise; and dislocation from arable land among some of the unintended but consequential effects of tourism development.

The most marginalized face numerous barriers to the advantages afforded by tourism, lacking language skills, even the most basic training, confidence and any familiarity with what is required. Appropriate, deliberate enabling support is necessary to leverage opportunities for the underprivileged. The hope has been that pro-poor tourism would prove a useful strategy, delivering benefits in least developed and developing countries (Harrison, 2008; Mitchell and Ashley, 2010). But without sound and very specific policy, tourism can readily further disadvantage those living in poverty, not only leaving behind the neediest, but actually increasing the gap. This can occur despite good intentions and broad policies of governments responsible for developing economies. The potential of tourism as a social and economic enabler requires close scrutiny and careful management. The vulnerable are also the most impacted by shocks to the local environment and/or economy. When economies are disrupted, be it by natural disaster, civil or political unrest, or as in the current circumstance, due to global pandemic, tourism demand can diminish overnight, as the world has witnessed with COVID. The least skilled, lowest paid and the unemployed experience the greatest burden of such disruptions, with no reserves or resources to draw on (ESCAP, 2016).

As mentioned already, tourism development frequently also impacts other dimensions of sustainable development, including the integrity of cultural and natural heritage, as tourism transfers their value into attractions, putting pressure on heritage sites and managers to prioritize visitor needs over conservation needs, with commodification processes influencing perceptions and rights.

We look to examples in Viet Nam, where tourism and heritage, in particular World Heritage, have become key elements in the government's recent strategic plans for development (Viet Nam Government, 2017). World Heritage listing of sites has become a significant trigger for economic development through tourism. These examples demonstrate the need for informed and deliberate policy, to educate and incentivize the private sector, for capacity building and ongoing support to help bridge gaps and address some of the issues already noted. We also highlight the significant role of partnerships in achieving successful outcomes, though these are not without their own challenges. A variety of partnerships, between international and national bodies, between different ministries, between the public and private sector and between formal and informal community sectors are identified as crucial.

It is well over 30 years since Viet Nam ratified the UNESCO *Convention Concerning the Protection of the World Cultural and Natural Heritage* (1972 World Heritage Convention) (UNESCO, 1972) in 1987. Viet Nam has now become one of the most active Member States in the Southeast Asian region, with eight World Heritage designated properties. Radical changes in the national development context over the last decade, has given rise to shifts in the allocation of domestic resources and collaboration with new stakeholders, especially the local private sector, in all dimensions of the economy and society. This includes both the heritage and tourism sectors. The Vietnamese Government, in focused partnership with UNESCO, actively participated in the formulation and implementation of the UNESCO (2015) *Policy on World Heritage and Sustainable Development.*

Viet Nam has shifted from a Low Income Country with a GDP of 575 USD per capita in 1987 to a Low Middle Income Country with a GDP of 2,715 USD per capita in 2019 (World Bank, 2014, 2019) and of 3,500 USD per capita in 2020 (IMF, 2021). At the end of 2018, Viet Nam had over 714,000 active private business entities with an average increase of 100,000 new business registrations per annum over the last decade (General Statistics Office, 2019).

Tourism has become one of three spearhead economic sectors of the country, with continual rapid growth of tourist arrivals to 2020. International visitation had grown from 3.78 million in 2009 to 18 million in 2019 (VNA, 2019) with heritage sites, especially World Heritage properties, becoming major hubs of tourism.

Viet Nam's World Heritage Sites (WHS) make huge contributions to local and national socio-economic development. The number of visitors and the revenue gained from ticket sales have increased between three to ten-fold over the ten-year period 2006–2016 (Hanh et al., 2018). The government also recorded 16 million arrivals (including 7 million international arrivals) visiting the eight World Heritage properties in 2017, bringing in 2,535 billion VND (110 million USD) from direct visitation revenues, and created millions of jobs. Because this rapid growth has been quite recent, Viet Nam has benefitted from the local UNESCO office actively participating in policy guidance, and working with hindsight from other regional offices, where heritage tourism has also been important in development strategies, including Cambodia, Laos and Myanmar. Integral to the growth of tourism at World Heritage sites in Viet Nam are targeted practices, co-developed between UNESCO, the International Labour Organization (ILO), (UNESCO and ILO, 2014), and the government, aimed at improving training and employment opportunities. The objective has been specifically to create a significant contribution from heritage tourism to the improvement of living standards in and around World Heritage sites (MoCST, 2018) and so provides useful insights to how heritage tourism can achieve the promise of a better future for all.

In this context, of very significant growth in tourism and unprecedented involvement of the private sector, policy makers and managers of World Heritage sites have faced both opportunities and development-related challenges. While Viet

Nam is reliant on international support in many areas to address the development gaps, pockets of poverty and inequalities, the national situation and realpolitik have radically changed. This is also true for development projects and interventions supporting heritage conservation, heritage site management and facilitating the local community's engagement. Heritage-site focused interventions have helped to save important built heritage, damaged during the war and neglected during the country's period of economic hardship. Now, more than ever, an integrated approach is necessary to deal with increasing multidimensional development pressures in the broader heritage sphere. These pressures are financial, geographical and political in nature. The dynamic business environment is part of the main challenge for sustainable development, but multi-stakeholder engagement is also a key part of the opportunity. This includes increased resources for reinvestment in heritage sites. However, the rise of the private sector has also witnessed the rampant and inappropriate installation of tourism and entertainment infrastructure in and around heritage sites. The competition, and race, is to invest in commercial and entertainment services that are lucrative, but most do not speak to heritage values, and are not focused on upskilling the most needy. As well, there has been considerable debate and controversy over certain concessions within several heritage sites. In a country with a non-democratic, central government, business connections are formidable. The leverage offered by a UN agency such as UNESCO cannot be underestimated. Without this, highly inappropriate development would be inevitable.

Collaborative support for the UN Sustainable Development Goals

The examples here, drawn from an ambitious UNESCO and ILO joint project supporting sustainable tourism in central Viet Nam (2014–2016) highlight lessons learnt about elements of success and some key challenges to enduring and productive partnerships, (UNESCO and ILO, 2014; Pham, 2016).

Several multi-sector partnerships involving knowledge and resource sharing were undertaken with the deliberate aim to support the UN SDGs (UNDP, 2021) in Viet Nam. The objective and mode of operation involved collaborations across public and private sectors (as per SDG 17); to improve the contributions of WHS to promote sustainable modes of tourism development (SDG 12B); to encourage opportunity and employment (SDG 8.5; 8.6), to support youth and providing training; and through all of these, to assist poverty reduction (SDG 1) by sustaining income growth for the bottom 40 per cent of the population. As a UNESCO project, important components were also supporting local culture and products (SDG 8.7); and reinforcing efforts to safeguard natural and cultural heritage (SDG 11.4).

The project was developed and implemented by the two UN agencies, UNESCO and ILO. The project operated at the highest level of agency commitment to cooperation, compared to the more usual generic format of joint programming between UN agencies. Various partnerships were involved between UNESCO Ha Noi Office, the ILO, the Ministry of Culture, Sports and Tourism

(MoCST), with Provincial and District governments and several local communities. National and international researchers supported UNESCO to monitor the progress and the outcomes. The ultimate goal was to improve decent work and income opportunities for local people, especially vulnerable groups in central Viet Nam (Quang Nam and Thua Thien-Hué provinces) through sustainable heritage tourism development.

The rationale of the two UN agencies are important in understanding the mode and success of the operation. Firstly, is the complementarity in areas of technical expertise and attention to each organizations priorities. UNESCO prioritized the sustainable preservation of WHS, enhancing benefits and participation of local people, with an integrated development strategy for heritage in the broader region. For example, UNESCO experts provided strategic destination planning, developing satellite attractions, and therefore, releasing pressures and the burden from tourism on the core heritage assets. They also worked with numerous local groups to ensure community-led culture products and services that will contribute to ongoing benefits to sustainable income generation and protect the intangible cultural heritage of the region. The ILO placed their attention on skills training, decent work and fairer benefit sharing from tourism, working through the tourism value-chain approach (ILO, 2016).

Secondly, the partnership approach was instrumental in reducing the cost of implementation. By reducing the many costs of duplicate project structures, taking advantage of various existing tools and each agency's in-house expertise, similar interventions helped the two organizations commit to the delivery of results at modest cost but with ambitious targets and results. A high level of efficiency was a key benefit of the partnership approach.

Thirdly, was the strong connection between the tourism sector and the heritage assets. Three WHS of Hué Citadel Complex of Monuments, Hoi An Ancient Town and the My Son sanctuary are obviously key heritage assets, but also constitute the core visitor economy assets of the destination and tourism value chain in central Viet Nam. See Figure 3.1. The living communities and the entire tourism value chain can benefit from heritage preservation and promotion of WHS, achieving the objectives of the ILO, and on the other hand, tourism adds values and generates resources for protecting and promoting the sites, in line with UNESCO objectives. With this shared vision, the two agencies were able to readily agree on the selection of the targeted locations and local partners for concerted actions.

The primary partnership of the two implementing UN agencies provided an important platform to engage a broad range of other partners, capitalizing on the multi-sector partnerships in project implementation at the ground level. Examples drawn from the joint project serve to demonstrate the success of mobilizing partnerships to support sustainable development through heritage tourism. Poverty reduction was targeted through the production of authentic local cultural products and the generation of decent job opportunities, while also reinforcing efforts to safeguard natural and cultural heritage.

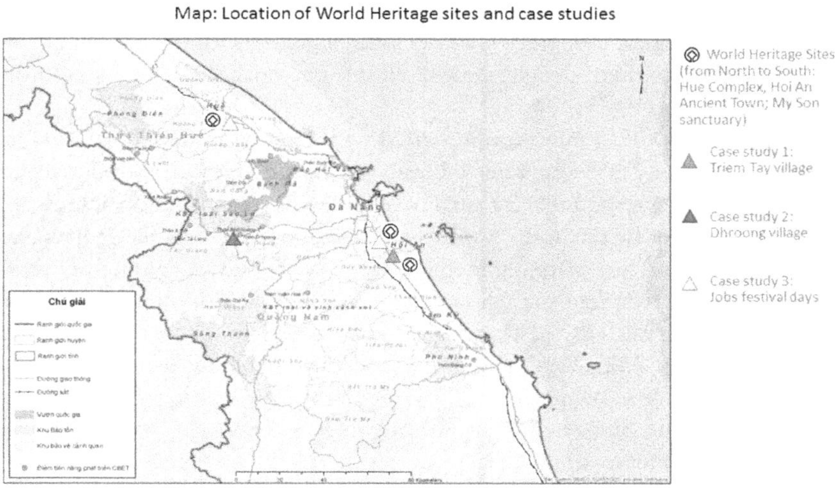

FIGURE 3.1 Map of Quang Nam and Thua Thien-Huế Provinces, home to three of Viet Nam's WHS and project targeted locations

Source: Map created by the author (Huong).

These examples highlight what is achievable with a sound partnership, where the parameters are carefully defined; the goals are clear and shared; the areas of responsibility are aligned to the strengths of the various partners; partners bring quite different strengths and expertise; and each partner has a good understanding of their roles and responsibility. Also, importantly, the budget, the timeline and the process all need to be discussed in detail, agreed and to be transparent.

The first example, from Triem Tay, a satellite village of the Hoi An WHS, is located just 15 minutes by boat across the Thu Bon river from the heritage town. Before the project intervention, the village of 750 inhabitants faced complex problems. All adults of working-age had left their home villages to seek work in nearby cities. The traditional craft of making sedge mats, that had previously made Triem Tay a wealthy community over hundreds of years, was declining and on the verge of collapse. Serious river bank erosion due to increasing flood events, and a lack of government attention, support or action added to the problem of survival for this small rural village. Collectively, the circumstances left the village extremely vulnerable. Local students had to travel to school in neighbouring communities, because the village school was closed along with the health clinic. Villagers lacked many public facilities. Traditional practices in organic farming had been discontinued. The village, despite its advantage of close proximity to the heritage core in which heritage tourism was booming, could not capitalize on their rich natural and cultural resources: an intact and authentic village landscape with typical setting of a Vietnamese rural countryside; a rich cultural-historic set of old houses and craft making traditions; abundant knowledge and wisdom in traditional folk songs and food making; and beautiful green walking paths, together with the friendliness and warm hospitality of local people. Despite all this potential, the village was in desperate circumstances.

The UNESCO–ILO intervention started with training to develop a task force of local facilitators. They were selected from the village together with district and commune agencies responsible for rural development, culture and tourism promotion. Once trained the task force was mentored and supported by the project team in applying a public-use planning methodology (Kohl, n.d.). A community action plan designed to revitalize the cultural resources and develop community-based tourism activities was created through a series of community meetings. A core group of 32 of the 152 village households gradually established a cooperative that played a central role in ownership of the community action plan, while the project team convened and supported them to bring in several partners at different levels in an integrated intervention.

Over a two-year period the partnership achieved many outcomes. This included a local cooperative shared by one third of village households, providing community tourism services and playing a facilitation role in multiple social activities; a local culture house was renovated and repurposed from the abandoned school; a tourism plan created by the village and directory of attractions; an interpretation framework reflecting the linkages with the Hoi An cluster region; a walking path was upgraded, connecting restored village temples, old houses and craft making households (see Figure 3.2); a community organic garden, river rest stops, and a bicycle trail connecting Triem Tay to a neighbouring woodwork village; a light bridge was installed over the river connecting with Hoi An; a new bamboo pier was installed for river boat access; strategic business contracts were established with tour operators; and a program was created for field trips by local schools, training institutions from cities and some foreign universities.

Given the limited project resource, less than 80,000 USD budgeted for this location (along with seven other targeted locations), such results would not have been possible without the wide range of partnerships.

At the local level, the District government contributed 60 per cent of the cost of the renovation of the abandoned school, transforming it into a culture house. The District also provided 100 per cent of the cost to upgrade the village trail by mobilizing political and financial support of the Provincial government through a rural development program. The District government also channelled resources from an agriculture program to support the public facilities (electricity, seeds and water supply) for the community organic garden. In addition, a vocational training program was adjusted to support skills training courses matching the needs of local people in hospitality.

At the provincial level, the Department of Culture, Sports and Tourism provided support in developing tourism maps and visitor guide information, promoting the location with tour operators, and including the community in their regular training and technical programs. The Provincial Cooperative Alliance

FIGURE 3.2 A local craft household opened as a part of the Triem Tay village tour

Source: Photo taken by the author (Huong).

brought in by the ILO, provided guidance, technical and business training, as well as financial support for the establishment of the local community-based tourism cooperative and its early period of operation. The local cooperative also benefited significantly from becoming a member of the Provincial Cooperative Alliance, providing access to interest free government loans. In addition, the Provincial Government multiplied its efforts in mobilizing government support from different programs to advance the construction of the new light bridge (for pedestrians, bicycles and motorbikes) connecting the village with Hoi An old town, and supported a project testing the consolidation of riverbanks with multiple wetland plantings.

Finally, the partnerships with the private sector, civil societies and training institutions contributed a vitally important piece to the picture and success of the project. The support from two responsible tour operators in Hoi An brought in small groups of visitors starting with half-day tours which helped to activate the community tourism services. Local non-governmental organizations (NGOs) including the Green Youth Collective, brought in volunteers and experts in organic farming and will maintain the long-term technical support and farming models. The first visitors, together with students from both local and foreign schools, helped the community services survive through the early stages, gaining experience and confidence for growth over time.

It has been a real success from where it started, but there is still a long way to go to make the enterprises sustainable, and considerable support at the District and Provincial level are still needed to ensure success.

Tourism as a tool for poverty reduction and promoting gender equity in Dhroong village

The second example, Dhroong village of the Ka Tu ethnic minority, is located in the Western area of Quang Nam Province, a 2-hour drive from Hoi An WHS, 2.5-hour drive from My Son WHS and a 3-hour drive from the Citadel Complex of Hué Monuments. The village is located along the Ho Chi Minh trail, with a spectacular tropical forest landscape at the south end of the huge Indochina karst mountain system, rich in ethnic cultural traditions and skills. However, the village is typical of a region left behind with the majority of the population living below the poverty line. Quang Nam provincial statistics indicated an annual GDP per capita of just 760 USD in the district in 2016 compared to the provincial average of 2,470 USD (Quang Nam Department of Planning and Investment, 2016). This village, like many other ethnic villages, could not improve their circumstances due to the lack of jobs or income opportunities. Most of the 30 households in the village were living in extreme poverty, relying mainly on subsistence from planting cassava and collecting food from the forest. The village had benefited from earlier international assistance with a community house functioning as a common space for local women to get together to learn to weave their traditional brocade textiles. But this generated little financial support for the small village.

They also faced critical social challenges, particularly stereotyping attitudes which precluded girls and women from education, instead taking on all the family duties, working on the farm, caring for babies and children, weaving and doing routinely hard work. Most of the villagers were illiterate.

The village was, however, assessed to have potential to be developed into a stopover along the Ho Chi Minh trail by the UNESCO–ILO community-based tourism project team. Additional income opportunities were considered feasible through the production of authentic, quality brocade craft products and becoming part of the adventure tour trails, which were receiving a gradual increase of cultural visitors willing to explore off the main tracks of the heritage site cluster, within a 3-hour drive.

The intervention was designed to take into account potential income generation, the social challenges, together with geographical and language barriers. The project began with some direct support to improve the communal space with better facilities, making it friendly and more convenient for local women to weave their brocade textile. Before the offer of skills training, the project engaged and cooperated with the local Women's Union and district authorities. This was essential to convince local families to enable women to attend classes to learn basic reading, writing and calculation skills, as well as participating in community sessions and discussions on gender roles. Two local women were provided with further training to become

FIGURE 3.3 Local women's group at the Dhroong community weaving space

Source: Photo taken by the author (Huong).

the focal points for the community. They then took on local facilitator roles in the formation of a local cooperative, assuming the accounting task and liaison with textile buyers from Hoi An.

Key results from the intervention over two years were the establishment of a basic level cooperative in brocade textile; a functional communal house used daily by local women for weaving, socializing and teaching each other their craft skills; a long-term contract with a high yield fashion designer in Hoi An; a retail craft-shop owned by the local cooperative in the front of the communal house; better information explaining their culture, craft skills and community was produced; partnerships with tour operators started bringing small groups of adventure and cultural visitors to the Western, guided trekking paths connecting this village and another Ka Tu ethnic village (Bhohoong) nearby; and cooking and village stay services are now provided by the local cooperative. The community business records show each cooperative member (all women) earned an additional annual income of 470 USD from brocade weaving products, not including their traditional earnings from farming, forestry and the other tourism-related activities such as cooking, trekking services. See Figures 3.3 and 3.4.

The support facilitated an enabling environment accounting for many of the benefits of the project, as well as the direct support in tourism product development. The partnerships were essential to prepare the community, providing readiness

FIGURE 3.4 A community workshop at the Dhroong community weaving space

Source: Photo taken by the author (Huong).

and enabling conditions for community tourism. The Women's Union and the Provincial Cooperative Alliance, closely monitored by the ILO, provided intensive support, mentoring, training, informal dialogue and counselling to encourage local women and their family's support to enable them to participate in the business training, bookkeeping and hospitality skills, and eventually working with the private sector. The dialogue around gender roles was essential to the process of developing local capacity and confidence and preparing the necessary conditions for local people to enter tourism-related activities. The Provincial Cooperative Alliance also provided the essential skills training such as bookkeeping, basic cooperative operations, procedures to access various government programs supporting ethnic minorities and start-ups. These areas were not strengths nor expertise of the two UN agencies. So, the local partnership was very important and complimentary, and undoubtedly the basis of the success. The two UN agencies were able to provide backstage support, giving priority to the development of the provincial tourism marketing strategy, interpretation framework, facilitation of press trips, initial visits of tour operators and guide training.

The District government and the Provincial Department of Culture and Tourism facilitated the dialogue, followed by a signed partnership agreement between the Dong Giang district and three neighbouring districts enabling inter-district sharing of security information and streamlining the required process for foreign visitors to the region which sits on the border between Viet Nam and Laos PDR.

The private sector also deserves mention, especially a highly committed social enterprise in fashion design and a joint adventure tour operator, and some other retail shops in Hoi An, which stimulated the business operations by sourcing the locally produced craft products and bringing in small groups of visitors.

Conclusion: the important role of partnerships

These examples provide insights into how to achieve successful heritage and tourism partnerships. Firstly, local people/beneficiaries should be positioned at the centre. Those who needed support were identified as facing multidimensional challenges: economic, social and cultural. The relevant strengths, advantages and areas of expertise of the different partners could then be mobilized accordingly for greater impacts with cost effectiveness. The partners represented many levels of governance and skills, including international (UN agencies) with focused areas of expertise, support and access to resources, as well as national, provincial, district, community and private sector partners. Each bought specific skill sets to the various partnerships and projects. But most importantly, the skills and areas of responsibility/influence matched the needs of the beneficiaries. The most marginalized face many barriers to the advantages afforded by tourism, requiring very concerted and ongoing effort and expertise to be effective.

Secondly, there must be capable facilitators as the catalyst for coordination and change. Ideally, they should be identified, grown and developed from locals, local existing entities and be well supported with capacity building, such as the local task-force and community cooperative (Triem Tay), and Women's Union (Dhroong). Equally important, is capacity building for managers and key personnel at middle level of management at the local district and provincial levels. This helps to ensure both the smooth implementation of projects and provides an exit strategy, leaving local capacity to sustain, replicate and to transition to others when the project team leaves.

Thirdly, the involvement of public–private partnerships is essential for a sustainable tourism model. The private sector can often be perceived as profit-oriented and thus have lesser roles in development projects or taking part in achieving the SDGs. However, in fact, the private sector possesses unique buying power, bringing in and influencing clients, visitors, creating jobs, and additionally, changing their own practices and influencing other private operators. This was a feature of both examples, but also in many other projects undertaken in the UNESCO-ILO initiative (Pham, 2016).

And finally, intensive support, mentoring and training is essential. This requires funding support and requires agencies like UNESCO and the ILO, with the expertise and focus to commit to seeing the projects succeed. The project implementers invested in the inception phase with careful situation analysis, stakeholder mapping, highlighting the local ownerships and using a culture-sensitive and site-specific approach. Without this initiation phase the projects would have no traction.

Despite the successes, these projects still face numerous challenges. A significant challenge relates to the degree of readiness of stakeholders. Often this can be quite low due to either low interest, low awareness or lack of any previous opportunity. In the first example, a business survey with 14 existing travel agencies before the intervention in Triem Tay village, showed that no one wanted to invest in the village, nor assessed it positively regarding tourism potential, claiming that it would require a huge investment on their behalf, because local people had no experience and very limited skills in hospitality service. This is the reason most tourism investors in most developing countries bring in their own qualified and experienced staff, and therefore locals miss out on the main opportunities. In the case of Triem Tay, the project had to: switch the order of intervention, with primary actions given initially to building capacity for the local community, and to support product development aiming at lower demanding segments of visitors (students, domestic locals, small groups interested in 'off track' experiences); engage with two pioneer travel companies in formulating the short day tour services; and partner with government agencies and media in promotion – all essential grounding activities before the location could become an attraction to regular travel agencies. This is an ongoing challenge.

Significant challenges can also arise from different personal agendas, including the timeline pressure of each stakeholder. Hence the success factors mentioned above were instrumental to overcome the challenges: the coordination, aligning the common priorities by positioning local beneficiaries at the centre and capitalizing on the advantages of the private sector through demonstrating to them the potential of new attractions, new tourism products and policy incentives. However, these projects are still not settled and have potential to fall over once the primary agencies leave the projects. This undoubtedly will be worse post COVID when all tourism has collapsed, and all local small businesses are struggling. Tourism unfortunately is an industry highly susceptible to market fluctuations.

Currently, in Viet Nam and other parts of South East Asia, the management of public-private partnerships around WHS is largely ad hoc, based on a case-by-case response to specific investment projects, rather than a strategic, proactive approach, centred around a long-term vision that promotes and protects the heritage values. The repeated emergence of development projects within, or in proximity to, core zones points to the planning framework needing to be fundamentally revised, providing greater regulatory control over the buffer zones. This situation is becoming more acute as the tourism sector grows. This is also the case throughout SE Asia. So, working with the private sector is not without problems. In order to gain maximum benefit and avoid irreparable damage to the integrity of WHS, it seems to be necessary to regulate and closely manage public–private partnerships.

Ongoing collaborative research, monitoring and strategic planning is an essential aspect of the partnership approach, not only to bring the international spotlight, and the strength of the UN to align heritage and tourism with sustainable development (Bushell, 2018) but also to develop more open communications, understanding of issues and to build trust. It is also essential to have more readily available and sound base data in order to adequately measure progress.

The politics of power and connection at the local and national levels is a constant that cannot be underestimated. So, while the partnerships, between different ministries, between the public and private sector and between formal and informal community sectors were identified as crucial, the dynamics of the business environment is equally a key challenge for sustainable development. The rise of the private sector, and with it, rampant and inappropriate tourism infrastructure in and around heritage sites remains problematic for UNESCO. Despite excellent connections at all levels of government, the level of influence of very senior business people remains dominant in decision-making processes. This has required UNESCO to tackle the problem quite laterally, by attempting to bring leading business people in as their partners and to attempt to influence their thinking and understanding of what constitutes appropriate and long-term strategic business. This is a slow process with limited success to date.

The work undertaken by UNESCO in Viet Nam is supporting the government at all levels, in both knowledge and resource sharing, as they work to achieve their SDG targets. While there remains much to do to improve the quality of life of the most disadvantaged, the progress has been impressive (Kozel, 2014). With all developing nations striving to achieve the SDGs, and in particular poverty alleviation via the development of tourism, progress has been encouraging but not without challenges. Tourism is not a panacea. It works in some places but not everywhere. And it is not without the many costs – social, cultural and environmental, as we outlined. These challenges are increased for both policy makers and practitioners when heritage is added to the tourism-led community development mix. This adds more complexity, more stakeholders, and requires even greater attention to planning, governance and monitoring.

The role of UN agencies, aid and development agencies and NGOs across South East Asia, and the partnership approach in promoting sustainable modes of tourism development has been very important and mostly productive. Heritage tourism as a past facing enterprise has the potential to provide new futures, especially for those in poverty. Despite its potential, however, tourism frequently fails to achieve development goals and objectives, particularly those linked to poverty.

While we have identified some important elements in the formulation of success, from our experience, to realize the potential requires pragmatic and forceful policies, interventions and stakeholders with considerable agency. A partnership-based approach is an important principle of sustainable development. World Heritage management involves many actors outside the heritage field. More needs to be done to engage stakeholders in other sectors to realize the broader social, economic and political importance of heritage protection.

References

Ashley, C., Roe, D. and Goodwin, H. (2001) *Pro-poor Tourism Strategies: Making Tourism Work for the Poor. A Review of Experience*. London: Overseas Development Institute.

Asian Development Bank (ADB) (2017) *Tourism Sector Assessment, Strategy and Road Map for Cambodia, Lao PDR, Myanmar and Viet Nam (2016–2018). Manila:* ADB

Bushell, R. (2018) 'Report to the Australian Dept Foreign Affairs and Trade, International Relations Grants Program: Australia-ASEAN Council', International workshop on *World Heritage and Sustainable Development in the Contemporary Context*, co-sponsored by Viet Nam Ministry of Culture, Sport and Tourism, UNESCO, and the Australian ASEAN Council.

Butcher, J. (2003) *The Moralisation of Tourism: Sun, Sand … And Saving the World?* London: Routledge.

de Kadt, E. (1979) (ed) *Tourism: Passport to Development?* New York: Oxford University Press.

Economic and Social Commission for Asia and the Pacific (ESCAP) (2016) *Facts and Trends at the Outset of the 2030 United Nations Development Agenda*. 2016 Statistical Yearbook for Asia and The Pacific. United Nations Economic and Social Commission for Asia and The Pacific. Available at: www.unescap.org/stat/data (Accessed 30 April 2022).

Edensor, T. (2001) 'Performing Tourism, Staging Tourism', *Tourism Studies*, 1(1), pp. 59–81.

General Statistics Office, (2019) 'White Book on Vietnam's Business sector'. Available at: www.gso.gov.vn/Default.aspx?tabid=382&ItemID=19273 (Accessed 30 April 2022).

Glotfelty, E. J. and Miles, G. M. (2018) '(S)Expectations Abroad: Male Traveler Interactions with Southeast Asian Economies', *Dignity: A Journal on Sexual Exploitation and Violence*, 3(3), https://doi.org/10.23860/dignity.2018.03.03.04

Hanh, D. B., Thuy, T. T. T., Huong, P. T., and Cuong, N. C. (2018) 'World Heritage and Sustainable Development in Vietnam', in Logan, S. and Larsen, B. L., (eds) *World Heritage and Sustainable Development: New Directions in World Heritage Management*. New York: Routledge, pp. 240–56.

Harrison, D. (2008) 'Pro-poor Tourism: A Critique', *Third World Quarterly*, 29(5), pp. 851–68.

Harrison, D. and Schipani, S. (2009) 'Tourism in the Lao People's Democratic Republic', in Hitchcock, M., King, T. and Parnwell, M. (eds) *Tourism in South East Asia Revisited*. Copenhagen: NIAS, pp. 165–88.

Hitchcock, M., King, V., and Parnwell, M. J. G. (1993) *Tourism in South East Asia*. London: Routledge.

Honey, M. (1999) *Ecotourism and Sustainable Development: Who Owns Paradise?* Washington: Island Press.

Hummel, J. (2015) 'The Rise and Fall of Tourism for Poverty Reduction within SNV Netherlands Development Organisation', Unpublished PhD Thesis, Wageningen University, The Netherlands.

ILO (2016) 'Value Chain Development Methodology'. Available at: www.ilo.org/wcmsp5/groups/public/---ed_emp/---emp_ent/---ifp_seed/documents/instructionalmaterial/wcms_434363.pdf (Accessed 30 April 2022).

IMF (2021) 'Countries Data, Viet Nam'. Available at: www.imf.org/en/Countries/VNM, (Accessed 30 April 2022).

Kohl, J. (n.d.) 'Public Use Planning. PUP Global Heritage Consortium'. Available at: http://pupconsortium.net/focusareas/pup/manual/ (Accessed 30 April 2022).

Kozel, J. (2014) *Well Begun But Not Yet Done: Progress and Emerging Challenges for Poverty Reduction in Vietnam (English)*. Washington, DC: World Bank Group. Available at: http://documents.worldbank.org/curated/en/898561468322131999/Well-begun-but-not-yet-done-progress-and-emerging-challenges-for-poverty-reduction-in-Vietnam (Accessed 30 April 2022).

Ministry of Culture, Sports and Tourism (MoCST) (2018) 'Report on the Protection and Preservation of Vietnam's Cultural Heritage for Sustainable Development, Hanoi', pp.9–10.

Mitchell, J. (2009) *Value Chain Analysis and Poverty Reduction at Scale*. Briefing Paper 49. London: Overseas Development Institute.

Mitchell, J. and Ashley, C. (2010) *Tourism and Poverty Reduction: Pathways to Prosperity*. Abingdon: Earthscan.

Pham, T. H., (2016). 'Final Evaluation Report VIE/13/08/LUX, ILO, Hanoi'. Available at: https://en.unesco.org/news/final-evaluation-report-project-responsible-tourism-development-central-viet-nam-vie1308lux (Accessed 30 April 2022).

Quang Nam Department of Planning and Investment (2016) 'Information Portfolio for Calling Investment in Dong Giang District'. Available at: www.dpiqnam.gov.vn/Portals/1/THONG%20TIN%20DAU%20TU/TH%C3%94NG%20TIN%20%C4%90%E1%BA%A6U%20T%C6%AF%20%C4%90%C3%94NG%20GIANG-QU%E1%BA%A2NG%20NAM.pdf (Accessed 30 April 2022).

Scheyvens, R. (2002) *Tourism for Development: Empowering Communities*. London: Longman.

Scheyvens, R. (2011). *Tourism and Poverty*. New York: Routledge.

Sevoz, L. (2016) *Sustainable Tourism: A Driving Force of Job Creation, Economic Growth and Development*. International Labour Organization. Available at: www.ilo.org/global/about-the-ilo/newsroom/news/WCMS_480824/lang--en/index.htm (Accessed 30 April 2022).

Sofield, T. H. B. (2000) 'Rethinking and Reconceptualizing Social and Cultural Issues in Southeast and South Asian Tourism Development', in Hall, C. M. and Page, S. (eds) *Tourism in Southeast and South Asia: Issues and Cases*, Oxford: Butterworth-Heinemann, pp. 45–57.

Szromek, A. R., Kruczek, Z. and Walas, B. (2020) 'The Attitude of Tourist Destination Residents towards the Effects of Overtourism—Kraków Case Study', *Sustainability* 12(1), 228 DOI:10.3390/su12010228

UNDP (2021) *UN Sustainable Development Goals*. Available at: https://bit.ly/3pjUBWL (Accessed 30 April 2022).

UNESCO (1972) *Convention Concerning the Protection of the World Cultural and Natural Heritage*. Available at: https://whc.unesco.org/en/conventiontext/ (Accessed 30 April 2022).

UNESCO (2015) *Policy on World Heritage and Sustainable Development*. Available at: https://whc.unesco.org/en/sustainabledevelopment/ (Accessed 30 April 2022).

UNESCO and ILO (2014) 'Joint Concept note for Technical Cooperation Project "Sustainable Tourism in Central Vietnam"', Hanoi. Available at: https://en.unesco.org/news/ilo-unesco-joint-concept-note-technical-cooperation-projects-viet-nam-2014-2015 (Accessed 30 April 2022).

Urry, J. (1995) *Consuming Places*. Routledge: London.

Viet Nam Government (2017) Decree 109 on the Management of World Natural and Cultural Heritage sites. Available at: https://datafiles.chinhphu.vn/cpp/files/vbpq/2017/09/109.signed.pdf (Accessed 05 May 2022).

Vietnam National Administration of Tourism, Ministry of Culture, Sports and Tourism, (VNA) (2019). Available at: http://vietnamtourism.gov.vn/english/index.php/statistic/international (Accessed 30 April 2022).

World Bank (2014) *Well Begun, Not Yet Done: Viet Nam's Remarkable Progress on Poverty Reduction and the Emerging Challenges*. Hanoi: World Bank. Available at: https://bit.ly/3SLqYLk (Accessed 30 April 2022).

World Bank (2016) Vietnam 2035: Toward Prosperity, Creativity, Equity, and Democracy. Available at: https://openknowledge.worldbank.org/handle/10986/23724. (Accessed 05 May 2022).

World Bank (2019) Available at: https://data.worldbank.org/indicator/NY.GDP.PCAP.CD?locations=VN (Accessed 30 April 2022).

World Tourism Organisation (UNWTO) (2002) *Tourism and Poverty Alleviation*. Madrid: WTO.

World Tourism Organisation (UNWTO) (2021) *Economic Contribution of Tourism and Beyond*. Available at: www.unwto.org/statistic-data-economic-contribution-of-tourism-and-beyond (Accessed 30 April 2022).

World Travel and Tourism Council (WTTC) (2017) *Travel and Tourism Global Economic Impact Report*. Available at: www.stb.gov.sg/content/dam/stb/documents/mediareleases/Global%20Economic%20Impact%20and%20Issues%202017.pdf (Accessed 05 May 2022)

4

INTANGIBLE CULTURAL HERITAGE, MARKETING AND INTELLECTUAL PROPERTY FOR SUSTAINABLE LIVELIHOODS

The Case of HIPAMS

Charlotte Waelde, Diego Rinallo, Ananya Bhattacharya, Harriet Deacon, Anindita Patra, Rajat Nath, June Taboroff and Benedetta Ubertazzi

Introduction

The commercialisation of intangible cultural heritage (ICH) is a politically sensitive subject, yet a reality for many heritage bearers. Of concern for the regulators is that over-commercialisation may occur resulting in the meaning of the ICH to the communities being lost, and 'profits' from commercialisation going to third parties. Yet for many communities and heritage bearers, commercialisation of their heritage is the only way to make a sustainable living. To investigate these tensions, the British Academy funded the interdisciplinary project 'Celebrating local stewardship in a global market: community heritage, intellectual property (IP) protection and sustainable development' in India. The project (short-titled HIPAMS, Heritage Sensitive Intellectual Property and Marketing Strategies [2018–2021]) asked the question: How can marketing and IP help marginalised communities harness their ICH to contribute to sustainable livelihoods while avoiding the perils of over-commercialisation?

This chapter will explain the academic and regulatory contexts for the HIPAMS project, highlighting the legal frameworks for IP and how these are quite different from those for the safeguarding of ICH. While both seek to regulate information, they do so with very different underpinning theories, goals and tools. It is when ICH and the market come together and claims of IP rights are made, that challenges for heritage bearer communities arise. The chapter will discuss how sustainable development through commercialisation of ICH has been addressed from within the 'ICH authorised discourse', and how that intersects with the IP regime. It will then illustrate, using the HIPAMS project as a case study, how IP can be used in practice as a tool to underpin marketing strategies when heritage bearer

DOI: 10.4324/9781003107361-5

communities commercialise their ICH. While the practical strategies chosen by the communities may not directly address the legal and regulatory concerns, they do show that IP can be a useful tool in pursuit of sustainable development.

The research environment

ICH safeguarding falls under the auspices of UNESCO which administers the 2003 *Convention on the Safeguarding of the Intangible Cultural Heritage* (henceforth 2003 Convention). According to the 2003 Convention, ICH includes practices, representations, expressions, knowledge, skills, which are to be found in oral traditions and expressions; performing arts; social practices, rituals and festive events; and traditional craftsmanship (UNESCO 2003, art. 2.1). These manifestations are neither mutually exclusive nor exhaustive, but examples of ICH. What binds them is their intangible nature. Each exists for a transient moment in time, and exemplifies the performative, fluid and processual nature of ICH as it is passed from generation to generation (Gibson, 2005). While the 2003 Convention does not address ownership of ICH, it places the community at the centre. The 2003 Convention's Ethical Principles state that the communities and groups concerned should be the ones to define what their ICH is, what value it has to them and how to manage it (UNESCO, 2015). ICH may be manifested in tangible objects, such as instruments, objects and artefacts (UNESCO, 2003, art. 2.2), but the operative word here is 'manifested'; the ICH is the intangible knowledge and skills which are manifested in these artefacts. The 2003 Convention along with the associated Operational Directives (ODs) (UNESCO, 2016) and the Ethical Principles establish a framework for safeguarding ICH. Safeguarding is directed towards adopting measures that ensure the viability of the ICH and can include identification, documentation and education (UNESCO 2003, art. 2.3).

This processual, intergenerational and community-oriented nature of ICH stands in contrast to the regime of IP which refers to creations of the mind and includes literary and artistic works, and symbols used in commerce. Led by the World Intellectual Property Organization (WIPO), the international IP regime is mainly driven by Western concepts and has been developing at the international level since 1883 with the *Paris Convention for the Protection of Industrial Property* (1883) for geographical indications (GIs), the *Berne Convention for the Protection of Literary and Artistic Works* (1886) (henceforth Berne Convention) for copyright and relatedly the *International Convention for the Protection of Performers, Producers of Phonograms and Broadcasting Organizations* (1961) (henceforth Rome Convention) for neighbouring performers rights.

The rationales for giving copyright protection to creative works are both economic and moral.[1] In terms of economic justification, it is to enable the owner to earn financial benefit from what they create. The theory is that as the author is able to earn a reward from exploitation of the work through exclusive rights in the work, there is an incentive to create more, which is of public interest benefit because creativity and innovation flourishes, and there is a broad range of creative outputs for general consumption (Landes and Posner, 1989; Fisher, 2001). There are also ethical or moral justifications which claim that the author has a natural or human right over the products of labour (Hughes, 1988; Drassinower, 2012), and instrumental justifications that focus on encouraging desirable activities (Hettinger, 1989). A GI by contrast is a sign used on products that come from a particular geographical place and that have particular qualities associated with that place. GIs exist primarily to communicate information: a GI 'is designed to break through the clutter of misleading messages about the origin of a good and connect customers with those goods which carry an authentic hallmark of Geographical Indications' (Kapur, 2016: 5).[2] Performers rights, like copyright, are intended to give to eligible performers the economic incentive to perform and also to enhance the reputation of the performer through being named (Arnold, 2015). The rights differ in content and in scope. Copyright, which last upwards of 50 years after the death of the author (Berne Convention, art. 7), arises mostly when the work is fixed in some tangible form, for instance when the book is written or the painting painted, vests initially in an individual and may be owned individually or in some jurisdictions by an institution (ibid., art. 3–4). A GI can generally be used by traders whose goods meet the specifications of the GI and may be administered by an association on behalf of the traders.[3] A GI can last forever so long as registered and used.[4] Performers' rights belong to the performer and generally last for 20 years after the fixation of the performance (Rome Convention, art. 13). Both copyright and performers rights have moral rights associated with them giving the author the right inter alia to claim to be identified as the author/performer of the work thus giving the possibility of enhancing reputation (Berne Convention, art. 6; *WIPO Performances and Phonograms Treaty*, 1996, art. 5; *Beijing Treaty on Audiovisual Performances*, 2012, art. 5).

The economic underpinnings of the IP system are clear. The IP system enables informational goods to be traded in the market, ready to be used as a communicative/promotional tool and/or defensive tools. In terms of communicative and promotional functions, for example, the communicative power of a GI is such that it can promote messages about the origin and attributes of the goods to which the GI is attached. In terms of a defensive tool, for example, the exclusive right of reproduction granted by copyright enables the owner to prevent others from reproducing a work protected by copyright without permission.

As Farah and Tremolada have noted, IP 'aims at protecting the proprietary rights and economic interests of individuals (human or corporate), whereas … [ICH] relies on the pre-preservation of the common heritage of a specific community or group' (Farah and Tremolada, 2015).

A key challenge for the ICH regime is the Western IP concept of the public domain. The public domain in IP is all of those parts of intellectual works over which there is no IP right. For example, when copyright protection expires, creative works fall into the public domain. As there is no IP right over works in the public domain, anyone may take these and reuse them without payment or permission. ICH generally does not meet the criteria for protection by IP for a number of reasons. These include that ICH does not have the requisite level of originality having been in existence for many generations, and that ICH is the knowledge and skills of the heritage bearers; knowledge and skills are not protectable by IP which generally only protects creations of recent origin and once they are fixed in some tangible medium. This leads many (Westerners) to believe that ICH is in the public domain. This can be seen in the activities of multinational corporations in the fashion field and elsewhere when contemporary high fashion is 'inspired' by Indigenous designs – commonly referred to as cultural appropriation.[5] Recent examples include the activities of Zara, Anthropologie and Patowl when Mexico alleged that Zara had used a pattern distinctive to the Mixteca community of San Juan Colorado; Anthropologie had used a design developed by the Mixe community of Santa Maria Tlahuitoltepec; Patowl had copied a pattern from the Zapoteco community in San Antonino Castillo Velasco (Reuters, 2021. See also: Lenzerini, 2008; Rimmer, 2015). In the appropriation of names, high fashion has also been found wanting when using Indigenous community names as trademarks to promote their products, such as Urban Outfitters use of 'Navajo' and 'Navaho' (*Navajo Nation v Urban Outfitters, Inc.* [2013]).

WIPO has for many years sought to develop *sui generis* IP protection at the international level for ICH thus removing any perception that it is 'in the public domain'. However, this has been unsuccessful in spite of 20 years of negotiation (Drahos, 2014; Wendland, 2019). In 1967 and 1971 attempts were made to introduce protection for folklore through a revision of the Berne Convention, but the attempt failed due to conceptual and definitional challenges.[6] Subsequently, and from the mid-1990s, WIPO embarked on a project to gather information about traditional cultural expressions (TCEs) and traditional knowledge (TK)[7] with a view to agreeing a treaty that would provide protection through IP. A draft treaty was produced in 2004 and has been amended several times since with the latest iteration being from 2019. Agreement still eludes the members of WIPO with a large number of issues remaining unresolved.

While it is unlikely that any new form of IP protection will emerge for ICH at the international level, the 2003 Convention and its ODs contemplate the use of existing IP rights by ICH communities. Article 13 of the 2003 Convention talks about State Parties adopting 'appropriate legal measures to ensure the safeguarding, development and promotion of the ICH present in its territory'. The ODs provide that it is through the application of, among other things, IP rights that States Parties should endeavour to ensure 'that the rights of the communities, groups and individuals that create, bear and transmit their ICH are duly protected when raising awareness about their heritage or engaging in commercial activities'. This suggests that if communities use IP rights as a legal measure, the two of the functions of IP noted above could be relevant: the communicative/promotional function when raising awareness, and both the defensive and communicative/promotional functions when engaging in commercial activities. However, the UNESCO Intergovernmental Committee (ICH committee) is keen to avoid any suggestion that the 2003 Convention introduces anything akin to a system of (intellectual) property. In its draft decision on the nomination of *Međimurska popevka*, a folksong from Međimurje (No. 01396) for inscription on the Representative List of the Intangible Cultural Heritage of Humanity (Representative List), the ICH committee noted that a proposed media campaign around the folksong would raise awareness about 'collective creativity and intellectual rights' clearly taking care to avoid a reference to intellectual *property* rights, and going on to stress that the 2003 Convention does not seek to establish a system of ownership 'such as through geographical indication and intellectual property' (UNESCO, 2018). IP rights therefore could be used as an instrument to help raise awareness when underpinning marketing strategies or to give some protection when developing commercialisation strategies, but not to create new rights in ICH. ICH in other words, should not be propertised and commodified via IP (Lenzerini, 2008; Rimmer, 2015).

It is against the background of these conflicting frameworks and regulatory positions that discussions have taken place with regard to the commercialisation of ICH and how that could contribute to economic sustainability.

ICH and commercialisation

In the lead up to the agreement of the final text for the 2003 Convention it was anticipated that safeguarding ICH could contribute to the sustainable economic development of bearer communities.

The 2003 Convention ODs contemplate the possibility that ICH communities will commercialise their ICH. Para 116 reads as follows:

> Commercial activities that can emerge from certain forms of intangible cultural heritage and trade in cultural goods and services related to intangible cultural heritage can raise awareness about the importance of such heritage and generate income for its practitioners. They can contribute to improving the living standards of the communities that bear and practise the heritage, enhance the local economy, and contribute to social cohesion. These activities and trade should not, however, threaten the viability of the intangible cultural heritage, and all appropriate measures should be taken to ensure that the communities concerned are their primary beneficiaries.

It is notable that the wording does not refer to the commercialisation of ICH as such, but that commercial activities can *emerge* from forms of ICH, and that goods and services *related* to ICH can generate income for the practitioners. Para 116 also concedes that commercial activities can result in positive economic and social impacts for bearer communities – but warns against the risks of negative impacts on the viability of the ICH and that third parties, external to the communities, might take the lion's share in the economic benefits. An attendant concern was that by embracing the market, over-commercialisation could occur, leading to commodification of ICH and loss of community control (Kirshenblatt-Gimblett, 2004; Lixinski, 2013; Akagawa and Smith, 2018; Harding, 2018). Paras 102 and 117 of the

Convention highlights the dangers that could arise from commercialisation. Para 102 states that commercialisation could:

> 1. de-contextualize or denaturalize the intangible cultural heritage manifestations or expressions concerned;
>
> [...]
>
> 4. facilitate the misappropriation or abuse of the knowledge and skills of the communities, groups or individuals concerned;
> 5. lead to over-commercialization or to unsustainable tourism that may put at risk the intangible cultural heritage concerned.

Para 117 emphasises what the response to these concerns should be: to avoid commercial misappropriation; to manage tourism in a sustainable way; to find a proper balance between the interests of the commercial party, the public administration and the cultural practitioners; and to ensure that the commercial use does not distort the meaning and purpose of the ICH for the community concerned.

Despite the hesitancy of UNESCO, over the years ICH has increasingly been commercialised. However, because of UNESCOs reluctance to expressly address commercialisation and how it could contribute to safeguarding and sustainable development for the benefit of the communities, commercialisation opportunities, and IP in the processes and products of those opportunities, are often claimed by others as foreshadowed in Para 116 (Lixinski, 2020). Well-known examples include the patenting of processes over TK by international organisations, such as the patent granted on turmeric for its healing properties by the USPTO for the University of Mississippi medical centre in 1995, later revoked when successfully challenged by the Indian government on the basis that it was not novel (Jayaraman, 1997). Other examples include Urban Outfitters' use of 'Navajo' and 'Navaho', and the use of Mexican Indigenous community designs by a range of multinational fashion corporations (*Navajo Nation v Urban Outfitters, Inc.* [2013]).

These examples illustrate two of the points above: first, that what is taken by these third parties is viewed, under the Western IP system, as being 'in the public domain'; and second, UNESCOs concern that ICH should not be propertised through IP claims. In these examples, and following on from Lixinski's point, property rights arise in the hands of third parties, and not those of the heritage bearers.

The HIPAMS project

While at the international level the politics and policies of UNESCO and WIPO lead in two different directions, they converge in an underlying belief that IP rights could be useful as tools to assist with the sustainable development of ICH communities engaging in commercialisation activities. The HIPAMS project hypothesised that marketing and IP could be brought together and used as tools to help communities strengthen sustainable livelihoods from their ICH, while avoiding over-commercialisation and commodification of their ICH – the worries articulated in the 2003 Convention and ODs.

The HIPAMS project team comprised academic experts in heritage, marketing and IP, along with an NGO called Contact Base (also known as Banglanatak dot com), based in Kolkata. At the heart of the project were three communities in West Bengal: Patachitra painters (patuas) from Naya village in Pingla in Paschim Medinipur; Chau dancers from Purulia and Chau mask-makers from Charida in Purulia; and Baul and Fakir community members from Nadia, Murshidabad.

- Patachitra is the practice of painting a story on a scroll which is unrolled as the *patua* performs the story through song, or *pater gaan*. Patachitra is said to date back more than 2,500 years. Stories depicted on the scrolls can now be religious or secular and often deal with ethics, morality or contemporary issues such as 9/11 and the Covid-19 pandemic.
- Purulia Chau is a dynamic, acrobatic dance in which the dancers wear ornate costumes representing characters from Indian epics. The dancers' costumes include elaborate masks made by the mask-makers from Charida. The masks are made by hand on a base of papier-mâché and clay, covered by cloth, paper and glue, and adorned with clay, glass beads, trinkets and straws.
- A person becomes Baul or Fakir after renouncing his/her religion and then becoming a part of a devotional (*bhakti*) community tradition influenced by Hinduism, Buddhism and Islam. Bauls develop an understanding of their philosophy through the guidance of a Guru during which they learn secret knowledge. Baul-Fakirs' musical performances and content have diversified in recent decades pushed by commercial demand for staged performances and audio recordings.[8]

The HIPAMS project accepted that for some communities, commercialisation of ICH artefacts through the market was essential for survival. The decision of whether, and how, to commercialise ICH was for the community members to make. There was recognition that not all ICH communities would be at a stage of development where it was possible to use IP and marketing tools in support of commercialisation.[9] Government support and the work of NGOs, notably Contact Base, had already assisted the Patachitra artists, Chau dancers and Charida mask-makers and Baul and Fakir communities to lift themselves out of abject poverty through targeted interventions including supporting heritage skills transfer within the community. As the communities were already making a living from their ICH, the HIPAMS team felt that it was appropriate to work with them to co-create targeted marketing interventions supported by IP to the extent desired by the communities. This would expand on the work already done by Contact Base while keeping the main focus on what the communities considered as important in their ICH. At every stage the communities were central to the work of the HIPAMS project and using methodologies including forum theatre and walking stories, the communities and the researchers worked together to develop the HIPAM strategies.[10]

The HIPAMS process and the role of marketing

Neither the 2003 Convention nor the ODs explicitly mention marketing, a body of knowledge deemed critical for the successful commercialisation of products, services, performances and other market offerings (Kotler and Keller, 2015). Over the years, marketing has been adapted to the needs and specific contexts of cultural, social and not-for-profit organisations. Activities such as awareness-raising or promotion can be understood as part of marketing. The HIPAMS project considered marketing as a possible 'missing link' between ICH safeguarding and its commercial valorisation, and sought to adapt core marketing principles and tools to the specific needs of heritage bearer communities.

In the academic context, marketing research has engaged very little with ICH-related research. Some work has adapted key marketing tools to the management of heritage attractions and sites (Misiura, 2006). Others have focused on how established brands can leverage their heritage as a source of competitive advantage, for example through digital storytelling initiatives, exhibitions or corporate museums (Rose et al., 2016). Insights from work in this area are however of limited help when modelling links between safeguarding and commercialisation of ICH. In the absence of this broader theoretical framework, the HIPAMS project built on the conceptual and applied work carried out in the context of the AlpFoodway Interreg Alpine Space project (2016–2019),[11] possibly one of the first to integrate insights from ICH safeguarding, IP protection and marketing in the context of ICH. The conceptual work during the first stages of the HIPAMS project also contributed to integrate ICH-related concerns into the development of marketing strategies and tactics, so as to seek to reduce the negative consequences of commercialisation.

More specifically, four key ideas underpinned the HIPAMS marketing strategies, bearing in mind that these should be heritage-sensitive. First, communities should be empowered to be the protagonists of their own marketing strategies. This aspect is particularly important when marketing interventions are designed or financially supported by NGOs or government agencies on behalf of the heritage bearers. In these cases, strategies should be co-created with the heritage communities, including their participation and consent at every stage of design, planning and implementation.

Second, social bonds inside the communities should be supported to mitigate the risk of intra-community tensions and competition. Traditional marketing knowledge is based to some extent on warfare metaphors (e.g., 'strategies' and 'tactics') and on the idea that rivals need to be defeated if a profit is to be made. Special caution is needed to reinforce intra-community solidarity, cooperation and learning. In this respect, marketing ideas such as 'finding one's market niche' or 'differentiating one's products' can result in complementary offerings that reduce the risk of excessive competition.

Third, heritage-sensitive market segments should be targeted. Segmentation is a key notion in marketing strategy, based on the idea that the marketplace consists of clients with different characteristics and needs. No individual or organisation can satisfy the needs of all market segments, and targeting specific segments can result in more effective marketing strategies, for example, in terms of pricing differentiation, ad hoc promotion and promotional tools. Thanks to market research, homogenous types of clients can be identified on the basis of specific characteristics such as demographic variables (e.g., gender, age, socio-economic status, place of residence, country of origin, languages spoken), lifestyles, ICH awareness and knowledge and sensitivity to specific heritage attributes of ICH-based offerings. Heritage bearer communities can decide not to serve client groups whose needs risk introducing dynamics that are dysfunctional to the goal of safeguarding important heritage attributes (e.g., tourists who demand cheap souvenirs but are not interested in learning about the heritage or willing to pay enough to provide a fair remuneration to the producers).

Fourth, individual and collective promotional approaches should be encouraged where community members support each other (Rinallo, 2020). Much like IP rights, marketing initiatives can be individual or collective (benefitting the entire community). Individual marketing initiatives in many cases need to be complemented by collective marketing efforts raising awareness about the ICH and the bearer communities. Celebrity ICH practitioners for example can be used to shed light on the community and the next generation of heritage bearers. Collective websites, media relations, museums, exhibitions and experiential showcases can contribute to educate public opinion and potential customers about the ICH and its cultural value, improving its reputation and, as a result, providing market opportunities for the community as a whole.

The HIPAMS project and the role of IP

In the HIPAMS project, the IP rights that were of most relevance were those introduced above – copyright, performers rights and GIs. Patents did not feature in the project at all; design rights featured only tangentially, while the use of registered trademarks was considered, but not pursued. As the discussion in the HIPAMS team developed, five factors helped to shape thinking about how marketing and IP might be brought together in the commercialisation strategy while also keeping the central focus on the ICH that was important to the communities and helping to safeguard that.

The first was that while HIPAMS was primarily an action research project (with an intended high level of impact), the theoretical frameworks within which IP rights are framed should inform how they were used. This relates both to the broad justifying frameworks for property rights in intangibles, as well as to the rationale for the individual rights used in the strategies. The HIPAMS IP strategies in other words, were not developed in a vacuum, but rather took heed of why the IP rights existed, and what work they were designed to do. Allied to this were the promotional/communicative and protective strategies that IP can support and how these might best be used in the project.

Against this background, the second factor was that the use of IP rights should underpin the marketing strategies that were co-created with the communities, which in turn were developed in response to what the communities considered vital in terms of their ICH. Echoing the discussion above, IP rights were used in HIPAMS to underpin marketing strategies mostly as a tool of positive protection and communication, rather than to carve out exclusive territory as a form of defensive protection divorced from the marketing imperatives. This strategy was also in response to the third factor, that of enforcement of IP. For some forms of IP, an example being a GI, an organisation has the responsibility to monitor infringements and take action. For other rights, including copyright and performers rights, it is up to the individual to take action against infringement. For the members of ICH communities that we worked with, such action would not be possible: enforcement action is expensive, lengthy and uncertain. Rather than developing IP strategies that relied on enforcement for their effectiveness, the strategies focused on positive communication and promotion.

The fourth factor, also core to the marketing strategy as noted above, was the community nature of ICH and the individual/collective nature of IP rights. Some IP rights, such as GIs and collective trademarks are communitarian by nature. A GI for instance may be used by those who meet the conditions for use of the GI. It can be used by all members of an ICH community who produce crafts to the specifications in the GI. A GI thus reflects and reinforces the community nature of ICH. Copyright and performers rights by contrast are individual by nature. Copyright for instance, is mostly owned by the individual who authors a work; performers' moral rights attach to the individual. Careful consideration was given to possible effects of the personalisation of ICH through the use of IP, and strategies underpinning marketing efforts tailored accordingly. Related to this was the fifth factor which was whether an association was in existence that represented the community. If an association was in place, then it was possible to think about collective IP rights that could be managed by the association. Where no community association existed, and imagining one was not an option, then collective IP rights would not be a feasible proposition.

Converging HIPAMS – the conceptual framework

During the first stages of the HIPAMS project, members of the team with marketing, heritage and legal expertise engaged in frequent comparison of perspectives, asking themselves questions such as: When does it make sense to register a trademark? What is the difference between a GI and a collective trademark? When ICH-related products do not benefit from high levels of awareness and are unlikely to be exported, is the investment required to legally protect and enforce IP justified? How should the risks of widespread copying of images linked to social media promotion be balanced with the benefits derived from increased visibility of ICH practitioners? How can new markets be developed without imperilling the community ICH?

An important turning point was when the team stopped saying 'from an ICH perspective', 'from a marketing perspective', 'from an IP perspective' when discussing a proposed action, and instead adopted ideas integrating their combined expertise. These ideas coalesced around four broad and interlinked themes each of which was designed to keep the ICH at the core of attention. The first was the imperative to maintain the heritage skills repertoire within the community. Early on when working with each of the communities, discussions took place with the community to find out what heritage attributes, skills and knowledge they considered core to their ICH. Action should then be taken to ensure that this repertoire was maintained, for instance through intergenerational training, and ensuring markets for traditional products made from these heritage skills. However, with a focus on marketing and increasing demand, it was understood that it would be likely that community members would innovate in the types of products they produced and performances they engaged in as they sought to meet new market demand. To address this, the second theme acknowledged that innovation should be encouraged, but that this should be heritage-sensitive; in other words, innovation should be rooted in heritage knowledge and skills. Such a strategy might show itself for example through *patuas* painting contemporary events on scrolls (such as about the Covid-19 pandemic)[12] but using traditional painting knowledge, skills and materials to do so; or Chau dancers performing a contemporary choreography using traditional steps, costumes and masks. The third theme focused on enhancing the reputation of the community and their heritage. This theme brought together ideas on how marketing and IP strategies could be used to increase the reputation of the community and their heritage. Once again, the ICH was at the core, with marketing input used to develop new audiences, and IP used as a tool to support the marketing strategies. An example was the use of a GI on packaging and promotional materials with the function of the GI being to help to increase the reputation of the community. The fourth theme focused on empowering the community in their relations with others. This brought to the fore the need for collective action in marketing and collective IP strategies such as developing ethical codes (also called art codes in the HIPAMS project) to be used by community members when dealing with third parties such as festival organisers, gallery owners and distributors. The ethical codes contain requests to these third parties drawn from IP law, general human rights norms and ethics such as to respect the ICH and to credit community members when circulating photographs of them and their work. The HIPAMS team represented this holistic strategy in the HIPAMS canvas shown in Figure 4.1.

The HIPAMS case study in practice

Prior to co-creating the marketing and IP strategies, the HIPAMS team spent time with the communities to find out what they thought of their ICH, what they believed their traditions to be, how these might have changed over time and what they did not want to change in the future. One of the tools that grew out of these encounters is the roots and fruits tool: the roots of the ICH enable the growth of fruits which manifest

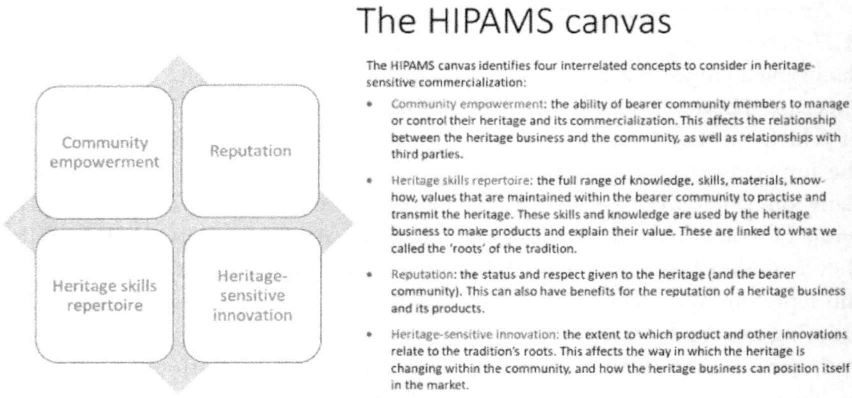

FIGURE 4.1 The HIPAMS canvas

Source: Illustration created by authors.

the ICH in different ways.[13] For instance, for the Charida mask-maker community, the ICH roots include the way in which Chau masks are made and the traditional masks; the fruits enable the community to use the knowledge and skills that make up the style not just for traditional masks, but for a whole range of contemporary masks – such as the one depicted in the HIPAMS roots and fruits tool.

One concern foreshadowed in the discussion above, is that using IP in connection with ICH would in some way commodify the ICH. However, the roots and fruits tool illustrates the benefits of the HIPAMS process in thinking through the relationship between traditions and products for sale, and highlighting cases where offering a product for sale, designing or creating a new product would damage the link to the roots of the tradition. What IP can then protect is the tangible manifestations of that ICH where the IP preconditions are met. For example, part of the patuas' ICH skill is in painting a particular style; the knowledge and skill encompassed in the painting style, and the style itself are unprotectable. What is protectable is the expression of those skills in the form of the traditional painting when on the scroll, or the umbrella, or the kettle, or of contemporary subject matter using the ICH skills such as Swarna Chitrakar's painting of a coronavirus.[14]

After focussing on the ICH as identified by the communities, and co-creating marketing strategies that met the needs and desires of the communities, the HIPAMS team overlaid this with co-created IP strategies that supported the marketing efforts and kept a focus on the ICH attributes important to the community. It also addressed the themes identified in the HIPAMS canvas. For example, a GI for *Bengal Patachitra* had been registered by Chitrataru, the community organisation for Patachitra in Naya village, as a handicraft in classes 16 (painting) and 24 (textiles) when the HIPAMS team started work with the community. The GI was identified as an important marketing tool for promotion and communication and to develop the reputation of the community in connection with their craft.

Enforcement of the GI arose as an issue for consideration. Practically, enforcement would likely be challenging as it is the registered owner and user who need to take enforcement action – a path unlikely to be pursued by Chitaratu or the patuas. For that reason, the HIPAMS team focused on thinking about the use of the GI and the communicative message that it can send, how it can differentiate handicrafts in the market and how it can indicate to consumers the origin of the products creating a link between the consumer and the patuas and their village. To this end, one of the strategies implemented by the community was to develop eco-packaging for their scrolls and other goods to which the GI was affixed. This not only gave a practical solution to the challenge of visitors transporting scrolls, but in addition created the important informational link. This packaging also contains a QR code which links to a performance by the patuas on their website. During a discussion with the patuas, the HIPAMS team discovered that while the pater gaan used to be central to, if not more important than, the scroll as the artists performed the song and unfurled the scroll, going from door to door in search of payment, over time the scroll had taken centre stage as the tangible objects sold to customers. The QR code on the packaging re-links the two, enabling the consumer to watch the performance while unfurling a scroll, even when not witnessing a live performance. This also helps to reduce the risk of commodification by linking the roots and fruits of the tradition.

During IP training, the *patuas* also learnt about what copyright and performers rights could do in underpinning their marketing efforts. With performers rights they could ask to be attributed as the performer of a performance; with copyright they could have rights in the recording of their performances (and the underlying work when original), and had the right to permit the taking of photographs of their paintings. As with GIs, enforcement is practically impossible. The HIPAMS team suggested that the community think about using Creative Commons licenses to permit consumers and visitors to take pictures and recordings of their work and circulate these on social media, and use the CC-BY-NC license. This would allow copies of the photographs and performances to be circulated for non-commercial purposes so long as the artists (and the village) are attributed. Such a strategy starts to teach the consumer that the patuas have rights in their work, but that they are giving permission for circulation of reproductions under the stated conditions. This circulation may in due course encourage more visitors to the villages as increasing numbers of people become aware of their work – helped by the requirement of attribution.

The ethical codes developed with the communities proved to be an important tool to empower the communities in their relations with others, as well as meeting marketing imperatives and the difficulties of IP enforcement. For the Chau community, the ethical code grew initially from a story told to the HIPAMS team by Moushumi Choudhury, a young female Chau dancer from Maldi in Purulia and winner of the 2019 Grand Prize in the Asia-Pacific Youth ICH Storytelling Contest for her photo story *Breaking the Glass Ceiling: One Step at a Time.*[15] Moushumi and her fellow Chau dancers had been contracted by a large Indian film-maker to perform, in full costume with masks, in a film called *Jobordokhol.* While Moushumi and her dancers received a payment for their performance, they were not credited in the film. Being credited is not only important for reputation, but it is also a right granted by performers rights laws. But it would have been difficult for Moushumi to negotiate her rights with the film-maker. The ethical code is designed to help to fill this void. It is based in the law, in human rights norms and in ethical frameworks and addresses the converged themes in the HIPAMS canvas. It can be used as a tool by Moushumi in relations with third parties with the hope and anticipation that in due course the principles that it embodies will be widely recognised by third parties in their interactions with the Chau (and other) communities.

Challenges

The project was evaluated by the team in 2021. While a difficulty with this timetable was the short timeframe for assessing impact of the use of IP and marketing on the commercialisation of ICH, the team hopes to return in five years for a follow-up inquiry. What the 2021 evaluation did find was that the project created new awareness among the tradition bearers about IP rights and the correlation with safeguarding and sustainable economic and social development through ICH. For instance, a Baul told us: 'when a photograph or work of any artist is being promoted, if the name of contact is given the artist also gets promoted with the art form' and a Chau dancer said:

> I worked in 7 movies … where our art was recognised but our names were not given. The names of the cast and crew are given but our names are nowhere to be found. Now I have understood, so I will claim the recognition whenever a booking comes.

However, the extent to which that knowledge translated into improved economic outcomes for the heritage bearers is extremely hard to gauge. An evaluation survey showed that the price of Patachitra products had increased 5–10% between 2019 and 2021 resulting in an increase in artists income.[16] Sixty per cent of the Baul Fakiri artists said that their fees or number of performances had increased between 2019 and 2021, while 100% of the Chau dancers said that their remuneration for every show as well the numbers of annual shows had increased over the same period. While it is tempting to claim that this is the result of the work of the project (despite the pandemic) it is of course not possible. But by using IP and marketing in service of the commercialisation of ICH while maintaining the rigour of the academic framework, what the project has done is to show how the communities can use these tools to their advantage.

Conclusion

The legal frameworks for ICH and IP start from two very different places: one, IP regulates the flow and exploitation of information products in the marketplace; the other, ICH, focuses on social and cultural processes. IP has innovation, economics and private (commercial) interests at core; ICH focuses on public interests and the relationship between heritage and the past (Bortolotto, 2020). At the legal regulatory level, these two regimes converge because both deal with information – information that without formal legal structures of control is both non-exclusive and non-rivalrous. IP provides that structure to grant exclusive but limited rights in contemporary information products. ICH has no such mechanism, resulting in the Western view that ICH is in the public domain. Related is UNESCO's concern that ICH should not be propertised through IP claims – that IP should not interfere with the processual intangible intergenerational nature of ICH. So far there is no (international) consensus on how IP and ICH could come together for the particular benefit of heritage bearers, resulting in continued (Western) taking from the 'ICH public domain', and the continuing concern that if they do converge, this would fossilise the intangible nature of ICH.

Yet on a practical level, IP can contribute in important ways towards the sustainable development of marginalised communities who wish to commercialise their ICH in pursuit of economic empowerment.[17] The HIPAMS project has shown that IP can underpin market orientated marketing strategies designed to help communities increase their income. Importantly, the communities need tools – such as the roots and fruits tool – to enable them to keep a focus on their ICH and what it is that is important to them about their ICH. Around this, tailored marketing strategies supported by IP tools specifically designed to spread communicative and promotional messages about the ICH and the heritage bearer communities, help communities to spread the word about the goods and services they offer which embody their ICH skills and knowledge. The HIPAM strategies do not fix or commodify the ICH skills and knowledge and so address one of the concerns of UNESCO. What HIPAMS do not do however is to directly address the takings from ICH perceived by some to be in the public domain. The hope is that over the longer term as communities increasingly develop commercialisation strategies that suit them and their ICH, that third parties will increasingly recognise that it is morally and ethically wrong to propertise heritage bearers' ICH in the pursuit of their own profit. In this way IP, as an integral part of the HIPAM, strategy will have played an important part.

Notes

1 The academic literature discussing justifications for IP is extensive. For a series of seminal essays see (Drahos, 1999).

2 None of the IP rights are without their critics. As seen in (Coombe and Chapman, 2020),

> GIs function ideologically to convey harmonious social imaginaries of territories that integrate production activities, communities, and natural environments, but in practice they enable forms of fetishization that may obscure and support unfair and exploitative labor conditions [...]. In India, for example, the GI for Darjeeling tea harnessed discourses of terroir and place-based distinction to fashion a luxury

commodity for global markets, but in the process, the exploitative, racialized labor relations of colonial-era tea plantations were further entrenched.

3 For the process in India see https://ipindia.gov.in/the-registration-process-gi.htm.

4 Time periods for protection vary depending on the sui generis legislation, but generally GI registration has to be renewed which can be every ten years.

5 There is extensive academic literature discussing cultural appropriation. For an edited collection bringing together a range of views see Ziff (1997).

6 The only amendment is in Article 15(4) which makes possible the protection of 'unpublished works where the identity of the author is unknown …'.

7 TCEs and TK are not synonymous with ICH but cover similar ground.

8 More information on each of the communities and their ICH is available in the case studies produced during the project. These are available at hipams.org.

9 The optimum stage of development for IP support is not clear, but, and recognising sociocultural differences, some insights may be gleaned from the Creative Fuse Project which considered in part at what stage of development small creative organisations might benefit from implementation of IP strategies. For more details, see: www.creativefusene.org.uk/project-overview/context/brighton-fuse/.

10 The HIPAMS team worked through specialists from Contact Base to overcome language barriers.

11 For more details, see: www.alpine-space.eu/projects/alpfoodway/en/home.

12 See this work here: https://folklife.si.edu/magazine/crisis-coronavirus-patachitra-scrolls-west-bengal-india?mc_cid=87ceb0bf9a&mc_eid=37a7018e06. Copyright would also subsist in the words of the song as they have been recorded.

13 One of the outcomes of the project is *The HIPAMS Toolkit: Community planning for sustainable development through intangible cultural heritage*, available at hipams.org See Part 3, Slide 15 of this Toolkit for more details. Available at hipams.org.

14 See note 12.

15 A full copy of the code can be found at hipams.org.

16 The average rate of inflation over the same period in India was 4.38%.

17 Policy briefs were prepared as one of the outcomes of the project. These briefs inform ICH, IP and other relevant policy makers in the country based on the HIPAMS learnings. Available at hipams.org.

References

Akagawa, N. and Smith, L. (2018) *Safeguarding intangible heritage*. London: Routledge.

Arnold, R. (2015) *Performers' rights*. 5th edition. London: Sweet & Maxwell.

Beijing Treaty on Audiovisual Performances (2012) Available at: https://treaties.un.org/Pages/showDetails.aspx?objid=08000002805985a3&clang=_en (Accessed 8 February 2022).

Berne Convention for the Protection of Literary and Artistic Works (1886) As revised 1967. United Nations Treaty Series, 828, p. 221. Available at: https://treaties.un.org/Pages/showDetails.aspx?objid=0800000280115ec9&clang=_en (Accessed 8 February 2022).

Bortolotto, C. (2020) 'Commercialization without over-commercialization: Normative conundrums across heritage rationalities', *International Journal of Heritage Studies*. doi: 10.1080/13527258.2020.1858441

Coombe, R. and Chapman, S. (2020) 'Ethnographic explorations of intellectual property' in *Oxford Research Encyclopaedia of Anthropology*. doi: 10.1093/acrefore/9780190854584.013.115

Drahos, P. (1999) *The international library of essays in law and legal theory: Intellectual property.* Dartmouth: Ashgate.

Drahos, P. (2014) *Intellectual property, indigenous people and their knowledge.* Cambridge: Cambridge University Press.

Drassinower, A. (2012) 'Copyright infringement as compelled speech', in Lever, A. (ed.) *New frontiers in the philosophy of intellectual property.* Cambridge: Cambridge University Press, pp. 203–24.

Farah, P. and Tremolada, R. (2015) 'Conflict between intellectual property rights and human rights: A case study on intangible cultural heritage', *Oregon Law Review*, 94, pp. 125–77.

Fisher, W. (2001) 'Theories of Intellectual Property', in Munzer, S. (ed.) *New essays in the legal and political theory of property.* Cambridge: Cambridge University Press, pp. 168–200.

Gibson, J. (2005) *Community resources: Intellectual property, international trade and protection of traditional knowledge.* London: Routledge.

Harding, S. (2018) 'Contemporary ICH and the right to exclude', in Waelde, C., Cummings, C., Pavis, M., and Enright, H. (eds) *Research handbook on contemporary intangible cultural heritage: Law and heritage.* London: Edward Elgar, pp. 78–105.

Hettinger, E.C. (1989) 'Justifying intellectual property', *Philosophy and Public Affairs*, 18(1), pp. 31–52.

Hughes, J. (1988) 'The philosophy of intellectual property', *Georgetown Law Journal*, 77(2), pp. 287–366.

International Convention for the Protection of Performers, Producers of Phonograms and Broadcasting Organizations (1961) United Nations Treaty Series, 496, p. 43. Available at: https://treaties.un.org/Pages/showDetails.aspx?objid=08000002800334e0&clang=_en (Accessed 8 February 2022).

Jayaraman, K.S. (1997) 'US patent office withdraws patent on Indian herb', *Nature*, 389, p. 6.

Kapur, A. (2016) *Made only in India: Goods with geographical indications.* London and New York: Routledge.

Kirshenblatt-Gimblett, B. (2004) 'Intangible heritage as metacultural production', *Museum International*, 56(1–2), pp. 52–65.

Kotler, P. and Keller, K.L. (2015) *Marketing management.* 15th edition. Upper Saddle River, NJ: Pearson Prentice Hall.

Landes, W.M. and Posner, R.A. (1989) 'An economic analysis of copyright law', *Journal of Legal Studies*, 18(2), pp. 325–63.

Lenzerini, F. (2008) 'Indigenous peoples' cultural rights and the controversy over commercial use of their traditional knowledge', in Francioni, F. and Scheinin, M. (eds) *Cultural Human Rights.* Martinus Nijhoff: Netherlands, pp. 119–49.

Lixinski, L. (2013) *Intangible cultural heritage in international law.* Oxford: Oxford University Press.

Lixinski, L. (2020) 'Commercializing traditional culture: Promises and pitfalls in the convergence of intellectual property law and cultural heritage law', *Annali italiani del diritto d'autore, della cultura e dello spettacolo (AIDA)*, 29, pp. 1–15.

Misiura, S. (2006) *Heritage marketing.* Burlington, MA: Butterworth-Heinemann.

Navajo Nation v. Urban Outfitters, Inc. [2013] 935 F. Supp. 2d 1147, 1161–9

Paris Convention for the Protection of Industrial Property (1883). As revised 1967. United Nations Treaties Series, 828, p. 305. Available at: https://treaties.un.org/Pages/showDetails.aspx?objid=080000028011642b&clang=_en (Accessed 8 February 2022).

Reuters (2021) 'Mexico accuses Zara, Anthropologie and Patowl of cultural appropriation', 31 May. Available at: www.reuters.com/world/americas/mexico-accuses-zara-anthropologie-patowl-cultural-appropriation-2021-05-30/ (Accessed 8 February 2022).

Rimmer, M. (2015) *Indigenous intellectual property: A handbook of contemporary research*. Cheltenham (UK) and Northampton (Mass.): Edward Elgar.

Rinallo, D. (2020). 'Heritage storytelling, community empowerment and sustainable development', *Pravovedenie*, 64(1), pp. 57–67. https://doi.org/10.21638/spbu25.2020.105

Rose, G.M., Merchant, A., Orth, U.R. and Horstmann, F. (2016) 'Emphasizing brand heritage: Does it work? And how?' *Journal of Business Research*, 69(2), pp. 936–43.

UNESCO (2003) *Convention for the Safeguarding of the Intangible Cultural Heritage*. Available at: https://ich.unesco.org/doc/src/01852-EN.pdf (Accessed 8 January 2022).

UNESCO (2015) *Ethical principles for safeguarding intangible cultural heritage*. Available at: https://ich.unesco.org/en/ethics-and-ich-00866 (Accessed 8 January 2022).

UNESCO (2016) *Operational directives for the implementation of the Convention for the Safeguarding of the Intangible Cultural Heritage*. Available at: https://ich.unesco.org/doc/src/ICH-Operational_Directives-6.GA-PDF-EN.pdf (Accessed 8 February 2022).

UNESCO (2018) *Decision of the intergovernmental committee: 13.COM 10.B.9*. Available at: https://ich.unesco.org/en/decisions/13.COM/10.B.9 (Accessed 8 February 2022).

Wendland, W. (2019) 'Protecting indigenous knowledge: A personal perspective on international negotiations at WIPO', *WIPO Magazine*. Available at: www.wipo.int/wipo_magazine/en/2019/06/article_0004.html (Accessed 9 January 2022).

WIPO Performances and Phonograms Treaty (1996) United Nations Treaty Series, 2186, p. 203. Available at: https://treaties.un.org/Pages/showDetails.aspx?objid=08000002800837ab&clang=_en (Accessed 8 February 2022).

Ziff, B. (ed.) (1997) *Borrowed power: Issues of cultural appropriation*. New Brunswick: Rutgers University Press.

PART 2

Heritage, Environment and Sustainable Development

5

HERITAGE IN URBAN DEVELOPMENT

Materialising Claims to Urban Space in Doha and Kingston

Clare Melhuish

Introduction

This chapter will explore the ways in which urban heritage narratives and practices are being deployed to mobilise the 'development' of cities formerly considered to lie at the 'periphery' of modernity. It will consider how those discourses influence urban planning decisions or become instrumentalised as mechanisms for urban regeneration (Pendlebury and Porfyriou, 2017) in order to produce both infrastructural and aesthetic transformations which contribute to the reimagining of cities as 'modern', and the further production of new discourses of cultural heritage which project alternative futures. It will examine the role played in these processes by different urban actors embedded in a global circulation of urban policy and practice (architects, masterplanners, planners, heritage experts, international agencies and investors, civic institutions, and ordinary citizens); and take a critical stance to consider how local heritage narratives and initiatives are mobilised in models of development which reflect the continuing influence of the Global North in shaping the characteristics of progress in former colonial and neocolonial contexts. Finally, and in this regard, it will draw attention to the threats posed to the stability and sustainability of urban communities, livelihoods, and lifeways by the implementation of such models of heritage-driven urban development.

The chapter presents research undertaken in Doha, Qatar between 2012 and 2015, as the city began to radically overhaul its urban infrastructure in preparation for the FIFA World Cup of 2022 and develops a comparative discussion through a critical evaluation of heritage-led regeneration discourses in Kingston, Jamaica, following the city's designation as a UNESCO City of Music in 2015. As a prefatory note to this discussion, I shall first draw attention to the different but interconnected inflections of the term 'development', dependent on context, in framing a critical perspective on the history of the relationship between development and heritage.

DOI: 10.4324/9781003107361-7

International development, urban development, and heritage

'International development' was spurred into being following the destruction of the world wars in the mid-20th century, shored up by a structure of international aid and financing led by the World Bank and International Monetary Fund, and delivered through a global network of non-governmental organisations (NGOs). It was designed to lift designated 'third world' countries out of poverty, including many newly independent, asset-stripped, postcolonial nation-states, and assist in the provision of essential infrastructure as well as establishing viable economies in the vacuum of 'under-development' left by colonial withdrawal. Later, as those same states became crippled by budgetary deficits, they were subjected to new loan conditions based on enforced changes to their political and governance structures. These were driven by free-market economic principles allied to US-led political positioning against socialism and designed to undermine the global alliances developed by the Soviet Union during the Cold War. By contrast, 'urban development' generally refers to commercial developer-led and/or state-led processes of property or real estate development in cities across the world, where it may also, but not necessarily be linked to the concept of 'urban regeneration', or 'place-based regeneration', specifically in the Global North: a process of redeveloping and improving urban fabric that has been designated as decayed, unsafe, or redundant, particularly in the former industrial areas of post-industrial cities. As Smith (2002) has described in his account of the new global 'revanchist' urbanism, this is an approach driven by the impetus to maximise land values in central and off-centre urban areas, attract inward investment, and materialise processes of social gentrification, resulting in a proliferation of homogenous mixed-use urban landscape complexes. It represents a model of neoliberal urbanisation driven by large-scale Urban Development Projects (UDPs) which Swyngedou, Moulaert and Rodriguez (2002: 199) further describe as 'the material expression of a developmental logic that views megaprojects and place-marketing as means for generating future growth and for waging a competitive struggle to attract investment capital'.

As such, urban development is largely complicit in the models promoted by international development across cities beyond the Global North. It is key to the emergence of new 'command centres' in the global economy (Sassen, 2005), new destinations for capital investment, and new campaigns for city marketing within the framework of economic modernisation and liberalisation promoted by international agencies across a global market economy. Most disturbingly, these driving international forces for local transformation play a defining role at increasingly numerous sites of post-disaster reconstruction, consolidating racial geographies, and perpetuating the long-term crisis of ecological degradation and climate breakdown brought about by colonial processes of extraction, settlement, and ecocide in vulnerable regions (Sheller, 2020).

These processes of evolution across the two connected fields of 'development' parallel an equally significant evolution in the field of heritage policy and practice between the immediate post-war years and the present. The perceived value of national and world heritage, and the need to put measures in place to preserve it, was heightened dramatically after the destruction of cities, museums, and historic sites wrought by the two World Wars and led to the creation of new policy frameworks and standards to ensure this could be achieved. International conventions (Venice Charter for Conservation and Restoration of Monuments and Sites, and creation of ICOMOS, 1964; UNESCO World Heritage Convention for the Protection of World Cultural and Natural Heritage, 1972; European Architectural Heritage Year, 1975) were created to intervene and arbitrate in processes of cultural heritage evaluation and preservation at an international level. These were founded in Global North scientific expertise and authority developed over the previous century in relation to colonial initiatives and experience, and in parallel with European nation-building. Over subsequent decades, European cities experienced a 'heritage boom' (Winter, 2013), whereby town planning policy became increasingly focused on issues around conservation and preservation of the historic built landscape. Indeed, 'By the 1990s, conservation had become a significant objective embedded at the heart of the land-use planning system, with a near-unchallenged consensus that the protection of the historic environment was a fundamental purpose of planning policy' (Pendlebury, 2015: 430), supported by the public consultation system. Property developers, urban designers, and architects began to embrace heritage discourses to promote narratives of historic continuity and urban identity that would support place-based regeneration (or place-making) and urban branding, embedded in the profitable redevelopment of central urban areas. Heritage was repositioned as part of the 'experience economy' (Klingmann, 2007; Böhme, 2013), and became a feature of the new landscapes of leisure and consumption described by Smith (2002) that were emerging through processes of city centre (downtown) redevelopment across the Global North, and increasingly in the last couple of decades at other sites around the world (Melhuish, Degen and Rose, 2016) – as this chapter will discuss.

Under Conservative, Labour, and Coalition governmental regimes in the UK, heritage has notably been instrumentalised beyond historic national identity-building discourses, to facilitate a range of policy purposes, particularly urban regeneration strategies aimed both at producing profit from property, and promoting social inclusion and citizenship (Pendlebury, 2015: 433–6), particularly in troubled inner-city areas during the New Labour years (Lees and Melhuish, 2013). However, heritage has also been mobilised at an international level as a driver of economic and social development, within a broadly neoliberal global market economy, as evidenced by the publication of UNESCO's 2011 Historic Urban Landscape Recommendation. This document opens up understandings of what constitutes heritage in an urban context, shifting away from the more rigid conservation approaches of the past focused on individual buildings and historic monuments. It positions 'urban heritage as a social, cultural and economic asset for the development of cities', explaining that

> the historic urban landscape approach moves beyond the preservation of the physical environment, and focuses on the entire human environment with all

> of its tangible and intangible qualities … cultural diversity, socio-economic and environmental factors along with local community values.
>
> *UNESCO, 2013: 5*

Psarra applauds the expanded definition of heritage through the historic urban landscape (HUL) concept, which dissolves the dualism between a traditional object-focused, and newer process-orientated approach – 'between architecture's traditional concern with intentional design and other areas of knowledge … approaching cities as entities that emerge out of multiple actions of people over time' (Psarra, 2018: 253). She proposes that it addresses the fundamental problem of architecture's role in urbanism, dating back to classical ideals resurrected in Renaissance Italy, which reduced the complexity of the city through a 'scenographic definition of urban space' intended as 'an instrument of urban control' (Psarra 2018: 253), and continuing through the tabula rasa approach of Modernist urban design – issues which remain relevant in the development of cities today.

The HUL definition addresses this, but also raises questions around the instrumentalisation of heritage and diversity for economic ends, based on a continuing privileging of aesthetic and material heritage values over the integrity and sustainability of living communities and the social fabric of evolving urban neighbourhoods. As Fouseki shows in her critical discourse analysis of the document, there is

> a paradoxical juxtaposition inherent in the text. On the one hand, the HUL Recommendation acknowledges the complexity and constant change of cities, and on the other, it highlights the need to 'freeze' those cities through preserving their integrity, authenticity and 'historic layering' from 'uncontrolled development' (para. 17).
>
> *Fouseki, 2019: 28*

As she points out, the document openly states the need to prioritise the needs and values of 'national and international communities' over those of local communities, which 'are expected to *respect* the former' (Fouseki, 2019: 30). As Fouseki describes in the case of the New Acropolis Museum project in Athens, and as we see repeatedly in large-scale urban development projects in European cities, this too often results in the fragmentation and dispersal of under-represented neighbourhood communities and livelihoods to make way for more powerful economic interests, reinforcing elite claims and management priorities, especially in urban centres and prime 'downtown' areas.

As these processes accelerate across cities beyond the Global North, heritage-led urban development has become further implicated with the principles of international development. This is true to differing extents of both the case studies discussed in this chapter. They raise the question of how heritage discourses might be mobilised differently within this context to promote a more ethical and inclusive approach to urban development, which both prioritises the needs and values of local communities, and highlights the discrepancies between localised colonial or neocolonial histories and hegemonic colonial heritage narratives which continue to support exploitation of local resources and local displacements, particularly 'black removal projects' (Asaka, cited Sheller, 2020: 9), in a context of postcolonial environmental catastrophe.

Grounds for comparison

I will now move to consider the grounds for comparison between two case studies that on first impressions might seem very different. Doha is an Islamic city located in the Arab world, with a short urban history dating back to the early 20th century. It originated in a pearl-fishing village on a desert peninsula in the Gulf, but today has a very high GDP derived from oil and gas reserves initially discovered in 1935. Its tiny minority native population represents a social elite sustained by the state, with a family- and tribe-based system of governance, while the majority of the population is made up of foreign guest workers, from labourers to professionals, who can never be recognised as citizens or nationals. Qatar was not a British colony but became part of the British protectorate in the Gulf in 1916. By contrast, Kingston is an old colonial city, laid out in 1703 by the British on a tropical island in the Caribbean Sea. It was a centre of the British plantation economy based on transported African enslaved labour to Jamaica, and a key node of the British Empire. It became an independent democracy in 1962, as part of the British Commonwealth, and has subsequently suffered political chaos and high levels of economic deprivation and violent criminal activity, rooted in the racial hierarchies and inequalities established by its history of white settler-colonialism and black enslavement. Migration between Jamaica and the British 'motherland', as it was historically understood, has been key to the dynamics of its economy since independence, when Britain actively recruited black Jamaicans to work in its public services as part of the country's post-war reconstruction, and settle in the UK with indefinite leave to remain.

The two cities however share some key characteristics, both having been historic key trading points in the global ocean-based economy, fundamentally shaped historically by the legacy of British urban planning systems and architectural design, and both having embarked in recent years on rebranding and city marketing initiatives, which have attracted the attention of international agencies and consultants, among which the British continue to maintain a strong presence. In that sense, both cities can be seen as historic and present-day destinations for international urban practice and policy expertise in what McCann, Ward and Roy (2013) have described as its global circulation around sites, with a particular link to British sources. Although the contrasting histories of the two cities' evolution suggest that urban heritage and collective memory have been shaped by very different forces and would take dissimilar forms in Doha and Kingston, the effects and continuing legacy of the British presence in the social and material construction of the urban are shared across these contexts, as this chapter will describe.

By comparing the ways in which heritage discourses have been mobilised around urban development initiatives in Doha and Kingston I hope firstly to provide some common insights into the implication of heritage in urban redevelopment as a platform for economic development, and its impact on local inhabitants and sustainable rooted communities. Secondly, I intend to draw attention, through a relational comparison (Ward, 2010), to the place of heritage discourses in the networks and flows that connect dissimilar cities beyond their geographical regions through mobilities of expertise and resources, and shape their reproduction.

Msheireb Downtown and downtown Kingston: an overview

The context for the Msheireb development in Doha is a globalising urbanity in which cities in Asia, South America, and the Gulf states now vie for international status with European and American urban centres (Acuto, 2014). However, there has also been a resurgence of interest in rediscovering local and vernacular styles, as cities seek to establish distinctive individual identities and, in particular, move away from received Western models of urbanisation (Melhuish, 2014). Doha has been reimagined and reinvented as a cultural and tourist destination through the implementation of large-scale, state-financed urban developments, framed by the Qatar 2030 Vision (Government of Qatar, 2008) for economic and social development and diversification. These include the waterfront, new museums and galleries, a multi-campus university site, Education City, and a radical reshaping of the historic centre with the Msheireb Downtown project. This agenda has been informed by a considerable investment in promoting a distinct Qatari identity, through architecture, urban design and cultural heritage (Sheikha Moza, 2012). The Msheireb project itself has been informed by several years of research into what might constitute a contemporary architectural expression of Qatari heritage and national identity, based on archaeological investigations and the remains of Doha's historic built fabric, which is limited by the nature of local building materials – primarily mud brick.

This $5.5bn mixed-use development, financed by the Qatar Foundation through its subsidiary Msheireb Properties, has now transformed a 34-ha site in the historic centre of Doha into a modern, mixed-use complex for living, working, shopping, and cultural consumption by middle- and upper-class Qataris and international professionals, displacing a long-standing community of low-income migrant workers to maximise land values in the city centre and attract inward investment. It emerged in 2005 as a central platform on which the dynamics of local, regional, and global identity and influence would be investigated and played out, at a culturally and politically significant site in the centre of the city, close to the reconstructed Souk Wakif (2005) and the Diwan al-Amiri, the seat of government. As one of our British architect respondents observed about the project, led by UK-based masterplanners Allies and Morrison and EDAW (now AECOM):

> It's been a three-way meeting of experience and expectation. One is the still point of Qatar, although it's not still because it's defining itself, the other is

the UK, with designers with more or less international experience but strong views about urbanism, and [thirdly] the people from Dubai, who are part of a great experiment of building things. We had to sort of play the role as the orchestrator in terms of place-making because it was not familiar territory for anybody else.

MDC architect

Thus, Msheireb offers a significant case study for a consideration of the complexities of postcolonial politics and cultural dynamics as they are played out through the representation of particular heritage discourses in urban development projects. In the context of the Gulf region, where cultural authority has been framed since the 18th century by Western 'orientalising' perspectives and colonising interventions (Said, 1978; Al-Sayyad, Bierman and Rabbat 2005), focused on the old regional centres of history, culture, and learning – Cairo, Beirut, and Baghdad – this interplay takes on a particular significance as new modern cities enter a battle for sophistication and culture within the region (Elsheshtawy, 2008), displacing the old hierarchies, and re-evaluating Arab culture and heritage as 'cultural capital that can be mobilised' (Serageldin, 2008: v).

Kingston, Jamaica, is also actively engaged in reimagining its identity, with aspirations to position itself as the cultural capital of the Caribbean, the 'pearl of the Antilles', after decades in which its image and reputation have been tarnished by crime and violence since independence. Its Urban Development Corporation (UDC) has been mobilising a regeneration imperative driven by a top-down urban waterfront and historic city centre development model of iconic buildings and public open spaces for leisure and consumption by affluent citizens. The renewed drive for redevelopment of the downtown area has been partly spurred by UNESCO's designation of the city as a Creative City for Music (2015) and the prospect of increased international visibility which it offers, based on the city's musical heritage, particularly the reggae genre, and its global impact. Under discussion with the Jamaica National Heritage Trust are proposals to designate downtown a protected Historic District, a heritage site which would also link to the Port Royal site across the harbour and create a cultural space to represent and communicate the identity of the city and its people. Port Royal has been on the Tentative List of UNESCO's World Heritage List for many years, pending the Jamaican government's attention to various parts of the submission, including its justification of Outstanding Universal Value and development of detailed Heritage Impact Assessments and management plans (UNESCO, 2019).

Like Doha, Kingston has looked to international consultants to implement these urban policy and design approaches, interlinked with heritage strategies, with a view to generating capital returns from land and attracting investment and tourism to the city centre. As reported by the national press, the government promised it would provide downtown Kingston with the economic driver it has lacked for half a century:

Minister Without Portfolio in the Ministry of Economic Growth and Job Creation, Daryl Vaz said recently that the revitalisation of downtown Kingston

> is critical to the process of attracting more investments in the country, and will ultimately lead to greater economic growth.'… We see the vast historical and cultural potential of downtown Kingston as a tourist destination,' he said. Prime Minister Andrew Holness has also expressed a desire for the waterfront to be 'the driving force for all of Kingston'.
>
> *(Henry, 2016)*

The decaying downtown area represents the first grid-plan colonial city laid out by the British in the Caribbean region, following the devastation of Port Royal by earthquake and fire – an embodiment of architectural and urban historical significance ripe for redevelopment. However, it is also surrounded by a ring of the city's poorest black neighbourhoods, politically-affiliated 'garrison' communities, reflecting the 'bi-polarity' of the city between this and the middle-class areas on Liguanea plain and into the hills (Clarke and Howard, 1999) which developed following the relocation of the port to Newport West in the 1960s, the British-financed remodelling of the waterfront by a newly formed Urban Development Corporation, and development of a new business commercial centre uptown in the 1970s (Figure 5.1). As an impoverished, politicised and 'racialised' space (Clarke and Howard, 1999) the proposed redevelopment raises important questions about the

FIGURE 5.1 Port Royal, Kingston, Jamaica: colonial heritage and poverty

Source: Photo taken by the author.

legacy of inequality inscribed into the city's built colonial heritage which demand attention.

In the next section I return to the Msheireb site to examine in closer detail how a heritage narrative specific to Qatari identity was constructed through the process of 21st century urban redevelopment, and the ways in which this was negotiated between international consultants and local client representatives through the technical apparatus of digital visualisations. I will then consider the links with Kingston through the cities' parallel histories of urban redevelopment by British consultants in the mid-20th century, and compare the potential for a postcolonial re-evaluation of heritage in the context of urban redevelopment, shaped by shifting constellations of tools, technologies, and expertise.

Negotiated heritage and the technical apparatus of urban reproduction in Doha

Findings from ethnographic research conducted between 2011 and 2013 on the Msheireb project (Rose, Degen and Melhuish, 2014; Degen, Melhuish and Rose, 2017; Melhuish, Degen and Rose, 2016) revealed the crucial role played by Computer Generated Images (CGIs) as a vehicle for the production and representation of a constructed concept of Qatari heritage and identity, which evolved into an image of hybrid, postcolonial and cosmopolitan urbanity, materialised in built form. As we observed and recorded the work of architects and visualisers on the scheme, the majority of whom had little or no knowledge of Doha or Qatar or its culture and all of whom were based in the UK or US, we became aware that the CGIs constituted a vital interactive platform for the development of an urban imaginary which, as we were told, had not existed before. It slowly emerged through a multistage process, involving many different actors, iterations, and software programmes – Microstation AutoCAD, 3DS Max, and Photoshop. This might involve cut and paste from other sources, e.g., internet libraries, photosharing websites, and offices' own archives of imagery from other projects, or digitally painting on effects, to produce a collaged and hybridised reproduction of Doha's downtown area.

This process was framed by an 'architectural language code' which had been developed from several years of research into local architectural forms conducted by the masterplanner and lead architect. It included elements such as rectilinear building volumes on a grid-based plan, combined with the use of traditional regional architectural patterns and features, e.g., *badgir* (wind chimneys), *liwan* (covered terrace or open-fronted room), *mashrabiyas* (window screens), and *mirzam* (projecting timber water spouts from roof edge). The ground plan of broad open boulevards is laced through with narrow shaded '*siqats*' (alleys) to give it an Arabic feel. At the heart of the development, however, following conventions of European and American urban design, is a large public square, addressed by a Cultural Forum at one end, a hotel at the other, and shops, restaurants, and outdoor seating lining each side. A series of grand new archive buildings faces the government palace (*Diwan al Amiri*) to the north; on the other side is a large open prayer ground, and cultural quarter of 'heritage houses', historic residences converted into museums. An extensive indoor shopping galleria, luxury shopping quarter, hotels, and offices comprise a substantial part of the development, along with residential apartments and townhouses for segregated Qatari and foreign residents on the north-west section of the site, with associated school and nursery facilities, and smaller open spaces. There are three mosques, and in phase 4, a concentration of high-rise office buildings and the first underground station of the new metro system which will bring public transport to Doha for the first time.

The new downtown visualised in the CGIs has then many similarities with the type of 'new landscape complex' elsewhere described by Smith (2002) but was conceived as a specific rebuttal to the Western-influenced model of 'Dubaisation'. It seeks to establish Qatari, as opposed to Emirati, cultural authority in the region, 'one of the pillars of brand Qatar' (client marketing officer), and a new approach to urban development which draws on a 'nostalgic image of Doha from the past', where tight streets expressed close social and family-based bonds: 'the essence of community' (client marketing officer). That memory of Doha is combined with another set of cultural references extending across a global network of places, spaces, and cities, which are also central to perceptions of identity in a now-affluent society 'used to the good things in life'. It is 'a way of thinking … being very modern yet very Qatari' (client marketing officer), expressive of 'the sort of real modernity and enjoyment of globalisation that is here' (architect) – a cosmopolitan urbanity overlaid onto the historic identity of a nomadic desert society.

This was not an easy process, but the technical apparatus of digital visualisation created an accessible platform for discussion and negotiation between the different parties involved. Most of the UK-based design architects and visualisers employed British or European (especially Spanish and Italian) staff who, as noted, had no knowledge of Doha. The client comprised a mixed group of mostly American, some British and Australian, and some Egyptian and Lebanese project managers and development managers and directors, many of whom had previous experience in Dubai and other parts of the Middle East including Kuwait and Beirut. However, the senior executive level was made up of Qataris from the civil service and ministries, answerable ultimately to the Chairperson of the Qatar Foundation, Sheikha Moza. Also on the development team were a handful of Qataris with training (commonly in Britain or the US) and some experience of working in architecture, urban, and interior design, in line with state directives on 'Qatarisation' (requirement to employ and train up a quota of local Qataris). At a more technical level, particularly IT support, roles were mainly filled by male employees from the Indian sub-continent, while PAs included a mix of nationalities (e.g., Russian, Indian), front-of-house receptionists were often Philipina women, and 'tea-boys' south Indians.

Some of the early architectural images had 'more orientalism' in them and the journey towards consensus was slow. As a visualiser respondent explained, they had to 'get the Arabic style [right]' but worked on it for a long time 'before the client started to say what they didn't like'. The work required to define the appropriate style and place-identity for the new development, in terms of its architectural and cultural references and atmosphere, grew out of a collective effort located in offices spread across a number of geographical locations, and staffed by a cosmopolitan mix of employees. Digital visualisation tools and technologies were critical to facilitating a postcolonial reinvention of the city based on a rejection of earlier Western-influenced approaches, and an embrace of discourses around national heritage and cultural identity that would mobilise the both the renewal of the city centre and the removal of its existing population of South Asian guest workers to the periphery (Figure 5.2).

Heritage shaping spatial inequalities in urban development

A substantial literature examines the ways in which urban planning and architecture have been used by states to reimagine and represent national and postcolonial identities following the end of empires and the recalibration of Western political and cultural influence around the world; (Mishra and Hodge, 1991; Yeoh, 2001; King, 2004). But postcolonial urban reinvention is often tied to nationalist narratives of state-building and cultural heritage which, as Jazeel (2013) argues, can also be exclusive of minorities and intolerant of cultural difference, resulting

FIGURE 5.2 CGI images on site at Msheireb Downtown, Doha: urban development shaped by narratives of national identity and heritage

Source: Photo taken by the author.

in continuing forms of urban segregation common to cosmopolitan postcolonial cities (Elsheshtawy, 2011 on Dubai). The Msheireb case is illustrative of the ways in which heritage discourses can be deployed on the one hand to establish new postcolonial urban identities through planning and architecture, but on the other to drive urban redevelopment projects influenced by the values of national elites and international stakeholders over and above the needs of local residents, reproducing patterns of colonial development in 'dual' or segregated cities (Edensor and Jayne, 2011: 19), 'divided into compartments' (Fanon, 1968: 37–40). This brings us back to the case of Kingston downtown, and a critique, based on archival research, of the historic legacy and continuity of urban development patterns through colonial and neocolonial interventions, which frame current heritage discourses linked to regeneration and 'development'.

Ruth Glass, the sociologist who founded UCL's original Centre for Urban Studies and coined the term 'gentrification' in her studies of London, noted the contrast between prosperity and impoverishment etched on Kingston's urban landscape, and emphasised the 'glaringly evident' impact of social segmentation resulting from the institution of slavery (Glass, 1989 [1962]: 216). Following the relocation of the port which was its interface with the world in the 1950s, supporting both the sugar and banana industries and tourism since the 19th century, a new waterfront zone was reclaimed by the UDC and designed in 1967 by British architects Shankland Cox as a means to 'improve the urban image', exploiting its potential to produce 'an exciting and dynamic image of a tropical downtown area against the sea … made up of efficient modern buildings … the whole complex providing an environment which will attract people' (Jamaica Architect, 1967: 45). Project lead Brooke Riley further elaborated that 'the downtown area … is choked, commerce is fading, the visual image is one of chaos, and culture has fled. Jobs and houses are far from plentiful. The blight of slum and obsolescence rings the city core'. He recommended that 'a social, economic and physical plan' for the development of the city be put in place (Riley, 1967: 48), while Shankland proposed that the city's development 'would be greatly encouraged by the development of a tourist magnet at the centre, and so for that matter would Jamaica's economy' (Gambrill, 1967: 15).

At around the same time in Doha, following the signing of a new Anglo-Qatari treaty of friendship and cooperation in 1970, another British planning consultancy Llewelyn Davies, fresh from their work on the high-profile masterplan for Milton Keynes, were invited to propose an expansion plan for the city to 1990, based on extension of the established ring-road system, and including land reclamation on the waterfront. The government purchased large tracts of land in the city centre from local families for clearance and redevelopment, providing the catalyst for the growth of a suburban hinterland of large free-standing family villas built with compensation money. This rupture with the traditional urban fabric contributed to the substantial material reshaping of the infrastructure and urban space of Doha from the 1950s onwards, harnessing the skills of international consultants, which led directly to the abandonment of low-rise buildings in the tight-knit central area around the bazaar, many built of mudbrick, and their occupation by immigrant workers. The emergence of an ethnicised landscape of disrepair, decay, and poor living standards at the heart of the historic city, was eventually to prompt the large-scale clearance and redevelopment initiative launched by the Msheireb Downtown scheme, as described in the previous section.

Similarly, British masterplanning intervention at the Kingston waterfront site in the name of economic development would contribute to a continuing decline of the historic grid city and racialisation of the urban landscape (Clarke and Howard, 1999). Today's regeneration initiative, framed as a multi-stakeholder initiative shored up by an MOU with China, focuses on the role of key cultural institutions – the Institute of Jamaica, the National Library, National Gallery, and the proposed new Music Museum – in the revival of the area as an economic driver for tourism driven by heritage discourses around Jamaican colonial and postcolonial identities. However, it does not offer a solution to the needs of the immediate local communities. Turning downtown into a heritagised cultural space to attract investment and tourism and generate new urban heritage narratives around Kingston as the cultural capital of the Caribbean, is unlikely to benefit low-income and disadvantaged black citizens who face the threat of potential displacement posed by large-scale urban regeneration schemes in cities all over the world.

By contrast, Gidel's comparison of the impacts of waterfront renewal projects on low-income communities in Port of Spain, Trinidad and Tobago (a former British colony), and Fort-de-France, Martinique (a former French colony, now Overseas Department of the French state), shows how in the latter case, urban policy developed by Letchimy as newly elected mayor from 2001 positively evaluated the contribution of its poorest citizens to the city's vitality and culture, and built that in to a comprehensive plan for reshaping the waterfront, of which five out of fourteen new projects focused on underprivileged communities located in the vicinity (Gidel, 2010: 43). Letchimy (2011) emphasised the role of a 'progressive [C]aribbean contemporary urbanism' in countering the *burden* of heritage, unshackling Caribbean societies from their colonial pasts, and shaping new urban models of universal relevance (Melhuish, 2019). However, many Caribbean cities have remained trapped in what Potter describes as 'spatially and socially polarized patterns of dependent urbanization' (Potter, 1989: 320; Clarke and Howard, 1999). Letchimy's inclusive approach to redevelopment, which respects citizens' 'right to the city' (Lefebvre, 1968), was led by a semi-public planning agency, while the Trinidadian 'mega-project', like Kingston's, was led by an Urban Development Corporation owned by the government. These contrasting structures for development, in which the control of urban space is diversified across a number of actors, are illustrative of the turn towards neoliberal urban policies (Jaffe, 2013) with direct implications for the spatial politics of urban inequality, as well as the creation of new forms of post-colonial national identity. Yet they are also rooted in the legacy of colonial and neo-colonial patterns of development, alongside hegemonic narratives of heritage and identity informed by international standards and systems of evaluation embedded in Western scientific discourse. For marginalised sectors of the population, this kind of heritage narrative, embedded in urban development, is often a threat and a burden, rather than an opening to new postcolonial futures.

Conclusion: constructing postcolonial heritage in Doha and Kingston

Ong and Roy (2011), in their discussion of 'worlding cities', have described a process of inter-referencing between 'other' cities within different networks, as Western points of reference become less relevant in a shifting global hierarchy. It reflects the enhanced fluidity and mobility of space and place which has occurred in postcolonial times, especially as it has been facilitated in more recent decades by digital technology and communications networks (Sheller, 2009). Colonial development processes were also mobile and transferable, but followed predictable trajectories from centre to periphery, and traditional modes of architectural and urban design and representation enshrined the authority of the architect and planner at the heart of such processes, with little opportunity for negotiation or democratisation of ideas and values. Digital visualising technologies used on the Msheireb project in Doha significantly contributed to the construction of new discourses of Qatari urban heritage based on collective memory and evidence of the city's identity prior to the discovery of oil and radical reshaping of the urban landscape through Western interventions. Furthermore, they facilitated the production of the project across sites and its wide circulation across international information platforms. However, the project has also relied on massive investment by the government which allowed the Qatari client to maintain control, notwithstanding the huge input by foreign consultants. In Jamaica such investment is not a possibility, opening the door wide to pressures from international agencies, assembled in multi-stakeholder consortia, to follow more predictable paths of development in which the negative heritage of colonial exploitation continues to shape the urban landscape in ways that counters its future vitality and autonomy.

While the narratives and power structures may shift between a city in the Gulf and cities in the Caribbean, the tools and references used to implement them are nevertheless often the same, and the results very similar, notwithstanding the underlying cultural and social differences. Networked processes of transnational architectural production facilitated by digital communications and software have fuelled the production of a commercial and often homogenising 'global architecture', critiqued by scholars such as Ren (2011) and McNeill (2009), accompanying the restructuring of historic city centres, or downtowns (Rotenberg, 2012). The roles played by different actors in the processes of urban change in which urban development is embedded range across investors, architects, planners, national and civic institutions, private sector companies, NGOs, citizens, and neighbourhood dons. These networks are sustained by constructed narratives around urban heritage and culture which increasingly underpin urban design strategies, and structure the inclusion or exclusion of different communities in the city, with the most vulnerable and least affluent always at risk.

Acknowledgements

Parts of this chapter relating to the Doha case study were first published in City and Society 2016, Vol. 28, no. 2, pp. 199–222: "The real Modernity that is here"; understanding the role of digital visualisations I the production of a new urban imaginary at Msheireb Downtown, Doha, by Clare Melhuish, Monica Degen, and Gillian Rose. Other parts, relating to the Kingston case study, were presented in early form at the conference Imagine Kingston: the regeneration of a city, Nov 9–12, 2017, hosted by the University of the West Indies (UWI), Kingston, Jamaica.

References

Acuto, M. (2014) 'Dubai in the "middle"', *International Journal of Urban and Regional Research*, 38(5), pp. 1732–1748.

Al Sayyad, N., Bierman, I. A. and Rabbat, N. O. (eds) (2005) *Making Cairo medieval*. Lanham MD and Oxford: Lexington Books.

Böhme, G (2013) *Architektur und Atmosphäre*. Munich: Wilhelm Fink Verlag.

Clarke, C. and Howard, D, (1999) 'Colour, race and space: residential segregation in Kingston, Jamaica, in the late colonial period', *Caribbean Geography*, 10(1), pp. 4–18.

Degen, M., Melhuish, C. and Rose, G. (2017) 'Producing place atmospheres digitally: architecture, digital visualisation practices and the experience economy', *Journal of Consumer Culture*, 17(1), pp. 3–24.

Edensor, T., Jayne, M. (eds) (2011) *Urban theory beyond the west: a world of cities*. Routledge, London.

Elsheshtawy, Y. (2008) 'Transitory sites: mapping Dubai's "forgotten" urban spaces', *International Journal of Urban & Regional Research* 32, pp. 968–988.

Elsheshtawy, Y. (2011) 'Urban (im)mobility: public encounters in Dubai', in Edensor, T., and Jayne, M. (eds) *Urban theory beyond the west: a world of cities*. London: Routledge, pp. 219–236.

Fanon, F., (1968) *Black skin, white masks*. New York: Grove Press.

Fouseki, K. (2019) 'Re-conceptualising "historic urban landscapes"', in Bharne, V. and Sandmeier, T. (eds) *Routledge Companion to Global Heritage Conservation*. London: Routledge, pp. 26–38.

Gambrill, T. (1967) 'Planning the city centre of the '70s', *Jamaica Architect*, 1, pp. 1–15.

Gidel, M. (2010) 'Fragmentation on the waterfront: coastal squatting settlements and urban renewal projects in the Caribbean', in Desfor, G., Laidley, J., Stevens, Q. and Shubert, D. (eds) *Transforming urban waterfronts: fixity and flow*. London: Routledge, pp. 35–54.

Glass, R. (1989 [1962]) 'The ashes of discontent: Jamaica today' in Glass, R. *Clichés of urban doom and other essays*. Oxford: Blackwell, pp. 210–216.

Government of Qatar (2008) *Qatar National Vision 2030*. Doha, Qatar: General Secretariat for Development Planning. Available at: www.gco.gov.qa/wp-content/uploads/2016/09/GCO-QNV-English.pdf (Accessed 19 December 2021).

Henry, B. (2016) 'Government fast-tracking plans to improve downtown Kingston', *Jamaica Observer*, 17 December.

Jaffe, R. (2013) 'The hybrid state: crime and citizenship in urban Jamaica', *American Ethnologist* 40(4), pp. 734–748.

Jamaica Architect (1967/8) 'The Kingston Waterfront Development scheme, by Shankland Cox and Associates', *Jamaica Architect* 1(3), pp. 37–47

Jazeel, T. (2013) 'Dissimulated landscapes: postcolonial method and the politics of space in southern Sri Lanka', *EPD: Society and Space* 31, pp. 61–79.

King, A. (2004) *Spaces of global cultures: architecture, urbanism, identity*. London: Routledge.

Klingmann, A. (2007) *Brandscapes: architecture in the experience economy*. Cambridge, MA: The MIT Press.

Lees, L. and Melhuish, C. (2013) 'Arts-led regeneration in the UK: the rhetoric and the evidence on urban social inclusion', *European Urban and Regional Studies*. doi: https://doi.org/10.1177/0969776412467474

Lefebvre, H. (1968) *Le droit à la ville*. Paris: Editions Anthropos.

Letchimy, S. (2011) 'L'urbanisme, d'hier à demain, ou l'art de la transmission', *Lyann Karayib: Cahier Ville Caraibe*, 1, pp. 8–11.

McCann, E., Ward, K. and Roy, A. (2013) 'Urban pulse – assembling/worlding cities', *Urban Geography*, 34(5), pp. 581–589.

McNeill, D., (2009) *The global architect: firms, fame and urban form*. Routledge, London.

Melhuish, C. (guest ed.) (2014) 'Heritage and renewal in Doha' [special issue], in Campkin, B. and Ross, R. (eds) *Urban Pamphleteer*, 4, p. 36.

Melhuish, C. (2019) 'Aesthetics of social identity: re-framing and evaluating modernist architecture and planning as cultural heritage in Martinique', *Planning Perspectives*, 34(2), pp. 265–283.

Melhuish, C., Degen, M. and Rose, G. (2016) '"The real modernity that is here": understanding the role of digital visualisations in the production of a new urban imaginary at Msheireb Downtown, Doha', *City and Society* 28(2), pp. 222–245.

Mishra, V. and Hodge, B. (1991) 'What is post-colonialism?' *Textual Practice*, 5, pp. 399–341.

Ong, A. and Roy, A. (2011) *Worlding cities: Asian experiments and the art of being global*. Oxford: Wiley-Blackwell.

Pendlebury, J. (2015) 'Heritage and policy', in Waterton, E. and Watson S. (eds) *The Palgrave handbook of contemporary heritage research*. Basingstoke: Palgrave Macmillan, pp. 426–441.

Pendlebury, J. and Porfyriou, H. (2017) 'Heritage, urban regeneration and place-making', *Journal of Urban Design*, 22(4), pp. 429–432.

Potter, R. (1989) *Urbanisation, planning and development in the Caribbean*. London: Mansell.

Psarra, S. (2018) 'The role of spatial networks in the historic urban landscape: learning from Venice in the fifteenth and sixteenth centuries', *The Historic Environment: Policy & Practice*, 9(3–4), pp. 249–273. doi: 10.1080/17567505.2018.1516380

Ren, X. (2011) *Building globalisation: transnational architecture production in urban China*. Chicago and London: University of Chicago Press.

Riley, B. (1967) 'The planning problems of downtown Kingston', *Jamaica Architect*, 1(3), pp. 48–50.

Rose, G., Degen, M., and Melhuish, C. (2014) 'Networks, interfaces, and computer-generated images: learning from digital visualisations of urban redevelopment projects', *Environment and planning D: Society and Space*, 32(3), pp. 386–403.

Rotenberg, R. (2012) 'Towards a genealogy of downtown', in McDonagh, G. and Peterson, M. (eds) *Global downtowns*. Philadelphia: University of Pennsylvania Press, pp. 29–47.

Said, E. (1978) *Orientalism*. New York: Pantheon Books.

Sassen, S. (2005) 'The Global City: introducing a concept', *Brown Journal of World Affairs*, XI(2), pp. 27–43.

Serageldin, I. (2008) 'Foreword', in Hassan, F., de Trafford, A. and Youssef, M. (eds) *Cultural heritage and development in the Arab world*. Alexandria, Egypt: Bibliotheca Alexandrina, pp. v–vi.

Sheikha Moza bint Nasser (2012) 'Message from Her Highness Sheikha Moza bint Nasser, Chairperson Msheireb Properties', *YouTube*, 19 July. Available at: www.youtube.com/watch?v=xeBeelno0iQ (Accessed 19 December 2021).

Sheller, M. (2009) 'Infrastructures of the imagined island: software, mobilities, and the architecture of Caribbean paradise', *Environment and Planning A*, 41, pp. 1386–1403.

Sheller, M. (2020) *Island futures: Caribbean survival in the Anthropocene*. Durham, NC and London: Duke University Press.

Smith, N. (2002) 'New globalism, new urbanism: gentrification as global urban strategy', in Brenner, N., and Theodore, N. (eds) *Spaces of neoliberalism: urban restructuring in North America and western Europe*. Oxford: Blackwell, pp. 80–103.

Swyngedouw, E., Moulaert, F. and Rodriguez, A. (2002) 'Neoliberal urbanization in Europe: large-scale urban development projects and the new urban policy', in Brenner, N., and Theodore, N. (eds) *Spaces of neoliberalism: urban restructuring in North America and western Europe*. Oxford: Blackwell, pp. 195–229.

UNESCO (2013) *New life for historic cities: the historic urban landscape approach explained*. Paris: UNESCO.

UNESCO (2019) *Decision: 43 COM 8B.39 The sunken city of Port Royal – a relict and continuing cultural landscape (Jamaica)*. Available at: https://whc.unesco.org/en/decisions/7402/ (Accessed 19 December 2021).

Ward, K. (2010) 'Towards a relational comparative approach to the study of cities', *Progress in Human Geography*, 34(4), pp. 471–487.

Winter, T. (2013) 'Clarifying the critical in critical heritage studies', *International Journal of Heritage Studies*, 19(6), pp. 532–545.

Yeoh, B.S.A. (2001) 'Postcolonial cities', *Progress in Human Geography*, 25, pp. 456–468.

6

FOOD HERITAGE FOR SUSTAINABLE FUTURES

Women's Cultures and Knowledge as Hidden Pillars of Alternative Foodways

Sandip Hazareesingh

Introduction

New directions in food heritage research tend to highlight community-based experiences of foodways valued from the past as renewable local commons, which represents a move away from the universalist discourses of global heritage agencies often deployed in the service of national-political objectives (Matta, 2019; Micarelli, 2021). This has been accompanied by renewed interest in the thousands of neglected and underutilised plant species (NUS) such as millets, cassava, and other traditional cereals, vegetables, and legumes which are popular with local communities but remain under researched by food systems actors (Padulosi et al., 2022). While the link between food systems, human health, and environmental sustainability has long been recognised, the urgency of food heritage research stems from mounting evidence that food production in the 'Anthropocene', dominated by just four corporations and three crops – rice, wheat, and maize, is one of the main drivers of planetary degradation, contributing to greenhouse gas emissions, biodiversity loss, and excessive freshwater use (Willett et al., 2019; Saladino, 2021; Weston and Watts, 2021).

This chapter presents a critical review of the state of play in the field of food heritage. It considers some of the main problems arising from the United Nations Educational, Scientific and Cultural Organization's (UNESCO) recent inclusion of food as part of humanity's 'intangible cultural heritage' and in particular, the marginalisation of women producers and local voices stemming from mainstream modes of national and global heritage governance. It also examines the status of food culture in heritage and development research literature, identifying a lack of attention to both cultural and gender issues. Suggestive examples of recent work highlighting the crucial cultural role of women in maintaining food heritage ecosystems are offered, reinforced finally by a case study of women's stewardship of

DOI: 10.4324/9781003107361-8

millet food systems in India which meets not only local consumer but also cultural, spiritual, and ecological needs. This chapter thus also contributes to an emerging research agenda aimed at achieving a stronger focus on women's knowledges crucial to the cultivation of a wealth of biodiverse plant species and crops. These NUS crops possess high nutritional value, are both carbon-absorbing and adaptable to climate change pressures, and keep local food traditions alive while being capable of sustaining future generations.

Food heritage, UN agencies, and the invisibility of women producers

The social and discursive construction of food as 'heritage' owes much to initiatives taken over the past couple of decades by UNESCO. The crucial landmark here was the appearance in 2010 of food in UNESCO's *Representative List of the Intangible Cultural Heritage of Humanity* following the organisation's establishment of the *Convention for the Safeguarding of Intangible Cultural Heritage* in 2003 (Brulotte and DiGiovine, 2016). Intangible Cultural Heritage (ICH) has generally been seen as a 'new heritage regime' which, departing from the focus on tangible cultural phenomena such as sites, monuments, and landscapes predominantly located in the Western world that characterised UNESCO's 1972 *World Heritage List*, also represented a less Eurocentric interpretation of cultural heritage. Hence, the Convention drew immediate interest from countries in the Global South, with African and Asian countries making up the first seven to ratify it (Romagnoli, 2019).

ICH is defined as 'the practices, representations, expressions, knowledge, skills – as well as the instruments, objects, artefacts and cultural spaces associated therewith – that communities, groups and, in some cases, individuals recognise as part of their cultural heritage'. It is 'transmitted from generation to generation, constantly recreated by communities and groups in response to their environment, their interaction with nature and their history, and provides them with a sense of continuity' (UNESCO, 2003). This definition has the merit of recognising or at least being open to hitherto ignored traditional knowledges, the value of cultural memory, the importance of local histories and environment, and significantly for the first time, the entangled relationship between the human and the natural world in the process of heritage-making. Moreover, the inclusion of food within the ICH framework of global governance has been seen as potentially enabling not only the safeguarding of traditional food products, but legal protection to producers such as farmers in the form of intellectual property rights, providing an alternative to World Trade Organization free trade market rules which have led to an impoverishment of agricultures and food cultures globally (Csergo, 2019).

However, in terms of its actual, contemporary practice of food heritagisation, UNESCO has come under sustained criticism for its primary reliance on national governments in the processes of heritage nomination, decision-making, and maintenance. This has meant the recognition, in practice, of established political regimes' sovereignty and control over 'their' peoples and cultural resources.

National governments have tended to perceive heritage as a commodified package of customary cultural practices with a view, primarily, to promoting tourism in alliance with private national tourist industries. This has often perpetuated the disenfranchisement of local peasant, Indigenous, and rural communities while paying lip service to their food-related cultural values and traditional knowledges (Matta, 2019). For instance, the nomination of Michoacán Mexican cuisine into the UNESCO ICH List in 2010 was accompanied by visual depictions of this cuisine as Indigenous, pre-Colombian, and based on women's traditional cooking. However, the people chosen by the Mexican State to publicise and represent this cuisine abroad with a view to encouraging tourism were not Indigenous women, who remained voiceless, but male restaurant-owning Mexican Chefs (Sammells, 2016). Here the past is deployed ideologically as visual persuasion to promote national-private interests, reinforcing in the process contemporary gender, race, and class inequalities.

Indeed, the official food heritage environment has stimulated the emergence of 'culinary nationalism' with governments competing for UNESCO recognition and its accompanying rewards (Matta, 2019). ICH has been 'instrumentalised' by nation states pursuing political and nationalist agendas and this has often involved conflicting claims over 'authentic' origins and ownership of particular dishes. Hostile neighbours Turkey and Armenia engaged in a bitter war of words following UNESCO's listing of a meat dish, *Keskek* as Turkish heritage in 2011 though it is also, as *Harisa*, a culinary tradition in Armenia. Here, the listing was perceived as cultural theft and UNESCO was blamed for supporting Turkey's bid to appropriate Armenian heritage (Aycan, 2016). Learning from this episode, UNESCO was at pains to ensure that the ICH adoption of *couscous*, the celebrated North African regional Berber dish, in 2020 was premised upon collaboration between the nations concerned. In 2016, Algeria attempted to nominate couscous on its own, drawing the wrath of its neighbour Morocco. But when it became clear that states possessing a shared heritage were required to submit a multinational nomination, the Magreb nations, Algeria, Morocco, Tunisia, and Mauritania, agreed to put aside their differences and submit a collective proposal. However, although this acknowledged the crucial role of women in the preservation of couscous heritage, referring to their 'fundamental role in the preparation and consumption of the dish and in practising and preserving the related symbolic value systems', media coverage was once again all about national pride and male celebrity chefs, even though one of them was prepared to confess that his expertise was based on 'decades of observing the mother, the sisters, and all North African women who are experts in this' (Al Jazeera, 2020).

While UNESCO encourages civil society involvement and participation in ICH identification and safeguarding, this process is firmly under the control of nation states who retain the power to determine the modalities of such social inclusion (or exclusion). In relation to food heritage, power differentials and conflicting interests (particularly in the context of the global advance of authoritarian regimes) ensure that vulnerable groups such as minorities and rural communities, and even more so the women of these communities, struggle to secure recognition of their heritage-making activities (Matta, 2019). As a result, official ICH nomination tends to be bestowed, as the examples above illustrate, on a commodified nation state-promoted version of food heritage primarily for tourist consumption and often even lacking a coherent framework of national safeguarding. These versions, as historian François Hartog (2017) has argued, tend to be overwhelmingly 'presentist', that is they relate to the past simply as an extension of the present and its concerns premised, in this context, upon the interests of short-termist national governments whose policies demonstrate only a limited concern for the future.

ICH processes and debates remain a world away from local communities quietly engaged in sustainable farming practices which include the safeguarding of traditional knowledge. Indeed, small farmers are increasingly perceived as crucial to heritage preservation and ecologically sustainable food futures. This entails the safeguarding of localised traditions and cultures of low-energy diversified cropping which create local autonomies from global capital flows (Smaje, 2020; Maass Wolfenson, 2013). These farming communities are often at variance with the economic and agricultural policies of their national governments intent on promoting the current global corporate food regime based on fossil fuel powered, climate warming fertilisers and pesticides (Brown, 2020). Instead, they are concerned with maintaining or reviving traditional food cultures as multiple, place-based 'commons' premised on the protection of life in all its diverse forms and supported by democratic and inclusive political arrangements (Vivero-Pol, 2017; Micarelli, 2021). This approach is seen as the only means of sustaining both human and non-human subjects in the context of climate change, biodiversity loss, and pandemics. Food commons crucially involve heritage, as crops and cuisines are created and sustained by local communities through cultural memory, oral transmission of knowledge between generations, and inherited cosmologies and rituals which they perform to give meaning to their lives as food producers and members of a social group (Hazareesingh, 2021).

Women are crucial to the production of food commons, not merely because they make up the majority of the world's small farmers and food producers (Sweetman, 1995; Smaje, 2020), but mainly because of their leading role as repositories of cultural memory which involves protecting, shaping, recreating, managing, and passing on place-specific (agri)cultural heritage pertaining to locally important seeds, plants, and foods (Nazarea, 1998, 2006). As holders of detailed farming knowledge relating to food and medicinal (but not cash) crops, they use their expertise to select and preserve seeds that will turn into nutritious and tasty foods and serve a variety of other farming and domestic purposes as well. For instance, in central Laos, women in Bolikhamsai province have been found to gather from local forests 37 types of plant food items, 68 types of medicinal products, 18 types of items for household use, and the same number for animal use (Ireson, 1997). In India these gendered modes of knowledge have put women smallholders at the forefront of the current millet revival social movement which will be explored in detail later in this chapter.

Yet such heritage-creating food practices remain 'invisible to the public eye' (Camacho, 2013) as women continue to be largely unheard in the formulation of heritage policies at national and global levels. A recent study on the subject found that although the achievement of 'gender equality' has received increasing attention in UNESCO's policies and programmes over the past decade, this was not reflected in World Heritage List documents, nor translated into action at the local, grassroots level of women farmers. An analysis of official documents pertaining to the nomination in 2011 of the vineyard landscapes of the Italian regions of Langhe-Roero and Monferrato as a World Heritage Site revealed that women's experiences and histories were marginalised with women wine producers declaring that they had not been directly involved in the identification of heritage values. As a result, two worlds of heritage were in existence but remained separate: one created by global heritage professionals through official, legal documents, the other a locally lived, undocumented 'women's heritage' shaped by their everyday cultural, social, and economic activities (Settimini, 2021).

A similar discrepancy between vision and actual implementation can be observed in another UN initiative, the much-praised 2015 Sustainable Development Goals (SDGs). This has received widespread acclaim as an inspiring blueprint for addressing, amongst other pertinent issues, the global challenges of food security and gender equality (SDGs 2 and 5). However, the failure of the UN agenda to recognise the foundational importance of culture to the achievement of these goals, expressed in the very scant references to either culture or heritage in the SDGs, has raised concerns. A recent report on their worldwide implementation found that the cultural dimension of sustainable development 'lags significantly behind' the main social, economic, and environmental priorities and that 'the potential to relate culture to the SDGs appears to remain largely untapped in national strategies to implement the SDGs' (Culture 2030 Goal Campaign, 2019: 4). This is particularly concerning in the light of the leading role of women in the creation and transmission of food cultural heritages in the Global South and the close interrelationship between culture and the realisation of gender equality.

As with UNESCO, the primacy of nation states and the dependent role assigned to civil society actors in the process of goal implementation has resulted, at best, in a conception of women as passive beneficiaries of equalising rights initiated by others rather than as active agents of change and empowerment themselves via cultural creativity and modes of self-organising. At worst, as in the case of India, national governments' control over the framework of SDG progress indicators has enabled them to leave out entire areas and issues deemed 'inappropriate'. The Indian government has excluded small farmers and their access to productive resources and nutritious foods from the monitoring process relating to SDGs 2 and 5 (Sharma et al., 2021). Given that farming accounts for the majority of working women who already face discriminatory inheritance laws and gender biased social norms which limit their access to and management control over farmland (Agarwal, 2018), this represents a severe setback for, if not an actual reversal of, progress towards gender equality. A recent study suggests that the Indian government has been able to domesticate the SDG framework for its own political and ideological ends and warns that empowering national governments in this way risks 'government capture' of the UN agenda in many parts of the world (Haustein and Tomalin, 2021).

Food culture in heritage and development-oriented academic literature

Mainstream heritage literature has so far shown little interest in the cultures of food. The leading English-language journal in the field, the *International Journal of Heritage Studies*, has published just two articles on the subject over the past decade. Perhaps the recent emergence of the concept of commons in critical heritage studies might provide an entry point for studies of food cultures. In a heritage context, 'commons' has been defined as local, collaborative processes of protection, (re)production, and ownership of cultural resources, 'in opposition to globalising and neoliberal currents' within mainstream heritage (Lekakis, 2020). Food has fared a little (but not much) better in the more 'niche' *International Journal of Intangible Heritage*, launched in the wake of the emergence of the Convention for the Safeguarding of the Intangible Cultural Heritage (CSICH) by the National Folk Museum of Korea. Here, Patricia Huang's analysis of Berber women's argan oil co-operatives in Morocco is one of the few to engage with the concept of 'sustainability'. The argan tree, and the traditional knowledge and practices relating to it, were adopted into the official ICH list in 2014. Oil extracted from the fruits of the tree play a crucial role in the diet and health practices of the Moroccan Berber communities who perceive it as 'the tree of life'. As in other food heritage contexts in the Global South, women remain the repository of the oral traditions that perpetuate intimate argan knowledges, which include the use of grinding millstones, a common Berber household item, to mix argan oil, honey, and almonds so as to make *amlou* the traditional Moroccan bread spread. Argan women co-operatives, selling a variety of oil products, emerged around the turn of the millennium, following research that established the oil's culinary, medicinal, and cosmetic virtues.

However, their story suggests that the granting of ICH status does little, on its own, to secure the long-term sustainability of a particular heritage product or to empower local women cultural producers. While UNESCO recognition boosted the co-operatives in the short-term, enabling more Berber women to enter the public sphere of paid employment, it has also had significant adverse effects. In particular, the co-operatives have faced fierce competition from private companies over oil sales, threatening their long-term viability, while 'ICH fame' has led to a rise in argan oil prices, reducing their use in Berber households and potentially putting into peril the preservation of this cultural heritage. Nor have the required national government initiatives to sustain the heritage safeguarding process been forthcoming. These include legislation to protect the argan tree under threat from ruthless harvesting by private companies, subsidising the co-operatives so that they can offer expanded job prospects to Berber women, and documenting the material culture of millstone use. (Huang, 2017).

Moreover, while the concept of sustainability has been at the heart of international development literature for some time now, its relevance and connection to food as cultural heritage has hardly ever been addressed. Issues pertaining to sustainable farming, agriculture, and food systems/regimes feature regularly in development journals such as the *Journal of Peasant Studies* and the *Journal of Agrarian Change*. However, these journals have tended to prioritise economic and political understandings of sustainability to the virtual exclusion of cultural aspects; recognising that farming is as much a cultural as an economic activity remains a bit of a struggle. Even the feminist-oriented *Gender and Development*, in the relatively few articles devoted to women in agriculture and food production over the past couple of decades, though strong in conveying the structural inequalities faced by women farmers, has had little to say about cultural processes. In a rare piece that, while unrelated to agricultural issues, did focus on the potential significance of cultural traditions for women's empowerment, the author observes that

> in the field of gender and development, an understanding of the influence that religious and cultural traditions have upon women's social status or economic opportunity is slowly being recognised as an important factor in the pursuit of female empowerment in developing countries.
>
> *Tomalin, 2006: 385*

But such recognition remains decidedly in the slow lane as far as development journals are concerned.

Culture, as histories, memories, stories, beliefs, rituals, and performances, is profoundly implicated in farming cycles of planting, gathering, harvesting, conserving, cooking, and eating, creating spaces of creativity and meaning that reveal a social group's most cherished values. Culture is therefore crucial to any holistic conception of sustainable development (Clammer, 2018). But even the literature on food as commons, including its major constituent dimensions of agroecology and food sovereignty, is essentially culture-light, as the contributions to the *Routledge Handbook of Food as a Commons* (2019) indicate. A recent survey of the literature on agroecology observes that this field 'does not take seriously its own calls to integrate culture and tradition into this socially transformative discipline' (Morgan and Trubek, 2020: 5). It found that 'tradition' in these writings referred predominantly to traditional food production rather than food preparation, neglecting in the process cultural meanings expressed through diets, cooking, and food choices. Similarly, food sovereignty literature tended to assume that people would choose local and traditional foods if only they had control over production. However, as rural diets are, in a globalised world, influenced by the availability of foods from elsewhere, there was no automatic link between traditional crops and traditional dishes. A more holistic approach, connecting the reciprocal spheres of production and consumption required 'place-based cultural investigations' (ibid.: 2) into the complex, often contradictory influences that determine how people arrive at their specific food eating choices. Such research, the authors suggest, might focus on women's roles in food preparation and household decision-making as they are 'some of the main movers in agroecology' but remain 'largely invisible' in publications (ibid.: 12).

This intervention highlights the crucial significance of place-based, women-led cultural contexts to any determination of sustainable farming and foodways. In turn, sustainable, biodiverse farming based on the widest range of crops is increasingly being recognised as crucial to human and planetary well-being and health (Willett et al., 2019; Padulosi et al., 2022). There is therefore real urgency to the suggested research in the context of the marginalisation of women's cultures both in institutions and academic literature broadly concerned with development. So far, the relatively scant work on food heritage and women's roles in farms, households, and local communities, and their significance for agroecological farming has tended to come from outside the formal heritage and international development disciplines. Hopefully, these emerging writings signal an expanding multidisciplinary future for food heritage studies involving concerns and methods drawn from (at least) anthropology, ethnobotany, history, archaeology, and gender studies.

In one such study particularly attuned to historical and cultural contexts, anthropologist Juana Camacho examines women's food cultivation practices as part of a wider process of place-making linked to political resistance. In a context defined by the legacies of slavery and contemporary armed conflict and dispossession, Afro-Colombian women in the Pacific Chocó coast of Colombia grow an impressive variety of culinary, medicinal, and ornamental plants on their home gardens based on traditional knowledge of plant use passed on through oral tradition and free community exchange of plants. Cultivation practices reflect agroecological values, aligning with the interactions and cycles of plants, animals, and nutrients in the natural world. These are part of a range of 'home making' practices whereby Chocó women sustain life, both materially and symbolically by constructing secure and safe places and performing a range of life cycle rituals. Such practices humanise localities designated by the government as 'empty' national lands, free to be used for energy, mining, and other enterprises. Occupying these territories becomes therefore crucial to the reconstruction of the social and cultural fabric of Afro-Colombian communities and to their assertion of place-defined citizenship rights (Camacho, 2013).

A few similar women-focused studies have occasionally appeared in the interdisciplinary journals *Culture, Food and Society* and *Culture, Agriculture, Food and Environment* which, as the title suggests, focuses on investigating the complex interrelationships between these four concepts. One study considers the leading role of women in cassava cultivation and accompanying rituals amongst two Indigenous Amerindian communities of Guyana. They are the acknowledged experts in cassava farming, possessing an intimate knowledge of the indigenous names, history, and distinct characteristics of each cassava landrace (traditional plant variety). This is significant as, turned into *farine* (flour) for making bread and porridge, cassava remains not only the preferred dietary staple of these communities but continues, as a sacred indigenous plant, to be central to their ontologies or belief systems. This is expressed in farming rituals and celebrations such as the annual, week-long 'young cassava' festival, which represents the high point of both the farming and religious calendars. Women also occupy leading roles in Indigenous worship practices based on pre-Colombian traditions, with some achieving the status of revered prophets. Farmers attempt to sustain cassava farming through experimentation, incorporating new, high-quality landraces arising from the reproduction process into their repertoire, and through exchange practices with other farmers. This enables the selection of landraces adaptable to different farming soils as well as to weather changes as happened following the El Niño droughts of 1995 and 2009 (Bulkan, 2019).

The evacuation of the realm of the cultural-historical in development literature concerned with food and farming means that the bulk of these writings also tend to comprehend these subjects through a presentist lens, one that, contingent upon viewing the socio-economic as the primary sphere of human activity, tends to view the present 'as the sole and ultimate dimension of reality' (Hellerma, 2020). In contrast, Sarah Osterhoudt's study of the village and people of Imorona on the north-eastern coast of Madagascar shows how farmers experience coextensive temporalities through their understanding that local agro-forestry landscapes are an assemblage of multiple time frames that weave together past, present, and future and that their own cultural memories shape how they farm their land and what they leave on it. Land is precious heritage and must therefore, as desired by ancestors, be passed on to the next generation as 'happy landscapes'. The complex knowledge required to successfully farm a diversity of indigenous crop and tree species relies on oral traditions passed down between generations which also emphasise other-than-human ontologies whereby ancestors, trees, and plants have agency and influence everyday cultivating practices. These heritage-derived cultural resources include the practice of *tantara*, a form of oral history which produces a shared, collective historical consciousness of place and community (Osterhoudt, 2017). An implicit critique of development presentism, this reflective and multivocal study invites a rethinking of the relationships between history, culture, and sustainable environments, and between humans and other beings.

Millets as women's food heritage in India

As outlined earlier, millets are undergoing a revival in India, particularly in the once dominant millet-growing regions of the south and north-east where they gradually gave way to rice following the Green Revolution of the 1960s and consequent government policies. However, water-guzzling rice cultivation has been affected by increasingly severe droughts over the past couple of decades consequent upon climate change. In this context, millets have re-emerged as one of the important foods of the future possessing a range of nutritional and environmentally friendly advantages in relation to rice, which include micronutrient richness, higher carbon absorption capacity, and drastically lower water usage (Hazareesingh, 2021).

In some southern and north-eastern States, millets have for centuries played a central role in the cultural life of Indigenous and local communities based not only on women's seed conservation and crop cultivating skills but also on their central role in farming cosmologies and rituals where cooking and eating millet foods have remained an important aspect of local celebrations and religious ceremonies. Over the past decade, women millet farmers have been mobilising and developing their organisational capacities with the support of NGOs, civil society organisations, and food, farming, and environmental activists. This has led to the emergence of an all India Millet Sisters Network made up of representatives of women millet farmers from 12 States. In May 2018, the Network issued a proclamation calling on the Indian government to 'recognise millets as our heritage crops' and 'their extraordinary value for providing food, nutrition, fodder, livelihood and ecological security in these climate-stressed times'. The declaration also demanded from government 'priority support to millet-based biodiversity agriculture practised by millions of small women farmers who are custodians of India's rich lore of millet farming practices' (All-India Millet Sisters Network, 2018: 1).

Conducting oral history interviews with women millet farmers in the locality of Kanakapura in the southern State of Karnataka at around the same time, it was significant that this 'lore of millet farming practices' encompassed everyday attachments to place and culture, to cooking and culinary knowledge as much as to farming skills. Unlike much of the existing academic literature that assigns separate disciplinary realms to studies of food culture on the one hand and farming practices on the other, they viewed these activities in a holistic continuum, as inseparable aspects of their lived experience. Seed saving lies at the heart of these endeavours, a care practice historically centred on women and passed down over the generations. Women nurture and preserve 'heirloom' or heritage varieties, helping communities maintain their food culture and security. As a common good, seeds adhere to both food and heritage commons. In the eyes of the women smallholders we spoke to, *nati* (local) seeds possess agency as entities with life-producing capacities, thus underlining the ontological relationship between the natural and human worlds whereby seeds reproduce both their own and human life by making food possible.

One of the farmers, Hombalamma, has acquired a public reputation as an eminent seed saver or *Beeja Matha* (Mother of Seeds). 'I have no education, but I have knowledge', she tells us. 'Men don't have this knowledge and they can't multi-task'. She perceives seeds as living, almost human, entities. 'They will not grow unless nurtured and loved like a child', she goes on. She explains how for the past 25 years, she has been preparing and using a pure, organic castor oil derived from castor seeds to coat seeds from indigenous millet and other food and medicinal plants, thus preserving them from pests and insects. Hombalamma and her family enjoy complete autonomy from the commercial seed market and are 'food sovereign', able to grow over 50 varieties of organic food crops at the optimal time on their biodiverse farm. Finger millet, pigeon pea, and other pulses predominate in a varied cropping system that also includes foxtail millet, hyacinth and broad beans, bottle gourd, pumpkin, tomato, and other fruits. These crops reach maturation at different times during the farming season, thus minimising risk to food security and ensuring a varied and nutritious diet (interview with Hombalamma 23 April 2018).

Seed saving was also linked to the tastiness of millet foods, and our team was often invited to share in a home-cooked meal of *ragi mudde* (finger millet soft balls). Taste, and the cultural practice of tasting, express a sensual appreciation of food quality by these women who also see themselves as the custodians of local cuisines and dishes. Taste may be perceived as an enabling and persuasive dimension of nutrition, and it is interesting that the women farmers also found it difficult to dissociate these two aspects of millet foods. From a food heritage perspective, taste functions as a form of 'sensory labour', a cultural knowledge practice that draws on family histories of discernment and facilitates the sustaining of vulnerable farming lives (Kantor, 2019). Indeed, our conversations with the women triggered their 'edible memories' (Jordan, 2015) of millet-based local pre-Green Revolution foods. Some narrated how they prepared delicious, fragrant millet 'rice' dishes from *arka* (kodo millet), *saame* (little millet), and *navne* (foxtail millet), eaten with *sambhar* (vegetable stew) made from a variety of local beans, with *avarekai* (hyacinth beans) particularly prominent on account of its nutrients and deep, rich scent. This combination of millets with stews was perceived as particularly wholesome and tasty by women in the villages of southern Karnataka.

The women were unanimous about the nutritional benefits of ragi as compared with rice. 'Rice is easily digested and passes through the body quickly, whereas ragi has more iron content, is digested very slowly, stays longer in the body and therefore provides more stamina and strength', Devaramma explains. But if ragi is so good, why has its household consumption declined in favour of rice, we ask. It's because rice became a status symbol, she replies, a desire not to be associated with 'the poor man's food' anymore. She goes on to describe one of the ways in which the cultural taste for rice was popularised in her village, recounting a story from her childhood about a rich local landowner who was attending the village *panchayat* (council) and had fixed a grain of rice on his moustache, pointing to it and telling people just how tasty rice was. So, in her family, they started eating more rice dishes than ragi which was reduced to one meal a day mainly because the government's Public Distribution System, set up in the wake of the Green Revolution, made it cheaper to buy rice than to grow ragi. But now this is changing, not only in her family but more generally in the villages as people have become more health conscious and been reminded by women elders of the nutritional benefits of millets (interview with Devaramma 12 March 2018).

But the revival of millets in the face of the dominance of rice as the main staple in rural India will require, amongst a range of enabling processes, an accelerated *praxis* of cultural action organised around events like food festivals with their rich potential for preserving and reinventing cultural heritage and community (Ascione and Fink, 2021). A useful model is provided by the North East Slow Food and Agrobiodiversity Society (NESFAS) and its food heritage activities in the State of Meghalaya. Established in 2012 as part of the International Slow Food Movement, NESFAS works with 130 local Indigenous communities to revive the desire and taste for traditional foods and cuisines, particularly millets, with the broader concerns to preserve Indigenous culture and knowledge, protect local biodiversity, and mitigate the impact of climate change. Women have played a crucial role in shaping the organisation as, in contrast to the dominant pattern elsewhere in India, they belong to matrilineal communities where property and farming knowledge are passed from mothers to daughters, providing a structural basis for agency and influence.

Over the past eight years, NESFAS has hosted 31 *Mei Ramew* (Mother Earth) food festivals and organised cooking workshops, seed fairs, and biodiversity walks. As a heritage food of all the Indigenous communities of the region, finger millet or *krai* in the local Khasi language, has featured prominently in these events. The festivals have attracted a large attendance and featured a series of interrelated cultural performances including cooking competitions and taste workshops which seek to encourage innovative recipes and dishes based on traditional knowledge. There have, for instance, been demonstrations of how to make *pakora* (fritter), *chapati* (thin wholegrain bread), and pancake from millet flour, as snacks that can be enjoyed 'on the go', seen as particularly relevant to young people (NESFAS, 2017). Two by-products of the festivals have been the emergence of Mother Earth Cafés in rural Meghalaya, serving meals prepared with local ingredients but from recipes offering a creative, contemporary twist (Global Alliance for the Future of Food, 2021); and monthly Mei Ramew Farmers' Markets, which enable farmers to sell their products directly to and engage with consumers and promote at the same time the appreciation of traditional foods more widely (Matters India, 2019).

The festivals brought together food cultures from over 150 villages, while related activities involved seed and plant exchanges as gifts. Such gifts function not only in the sense suggested by Mauss, as a mode of anti-commodity exchange designed to develop close, personal inter-communal relationships (Gregory, 1982) but also to imbue receivers with the sacredness of the land from which the gifts originate, transmitting a responsibility of care for the local biodiversity into the future. For these Indigenous communities, the commoning of food rests on shared emotional connections expressed through reciprocity and solidarity. Another related feature of the festivals is the performance of the traditional farming songs and dances of the local villages, including songs that accompany the cycle of everyday millet production. These much enjoyed and acclaimed performances underline the significance of culture and emotions in local farming lives, contributing to the realm of gift exchange and renewing people's attachment to places and heritages.

Food festivals are inevitably linked with tourism as 'branded culinary destinations' (Yang et al., 2020) to which NESFAS is not opposed though it perceives the festivals and cafés as promoting 'sustainable' forms based on bringing together local producers, entrepreneurs, and consumers interested in renewing and promoting healthy traditional foods, thus benefiting the rural economy. Essentially, the organisation aims to encourage ethical and responsible consumption and sustainable ecotourism (NESFAS, 2020). However, the festivals are supported by the State government of Meghalaya which has a somewhat different perspective. A major international NESFAS event was the highly successful second Indigenous Terra Madre festival held in November 2015, which showcased, celebrated, and shared produce from indigenous food systems across the world, attracting over 600 participants from 58 countries.

However, the government perceived the festival as evidence that cultural heritage can be leveraged to achieve 'growth and prosperity' through the opening up of a remote region to international tourism. This has resulted in land grabs by tourist entrepreneurs and environmental damage to local landscapes due to the unregulated influx of tourists (Nongkynrih, 2019). At the same time the tourism industry has always kept a keen eye on food festivals as part of destination branding strategies and the annual Mei Ramew event is now listed in the *Lonely Planet* and other tourist guides. Indian tour operators have also reportedly added that festival to their culinary tourism itineraries (Chawla, 2021). Moving forward, there are real dangers that a region whose very remoteness has helped preserve its traditional, sustainable foodways may suffer the blight of modern 'development', with places and ways of life transformed by the requirements of surging waves of global visitors. While local food festivals' potential to generate 'sustainable tourism' has received much favourable scholarly attention recently, there remains in Meghalaya a stark contrast between the high status and reputation of Indigenous women as food producers and their confinement to low-skilled, low-paid, and often unsafe jobs in the tourist industry (De, 2013).

Conclusion

In India and much of the Global South, women's place-based farming heritage, encompassing local knowledge of biodiversity, cultural memory, and cosmological frameworks of values and beliefs, are crucial to the production of sustainable food systems. As in the cited case of millets, heritage includes seed preservation practices, knowledge of crop cultivation and of food preparation through memories and recipes as women manage family nutrition, dietary choices and tastes, as well as changes and innovations within specific cultural contexts. Moreover, sustainable farming based on the full range of the thousands of neglected food crops across the world is now seen as essential to the well-being of the earth's life support system and to a move to a post-Anthropocene era. Yet rural women's cultural heritages, and their crucial role in driving potentially wholesome food futures remain, for different reasons, ignored by global and national heritage agencies as well as by the bulk of heritage and international development literature.

The alternative paradigms of food commons and agroecology within international development need both to give far greater attention to gender and to reach out beyond their comfort zone in the social sciences to arts and humanities methods and approaches broadly concerned with the realms of history and culture. The formal discipline of Heritage, on the other hand, must take greater interest in food cultures particularly from the vantage point of rural women, with research on the oral traditions that lie at the heart of women's knowledge being especially urgent in view of their endangerment from the vicissitudes of both societal neglect and time. Indeed, the vast range of traditional nutritious foods and their associated local cultures and knowledges remain endangered, representing a fundamental aspect of the larger species extinction crisis unfolding across the planet. They have not so far attracted much interest from mainstream heritage actors, and there is certainly room for UNESCO to do much more here, potentially through its 'Man (sic) and the Biosphere' programme.

Nonetheless, there are reasons to be cautiously optimistic at least about the prospects of millet revival in India (and potentially sub-Saharan Africa): the Karnataka-based social movement dedicated to achieving this, made up of farmers, NGOs, nutritionists, and academics has had significant influence, including the active support and patronage of the agriculture minister and department of the previous State government in office until 2019. One policy outcome has seen the FAO nominate 2023 as the International Year of Millets, with the UN General Assembly adopting a resolution to this effect in March 2021 as part of the UN's Decade of Action on Nutrition. This represents a significant boost to the campaign and, with increasing pro-millet stories in the national press and on social media, promises to lead to a greater global awareness of the benefits of these foods which are back on restaurant menus. FAO recognition will also open up new spaces for action and influence: but to be ultimately successful, the millet revival campaign will need to use these emerging opportunities judiciously. In particular, it will be crucial to promote local cultural action programmes such as those initiated by NESFAS so as to reactivate the *desire* to eat millets amongst new generations. In these events, women producers, cooks, and food enthusiasts must be given a leading role and voice.

References

Agarwal, B. (2018) 'Gender equality, food security and the sustainable development goals', *Current Opinion in Environmental Sustainability*, 34, pp. 26–32.

Al Jazeera (2020) 'UNESCO adds couscous to list of intangible world heritage', *Al Jazeera*, 16 December. Available at: www.aljazeera.com/news/2020/12/16/unesco-adds-couscous-to-list-of-intangible-world-heritage (Accessed 9 June 2021).

All-India Millet Sisters Network (AIMS) (2018) *Umiam Declaration of Millet Sisters*. Available at: https://milletindia.org/wp-content/uploads/2017/03/Umiam-Declaration-English.pdf (Accessed 18 March 2022).

Ascione, E. and Fink, C. (2021) 'Italian *sagre*: preserving and re-inventing cultural heritage and community through food festivals in Umbria, Italy', *Food, Culture & Society*, 24(2), pp. 291–308.

Aycan, B. (2016) 'The politics of intangible cultural heritage and food fights in Western Asia', *International Journal of Heritage Studies*, 22(10), pp. 799–810.

Brown, T. (2020) 'When food regimes become hegemonic: agrarian India through a Gramscian lens', *Journal of Agrarian Change*, 20, pp. 188–206.

Brulotte, R.L. and Di Giovine, M.A. (2016) 'Introduction. Food and foodways as cultural heritage', in Brulotte, R.L. and Di Giovine, M.A. (eds) *Edible identities: food as cultural heritage*. Abingdon and New York: Routledge, pp. 1–28.

Bulkan, J. (2019) 'The place of bitter cassava in the social organization and belief systems of two indigenous peoples of Guyana', *Culture, Agriculture, Food, and Environment*, 41(2), pp. 117–128.

Camacho, J. (2013) 'People, place, and plants in the Pacific coast of Colombia', in Nazarea, V.D., Rhoades, R.E. and Andrews-Swann, J.E. (eds) *Seeds of resistance, seeds of hope.* Tucson: The University of Arizona Press, pp. 115–150.

Chawla, P. (2021) *Culinary tourism: Exploring India's enormous treasure grove.* Available at: https://mediaindia.eu/tourism/culinary-tourism-india/ (Accessed 14 June 2021).

Clammer, J. (2018) *Art, culture and international development.* Abingdon and New York: Routledge.

Csergo, J. (2019) 'Food as a collective heritage brand in the era of globalization', *International Journal of Cultural Property*, 25, pp. 449–468.

Culture 2030 Goal Campaign (2019) *Culture in the implementation of the 2030 agenda: a report.* Available at: https://culture360.asef.org/resources/culture-implementation-2030-agenda-report-culture-2030-goal-campaign/ (Accessed 15 June 2021).

De, U.K. (2013) 'Sustainable nature-based tourism, involvement of indigenous women, and development: a case of North-East India', *Tourism Recreation Research*, 38(3), pp. 311–324.

Global Alliance for the Future of Food (2021) *North East Slow Food & Agrobiodiversity Society (NESFAS): an innovative approach in support and celebration of Indigenous Food Systems.* Available at: https://futureoffood.org/insights/north-east-slow-food-agrobiodiversity-society-nesfas/ (Accessed 16 June 2021).

Gregory, C. (1982) *Gifts and commodities.* London: Academic Press.

Hartog, F. (2017) *Regimes of historicity: presentism and experiences of time.* New York and Chichester: Columbia University Press.

Haustein, J. and Tomalin, E. (2021) 'Religion, populism, and the politics of the Sustainable Development Goals', *Social Policy & Society*, 20(2), pp. 296–309.

Hazareesingh, S. (2021) '"Our grandmother used to sing whilst weeding": oral histories, millet food culture, and farming rituals among women smallholders in Ramanagara district, Karnataka', *Modern Asian Studies*, 55(3), pp. 938–972.

Hellerma, J. (2020) 'Negotiating presentism: toward a renewed understanding of historical change', *Rethinking History*, 24(3–4), pp. 442–464.

Huang, P. (2017) 'Liquid gold: Berber women and the argan oil co-operatives in Morocco', *International Journal of Intangible Heritage*, 12, pp. 140–155.

Ireson, C. (1997) 'Women's forest work in Laos', in Sachs, C.E. (ed.) *Women working in the environment.* Washington: Taylor & Francis, pp. 15–30.

Jordan, J.J. (2015) *Edible memory. The lure of heirloom tomatoes and other forgotten foods.* Chicago: The University of Chicago Press.

Kantor, H.S. (2019) 'A body set between hot and cold: everyday sensory labor and attunement in an Indian Village', *Food, Culture & Society*, 22(2), pp. 237–252.

Lekakis, S. (2020) 'Cultural heritage in the realm of the commons. Reading a letter from the future', in Lekakis, S. (ed.) *Cultural heritage in the realm of the commons. Conversations on the case of Greece.* London: Ubiquity Press, pp. 1–14.

Maas Wolfenson, K.D. (2013) *Coping with the food and agriculture challenge: smallholders' agenda.* Rome: Food and Agriculture Organization of the United Nations.

Matta, R. (2019) 'Heritage foodways as matrix for cultural resurgence: evidence from rural Peru', *International Journal of Cultural Property*, 26, pp. 49–74.

Matters India (2019) 'First Mei-Ramew Farmers' Market of 2019 a big hit', *Matters India*, 15 April 2019. Available at: https://mattersindia.com/2019/04/first-mei-ramew-farmers-market-of-2019-a-big-hit/ (Accessed 17 June 2021).

Micarelli, G. (2021) 'Feeding "the commons": rethinking food rights through indigenous ontologies', *Food, Culture & Society*, 24(3), pp. 446–463.

Morgan, C.B. and Trubek, A.B. (2020) 'Not yet at the table: the absence of food culture and tradition in agroecology literature', *Elementa: Science of the Anthropocene* , 8(40), pp. 1–12.

Nazarea, V.D. (1998) *Cultural memory and biodiversity*. Tucson: The University of Arizona Press.

Nazarea, V.D. (2006) 'Local knowledge and memory in biodiversity conservation', *Annual Review of Anthropology*, 35, pp. 317–335.

Nongkynrih, A.K. (2019) 'Sustainable tourism in the context of Meghalaya: a sociological perspective', *Explorations*, 3(1), pp. 27–44.

North East Slow Food & Agrobiodiversity Society (NESFAS) (2017) *Annual report 2016–2017*. Available at: www.nesfas.in/wp-content/uploads/2018/10/Nesfas-ar-low-res.pdf (Accessed 28 March 2022).

North East Slow Food & Agrobiodiversity Society (NESFAS) (2020) *Annual report 2019–2020*. Available at: www.nesfas.in/wp-content/uploads/2021/03/Annual-Report-2019-2020.pdf (Accessed 28 March 2022).

Osterhoudt, S.R. (2017) *Vanilla landscapes. Meaning, memory, and the cultivation of place in Madagascar*. New York: New York Botanical Garden Press.

Padulosi, S., Oliver King, E.D.I, Hunter, D., and Swaminathan, M.S. (2022) *Orphan crops for sustainable food and nutrition security: promoting neglected and underutilized species*. London and New York: Earthscan from Routledge.

Romagnoli, M. (2019) 'Gastronomic heritage elements at UNESCO: problems, reflections on and interpretations of a new heritage category', *International Journal of Intangible Heritage*, 14, pp. 157–171.

Saladino, D. (2021) *Eating to extinction. The world's rarest foods and why we need to save them*. London: Jonathan Cape.

Sammells, C.A. (2016) 'Haute traditional cuisines: how UNESCO's list of intangible heritage links the cosmopolitan to the local', in Brulotte, R.L. and Di Giovine, M.A. (eds) *Edible identities: food as cultural heritage*. Abingdon and New York: Routledge, pp. 141–158.

Settimini, E. (2021) 'Women's representation and participation in UNESCO heritage discourses', *International Journal of Heritage Studies*, 27(1), pp. 1–15.

Sharma, N., Reddy, S., Clammer, J.R., Kostakos, G. and Ladi, S. (2021) *Implementing the SDGs in India: poverty, hunger, and gender*. Brussels: Foundation for Global Governance and Sustainability.

Smaje, C. (2020) *A small farm future. Making the case for a society built around local economies, self-provisioning, agricultural diversity and a shared Earth*. White River Junction, VT: Chelsea Green Publishing.

Sweetman, C. (1995) 'Editorial', *Gender & Development*, 3(1), pp. 1–6.

Tomalin, E. (2006) 'The Thai Bhikkhuni movement and women's empowerment', *Gender & Development*, 14(3), pp. 385–397.

UNESCO (2003) *Text of the Convention for the Safeguarding of the Intangible Cultural Heritage*. Available at: https://ich.unesco.org/en/convention (Accessed 28 March 2022).

Vivero-Pol, J.L. (2017) 'Food as commons or commodity? Exploring the links between normative valuations and agency in food transitions', *Sustainability*, 9(42), pp. 1–23.

Vivero-Pol, J.L., Ferrando, T., De Schutter, O., Mattei, U. (eds) (2019) *Routledge handbook of food as a commons*. Abingdon and New York: Routledge.

Weston, P. and Watts, J. (2021) 'The cow in the room: why is no one talking about farming at COP26?' *The Guardian*, 9 November. Available at: www.theguardian.com/environment/2021/nov/09/the-cow-in-the-room-why-is-no-one-talking-about-farming-at-cop26-aoe (Accessed 10 November 2021).

Willett, W. et al. (2019) 'Food in the Anthropocene: the EAT-Lancet Commission on healthy diets from sustainable food systems', *The Lancet* 393, pp. 447–492.

Yang, F.X., Wong, I.A., Tan, X.S., and Chi Wai Wu, D. (2020) 'The role of food festivals in branding culinary destinations', *Tourism Management Perspectives*, 34, pp. 1–11.

7

LEARNING FROM THE DEEP PAST

Critical Perspectives on Biocultural Heritages for Well-Tempered Futures

Paul J. Lane and Federica Sulas

Introduction

At least since the Bretton Woods agreements in 1944 (Helleiner, 2014) and the establishment of a new international monetary regime in the immediate post-World War II era following the creation of the International Monetary Fund and the World Bank (Rosenstein-Rodan, 1944), most international development policies and interventions have been driven by present- and future-oriented perspectives. Less attention has been given to the role an understanding of the past might play in addressing contemporary challenges, in particular environmental issues such as combatting soil erosion, deforestation, and desertification. Proposed solutions have commonly relied on technical interventions based on the skills and knowledge of external actors (Elzinga and Landström, 1996), creating rather than reducing relations of dependency between the so-called 'developed' global centre and 'developing' periphery (Mabogunje, 1980; Dei, 1993). Many of these interventions have also been informed by singular narratives of the causes of environmental 'problems' and unexamined assumptions that they were of recent origin. The roots of this approach, however, lie much earlier during the era of European colonial rule (Beinart and Hughes, 2007; Burk and Davis, 2011; Ax et al., 2014), when negative attitudes regarding the abilities and competence of non-Western peoples in managing their environments and natural resources became entrenched in colonial environmental governance (e.g., Kull, 2000; Davis, 2005; Urzedo and Chatterjee, 2021). These have often been perpetuated in postcolonial contexts, and continue to hinder efforts aimed at securing sustainable development and resilient livelihood strategies (e.g., Carswell, 2003; Randeria, 2007; Smith and Dressler, 2020). As research on these environmental histories and political ecologies has advanced in recent decades, it has become increasingly apparent that an understanding of the deep histories of human–environment interactions can play a fundamental role

DOI: 10.4324/9781003107361-9

in planning for and enabling more sustainable futures (e.g., Costanza et al., 2007; Chase and Scarborough, 2014; Adamson et al., 2018; Jackson et al., 2018). In this chapter, we explore such arguments with reference to the concept of biocultural heritage and its synonyms.

Biocultural heritage

Biocultural heritage is a relatively new conceptual framework for understanding cultural landscapes that emerged from recognition that many species-rich and biologically diverse landscapes have long histories of human intervention and modification (Rotheram, 2015 and references therein). Far from being pristine landscapes that need to be protected at all costs from the 'damaging hand of humans', these landscapes, which can vary in spatial scale from small, sacred groves and watering points to extensive steppe and savanna grasslands, tropical rainforests, and agricultural landscapes, have been shaped by processes of ecological mutualism linking the actions of humans and other non-human co-inhabitants (Hill et al., 2011; Arnaiz-Schmiz et al., 2018; Seele et al., 2019). Moreover, as the results of long-term biological and social relations that have shaped the dominant biophysical processes, these places also represent a materialisation of the cultural knowledge, experiences, and memories invested in them over generations (Lindholm and Ekblom, 2019 and references therein). As the term has come to acquire some traction within the heritage field, different definitions of biocultural heritage have emerged. Eriksson (2018: 1), for example, proposes an operational definition based on niche construction theory whereby biocultural heritage refers to 'biological manifestations of culture, reflecting indirect or intentional effects, or domesticated landscapes, resulting from historical human niche construction'. Such an operational definition bridges UNESCO's concept of cultural landscapes (as the 'combined works of nature and man (*sic.*)', 1972, art. 1), while recognising the changing nature of the values and meanings people assign to material manifestations of culture. In contrast, UNESCO's definition of biocultural heritage as 'living organisms or habitats whose present features are due to cultural action in time and space' (2008: 8) appears somewhat at odds with the passing of time, and how cultural materials and values change. As remarked by Lindholm and Ekblom (2019), historic dynamics shaping biocultural heritage remain largely ignored in current approaches to rural development and conservation. The outcome is the alienation of knowledge and experience matured over time and across change from conservation activities, landscape planning, and the enabling of sustainable livelihoods.

As loss of biodiversity deepens, there is increasing awareness that environmental health is essential to a sustainable planet and human and other forms of life and, ultimately, that our species and our planet are interdependent. Yet, biodiversity remains largely portrayed as distinct from cultural diversity. For the Convention on Biodiversity and UNESCO, for example, biological diversity is the variability among all living organisms, within and between species and ecosystems, whereas cultural diversity refers to human communities, their ethnicities, history, languages, practices, knowledge, and value systems (CBD and UNESCO, 2010: 1). Underpinning such a distinction are two fundamental assumptions rooted in Western thought: (i) culture is broadly consistent over time (and does not belong to 'bio-', from ancient Greek βίος, 'bios' meaning 'life'); (ii) humans stand in distinction to and separated from nature. Such separations often contrast with traditional worldviews and Indigenous knowledge systems wherein people, culture, and nature are regarded as living parts of the same entity, and time and space are constantly negotiated.

Concepts of 'heritage' associated with relational ontologies of this kind also diverge from the natural versus cultural binary that has underpinned Western approaches to heritage management and wildlife conservation for at least 150 years, and more recent distinctions between tangible and intangible heritage. For the Aboriginal cultures of Victoria, Australia, for example, cultural heritage embodies the knowledge, practices and people, objects and places that shape identity and, as such, heritage is a lived spirituality fundamental to the well-being of communities through connectedness across generations (Victorian Aboriginal Heritage Council, 2021). This definition is not too far from the one promoted by many other Indigenous communities across the globe (e.g., IIED, 2005), including the very few entrusted with the management and preservation of their heritage under UNESCO World Heritage status. A poignant case study is Taos Pueblo, New Mexico: the only Native American inhabited settlement designated as a UNESCO World Heritage Site (Taos Pueblo, 2022). Here, a Tao-speaking Pueblo community practices a traditional way of life in adobe houses, with neither piped water nor electricity (Trujillo, 2019), and performs rituals in their sacred groves and at sacred sites. Nonetheless, this does not prevent the Taos Pueblo community from sending their children to schools, driving cars, or running lucrative ski resorts outside their private living space. The separation between public and private spheres is perhaps the recipe for nurturing a culture with deep historical roots and a heritage of material and spiritual values. However, Taos Pueblo remains an inspiring exception, as local and Indigenous communities are often excluded by, and even alienated from, external interventions aimed at the protection and conservation of their heritage.

Recent assessments find higher biodiversity rates in areas managed by Indigenous people and local communities (IPBES, 2019)—a finding that is informing policy making (Bridgewater 2017; Swiderska et al., 2020). Whilst welcomed as a new finding in development and environmental assessment arenas, the role of local communities in fostering biodiversity has long been recognised in historical ecology (Figure 7.1). By engaging with local knowledge systems and practices, historical ecology captures the entanglement and interdependency driving cultural and ecological diversity. In recent years, comparative research has shed light on the nature and patterns of socioecological processes that create and maintain such diversity (see e.g., Cevasco et al., 2015), a process itself described as biodiversification (Ingold, 2000).

In historical and political ecology, investment in modifying, creating, and adapting landscapes to support livelihoods has been considered in terms of *landesque capital*, a concept describing land improvements by people that endure through maintenance, and can also support further improvements through innovation (Widgren and Håkansson, 2014). The lasting human influence on the biosphere, whether resulting from land practices of *landesque capital* or interactions with other species, has been described as a process of 'landscape domestication' (Terrell et al., 2003; Erickson, 2006; Clement, 2014). Other scholars consider these intersections as examples of 'niche construction' (Clement et al., 2020), or 'ecological engineering' (Storozum et al., 2021). As suggested by Erickson (2006), through intentional and unintentional activities and practices people transform local environments into productive and cultural landscapes. These concepts offer theoretical and practical frameworks for understanding (human) landscapes as palimpsests of enduring cultural and environmental interactions that create and enhance biodiversity over time and space. In doing so, they introduce a spatio-temporal dimension to examining how and why people make sustainable investments of time and energy in land, land use history, and current practices of food production that are culturally and environmentally sustainable (see Widgren and Håkansson, 2014).

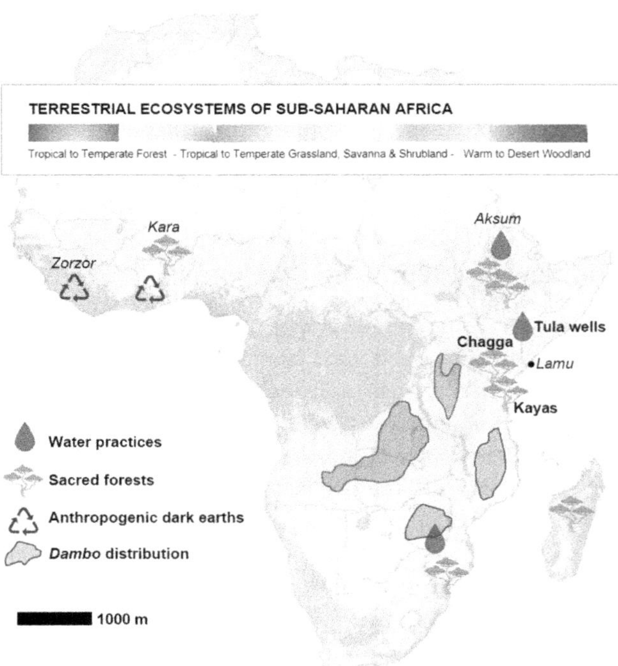

FIGURE 7.1 Location of biocultural heritage in sub-Saharan Africa discussed here. Base map adapted from Standardized Terrestrial Ecosystems of Africa, American Association of Geographers (2013) (Available at: www.aag.org/cs/publications/special/map_african_ecosystems)

Source: Image by the authors.

Comparative analyses of traditional agro-pastoral practices across profoundly different environmental and cultural contexts identify some important commonalities. For example, Agnoletti and colleagues (Agnoletti et al., 2015) have shown how traditional farming systems in Morocco, Cuba, and South Italy all share complex landscape mosaics, whereby most of the land is highly fragmented in small-sized plots under different uses ranging from mixed crop farming and gardening to wooded pastures and mixed forests. In eastern Africa, livestock herding practices have a deep-time history, preceding the development of crop cultivation. Transitions to food production took different paths, creating and reconfiguring diverse cultures, languages, ethnicities, ecologies, and lifeways over time. Such a process produced enduring, distinctive biocultural niches and landscape mosaics, some of which persist to this day (Boles et al., 2019). By creating and enabling these mosaics, traditional systems create high spatial heterogeneity and connectivity between land uses and habitats that maintain and promote biological diversity.

In this chapter, we examine how the deep past relates to traditional practices and know-hows that can, in turn, inform pathways to well-tempered futures. To do so, we take a backward journey starting with the most widespread development interventions since the mid-20th century: reforestation to rehabilitate land and the construction of dams to increase/secure food production and generate energy. Having outlined the historical and economic contexts spearheading reforestation and dam construction programmes, we consider the impact of these solutions in sub-Saharan Africa in contrast to smaller-scale, locally embedded interventions to achieve the same goals that have deeper historical roots and cultural associations.

Heritage and development: land and water

Past know-hows concerning resource uses have been overlooked in heritage discourses, traditionally concerned with tangible, material remains. If remains of built infrastructures such as Roman aqueducts or Incan terrace systems have long been cherished and preserved as heritage of global significance (Mays, 2010; Castro et al., 2019), the know-hows and practices of past resource management have until recently been ignored. On the one hand, heritage thinking developed within Western contexts has shaped our perception of the footprint of past land and water management, whereby the remains of a stone-built fountain are readily recognised as part of this heritage, whereas the ephemeral traces of past arable farming have often remained invisible to the non-expert eye. On the other hand, know-hows and practices that have endured through time persist to the present as traditional and/or Indigenous knowledge. The historical depth of Indigenous practices is, however, often masked by the ways in which they are described and understood as 'traditional practices' with no consideration of their temporal dimensions and possible transformations over time (Stump, 2010). More recent recognition of intangible cultural heritage, nonetheless, has brought the value of community knowledge, practices, and skills to the fore. Initially sparingly addressed by individual countries since the 1950s (Lenzerini, 2011), the UNESCO Convention for the Safeguarding of Intangible Cultural Heritage in 2003 defined the parameters of intangible cultural heritage as the 'practices, representations, expressions, knowledge, skills—as well as the instruments, objects, artefacts and cultural spaces associated therewith—that communities, groups and, in some cases, individuals recognize as part of their cultural heritage' (UNESCO, 2018, art. 2). This definition recognises that intangible heritage is transmitted from generation to generation, enduring through an ongoing negotiation that communities and groups entertain with their environment and history, promoting respect for cultural diversity and human creativity. Engaging and recognising intangible cultural heritages has inevitably stimulated reflection on the relationship between cultural practices and landscapes. Rather than being seen as a canvas for human agency, landscapes are considered as both product and process of tangible and intangible heritage making (Roe, 2016), providing the optimal scale for appreciating the interactions between community practices and environmental resources.

Since the late 19th century, 'modern' development has focused on maximising productivity of food and energy to support economic growth. The 1880s saw major developments in science and technology supporting colonial expansion of Western powers into Africa and Asia (Headrick, 1979). Among the challenges and opportunities created by these developments were the needs of fast-growing industries and urban centres in the colonies themselves and the homeland, with the regular supply of timber, food, and water, to mention but three key resources, being especially central. To meet these needs, investment focused on tree-planting for timber and charcoal supply, the introduction of extensive cash crop monoculture and industrialisation of farming, and dam building to support large-scale irrigation agriculture. In these solutions, it is not difficult to see the vestiges of distant imperial successes: the *latifundia* feeding Roman empires, the irrigation agriculture supporting Pharaonic kingdoms.

Three of the prime tools of these development interventions were eucalyptus tree species, economic crops (maize, wheat, cotton, and sugar cane), and masonry gravity dams. From Mediterranean coastal regions to African highlands and the prairies of North America, landscapes of deep historical significance were reshaped by the planting of non-native trees and crops, and the damming of rivers and water courses. Interventions were framed as being democratic in scope and reach by employing the same criteria for assessing, planning, and implementing land development programmes. Eucalyptus plantations, for example, followed coherent seedling patterns of planting rows, perpendicular to the slope if on a gradient, and defined by stone terraces whether in South Italy or Northern Ethiopia. On dams, following the success of the First Aswan Dam in Egypt established in 1902, the 1950s and 1960s initiated a period of grand dam building with a handful of Western firms leading the field. The Italian company Salini Costruttori (now rebranded as Webuild), for example, built about 60 large dams across Africa in the 1950s and 1960s, including some of the largest ones such as the Kariba Dam (Zambia and Zimbabwe) in 1959, and is now completing the Grand Ethiopian Renaissance

Dam. Standardised development policies and interventions, which ignore and are insensitive to local practices and contexts, persist to the present day in the face of increasing debate on the shortfalls of planning and implementation for reforestation and restoration (Bond et al., 2019; Fagan, 2020), mega-dams and hydropower (Showers, 2011), and their impacts on both tangible and intangible heritage (King and Eoin, 2014).

Case studies

Integrated water practices

In sub-Saharan Africa, distinctive food production systems supported past social development across a wide range of geographical, ecological, and cultural diversity. These food production systems were inherently attached to specific water practices, ranging from wetland and soil moisture management to water storing and distribution. In the Ethiopian-Eritrean highlands, for example, the Aksumite kingdom emerged in the late first millennium BCE from a long trajectory of mixed farming and sedentism (Fattovich, 2010; Phillipson, 2012). In a landscape of fertile, volcanic soils and woody savannah vegetation, and supported by two rainy seasons, plough agriculture and livestock herding enabled social complexity and urbanism to flourish for centuries. Negotiating the opportunities and challenges offered by the rich ecological diversity of the highlands, Aksumite farmers dealt with changing rainfall controlled by the Monsoon winds and fertile but clayey, swelling soils to secure food and water for a burgeoning urban population of administrative and religious elites, craft workers, and traders across the kingdom. Ox-drawn ploughs could control drainage and soil erosion, and prepare the land for sowing wheat, sorghum, and indigenous teff just before the first rains. Ploughing and crop rotation maintained soil moisture and fertility for rain-fed farming, while reservoirs, wells, and springs supplied water for domestic, economic, and ritual services. Cut into the shallow bedrock, large reservoirs captured rainfall, tapped groundwater, and controlled water infiltration to supply core residential areas (Figure 7.2), while springs and wells dotted the agro-urban landscape (Sulas, 2018). The grains and pulses grown from the late first millennium BCE remain the backbone of food security in parts of the Ethiopian-Eritrean highlands today, where some of the ancient reservoirs continue to provide the most reliable water supply for local communities. In these highland environments, rain-fed farming meant that water storage could maximise supply for human and animal subsistence, and ritual needs during the dry season.

In contrast, water storing becomes central to food production, subsistence, and socioecological services in lowland environments, where rainfall is often low and evapotranspiration high. In the transboundary lowlands between southern Ethiopia and northern Kenya, Borana pastoralist lifeways have long been linked to a distinctive water well system, known as *tula* wells (Tiki et al., 2011; Oba, 2019; Ochungo et al., 2022). Where rainfall is low and variable, and surface water

FIGURE 7.2 Example of an Aksumite water reservoir still in use today, Tigray, Ethiopia

Source: Photo taken by the author (Sulas).

lacking, Borana have engineered this well system to reach highly productive but very deep aquifers by cutting through hard bedrock (limestone) and lifting water through a chain of human-carriers. *Tula* wells are found in clusters and managed by different Borana clans under shared customary laws through generations. These wells represent the only reliable, and often the only available, source of water for human and animal subsistence, and food production. But *tula* wells also contribute to fertility, continuity of lineages, clan solidarity, and peace. The building, maintenance, and productivity of these wells is reliant on social cooperation as much as on human–environmental interplay.

In environments characterised by strong seasonality, community experience can turn otherwise unproductive landscape features into niches of food production, biodiversity, and social cohesion. For example, *dambos* have long supported cultivation, grazing, and fish farming while providing a source of water in dry periods, buffering rainfall erosion and flooding risks. *Dambos* are low-lying, shallow, seasonally or interannually waterlogged depressions found in large floodplains across intertropical Africa (Roberts, 1988; Burrough et al., 2015). Due to their changing nature—from waterlogged to dry—*dambos* represent a highly versatile environmental resource for ecological and cultural services. Whilst their origin remains debated, *dambos* have been managed by local communities across different environments for generations (Roberts, 1988). In southern Zimbabwe, for example, *dambos* supply micro-irrigation for cultivation but also provide shallow watering points for livestock. In central Zambia, *dambos* support small-scale cultivation and vegetable gardens, and fish farming.

Sacred groves and agroforestry

Sustained research over the last two decades has brought international attention to the biodiversity generated by distinctive community forestry and practices creating sacred forests, which can be considered as examples of biocultural heritage.

Sacred forests and groves are often perceived as pockets of pristine nature by outsiders—fragments of primordial Eden that have escaped the domesticating endeavours of humankind. In fact, these spaces are sources of spiritual and economic well-being nurtured by local communities over generations (Heckenberger et al., 2007; Fraser et al., 2016). Sacred groves (Figure 7.3) are common throughout Africa's diverse environments (Sheridan and Nyamweru, 2007). In the densely settled Kara region of northern Togo, for example, Kossi and colleagues (Kossi et al., 2021) have recorded over a 100 sacred groves of different types and extent nestled within and around old villages, serving as places of initiation ceremonies for the inhabitants of long-established settlements, but also community members who now live elsewhere. The diversity of sacred groves is shaped by the different management practices local communities perform and adapt through time and across space, ranging from ritual fires and woodcutting to creating firewalls and full protection. Whilst the historical depth of sacred groves remains largely unknown, they are biodiversity hubs created by Indigenous practices transmitted over generations. As in the case of small-scale tropical agroforests more generally (Scales and Marsden, 2008), the type, duration and intensity of management practices can have significant influences on species richness and abundance, and it is important to establish empirically whether management practices, including taboos restricting use and access, do indeed enhance biodiversity. Nonetheless, it is also important to recognise that the species composition of sacred groves is the consequence of intimate human–environment interactions over the long term and, in this sense, they are biocultural entities and constructs, rather than merely fortuitously preserved and protected patches of pristine, primordial 'nature'. Numerous other examples of sacred groves have been documented across the African continent, including the *kayas* found throughout the remaining patches of coastal forest in Kenya and northern Tanzania (Metcalfe et al., 2009)[1]; diverse categories of sacred forests in Mozambique (Virtanen, 2002) and Madagascar (Tengö et al., 2007); and the church forests in highland north-western Ethiopia associated with Ethiopian Orthodox Tewahedo churches and monasteries (Ruelle et al., 2018).

Certain categories of small-scale agroforests have also been identified as creating distinct habitats that require recurrent human intervention and management yet, through the unintended creation of particular relations of ecological mutualism, can also enhance localised biodiversity (Wiersum, 2004). One of the best studied examples of these are the forest gardens created and maintained by the Chagga extending almost 100 km across the southern and eastern slopes of Mount Kilimanjaro, Tanzania, roughly between the 1000 m and 1800 m contours. These areas have been farmed for perhaps two millennia, although according to their oral traditions the Chagga settled here much more recently and bananas, which are the main staple and now also an important cash crop, were probably also only introduced from South East Asia in the mid-to-late first millennium CE (Stump and Tagseth, 2009). Historically, the Chagga agricultural landscape comprised an intricate and integrated mosaic of forest gardens, agricultural terracing, irrigation channels, ponds, and water storage reservoirs (*ndiva*). Many of these elements

FIGURE 7.3 Example of integrated protection of the cultural and natural heritage of the Sacred Mijikenda Kaya Forests by National Museum of Kenya. Image: V. Ochieng

Source: Wikimedia Commons, CC BY-SA 2.0. Image available here: https://commons.wikimedia.org/wiki/File:Kaya-skog.jpg.

survive, although wider economic, social and demographic pressures have seen a decline in use and maintenance of many of these, including felling of shade trees and the expansion of monocropping. Where they survive, Chagga forest gardens exhibit a complex vertical vegetation structure that closely mimics that of tropical montane gallery forest, with a relatively open upper canopy formed by shade trees such as *Albizia schimperiana* that support a wide range of epiphytes and lianas, and below this closely planted bananas forming a dense upper shrub layer, interspersed with coffee trees (*Coffee arabica*) and cocoyam (*Colocasia esculenta*) comprising a lower shrub layer with a herb layer at ground level comprised of diverse ruderal species (Hemp, 2006: 1201, Table 7.1.). As well as exhibiting considerable plant diversity, these forest gardens support a rich assemblage of Saltatoria fauna, sharing around 70% of the species in common with the adjacent forest (Hemp, 2006). Regular recycling of plant matter supplemented by the addition of animal manure from stall-fed domestic livestock also helps sustain the microbial properties of the soil over the long-term (Mganga et al., 2016).

Anthropogenic dark earths

Anthropogenic dark earths are remnants of very fertile, carbon- and nutrient-rich, black soils created by past Indigenous practices. They were first recognised scientifically in Amazonia, where they are referred to as *terra preta de índio* or Amazonian Dark Earths (ADEs), and have been shown to be associated with ancient settlements from over two thousand years ago (Woods and Deneval, 2009). These anthropogenic soils are characterised by high concentrations of (pyrogenic) carbon and domestic waste that retain nutrients and moisture, making them highly fertile. Keeping a productivity higher than the one afforded by surrounding soils even today, Amazonian Dark Earths are considered a potential model for sustainable

FIGURE 7.4 Women manuring soil in the Lawre district, Ghana; April–May 2013

Source: Photo: C Peterson (CIAT/CCAFS). Used under the licence CC BY-NC-SA 2.0. Image available here: www.flickr.com/photos/cgiarclimate/8855722436/in/album-72157633739804144/.

agriculture as well as carbon store and sink in Amazonia and beyond (Glaser et al., 2001; Sombroek et al., 2003; Heckenberger et al., 2007). Similar anthropogenic dark earths (Figure 7.4) have been recorded in West Africa (Fraser et al., 2014; see also Kreike, 2013, esp. pp. 63–101), and beyond (e.g., Wiedner et al., 2015). In Liberia and Ghana, for example, Indigenous practices transform highly weathered and infertile, yellow to red tropical soils into black, highly fertile, and carbon-rich soils by upcycling the waste from household and other activities (Frausin et al., 2014; Solomon et al., 2016). Organic residues from cooking and food preparation, crop harvest, processing of palm oil, and production of handmade soap, are all deposited on soils around old and abandoned settlements. This continuous and intense input of nutrients and carbon transforms otherwise nutrient-poor local soils into highly fertile and carbon-rich anthropogenic dark earths to support intensive farming of diverse crops, including staple ones such as plantain, cassava and taro, and multi-storey home gardens. In the Zorzor district of Liberia, Solomon and colleagues (Solomon et al., 2016) report that almost a third of farm household income comes from crops grown on dark earths. Here, oral histories and radiocarbon dating of buried dark earths show that these practices have been in place for over five hundred years (Solomon et al., 2016).

Discussion

Modernist approaches to land and water development share a number of common traits. First, development initiatives tend to be large scale, standardised, and highly engineered, independent of the socioecological contexts of the problem to be solved, its causes, and where and when it emerged (Table 7.1). Second, large-scale systems are by nature labour- and energy-intensive and characterised by rigidity. A few thousand hectares of eucalyptus tree seedlings or flood capture cannot swiftly adjust to changing rainfall patterns. Indeed, overbank flooding following exceptionally heavy rains has become the rule rather than the exception for large-scale dams, whether in Italy (Bocchiola and Rosso, 2014) or Zimbabwe (Samu and Kentel, 2018). Maintenance quickly becomes a liability rather than an insurance. Third, modern development initiatives are borne out of office planning with no cultural or spiritual meaning for the communities most affected by these interventions. This in part explains the reluctance shown by local communities to embrace water boreholes, large-scale irrigation, reforestation, mega-dams, and mining projects (Evers and Seagle, 2012; Cock, 2019; Zeitoun et al., 2019). A traditional well in southern Zimbabwe rarely runs dry as local Shona communities ensure respectful use of above and underground water and rigorous regulation of access to the well, alongside other controls. In southern Zimbabwe, as in the Aksum area and elsewhere, access to borehole or piped water has become a privilege for the few who live where these infrastructures are in place and functioning. Conversely, most people reside in areas where these are either not available or working, and often experience water challenges as the social network of water governance gradually erodes (Pikirayi et al., 2016).

While different in nature, the examples of past land and water management from sub-Saharan Africa surveyed above suggest that a deep knowledge and tailored management of local ecological conditions were key to ensuring food and water security for both urban and agro-pastoral-fishing societies in the past. While changing geopolitical and trade conditions took a dramatic toll on sub-Saharan Africa's ancient societies, farming and herding communities were able to adjust and mitigate major changes. Their continuing interventions and improvements, such as turning poor soils into productive dark earths, can be considered expressions of *landesque capital* investment to satisfy contingent needs—supplying food to local communities—while maintaining returns over the long term by preserving and creating soil fertility, crop productivity, and human and environmental health. These constant, transformative processes rely on regular input of organics as much as the biophysical reactions stimulated by these additions into the soil biome. Similarly, sacred groves depend on practices and actions that preserve and enhance plant

TABLE 7.1 General properties and conditions of biocultural heritage *vis-à-vis* those of modern development

Category	Environment and ecology	Technology	Governance	Value	Trade-off
BIOCULTURAL HERITAGE	Context-specific Access-oriented Multiple forms of resource	Local materials Low maintenance Adaptive to change Regenerative	Bottom-up Culture-specific Cooperative	Cultural Spiritual Economic	High biodiversity Soil health Social cohesion
MODERN DEVELOPMENT	Large-scale Planning-driven Selective resource forms	Imported materials High maintenance Rigid Input-dependent	Top-down State/Inter-state agencies	Economic (Political)	Energy supply Income generation Trade

Source: The table was produced by both authors.

diversity over time. Time coupled with cultural/social agency can be considered the quintessential ingredients of enduring practices.

In contrast to the modernist emphasis on centralised and large-scale land and water management, community-driven practices in the past and in the present share dynamic and flexible approaches to using, producing, and conserving resources (Table 7.1). Whether a water reservoir or a cultivated plot, food and water security is tied to specific topographic positions for maximising harvesting, conservation, distribution, and use. Rather than focusing on one particular resource, such as rainwater or cattle, diversified agro-ecological practices appear to have sustained foodway diversity and security at times of stability as well as during major sociopolitical shifts.

Conclusion

By engaging with local knowledge, experience, and memory, biocultural heritage approaches offer unique potential for bridging local communities, heritage conservation, and development planning. Local communities are those most impacted by biodiversity loss, destruction of heritage sites, climate change, and economic crises. Yet, planning and implementation of responses to these hazards typically rest in the hands of groups and individuals who are only indirectly affected by these trends. If legal and rights issues have polarised much debate about intangible heritage to date, biocultural heritage approaches can steer thinking and interventions informed by the deep past and the traditional knowledge systems that enabled communities to develop, prosper, and mitigate change. Rather than being a resource for ticket-paying tourism industries, community biocultural heritages are assets in constant evolution to secure the subsistence, health and well-being of societies and environments.

In this regard, there have been important developments in recent years, as Indigenous peoples and local communities have begun to work, in collaboration with groups such as Natural Justice (see Natural Justice, 2021) and more recently the International Union for Conservation of Nature, on formally documenting the rules, regulations, and procedures they were used historically to govern their territories and natural resources usage. Termed 'biocultural community protocols', these have proved on occasion to be powerful tools offering a rights-based approach to protecting the historical knowledge underpinning these practices, the intellectual property of communities, and the landscapes in which the biocultural heritage took root (Jonas et al., 2010). A notable sub-Saharan African example is that prepared by a consortium of stakeholders around Lamu, northern Kenya (Save Lamu, 2018) to contest the construction of a coal-fired electricity generating plant by the Kenya Government resulting in a High Court decision to halt the project[2] and, following a decision in a lower court, also an order to pay compensation of US$170 million to c. 4600 fishermen displaced from Manada Bay, Lamu (Chome, 2020).

The Lamu case, associated as it is with a large-scale infrastructure development project aimed at enhancing economic prosperity and livelihoods across some of the most disadvantaged sectors of Kenya, brings into focus the need to reappraise the roles that heritage might play in the development process in sub-Saharan Africa.

There can be no doubt that the planned development corridor, of which the construction work at Lamu is a part, will help enhance incomes and employment opportunities. However, its implementation, with limited due regard to the existing biocultural heritage assets of the communities this 'development' is intended to serve, has not only created social and political frictions, but also seen the destruction of habitats and the sustainable practices associated with them. Such issues ultimately bring to the fore questions central to ensuring mutually beneficial interdependencies between development and heritage: 'Development of what and for whom?', and 'Whose and which heritage is to be valued and protected, and why?'.

The examples of biocultural heritage practices surveyed above speak volumes to the fundamental roles that time and local communities can play in tempering the present for securing a better future. They show that heritage is a process as much as a product of community engagement with their surroundings, where relations, tensions, and equilibria are in flux through time and space. In acknowledging the fundamental contribution biocultural heritage makes to sustaining communities and environments, it is hard to find logic in approaches to economic or community development that rely on either singular causal explanatory models of the 'problem' that needs solving, or those that expect proposed solutions to have universal applicability and potential to effect positive change.

There is tremendous opportunity to realise the potential of biocultural heritages for supporting environments and communities across sub-Saharan Africa, while mitigating increasing vulnerabilities to socioecological distress. As the pace of infrastructure development increases in response to such vulnerabilities, it is imperative to recognise and engage—appropriately and efficiently—local communities and their ways of creating development through time. This will also require more concerted research and dialogue because the path to well-tempered lives runs through collaboration with communities over policies, implementation, and 'future making'. Development must better integrate their insights and concerns giving greater attention to the temporal depth of biocultural heritage because, as the old adage has it, 'only time will tell'.

Acknowledgements

We are grateful to Charlotte Cross and John Giblin for inviting us to contribute to the volume, and their extended support throughout the development of this chapter. Federica Sulas is grateful to the A. G. Leventis Foundation, sponsoring her research at the time of writing.

Notes

1 These include the Sacred Mijikenda Kaya Forests added to the UNESCO Cultural Landscapes list in 2008 (UNESCO, 2022).

2 See Petition 22 of 2012 Mohamed Ali Baadi and others v Attorney General & 11 others [2018] eKLR, available at: http://kenyalaw.org/caselaw/cases/view/156405 (Accessed 30 May 2021).

References

Adamson, G.C.D., Hannaford, M.J. and Rohland, E.J. (2018) 'Re-thinking the present: the role of a historical focus in climate change adaptation research', *Global Environmental Change*, 48, pp. 195–205.

Agnoletti, M., Tredici, M. and Santoro, A. (2015) 'Biocultural diversity and landscape patterns in three historical rural areas of Morocco, Cuba and Italy', *Biodiversity & Conservation*, 24, pp. 3387–3404.

Arnaiz-Schmitz, C., Herrero-Jáuregui, C. and Schmitz, M.F. (2018) 'Losing a heritage hedgerow landscape. Biocultural diversity conservation in a changing social-ecological Mediterranean system', *Science of the Total Environment*, 637, pp. 374-384.

Ax, C.F., Brimnes, N., Jensen, N.T. and Oslund, K. (eds) (2014) *Cultivating the colonies: colonial states and their environmental legacies*. Athens: Ohio University Press.

Beinart, W., and Hughes, L. (2007) *Environment and empire*. Oxford: Oxford University Press.

Bocchiola, D. and Rosso, R. (2014) 'Safety of Italian dams in the face of flood hazard', *Advances in Water Resources*, 71, pp. 23-31.

Boles, O.J.C., Shoemaker, A., Courtney Mustaphi, C.J., Petek, N., Ekblom, A. and Lane, P.J. (2019) 'Historical ecologies of pastoralist overgrazing in Kenya: long-term perspectives on cause and effect', *Human Ecology*, 47, pp. 419–434.

Bond, W.J., Stevens, N., Midgley, G.F. and Lehmann, C.E.R. (2019) 'The trouble with trees: afforestation plans for Africa', *Trends in Ecology & Evolution*, 34(11), pp. 963-965.

Bridgewater, P. (2017) 'The intergovernmental platform for biodiversity and ecosystem services (IPBES) – a role for heritage?', *International Journal of Heritage Studies*, 23(1), pp. 65-73.

Burke, E. and Davis, D.K. (2011) *Environmental imaginaries of the Middle East and North Africa*. Athens: Ohio University Press.

Burrough, S.L., Thomas, D.S.G., Orijemie, E.A. and Willis, K.J. (2015) 'Landscape sensitivity and ecological change in western Zambia: the long-term perspective from dambo cut-and-fill sediments', *Journal of Quaternary Science*, 30, pp. 44–58.

Carswell, G. (2003) 'Continuities in environmental narratives: the case of Kabale, Uganda, 1930-2000', *Environment and History*, 9(1), pp. 3–29.

Castro, J., Vallejo, L.E., and Estrada, N. (2019) 'The optimal design of the retaining walls built by the Incas in their agricultural terraces', *Journal of Cultural Heritage,* 36, pp. 232–237.

CBD (Convention on Biodiversity) and UNESCO (2010) *A Proposed Joint Programme of Work on Biological and Cultural Diversity Led by the Secretariat of the Convention on Biodiversity and UNESCO. Working Paper.* Available at: https://www.cbd.int/doc/meetings/development/icbcd/official/icbcd-scbd-unesco-en.pdf (Accessed 6 April 2021).

Cevasco, R., Moreno, D. and Hearn, R. (2015) 'Biodiversification as an historical process: an appeal for the application of historical ecology to bio-cultural diversity research', *Biodiversity & Conservation*, 24, pp. 3167–3183.

Chase, A.F. and Scarborough, V. (2014) 'Diversity, resiliency, and IHOPE-Maya: using the past to inform the present', *Archaeological Papers of the American Anthropological Association*, 24(1), pp. 1–10.

Chome, N. (2020) 'Land, livelihoods and belonging: negotiating change and anticipating LAPSSET in Kenya's Lamu county', *Journal of Eastern African Studies*, 14(2), pp. 310–331.

Clement, C.R. (2014) 'Landscape domestication and archaeology', in Smith, C. (ed.) *Encyclopedia of global archaeology*. New York: Springer. doi: 10.1007/978-1-4419-0465-2_817

Clement, C.R., Levis, C., Franco-Moraes, J. and Junqueira, A.B. (2020) 'Domesticated nature: the culturally constructed niche of humanity', in Baldauf, C. (ed.) *Participatory biodiversity conservation*. Cham: Springer, pp. 35–51.

Cock, J. (2019) 'Resistance to coal inequalities and the possibilities of a just transition in South Africa', *Development Southern Africa*, 36(6), pp. 860–873.

Costanza, R., Van Der Leeuw, S., Hibbard, K., Aulenbach, S., Brewer, S., Burek, M., Cornell, S., Crumley, C., Dearing, J., Folke, C. and Graumlich, L. (2012) 'Developing an integrated history and future of people on Earth (IHOPE)', *Current Opinion in Environmental Sustainability*, 4(1), pp.106–114.

Davis, D.K. (2005) 'Potential forests: degradation narratives, science, and environmental policy in protectorate Morocco 1912–1956', *Environmental History*, 10(2), pp. 211–238.

Dei, G.J.S. (1993) 'Sustainable development in the African context: revisiting some theoretical and methodological issues', *Africa Development / Afrique et Développement*, 18(2), pp. 97–110.

Elzinga, A. and Landström, C. (eds) (1996) *Science and internationalism*. London: Taylor Graham.

Erickson, K.L. (2006) 'The domesticated landscapes of the Bolivian Amazon', in Balée, W.I. and Erickson, C.L. (eds) *Time and complexity in historical ecology: studies in the neotropical lowlands*. New York: Columbia University Press, pp. 235–278.

Eriksson, O. (2018) 'What is biocultural heritage and why should we care about it? An example from Swedish rural landscapes and forests', *Nature Conservation*, 28, pp. 1–32.

Evers, S.J.T. and Seagle, C. (2012) 'Stealing the sacred: why "global heritage" discourse is perceived as a frontal attack on local heritage-making in Madagascar', *Conservation & Development*, 7(2S), pp. 97–106.

Fagan, M.E. (2020) 'A lesson unlearned? Underestimating tree cover in drylands biases global restoration maps', *Global Change Biology*, 26(9), pp. 4679–4690.

Fraser, J.A., Diabaté, M., Narmah, W., Beavogui, P., Guilavogui, K., De Foresta, H. and Junqueira, A. (2016) 'Cultural valuation and biodiversity conservation in the Upper Guinea forest, West Africa', *Ecology and Society*, 21(3), p. 36.

Fraser, J.A., Leach, M. and Fairhead, J. (2014) 'Anthropogenic dark earths in the landscapes of Upper Guinea, West Africa: intentional or inevitable?' *Annals of the Association of American Geographers*, 104(6), pp. 1222–1238.

Frausin, V., Fraser, J.A., Narmah, W., Lahai, M.K., Winnebah, T.R.A., Feirhead J., and Leach, M. (2014) 'God made the soil, but we made it fertile': gender, knowledge, and practice in the formation and use of African Dark Earths in Liberia and Sierra Leone', *Human Ecology*, 42, pp. 695–710.

Glaser, B., Haumaier, L., Guggenberger, G. and Zech, G. (2001) 'The "Terra Preta" phenomenon: a model for sustainable agriculture in the humid tropics', *Naturwissenschaften*, 88, pp. 37–41.

Headrick, D.R. (1979) 'The tools of imperialism: technology and the expansion of European colonial empires in the nineteenth century', *The Journal of Modern History*, 51(2), pp. 231–263.

Heckenberger, M.J., Russell, J.C., Toney, J.R. and Schmidt, M.J. (2007) 'The legacy of cultural landscapes in the Brazilian Amazon: implications for biodiversity', *Philosophical Transactions of the Royal Society B*, 362, pp. 197–208.

Helleiner, E. (2014) *Forgotten foundations of Bretton Woods*. Ithaca, NY, and London: Cornell University Press.

Hemp, A. (2006) 'The banana forests of Kilimanjaro: biodiversity and conservation of the agroforestry system of the Chagga home gardens', *Biodiversity & Conservation*, 15(4), pp. 1193–1217.

Hill, R., Cullen-Unsworth, L.C., Talbot, L.D. and McIntyre-Tamwoy, S. (2011) 'Empowering Indigenous peoples' biocultural diversity through World Heritage cultural landscapes: a case study from the Australian humid tropical forests', *International Journal of Heritage Studies*, 17(6), pp. 571–591.

IIED (International Institute for Environment and Development) (2005) *Protection of traditional knowledge and cultural heritage – the concept of collective bio-cultural heritage. Report of the Working Group on Indigenous Populations, 23rd session: IIED.* Available at: https://pubs.iied.org/g01067?k=heritage%20territories (Accessed 20 April 2021).

Ingold, T. (2000) *The perception of the environment: essays on livelihood, dwelling, and skill.* London: Routledge.

IPBES (Intergovernmental Science-Policy Platform on Biodiversity and Ecosystem Services) (2019) *Global assessment report on biodiversity and ecosystem services of the Intergovernmental Science-Policy Platform on Biodiversity and Ecosystem Services.* Bonn: IPBES secretariat. Available at: https://ipbes.net/global-assessment (Accessed 12 April 2021).

Jackson, R.C., Dugmore, A.J. and Riede, F. (2018) 'Rediscovering lessons of adaptation from the past', *Global Environmental Change* 52, pp. 58–65.

Jonas, H., Shrumm, H. and Bavikatte, K. (2010) 'Biocultural community protocols and conservation pluralism', *Policy Matters*, 17, pp. 102–112.

King, R. and Eoin, L.N. (2014) 'Before the flood: loss of place, mnemonics, and "resources" ahead of the Metolong Dam, Lesotho', *Journal of Social Archaeology*, 14(2), pp. 196–223.

Kossi, A., Mazalo, K.P., Kossi Novinyo, S. and Kouami, K. (2021) 'Impacts of traditional practices on biodiversity and structural characteristics of sacred groves in northern Togo, West Africa', *Acta Oecologica*, 110, 103680.

Kreike, E. (2013) *Environmental infrastructure in African history: examining the myth of natural resource management in Namibia.* Cambridge: Cambridge University Press.

Kull, C.A. (2000) 'Deforestation, erosion, and fire: degradation myths in the environmental history of Madagascar', *Environment and History*, 6(4), pp. 423–450.

Lenzerini, F. (2011) 'Intangible cultural heritage: the living culture of peoples', *European Journal of International Law*, 22(1), pp. 101–120.

Lindholm, K.-J. and Ekblom, A. (2019) 'A framework for exploring and managing biocultural heritage', *Anthropocene*, 25, 100195.

Mabogunje, A.L. (1980) 'The dynamics of centre-periphery relations: the need for a new geography of resource development', *Transactions of the Institute of British Geographers*, 5(3), pp. 277–296.

Mays, L.W. (2010) 'A brief history of Roman water technology', in Mays, L.W. (ed.) *Ancient water technologies*. Dordrecht: Springer, pp. 115–137.

Metcalfe, K., Ffrench-Constant, R. and Gordon, I. (2009) 'Sacred sites as hotspots for biodiversity: the Three Sisters Cave complex in coastal Kenya', *Oryx*, 44(1), pp. 118–123.

Mganga, K.Z., Razavi, B.S. and Kuzyakov, Y. (2016) 'Land use affects soil biochemical properties in Mt. Kilimanjaro region', *Catena*, 141, pp. 22–29.

Natural Justice (2021) *Conservation and Customary Use.* Available at: https://naturaljustice.org/programme/conservation-and-customary-use/ (Accessed 30 May 2021).

Oba, G. (2019) 'Transforming labour and technology of the ancient *tula* wells for watering livestock in Borana, Southern Ethiopia', *Nomadic Peoples*, 23(2), pp. 218–240.

Ochungo, P., Khalaf, N., Merlo, S., Beldados, A., M'Mbogori, F.N., Tiki, W., and Lane, P.J. (2022) 'Remote sensing for biocultural heritage preservation in an African semi-arid region: a case study of indigenous wells in Northern Kenya and Southern Ethiopia', *Remote Sensing*, 14, 314.

Phillipson, D.W. (2012) *Foundations of an African civilisation Aksum & the northern Horn, 1000 BC–AD 1300.* Oxford: James Currey.

Pikirayi, I., Sulas, F., Musindo, T.T., Chimwanda, A., Chikumbirike, J., Mtetwa, E., Nxumalo, B. and Sagiya, M.E. (2016) 'Great Zimbabwe's water', *WIREs Water*, 3(2), pp. 195–210.

Randeria, S. (2007) 'Global designs and local lifeworlds: colonial legacies of conservation, disenfranchisement and environmental governance in postcolonial India', *Interventions*, 9(1), pp. 12–30.

Roberts, N. (1988) 'Dambos in development: management of a fragile ecological resource', *Journal of Biogeography*, 15, pp. 141–148.

Roe, M. (2016) 'Landscape and intangible cultural heritage. Interactions, memories and meanings', in Stefano, M.L. and Davis, P. (eds) *The Routledge companion to intangible cultural heritage*. Abingdon: Routledge, pp. 342–355.

Rosenstein-Rodan, P.N. (1944) 'The international development of economically backward areas', *International Affairs*, 20 (2), pp. 157–165.

Rotherham, I.D. (2015) 'Bio-cultural heritage and biodiversity: emerging paradigms in conservation and planning', *Biodiversity and Conservation*, 24(13), pp. 3405–3429.

Ruelle, M.L., Kassam, K.A. and Asfaw, Z. (2018) 'Human ecology of sacred space: church forests in the highlands of northwestern Ethiopia', *Environmental Conservation*, 45(3), pp. 291–300.

Samu, R. and Kentel, A.S. (2018) 'An analysis of the flood management and mitigation measures in Zimbabwe for a sustainable future', *International Journal of Disaster Risk Reduction*, 31, pp. 691–697.

Save Lamu (2018) *The Lamu County Biocultural Community Protocol*. Available at: www.savelamu.org/wp-content/uploads/2019/07/LAMU-COUNTY-BIOCULTURAL-COMMUNITY-PROTOCOL-24-June.-1.pdf (Accessed 30 May 2021).

Scales, B.R. and Marsden, S.J. (2008) 'Biodiversity in small-scale tropical agroforests: a review of species richness and abundance shifts and the factors influencing them', *Environmental Conservation*, 35(2), pp. 160–172.

Seele, B.C., Esler, K.J. and Cunningham, A.B. (2019) 'Biocultural diversity: a Mongolian case study', *Ecology and Society*, 24(4), 27.

Sernicola, L. (2017) *Ancient settlement patterns in the area of Aksum (Tigray, northern Ethiopia) – Ca. 900 BCE–800/850 CE*. Oxford: Archaeopress. BAR International Series 2860.

Sheridan, M.J. and Nyamweru, C. (2007) *African sacred groves: ecological dynamics and social change*. Oxford: James Currey.

Showers, K.B. (2011) 'Electrifying Africa: an environmental history with policy implications', *Geografiska Annaler. Series B*, 93(3), pp. 193–221.

Smith, W. and Dressler, W.H. (2020) 'Forged in flames: Indigeneity, forest fire and geographies of blame in the Philippines', *Postcolonial Studies*, 23(4), pp. 527–545.

Solomon, D., Lehmann, J., Fraser, J.A., Leach, M., Amanor, K., Frausin, V., Kristiansen, S.M., Millimouno, D. and Fairhead, J. (2016) 'Indigenous African soil enrichment as a climate-smart sustainable agriculture alternative', *Frontiers in Ecology and the Environment*, 14(2), pp. 71–76.

Sombroek, W.G., Ruivo, M.L., Fearnside, P.M., Glaser, B. and Lehmann, J. (2003) 'Amazonian Dark Earths as carbon stores and sinks', in Lehman, J., Kern, D.C., Gaser B. and Woods, W.I. (eds) *Amazonian Dark Earths: origins, properties, management*. Dordrecht, Netherlands: Kluwer, pp. 125–139.

Storozum, M.J., Goldstein, S.T., Contreras, D.A., Gidna, A.O., Mabulla, A.Z.P., Grillo, K.M. and Prendergast, M.E. (2021) 'The influence of ancient herders on soil development at Luxmanda, Mbulu Plateau, Tanzania', *Catena*, 204, 105376. doi: 10.1016/j/catena.2021.105376

Stump, D. (2010) '"Ancient and backward or long-lived and sustainable?" The role of the past in debates concerning rural livelihoods and resource conservation in Eastern Africa', *World Development*, 38(9), pp. 1251–1262.

Stump, D. and Tagseth, M. (2009) 'The history of precolonial and early colonial agriculture on Kilimanjaro: a review', in Clack, T. (ed.) *Culture, history and identity: human-environmental relations in the Mount Kilimanjaro area, Tanzania*. Oxford: Archaeopress, pp. 107–124.

Sulas, F. (2018) 'Traditions of water in the northern Horn of Africa', in Sulas, F. and Pikirayi, I. (eds) *Water and societies*. London: Routledge, pp. 155–175.

Swiderska, K., Argumedo, A. and Pimbert, M. (2020) 'Biocultural heritage territories: key to halting biodiversity loss', *IIED Briefing*, July 2020.

Taos Pueblo (2022) *Taos Pueblo: Over 1000 Years of Tradition*. Available at: https://taospueblo.com/ (Accessed 7 January 2022).

Tengö, M., Johansson, K., Rakotondrasoa, F., Lundberg, J., Andriamaherilala, J.A., Rakotoarisoa, J.A. and Elmqvist, T. (2007) 'Taboos and forest governance: informal protection of hot spot dry forest in southern Madagascar', *Ambio*, 36(8), pp. 683–691.

Terrell, J., Hart, J., Barut, S. et al. (2003) 'Domesticated landscapes: the subsistence ecology of plant and animal domestication', *Journal of Archaeological Method and Theory*, 10(4), pp. 323–368.

Tiki, W., Oba, G., and Tvedt, T. (2011) 'Human stewardship or ruining cultural landscapes of the ancient "Tula" wells, southern Ethiopia', *Geographical Journal*, 177(1), pp. 62–78.

Trujillo, A. (2019) 'Exploring living heritage conservation: an ethnography of Taos Pueblo, New Mexico', *Ursidae: The Undergraduate Research Journal at the University of Northern Colorado*, 6(2), Article 11. Available at: https://digscholarship.unco.edu/cgi/viewcontent.cgi?article=1230&context=urj (Accessed 25 August 2022).

UNESCO (1972) *Convention Concerning the Protection of the World Cultural and Natural Heritage*. Available at: https://whc.unesco.org/en/conventiontext/ (Accessed 6 April 2021).

UNESCO (2008) *Links between biological and cultural diversity-concepts, methods and experiences, Report of an International Workshop, UNESCO, Paris 2008*. Available at: https://unesdoc.unesco.org/ark:/48223/pf0000159255 (Accessed 25 August 2022).

UNESCO (2018) *Basic Texts of the 2003 Convention for the Safeguarding of the Intangible Cultural Heritage*. Paris: UNESCO, Intangible Cultural Heritage. Available at: https://ich.unesco.org/doc/src/2003_Convention_Basic_Texts-_2018_version-EN.pdf (Accessed 12 April 2021).

UNESCO (2022) *Sacred Mijikenda kaya forests*. Available at: https://whc.unesco.org/en/list/1231 (Accessed 7 January 2022).

Urzedo, D., and Chatterjee, P. (2021) 'The colonial reproduction of deforestation in the Brazilian Amazon: violence against Indigenous peoples for land development', *Journal of Genocide Research*, 23(2), pp. 302–324.

Victorian Aboriginal Heritage Council (2021) *Aboriginal cultural heritage keeps us strong*. Available at: www.aboriginalheritagecouncil.vic.gov.au/aboriginal-heritage (Accessed 11 April 2021).

Virtanen, P. (2002) 'The role of customary institutions in the conservation of biodiversity: sacred forests in Mozambique', *Environmental Values*, 11(2), pp. 227–241.

Widgren, M. and Håkansson, N.T. (2014) 'Introduction: landesque capital: what is the concept good for?' in Håkansson, N.T. and Widgren, M. (eds) *Landesque capital: the historical ecology of enduring landscape modifications*. Walnut Creek, CA: Left Coast Press, pp. 9–30.

Wiedner, K., Schneeweiß, J., Dippold, M.A., and Glaser, B. (2015) 'Anthropogenic Dark Earth in northern Germany —The Nordic analogue to terra preta de Índio in Amazonia', *Catena*, 132, pp. 114–125.

Wiersum, K.F. (2004) 'Forest gardens as an "intermediate" land-use system in the nature-culture continuum: characteristics and future potential', in Nair, P.K.R., Rao, M.R. and

Buck, L.E. (eds) *New vistas in agroforestry. Advances in agroforestry, vol 1.* Dordrecht: Springer, pp. 123–134.

Woods, W.I. and Denevan, W. (2009) 'Amazonian Dark Earths: The first century of reports', in Woods, W.I., Teixeira, W.G., Lehmann, J., Steiner, C., WinklerPrins, A. and Rebellato, L. (eds) *Amazonian Dark Earths: Wim Sombroek's Vision.* Dordrecht: Springer. doi:10.1007/978-1-4020-9031-8_1

Zeitoun, M., Dirar, A., El Moghraby, A. and Hashim, M.J. (2019) 'A "justice" reading of the trans-national struggle of the people displaced by the Merowe Dam', *Local Environment*, 24(2), pp. 129–145.

8

MARINE CULTURAL HERITAGE AND SUSTAINABLE DEVELOPMENT

Mark Lamont

Introduction

Marine Cultural Heritage (or MCH) faces a public relations issue. There is a widely established view that MCH is too specialised to be of broad use to global development. This is an ongoing public relations problem that the chief promotors of MCH, by and large marine archaeologists, face in convincing others that the biocultural heritage of the seas matters and, indeed, can contribute to the global ocean's most pressing environmental and development challenges (Henderson, 2019; Trakadas et al., 2019). Like most public relations issues, the challenge for MCH is to make itself more visible beyond the professional networks of marine archaeology, their ocean science counterparts, and stakeholders drawn from various marine industries.

A key challenge in making MCH more visible within the global development landscape, including the 2030 Agenda for Sustainable Development, parallels efforts to enhance 'ocean literacy', making human relationships to the oceans, over time and across cultures, more explicit, relevant, and measurable. For this to happen, innovative methodologies of working with maritime and coastal communities who are seeking more sustainable pathways to development have been proposed by major new research hubs. One of these is the Global Challenges Research Fund (GCRF) network, 'Rising from the Depths' (RftD), which aimed to engage MCH with critical challenges of sustainable development in the Western Indian Ocean states of Kenya, Tanzania, Mozambique, and Madagascar. Proposals to integrate MCH into development depend upon creating inclusive and transformative pathways through which different members of maritime and coastal communities are able to 'see' that MCH can generate new kinds of values through its greater visibility.

Marine archaeologists may find perceptions that MCH is not very useful to development difficult to shake off, but transformations in ocean science and environmental governance have brought about changed understandings of the complex

DOI: 10.4324/9781003107361-10

and dynamic ways in which natural and human ecologies interact in and across deep time. Deep time is an emerging transdisciplinary concept that looks at the ways in which planetary history and geological temporalities far outstrip social experiences of time, the here and now, so to speak, but in ways that intersect some of the most pressing social challenges, such as the depletion of biodiversity and threats to ecosystem resilience (see Irvine, 2020; see also Lane and Sulas, this volume). As an emerging process, MCH engages with ocean science to provide further evidence of how human agency and materiality shapes oceans and coasts and how these powerful natural geologies shape humanity. Here, marine archaeology has long standing partnerships with other geophysical scientists and the local people that provide them with critical access to the fieldsites where they work. Yet these relationships were not sufficient to prove that MCH could be of value to development.

This growth of interest in how MCH can be integrated in development is spearheaded by an increasingly critical, interdisciplinary, and socially engaged marine archaeology. This new area of heritage is shaped by wide and serious discussions about how the politics of scientific knowledge production can either help or hinder the heterogeneous communities that live in areas of significant scientific importance or alongside recognised and scheduled cultural heritage assets. As consultants, archaeologists now occupy unique 'brokerage' spaces between communities and commercial organisations. Coming out of their scientific work, archaeologists' focus on the historical and geological transformation of landscapes (including seascapes) makes them keen observers of deep time, ecological histories, and the rise and fall of maritime powers over millennia. These theoretical perspectives have encouraged marine archaeologists to look for ways in which MCH can be made more visible, accessible, and inclusive.

This chapter will first outline MCH, before providing overviews of how MCH has engaged with the intensification of ocean industrialisation, marine spatial planning, and the role of marine archaeologists in carrying out work in these contexts. It examines how marine archaeologists work with other scientists and ocean stakeholders to address climate change through learning from the deep past as part of a recognition of biocultural heritage. It then moves on to a discussion about how UNESCO and the SDGs promote value within MCH at a range of scales in order to link it to the global sustainable development agenda. Finally, these issues are linked to a case study of a community project in coastal Kenya that explicitly tied MCH to development.

Conceptualising MCH

'[A]ll past human action on the coasts as well as directly on the sea can be combined to constitute Marine Cultural Heritage', writes Jon Henderson, in an important review article on the wider applications of marine archaeology to challenges within the sustainable development agenda (Henderson, 2019: 4). While shipwrecks, submerged and coastal settlements, ports and harbours, as well as the surrounding ecologies shaped by maritime peoples are considered 'tangible culture', Henderson (2019) also recognises those 'intangible' categories of MCH in the form of cultural practices, artistic and linguistic expressions, local skills, and traditional and historical knowledge of the marine environment. In this scheme of things, sea shanties, fishing grounds, marine places, the capricious actions of ocean spirits, knowledge of wind and tides, as well as boat maintenance can all be considered MCH. This expanded definition of MCH permits interdisciplinary research on the sea from scientific, humanities, and social science perspectives.

Variations of this definition of MCH have withstood debate among scholars since Christer Westerdahl's (1992) notion of a 'maritime cultural landscape' expanded the scope for collaboration between archaeologists, historians, and other social scientists. For the past 30 years, the cultural landscape approach has been influential in maritime studies, even being the dominant theoretical perspective within which MCH has been promoted.

At the forefront of this has been the concept of biocultural heritage (Ekblom et al., 2019). Biocultural heritage aims at integrating 'conventional boundaries between biological and heritage conservation, rural development, and local participation' through understanding cultural landscapes as the outcome of 'long-term biological and social relationships, shaping the biological and material features of the landscape and also memory, experience, and knowledge' (Lindholm and Ekblom, 2019: 2). Archaeologists have identified this as an integrated landscape approach to biocultural heritage and applied it to both terrestrial and maritime spaces (Lane, 2010; Lane, 2015). Greater collaboration between ecologists and archaeologists has contributed to the widening of the archaeological reconstruction of historical ecologies.

This approach has led to making biocultural understandings of past marine environments relevant to contemporary concerns. One example includes archaeological studies of the social and environmental impact of ancient tsunamis in the Indian Ocean (Maselli et al., 2018; Mjema, 2018). These have been critical in providing a baseline for comparing the damage and costs of the 2004 Indian Ocean Tsunami, while also feeding into future disaster mitigation planning along the coasts of the Western Indian Ocean. There are, however, newer challenges to the maritime cultural landscape approach, indicating a theoretical unease with using the land as a basis for framing the sea as an object. Within archaeology there are philosophical calls to consider the sea as a *hyperobject*, where the sea is seen neither as a 'landscape or facilitator of human activity,' a surface that acts as a stage for human mobility and cultural connectivity, but an 'entity of vast geographical and temporal scale that possesses agency' (Campbell, 2020). It remains to be seen, in this context of climate change whether this philosophical turn in marine archaeology will have an impact on MCH in its engagements with development contexts. These archaeological debates about interpreting ocean spaces, as either a stage of human activity or agent of transformation, resonate with wider discussions and disagreements about the nature of the global oceans themselves.

Several converging visions of the global ocean are represented in journalistic, scientific, and grey literatures: the transformation of ocean governance as the seas become a 'new economic and development frontier'; the recognition of the ocean as 'humanity's natural and cultural heritage'; and the diffusion of movements to conserve fragile marine ecosystems and preserve ocean resilience in the face of climate change (Arbo et al., 2018). These debates have pivoted around an emerging scientific division of labour: one aligning with engineering and technical innovation in infrastructure, transport, and resource extraction; the other allied to environmental protection and the conservation of marine spaces. This contrasting division of technical and scientific labour is leading to new development concepts for the harnessing of the ocean's resources to the global political economy. Marine archaeologists have found themselves situated at the edges of this scientific division of labour. This is because marine archaeology is a technologically engaged humanities field that is keenly attuned to the deep time of the Anthropocene, but which works with the private and governance sectors to usher in economic innovation and adaptations. At the forefront of these new relationships between development and ocean science has been the Blue Economy, a model of sustainable growth in marine-based industries.

Blue Economy

This context of competing visions of the global oceans' future role in global development witnesses not only 'green' and 'blue' models for conservation, but also the rhetorical rise of the Blue Economy as an economic growth model. Blue Economy is an ocean based economic growth model. It focuses on promoting the oceans as a new economic and development frontier (Arbo et al., 2018; Lehman, 2018). 'Blue growth' is most strongly defined with plans to develop aquaculture, renewable energy, coastal and maritime tourism, marine biotechnology, and deep seafloor mining. This vision of the ocean as a frontier is intricately linked to shifts in the global political economy that is ushering in a disruptive energy transition, a scramble for new sources of food security, and the commodification of the global ocean commons.

As an extremely contested model of development, the Blue Economy is generating considerable debate about how the global oceans and maritime spaces can sustainably produce value within planetary limits. While driving innovation in the exploitation of marine spaces and their resources, marine social scientists warn that 'blue growth' runs up against strong environmental concerns (Arbo et al., 2018: 295). Literature that promotes the Blue Economy typically endorses a loose alliance between 'blue growth' planning and the United Nations' (UN) SDGs, specifically SDG 14 'Life Below Water'. A more critical literature points to the Janus-faced character of 'blue growth' as both driver of development and innovation as well as a 'power grab' for the ocean's natural resources and its strategic geopolitical assets (Barbesgaard, 2018). Culture and heritage, like ecology, provoke archaeologists to debate how they will approach and negotiate the conflict in these competing visions of ocean development, sustainability, and conservation.

Marine archaeology and the Blue Economy

Marine archaeologists' responses to Blue Economy planning have been situated within the expanded work of heritage consultancy and environmental impact assessments (EIA) for government and private sector stakeholders in the marine environment. Archaeological consultants find an expanded role in marine development as the exploitation of coastlines, the seabed, and intertidal areas like estuaries is intensified. Examples from the United Kingdom might include, for instance, EIAs that contract archaeology firms to produce evidence and reports for the renewable energy industry, as when investors apply for licensing to drive new infrastructure projects, such as offshore wind turbines. Sand harvesting in the intertidal areas, where there may be risk of damaging or destroying submerged cultural heritage, such as shipwrecks or air wrecks is also a prime area of archaeological involvement in development. Cabling, new port facilities, and dredging are also areas where archaeologists are drawn more closely to the challenges of sustainable development.

While scientists may frequently experience an awkward relationship with the private sector and government, they are important intermediaries for cultural resource management. This is an increasingly expanding area of concern as scientists, communities, and the private sector are encouraged to adopt more inclusive and participative models of development planning, and as regulations formed around sustainability receive more legal dimensions and weighting. Global development puts tremendous pressures on ocean resources, leading to new interdisciplinary scientific engagements with multiple stakeholders who have vested interests in the conservation or exploitation of the marine environment.

Networks, MCH, and global development

MCH's entry into sustainable development, 'blue growth', and ocean industrialisation comes about in what we might wish to term a consultancy complex. Marine archaeologists are promoting the wider goals of MCH in consultancies that cross various scientific, governance, and industrial sectors. Research grants from national research councils and larger funders like the European Union or the National Oceanic and Atmospheric Administration (NOAA) in the United States have been critical accelerators for MCH's engagement with development. The future sustainability of these funded projects rests largely in the longevity of private sector and community efforts to keep heritage initiatives going once government-sourced funding ends.

Archaeology is enmeshed in a complex interplay of professionals and communities working to execute plans not only to intensify but also merge economic exploitation with the ecosystem management of coastal landscapes and marine spaces. Marine archaeologists play a prominent and increasingly influential role in promoting policy and practices relating to cultural resource management in the context of sustainable marine and coastal development.

Transformations within global development, however, are carving out new roles for marine archaeologists. A distinctively new focus on ocean resilience in the face of climate change is bringing about an urgent need to understand how human beings impact upon the planet's ecologies in deep time. A precursor to this concern for historicising the global oceans is the field of historical marine ecology which aims to reconstruct anthropogenic and natural changes in the marine environment (Lotze et al., in Jackson 2011: 137; Shackeroff et al., 2011; Kittinger et al., 2015). It is this widening of scientific work with implications for developing sustainable practices that has brought marine archaeologists to work more closely with ocean scientists.

The 2020 rollout of the UN Decade of Ocean Science for Sustainable Development (or Ocean Decade) ushered MCH into emerging and rapidly changing debates about the conservation of fragile marine ecosystems, healthy oceans, and sustainable development. The 'Ocean Decade' proposes to work closely with SDG 14 'Life Below Water' and is mobilising ocean scientists to create networks to monitor degradation within marine ecosystems and to propose how to best mitigate these impacts. Marine archaeologists have identified a lack of integration between cultural heritage, ocean science, and sustainable development, although a growing number of MCH networks aim to change this (Trakadas et al., 2019: 155).

Out of this engagement with the SDGs, the Ocean Decade Heritage Network (ODHN) was officially endorsed by the UN Ocean Decade in June 2021, aiming to integrate heritage and ocean science, facilitate co-design with community stakeholders, manage data and knowledge, develop capacity in MCH and development, enable greater diversity and representation, and contribute to educational platforms and ocean literacy. ODHN is interested in inclusive development and has an active programme of research in to how archaeological or deep-time perspectives on climate change can inform decision making in the marine ecosystem environment.

Creating value through visibility

The relationship between cultural heritage and values derived from development has been presented as a problem that has challenged economic theory, inviting interdisciplinary perspectives that borrow as freely from anthropology as they do from ecology (De la Torre, 2002). A new discourse of 'benefits,' 'assets,' and 'values' is replacing older visions of a static line separating cultural heritage from development, one past-oriented and the other looking to the future (see Basu and Modest, 2014; Cross and Giblin, Chapter 1, this volume). Value is a significant aspect to heritage and the desire to conserve sites, objects, and landscapes of cultural significance is a fundamental goal for heritage organisations, hence the need to define 'value' and 'benefits' in a range of monetary and non-monetary scales (De la Torre, 2002: 3). Yet the proliferation of these different scales of value is a significant challenge that faces heritage-as-development projects.

These diverse values are complexly arranged across many differing kinds of activities, including a range of bureaucratic ones related to ocean governance. MCH is factored into these as an income earner through heritage tourism and community science. There is a huge knowledge gap regarding how scientific activities bring income to communities that live in areas of scientific interest, although considerably more attention has been paid to how heritage brings income to local communities. As one report on the potential of MCH for development states, 'these social and economic benefits are already occurring, but they are obscured or unrecognised', adding that such benefits have 'potential to be enhanced' (Firth, 2015: 5). Thus, value is not just out there, but it needs to be created and sustained. Enhancing the social and economic benefits of heritage in marine spaces depends upon previous work to establish the value of culture in socio-economic development, work pioneered by UNESCO in the 1980s.

UNESCO has advocated for the inclusion of 'culture' in sustainable approaches to development since the declaration of a World Decade for Cultural Development in 1988 (Dobrosława, 2020: 313). Marine archaeology's links to the culture-development nexus have grown out of complex interrelations between an expanding marine economy and the legal requirements of ocean-based industries to undertake expert EIAs. There is an increased space for archaeological consultancies in industrial development as an outcome of the legal (and moral) requirements of corporations to comply with sustainable practice. Marine and underwater archaeologists are likely to be contracted to evaluate industrial development and its risks to biocultural and ecological systems and services. This is a normative value, but there are also additional and more derivative values that MCH promotes, values that have much to do with advancing our understandings of past, present, and future ocean and coastal environments.

In the Western Indian Ocean, for example, archaeologists are contracted to gather systematic evidence on the potential impacts of constructing new coastal infrastructures like bridges, breakwaters, and harbours upon the submerged historical environment. Often the work of marine archaeologists is linked to wider extractive industries, such as oil and natural gas, or else connected to broader developments in extending pipeline networks or laying ICT cables across the seafloor. Nation-states like Kenya, Tanzania, Mozambique, and Madagascar are increasingly drawn to their considerable ocean resources for new kinds of development opportunities. Each of these states are active participants in Blue Economy development planning (Attri, 2018).

With accelerating change to marine ecologies now recognised as a global problem, and as Blue Economy planning gains pace and political support in the Western Indian Ocean, marine archaeologists recognise the need to address the global politics of cultural heritage and development. Questions such as 'How much development? At what cost?' become issues for debate among heritage and archaeological professionals and their networks. Warnings from the excessive damage of coastal development upon heritage assets in the United States and Europe – areas where significant resources have been allocated to heritage – is now being embedded into capacity building and training programmes for marine archaeologists in the Global South. The development of mega-cities along China's coasts, for instance, have been seen as coming at a deleterious and irreversible cost to submerged and coastal heritage. In response to a range of urgent global problems, such as climate change, rising sea level, and depleted ocean health, marine archaeologists are seeking to align their research strategies with the funding priorities of the Global North. Self-conscious of the need to 'do good, better' and join in with the aims of a range of SDGs, marine archaeologists and their heritage counterparts endeavour to work more closely and collaboratively on inclusive and community-focused projects, seeking to enhance the benefits that research can stimulate in areas of local scientific or historical importance. In making the case for the importance of cultural heritage in the form of 'shared histories, place-making, traditions and livelihoods' to the long-term sustainability of the region's communities, marine archaeologists have increasingly prioritised the co-design and co-production with partners in the Global South (Henderson et al., 2021: 1027). Reflecting critical awareness of the place of Indigenous design in sustainable development, these practitioners are now promoting engagement with local communities as good practice. In practical terms, this means that marine archaeologists are now co-opting some aspects of development discourse, such as that of 'community participation', as a legitimising factor in their promotion of the heritage-as-development turn.

The recognition of 'culture' indicators within the 2030 Agenda for Sustainable Development set the stage to bring marine archaeologists, and their funding bodies, into closer rapport with the SDGs and its sustainability narratives. Yet at the very centre of these concerns, the value of culture is measured differently by heritage and development professionals. Heritage studies' bifurcated approach to culture, seeking to disaggregate the complexities of biocultural heritage into vague categories of the 'tangible' and 'intangible', falls short of producing economic benefits for local heritage projects organised 'from below' or co-designed with global partners. Heritage values are not wholly capable of instrumentalising culture towards the goals and aims of sustainable development policy. Culture – as marine archaeologists would understand it – needs to be translated into a language that development practitioners use and understand. It was not, however, the formal development policy clusters such as 'prosperity and livelihoods', 'knowledge and skills', and 'inclusion and participation' that were the drivers of MCH's new relationship to development (Hosahrahar, 2019). It was marine archaeologists' close relationships with other biophysical scientists and work within EIAs that shape an alternative understanding of heritage value, that is, a value that is frequently non-monetary and embedded in the politics of knowledge production.

The idea of 'benefit' derived from MCH owes much to a prior reworking of the biological concept of 'ecosystems service' which describes how human well-being is provided for by the environment and ecosystems (Daily et al., 1997). It is widely understood that ecosystem services are relational and dependent upon context, that is to say, culturally constructed (Milcu et al., 2013; Allen et al., 2021: 7). Heritage's value has been measured, in some literature, through the parallel concept of 'cultural ecosystem service' (CES), defined as the 'non-material benefits (e.g. experiences, capabilities) that people derive from human-ecological relations' (Chan et al., 2011: 206). As well-being is now a recognisable index of development, the promotion of heritage's 'benefits' upon identity, belonging, and aesthetics echoes what the natural environment is understood to do for human beings. While well-being remains difficult to measure, it is left to those locally engaged with heritage projects to determine how such value is to be translated into income generation, community organisation, and development planning.

To understand how these stakeholders have come to MCH as a potential focus point for both conservation and entrepreneurship, it is important to identify how deep concerns over the ocean's environmental resilience are coupled with ocean industrialisation (Arbo et al., 2018). Research on these tensions between 'saving the planet' and 'business as usual' have typically identified the Blue Economy, or 'blue growth,' as a focal point through which to theorise what is occurring in the global oceans as a unified, albeit immensely diverse context. This dual focus on conservation and entrepreneurship presents a complex portrait of heritage values within development contexts. On the one hand, the identification of stabilised and protected cultural heritage 'assets' is required by archaeological and heritage professionals, whilst values are also expected to be generated by local stakeholders or 'community champions' through tourist and visitor-related activities, such as guiding school or public groups through a heritage site or offering interpretive services at museums or other similarly curated venues. In what follows, a brief example is provided where a local community was charged with generating value that could count as development in the normative sense of generating income from a MCH project.

Rising from the Depths

A focus within MCH is training and capacity building (Blue and Breen, 2019). This has been an important strand of rationalising funding and ties MCH to sustainable development within maritime communities. At least one of the networks discussed in this review, RftD, was explicitly linked to the 2030 Agenda for Sustainable Development and its 17 SDGs. As outlined above, another network, ODHN, responds to the UN Ocean Decade 2021–2030 (Trakadas et al., 2019). While most of the professionals leading these networks are colleagues and work together to define clearer objectives and goals for MCH within sustainable development, the 'beneficiaries' of these networks are envisioned to be marine archaeologists, heritage professionals, educators, and community leaders in the Global South.

MCH is gaining momentum among a broad range of coastal and maritime communities in eastern and southern Africa. Although MCH projects are modest in number, they benefit from current visions among global development practitioners to 'do good, better,' through inclusive innovation, and an increasing appetite to 'bring science back to the community' through collaboration and co-design between visiting scientists and local community-based organisations (CBOs). These are projects that are aware of the histories of colonialism and the politics of exclusion and expulsions that have marked these eastern and southern African communities' encounters with a range of governments, scientists, and business operators.

The focus of the RftD research hub was on bringing communities to engage with MCH as a meaningful pathway for sustainable cultural, development-oriented, and educational impacts. Funded through the GCRF, RftD seed-funded smaller 'innovation projects' in maritime communities in Kenya, Tanzania, Mozambique, and Madagascar. These projects were co-designed by academics, community leaders, and local people who make their livings, in one way or another, from the marine resources available to them.

One of these projects, 'MUCH (Maritime and Underwater Cultural Heritage) to Discover in Mida Creek,' will be presented as a limited case study, as the author was directly involved in its co-design and made contributions to the project during its lifetime. Stakeholders including a CBO, a women's group called *Bidii na Kazi* (Effort and Work), and the National Museums of Kenya worked with marine archaeologists and social anthropologists from the United Kingdom (University of Ulster/British Institute in Eastern Africa) and a Finnish digital creative.

Co-created with several local stakeholders, the project idea proposed to generate incomes from creating alternative and additional livelihoods (AALs) through creating 'value' by making MCH visible. That project was founded on the challenge of making MCH more inclusive and accessible, building on insights won from recent efforts in 'ocean literacy' linked to the UN Ocean Decade (Lee, 2019). Drawing on a biocultural framing of MCH, which strongly underscored the need for local stewardship in the management of ecosystems and landscapes, the project envisioned how heritage could be instrumental as a pathway to community resilience and sustainable development. It brought together local community activists, women's groups, educators, government conservationists, marine and underwater archaeologists, digital creatives, Beach Management Units (BMUs), hoteliers, tour operators, local government officers, and anthropologists. While some of these stakeholders are directly engaged in resource governance, such as the BMUs that manage fisheries catches, auctions, and licensing at known landing sites, others shape governance through critique and transformations to the communities of practice in which heritage interventions are made. Based on the threat of expulsions of both fishers and farmers from the collapse of local ecosystems, despite being in a 'triangle' of national parks, the focus of the RftD-funded project became fixed on the potential value of biocultural heritage as a way of bringing nature conservation, landscape management, and development goals together in a community-based project.

The proposed project built on a complex legacy of value construction that comes through the bringing together of several relatively recent concepts used in conservation management: that values can be derived from ecosystem services, such as carbon sequestration of mangrove forests; the renegotiated place for 'sustainable' tourism in 'blue growth' economics, such as ecotourism or cultural tourism; and the emergence of a new conceptual framework for biocultural heritage as it is applied to nature conservation and development goals (Lindholm and Ekblom, 2019).

A key objective was adding a MCH interpretive centre and involving community members to construct local in-shore boats, dug-out canoes (*mtumbwi*), and a lateen sail dhow (*dau*) based on traditional environmental knowledge. This approach was designed to bring in additional and alternative incomes to the *Bidii na Kazi* CBO. Modest revenues were generated from a series of AALs, including the building of the Dhow-Restaurant, an eating place located in Mida Creek's extensive mangrove forest, accessible by boat and walkways elevated above the ebb and flow of the creek's dramatic tides. This project endured several challenging circumstances. One of these included a logging moratorium lasting the life of the project which made sourcing local timber for the boatbuilding and restaurant construction an impossibility. The other was dramatic spring tides that severely limited a reforestation project, as these high waters washed mangrove propagules out to sea. The loss of *Bidii na Kazi*'s champion, Bi Arafa Salim Baya, who passed away towards the end of the project, also muted a growing complaint about the gender dynamics of projects within Mida Creek, and the need to co-design research with local intersectionalities at the forefront.

While all these dynamics reveal the internal politics of development projects within communities – taking community to be defined as a heterogenous group of people who are shaped as a community by argument, difference, and history – the project was largely viewed as successful in making MCH visible, both to the local people living in Mida Creek, as well as among national and global stakeholders. The material markers of this success such as the restaurant, the dhow, the website, the interpretive centre, and the fishing traps echoed the training and capacity building that was evidenced through workshop attendance feedback forms and follow-up reporting on impact. Yet more subtle echoes of value could be heard among the archaeologists involved in the project who contemplated the possibility of finding evidence of the long-hypothesised theory that Mida Creek was the principal port for the historic town of Gedi. Value was also measured in the increased capabilities of local youth who learn wooden boat-building skills (Figures 8.1 and 8.2) and the local woman's group who incorporated accounting practices into their existing business management skills. Into such evaluations of the project's success, the usual distinctions of tangible and intangible cultural heritage lost their distinctiveness and usefulness.

Yet these successes were, on the balance, unmeasurable, and cannot be easily translated into the clean development indices of CES values. A community like Mida Creek remains excluded from many development pathways. A depleted Indian Ocean fishery has had a harmful impact on the social resilience of fisher communities. The loss of reproducing fish stocks has led to grim socio-economic insecurity in many fisher communities. Associated with transformations within global fisheries, especially the presence of industrial, 'foreign' fishing fleets off

FIGURE 8.1 Traditional boat-building workshop with students from Pwani University and Kenya National Museums staff, Mida Creek, Kilifi County

Source: Photo taken by MUCH to Discover in Mida Creek project, specifically Wes Forsythe. Permission supplied by email.

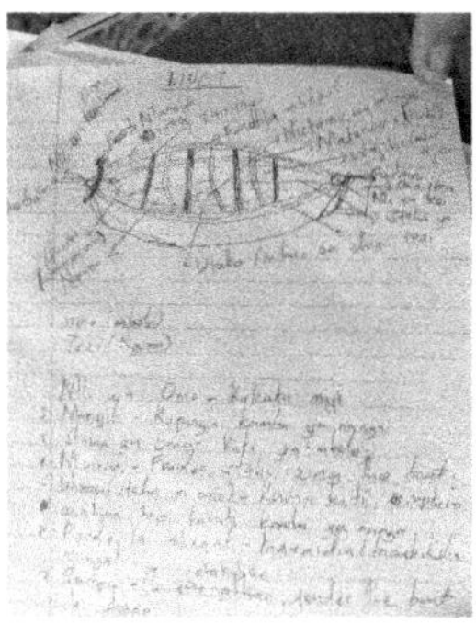

FIGURE 8.2 One outcome of boat-building sessions as Mida Creek was the guided rediscovery of Swahili maritime culture and nautical terms

Source: Photo taken by MUCH to Discover in Mida Creek project, specifically Wes Forsythe. Permission supplied by email.

or within national waters, these coastal and maritime communities have undergone tremendously arduous social and cultural changes. With the long-term but accelerating loss of biodiversity in the marine and intertidal zones, there is a general anxiety that cultural knowledge of the sea and its resources – including Indigenous fishing practices that were explicitly and conscientiously 'sustainable' – will be lost to future generations. The broader point that projects like that of Mida Creek bring home is that the challenges occur simultaneously at a variety of local, national, and global scales, such that the rent seeking policies of Kenyan governments, which issue fishing licenses within their national waters to foreign fishing fleets, come to undermine policies that promote community cohesion through initiatives such as cultural heritage or even gender-focused resource management schemes.

Conclusion: MCH and ocean governance

Engaging with SDG 14, 'Life Below Water', MCH research proposes to add a deep historical perspective on the sustainable use of marine resources within oceans that are profoundly impacted by humans. Countering narratives that treat oceans as lacking history, or which represent the oceans either as a vast asocial planetary space (Steinberg, 2018), as frontier (Lehman, 2018), or as a microscopic 'alien ocean' (Helmreich, 2009), MCH's engagements with the challenges of sustainable development recognise new sensitivities around the Anthropocene as political (Barry and Maslin, 2016). The move to efface history from the ocean is a very real one. While national scientific organisations like NOAA now appeal to the global reach of the environmental threats to ocean health by claiming 'There is only *one* global ocean', there has been a total shift in the commodification and governance of the world's oceans through the lens of property relations (Helmreich, 2009). Once the global ocean is viewed as something that must be either conserved or exploited, the logic of the market and private property can gain a foothold upon the commons. MCH can bring back into the discussion of a singular, global ocean how history has shaped how people develop ocean spaces in the present, both on its surfaces and within its depths. MCH can offer a critical view of the ocean as a form of private property, exposing the many ways through which past communities have tried to lay claim to it through their relationships to the sea and coast.

Against this new governance dialogue of the world oceans as property, older discourses about the commons are quickly fading from view, damaging myriad coastal communities who depend upon the sea for their livelihoods, their material culture, and their identities. Although heritage also plays around with this political idea of the commons, as in claims for the universal value of cultural heritage, the new geopolitics of the oceans – opened by novel partnerships between scientific researchers, private interests, and non-state organisations, as well as nation-states – promotes a global sea that effaces the tremendously diverse adaptations to marine spaces and aquatic ecosystems by human societies.

As the implementation phase starts for the UN Ocean Decade (2021–2030) such governance issues will be increasingly important. MCH is seeking to engage with ocean science to begin new dialogues about the uses and ends of scientific knowledge. Through new models of funding projects that seek to promote 'healthy oceans' by co-designing research with its users, broader understandings of MCH encourage placing community participation at the centre of sustainable fisheries and aquatic ecosystems, hence, redirecting the tendency to exclude 'life above water' in debates about ocean governance (Jentoft, 2020). Emerging discourses about ocean governance are critical to MCH's engagement with global development, concerned as they are with a certain polarisation within policy that seeks either to 'conserve' or 'exploit' oceanic 'resources' or 'assets' (Hannigan, 2016).

References

Allen, K., Castellano, C. and Pessagno, S. (2021) 'Using dialogue to contextualize culture, ecosystem services, and cultural ecosystem services', *Ecology and Society*, 26(2). doi:10.5751/ES-12187-260207.

Arbo, P. et al. (2018) 'The transformation of the oceans and the future of marine social science', *Maritime Studies*, 17(3), pp. 295–304.

Attri, V.N. and Bohler-Muller, N. (eds) (2018) *The blue economy handbook of the Indian Ocean region*. Pretoria: Africa Institute of South Africa.

Barbesgaard, M. (2018) 'Blue growth: savior or ocean grabbing?', *The Journal of peasant studies*, 45(1), pp. 130–149.

Barry, A., and Maslin, M. (2016) 'The politics of the anthropocene: a dialogue', *Geo: Geography and Environment*, 3(2), e00022.

Basu, P., and Modest, W. (eds) (2014) *Museums, heritage, and international development*. Abingdon: Routledge.

Blue, L. and Breen, C. (2019) 'Maritime archaeology and capacity development in the global south', *Journal of Maritime Archaeology*, 14(3), pp. 321–332.

Campbell, P.B. (2020) 'The sea as a hyperobject: moving beyond maritime cultural landscapes', *Journal of Eastern Mediterranean Archaeology & Heritage Studies*, 8(3–4), pp. 207–225.

Chan, K.M.A., Goldstein, J., Satterfield, T., Hannahs, N., Kikiloi, K., Naidoo, R., Vadeboncoeur, N. and Woodside, U. (2011) 'Cultural services and non-use values', in Kareiva, P., Tallis, H., Ricketts, T.H., Daily, G.C. and Polasky, S. (eds) *Natural capital: theory and practice of mapping ecosystem services*, pp. pp. 206–228. Oxford: Oxford University Press. doi: 10.1093/acprof:oso/9780199588992.003.0012

Daily, G.C., Alexander, S., Ehrlich, P.R., Goulder, L.H., Lubchenco, J., Matson, P.A. and Mooney, H.A. (1997) *Nature's services: societal dependence on natural ecosystems*. Washington D.C.: Island Press.

De la Torre, M. (ed.) 2002 *Assessing the values of cultural heritage: research report*. Los Angeles, CA: Getty Conservation Institute.

Dobrosława, W-M. (2020) 'What role for culture in the age of sustainable development? UNESCO's advocacy in the 2030 Agenda negotiations', *International Journal of Cultural Policy*, 26(3), pp. 312–327.

Ekblom, A., Shoemaker, A., Gillson, L., Lane, P. and Lindholm, K.J. (2019) 'Conservation through biocultural heritage—examples from sub-Saharan Africa', *Land*, 8(1), 5.

Firth, A. (2015) *Social and economic benefits of marine and maritime cultural heritage*. Fjordr Ltd for Honor Frost Foundation, London.

Hannigan, J. (2016) *The geopolitics of deep oceans*. Cambridge: Polity.

Helmreich, S. (2009) *Alien ocean: anthropological voyages in microbial seas*. Oakland, CA: University of California Press.

Henderson, J. (2019) 'Oceans without history? Marine cultural heritage and the sustainable development agenda', *Sustainability*, 11(18), 5080.

Henderson, J. et al. (2021) 'Rising from the depths network: a challenge-led research agenda for marine heritage and sustainable development in Eastern Africa', *Heritage*, 4, pp. 1026–1048.

Hosagrahar, J. (2019) *Culture/2030 Indicators.* UNESCO: Paris, France.

Irvine, R. (2020) *An Anthropology of Deep Time: Geological Temporality and Social Life*. United Kingdom: Cambridge University Press.

Jackson, J. et al. (2011) *Shifting Baselines: The Past and the Future of Ocean Fisheries*. Island Press: Washington; Covelo; London.

Jentoft, S. (2020) 'Life above water: small-scale fisheries as a human experience', *Maritime Studies*, 19(4), pp. 389–397.

Kittinger, J.N., McClenachan, L., Gedan, K.B., and Blight, L.K. (eds) (2015) *Marine historical ecology in conservation: applying the past to manage for the future*. Oakland, CA: University of California Press.

Lane, P.J. (2010) 'Developing landscape historical ecologies in Eastern and Southern Africa: opportunities and challenges', *African Studies*, 69, pp. 299–322.

Lane, P.J. (2015) 'Archaeology in the age of the Anthropocene: a critical assessment of its scope and societal contributions', *Journal of Field Archaeology*, 40(5), pp. 485–498.

Lee, Y.H. (2019) 'Ocean cultural heritage and ocean literacy programs in the UN Decade of Ocean Science for Sustainable Development (2021–2030)', *Journal of Ocean and Culture*, 2, pp. 136–146.

Lehman, J. (2018) 'Marine cultural heritage: frontier or centre?', *International Social Science journal*, 68(229–230), pp. 291–301.

Lindholm, K.J., and Ekblom, A. (2019) 'A framework for exploring and managing biocultural heritage', *Anthropocene*, 25, 100195.

Lotze, H. et al. (2011) 'Uncovering the ocean's past', in Jackson, J. and K. Alexander and E. Sala (eds) *Shifting Baselines: The Past and the Future of Ocean Fisheries*, pp. 137–161. Island Press: Washington; Covelo; London.

Maselli, V., Oppo, D., Moore, A.L., Gusman, A.R., Mtelela, C., Iacopini, D., Taviani, M., Mjema, E., Mulaya, E., Che, M., Tomioka, A.L., Mshiu, E. and Ortiz, J.D. (2020) 'A 1000-yr-old tsunami in the Indian Ocean points to greater risk for East Africa', *Geology*, 48(8), pp. 808–813.

Milcu, A.I., Hanspach, J., Abson, D. and Fischer, J. (2013) 'Cultural ecosystem services: a literature review and prospects for future research', *Ecology and Society*, 18(3). doi:10.5751/ES-05790-180344

Mjema, E. (2018) 'Catastrophes and deaths along Tanzania's Western Indian Ocean coast during the Early Swahili period, AD 900-1100', *Azania*, 53(2), pp. 135–155.

Shackeroff, J.M., Campbell, L.M. and Crowder, L.B. (2011) 'Social-ecological guilds: putting people into historical marine ecology', *Ecology and Society*, 16(1), 52.

Steinberg, P.E. (2018) 'The ocean as frontier', *International Social Science Journal*. English edition, 68(229–230), pp. 237–240. doi:10.1111/issj.12152

Trakadas, A. et al. (2019) 'The Ocean Decade Heritage Network: integrating cultural heritage within the UN Decade of Ocean Science 2021–2030', *Journal of Maritime Archaeology*, 14(2), pp. 153–165. doi:10.1007/s11457-019-09241-0

Westerdahl, C. (1992) 'The maritime cultural landscape', *International Journal of Nautical Archaeology*, 21(1), pp. 5–14.

PART 3

Heritage, Health and Development

9

HERITAGE, DEVELOPMENT, AND MENTAL HEALTH

Yolana Pringle and Seggane Musisi

Introduction

Mental health occupies an increasingly central place within international development agendas. Mental ill health is regarded as an obstacle to economic and social development, while development is framed as a prerequisite for mental health. This 'psychic turn' within the development arena is visible in the creation of 'happiness' and well-being targets, the inclusion of mental health in the UN Sustainable Development Goals (SDGs), and the mobilisation of the behavioural and psychological sciences in such areas as child development, poverty reduction, humanitarianism, and peacebuilding. However, this conceptualisation has been criticised for promoting Western notions of individual subjectivity, as well as for depoliticising and decontextualising development. The place of heritage within the framing of mental health as a global priority has also received less critical attention. This is despite rich literatures on the importance of heritage projects for memory work and healing in post-conflict settings, as well as the relationship between cultural heritage and individual and collective well-being. Questions of heritage have similarly often been overlooked in the broader historical literature on psychiatry and mental health. This has occurred despite increased attention to colonial histories of development, the ongoing reliance on colonial institutions of psychiatry in contemporary mental health systems across the Global South, and growing interest in the cultural heritage significance of healthcare institutions. This chapter outlines the ways that mental health has become a key part of global health, development, and peacebuilding agendas. Heritage is increasingly implicated in these debates, with heritage regarded as contributing to mental health as a development outcome. This case study—heritage, development, and mental health in Uganda—draws out the relevance of these wider themes and developments in further depth, with a focus on: heritage and healing in post-conflict Uganda; the place of communities and

DOI: 10.4324/9781003107361-12

heritage in mental health projects; and colonial heritage and its impact on mental health. The aim is not to propose a single framework for heritage, development, and mental health, but to suggest new connections between often disparate bodies of research and practice, and to advocate for the recognition of the creative power of communities.

Mental health, well-being, and international development

Since the early 1990s, there has been growing concern about the social and economic burden of Mental, Neurological, and Substance use disorders (MNS) (Prince et al., 2007). Studies by the World Bank and the World Health Organization (WHO) highlighted that previous approaches to the burden of disease, focusing on death rates rather than disability, meant that the burdens of mental health conditions had been 'seriously underestimated', accounting for almost 11 per cent of the total disability-adjusted life years lost (World Bank, 1993; Murray and Lopez, 1994). This economic framing of mental health problems has linked mental health with poverty: mental health is not only an obstacle to economic and social development, but impossible to secure without also tackling poverty. While absent from the Millennium Development Goals, which focused almost exclusively on communicable diseases, and largely neglected in broader development objectives, its inclusion in the SDGs signals that mental health has now become a global priority. It has been lauded as a long overdue step towards redressing historical biases towards physiological needs, while also criticised for promoting Western notions of individual subjectivity, as well as for depoliticising and decontextualising development (Klein and Mills, 2017; Mills and Fernando, 2017).

The growth of the Movement for Global Mental Health, as well as research and advocacy by the WHO, has led to a proliferation of mental health interventions in the Global South. The WHO's Mental Health Gap Action Programme (mhGAP) (2008) aims to reduce the gap between the burden of MNS use disorders, and the availability of specialist services needed to alleviate them (WHO, 2008). They have since published a suite of tools, including an intervention guide, training manual, and an app offering diagnostic algorithms, which foreground universality and commensurability. Sociologists point out how such tools are 'built for expansion', particularly in the digital age, with 'adaptability' limited largely to translation, training options, and adjustments depending on the organisation of health systems and availability of resources and personnel. Little attention is given, moreover, to the 'social life' of these tools—the ways they are used in local contexts, and how this 'might disrupt or question the underlying logic and epistemology' (Mills and Hilberg, 2019). Historians would also situate such tools in a longer trajectory of attempts to define universal standards, including decades of development and testing (Vaughan, 2016; Wu, 2021). Such manuals, as well as project evaluations, scientific meeting reports, and conference papers, represent some of the tangible heritage of global mental health that can be found in offices, libraries, medical schools, and now mobile phones across the Global South.

The growing authority of the 'psy' disciplines more generally has seen the mobilisation of the behavioural and psychological sciences in such areas as child development, poverty reduction, and societal cohesion. The World Bank's *Mind, Society, and Behaviour* (2015) argues that development policies and interventions, including health outcomes and poverty reduction, could be improved by applying insights from psychology and behavioural economics (Mills, 2018). The language of hope, well-being, and happiness is also increasingly seeping into public policy and political objectives at both national and international levels. This has involved a search for statistical indicators that more adequately address societal well-being not just through economic conditions or GDP, but its environmental, as well as social dimensions (Stiglitz et al., 2009; Helliwell et al., 2012). Bhutan's Gross National Happiness (GNH) index, for example, centres societal well-being in public policy, offering a multidimensional measure across the domains of psychological well-being, health, time use, education, cultural diversity and resilience, good governance, community vitality, ecological diversity and resilience, and living standards in public policy objectives (Ura et al., 2012). Governments in South America—particularly Bolivia and Ecuador—meanwhile, have co-opted and operationalised discourses of *buen vivir* (good living) since the 2000s as a radical alternative to neoliberalism (Vanhulst and Beling, 2014; Domínguez et al., 2017). The different ways in which these are being pursued not only highlights the lack of consensus over discourses of sustainable development and the 'Green Economy', but the difficulties of developing subjective measures of well-being, and the ways these relate to individual and communities' capabilities (Pouw and Gilmore, 2012). This has been compounded by the ways 'happiness' has been conceptualised and operationalised in places with limited or no freedom of expression, such as in the United Arab Emirates (Fanti, 2020).

In the context of the emergence of a 'security-development nexus', in which security and development are regarded as interlinked and mutually necessary for sustainable peace (Duffield, 2007), mental health and psychosocial well-being has been suggested as an entry point for achieving sustainable peace in post-conflict settings (Bubenzer et al., 2017). Based on the notion that exposure to traumatic events undermines social cohesion, trust in peace and reconciliation processes, and fuels long-term 'cycles of violence', mental health and psychosocial support (MHPSS) interventions appear to offer an entry point to social and political transformation (Pham et al., 2010; Tankink et al., 2017). This reinforces the authority of psychological expertise in the management of violent conflict and risk, despite critiques from scholars that this depoliticises violence and pathologises communities' needs and responses to traumatic experiences (Pupavac, 2001; Fassin and Rechtman, 2009; Howell, 2011).

MHPSS activities, which have proliferated since the 1990s, range from narrative-exposure therapy and cognitive behavioural therapy, to the now ubiquitous psychosocial approaches of basic counselling of individuals, groups, and families, community-based support projects, mental health education, and the provision of child-friendly spaces (Miller and Rasmussen, 2010; Tol et al., 2011a). Arts-based approaches, including dance and musical performance, creative writing, clay modelling, photovoice, narrative theatre, and storytelling are growing in prominence, and have been noted for their potential for providing holistic psychosocial support, particularly among societies or groups that might have difficulties expressing themselves verbally (Tankink et al., 2017). While there is growing consensus on the aims and guiding principles of MHPSS, the field remains divided between the trauma approach, which focuses on post-traumatic stress disorders (PTSD) and the psychosocial approach, which is more holistic and community-based. Much of the debate centres on the extent to which knowledge is generalisable or unique between cultural contexts, and whether interventions should be targeted at specific 'vulnerable' groups or are community-wide (Ager, 1997; Miller and Rasmussen, 2010). It is exacerbated by a weak evidence-base for the effectiveness of MHPSS approaches, particularly the collective impact of psychosocial support. This lack of consensus is problematic because ill-conceived MHPSS interventions have the potential to cause harm by undermining local coping strategies, invalidating local political agency, and prioritising individual diagnosis and treatment over justice and accountability processes (Wessells and van Ommeren, 2008).

Researchers and practitioners stress the need for more attention to the social, cultural, and political context in which MHPSS operates, and particularly whether interventions address locally perceived needs (Tol et al., 2011b). This is where closer dialogue between those engaged in MHPSS and those within the fields of heritage, healing, and memory could be productive. These bodies of literature have remained largely separate, despite the latter offering important insights into the contextually and historically varied ways that communities affected by violence manage the past, and how this shapes the ways they handle the present. This includes reconciliation and healing through complex rituals, notably funerals and last rites, often difficult to observe fully in conflict and post-conflict settings (Lan, 1985; Reynolds, 1990; Englund, 1998). It also includes the ways that orature and other forms of cultural heritage serves as a resource for communities—for public expression, dissent, and resistance, as well as for well-being (Chimombo, 1987; Lwanda, 2008; Wanjiru et al., 2015; Carcelén-Estrada, 2018). Indeed, this has led some heritage researchers and practitioners to point to the productive potential of cultural heritage, often as part of an emancipatory framing of development in which individuals and communities 'determine their own values and their own aspirations' (Basu and Modest, 2014: 14). In this way, heritage offers an entry point for bringing together often disparate literatures and practices on global health and development, and for more critical reflection on the ways that the past—in its multiple, and ever-present forms—can offer new ways of thinking about what mental health means, and how to achieve it.

Mental health and healing in heritage

The language of healing—whether economic, social, political, or cultural—permeates much of the rhetoric on the value of heritage, particularly in post-conflict settings. This tends to frame heritage as a 'thing' or set of 'things' (Giblin, 2014) that can help communities negotiate or mediate pain, whether deployed in support of reconciliation, peacebuilding, entertainment, justice, or MHPSS initiatives. UNESCO's (2019: 3) *Promoting Culture in Emergencies* highlights that 'the rehabilitation of heritage can contribute towards healing the scars of war and disasters by allowing communities to recover a sense of hope, dignity and empowerment' and 'can be a powerful tool for reconciliation and a building block for social cohesion'. This productive potential for heritage-healing can be seen in a range of projects, including the Building Resilience Through Heritage (BReaTHe) project in Jordan, which is using virtual or digital heritage for 'community resilience-building' and to create a space for diverse communities—many of whom have been displaced—to come together (BReaTHe, 2019). In the national context of South Africa, moreover, politicians and heritage practitioners have moved to pass post-apartheid heritage legislation that is more inclusive, while also tied up with attempts to recraft the past in terms of shared nationhood. This approach to heritage-healing highlights how heritage can be used to perform and reshape the past, address cultural trauma, and represent a form of therapy, particularly for those who are 'disempowered, dislocated and disadvantaged' (Meskell and Scheermeyer, 2008). Yet much of this literature, and related projects and policy, has focused on questions of whether heritage 'helps' or 'harms', something that has been critiqued as a distraction from deeper understandings of the role heritage can play in negotiating and reimagining the past (Giblin, 2014).

The instrumentalisation of heritage in post-conflict settings is mirrored in the use of arts-based approaches both for public health-led interventions and development initiatives encompassing health. These commonly use arts that would fall under a broad heading of cultural heritage—theatre, music, the visual arts, storytelling, and other literary traditions—viewing them as a channel for the communication of public health messages, particularly those around HIV/AIDS and communicable diseases—some with demonstrable efficiency (Bunn et al., 2020). The best of these initiatives are developed in partnership and in dialogue with local communities, taking into account the context in which these arts operate, and working to 'transform social structures and other conditions that work to thwart democratic participation' (Abdulla, 2016; see also Kamlongera, 1982). Indeed, as scholars and others in the Global South point out, connections between the arts and health are not new. Storytelling traditions in many parts of Africa, for example, historically included health messaging and education, yet have been disrupted by colonial policies that deliberately undermined indigenous practices (Abdi, 2007; Mawere and Awuah-Nyamekye, 2015). This reinforces the significance of critiques of practices such as 'Theatre for Development', in promoting globalisation and undermining the opportunities that Indigenous theatre might offer for grassroots activism and change (Ahmed, 2002). Yet such arts-based approaches to health nevertheless have the potential to reach wider audiences, promote well-being, and inform research, when approached ethically and responsibly (Bunn et al., 2020). While theatre and storytelling, for example, is increasingly lauded for its emancipatory potential, informing participatory action research methodologies and producing more ethical and locally-relevant research, it should not be used merely to extract knowledge (Caxaj, 2015; Wasamba, 2015).

Arts-based approaches to public health have tended to neglect mental health messaging, with well-being and happiness regarded as secondary or tangential outcomes for participants (Wingham et al., 2020). Yet mental health and well-being are central to narratives on the importance of intangible cultural heritage. In broad terms, this is reflected in the medicalised language used to describe intangible cultural heritage: it is both a 'diagnosis' for economic, political, technological, and demographic changes that are said to threaten the viability of cultural practices, as well as a 'treatment' in the form of 'safeguarding' (Hafstein, 2018). More specifically, many of the entries on the UNESCO Representative List of the Intangible Cultural Heritage of Humanity refer to mental health, whether through Indigenous medical knowledge and healing practices around mental illness or mental distress, or through the broader psychosocial and mental health aspects of dances, festivals, and folk media (UNESCO, 2020). In China, physicians have argued that intangible cultural heritage not only has a role in treating mental and neurological conditions (such as the use of Miao medicine for epilepsy), but has an aesthetic and artistic value, inspiring nationalism and cultural self-confidence, helping to build communities, and providing opportunities for more inclusive mental healthcare systems (Liu and Li, 2020). With colonial Witchcraft Acts, enacted in large parts of the Global South in the early 20th century to outlaw cultural practices associated with the spirit world, such efforts to recognise and promote Indigenous cultural heritage have also been ascribed a recuperative role (Musisi, 2021, see also Fadeyi, this volume). Yet the manner in which this is being done is subject to critique. This includes concern about the top-down approach to heritage as well as the Eurocentrism of definitions in instruments such as the World Heritage Convention, which draws a distinction between 'natural' and 'cultural' heritage in ways that negate Indigenous peoples' conceptions of heritage, particularly when it comes to healing heritage (Munjeri, 2004; Disko, 2017). Efforts around the 'protection' of Indigenous healing knowledge are also problematic. Among the Sámi, as in many Indigenous societies, concepts of secrecy and inner experiential knowledge are an integral part of Indigenous healing knowledge, and thus conflict with UNESCO's goals of knowledge 'transfer' and 'revitalisation' (Helander-Renvall and Markkula, 2017). The inscription of Vimbuza—an illness and a healing ritual practised among the Tumbuka people in northern Malawi—on the UNESCO list also highlights tensions between ritual and non-ritual forms of intangible heritage, particularly among those that would prefer recognition of Vimbuza as ritual from religious, legal, and health authorities in Malawi (Gilman, 2015).

The recognition that cultural heritage can help think through what it means to be healthy in a holistic sense is reflected in increasing calls for the built environment, or 'healing environment', to be considered in sustainable hospital design. At the Seoul National University Medical Campus and Hospital, this has involved consideration of the multilayered nature of heritage on campus, spanning modern buildings and open spaces, as well as cultural heritage sites from the Chosun

Dynasty, Daehan Empire, European and Japanese colonial occupation, and the postcolonial era. Approaching spaces such as these as healing environments requires moving beyond a focus on the function of Western medicine, or an emphasis on green spaces, to discussions on how to harmonise the space in ways that help create new meanings and feelings for visitors (Jeong, 2019). This has entered proposals for reimagining psychiatric institutions in places like Kenya through 'supportive design', suggesting important avenues for future research (Cheruiyot, 2018). Such proposals are pertinent because many psychiatric institutions in formerly colonised countries evolved from colonial prisons—often overcrowded and run down, and recognised even at the time as offering little more than confinement (Mahone and Vaughan, 2007; Pringle, 2019; Rajpal, 2020). Colonial debates over buildings and space, moreover, were informed by the desire to reproduce and maintain the social and racial order (Deacon, 2000; Jackson, 2005). The ongoing use of former colonial institutions means that those that use their services need to negotiate what might be seen as a heritage of psychiatry—sites of memory, nostalgia, and a 'border zone' between 'the colonial and the postcolonial, between local exegeses of mental distress and Western psychiatry' (Kilroy-Marac, 2019)—often in contexts where there are ongoing inequalities of power and resources.

In approaching the topic of healing environments, heritage and health practitioners can draw on wider literature on the ways people engage with landscape elements. This includes natural landscapes in which public healers have negotiated and drawn on the power of ancestors (Schoenbrun, 2006; Kodesh, 2010), as well as rich debates on the built heritage of colonialism. These have located colonial buildings, street names, and statues as lying in a landscape of 'power struggle'—as traces of the 'attempt to forge legitimacy and erase memory of the indigenous people' (Mawere and Mubaya, 2016: 57) as well as 'colonial debris' that can traumatise (Mhango, 2015). Such debates about built heritage are not new, however, long being tied up with nation building projects and attempts to establish national dignity and pride (McGregor and Schumaker, 2006). In early postcolonial Kenya, street names and public spaces were 'sites for justice restitution and reputational politics', and offered opportunity to promote both diversity and unity (Wanjiru and Matsubara, 2017: 20). Ongoing debates in South Africa today similarly point to the ways that statues have the potential both to 'evoke hope' as well as to 'act as a reminder of the brutal past' (Mhango, 2015: 89). In doing so, this wider literature serves as a reminder of the importance of understanding heritage as something that is performed and constantly being reshaped. It is this that offers its potential to stir a 'gentle politics' through participation and everyday living (Crouch, 2015).

Heritage and mental health in Uganda

Heritage is vitally important to understanding Uganda's mental healthcare landscape, and the ways the legacies of colonialism and development perpetuate health inequalities and inequities today (Musisi, 2021). This includes a deliberate undermining of healers' shrines by colonial officials—spaces for public healing, collective well-being and memory, as well as politics (Kodesh, 2007), in addition to the denial of communities' rights to participate in health governance (Mulumba et al., 2021). Uganda's Mental Health Act, last revised in 1964 operated until 2019, contained outdated, derogatory, and stigmatising language, despite attempts at legislative reform in recent years (Nyombi et al., 2014). For over 35 years, even after independence, it continued to fail to adequately protect people with mental disorders from violence and discrimination (Ssanyu, 2007; Kigozi et al., 2010). Colonial mental healthcare policies, moreover, focused on centralised institutions, with little invested in community public mental health initiatives, and the sidelining of traditional healers (Musisi, 2021). This institutional mindset, in particular, has been difficult to overcome. When the Uganda government looked to rehabilitate mental health services in the late 1980s and 1990s, following decades of neglect and underdevelopment, they retained the decades-old focus on institutionalisation, rather than reimagining mental health policy by drawing on community public mental health approaches (MacRae, Zwi, and Gilson, 1996; Boardman and Ovuga, 1997). Such legacies have continued to hamper fresh thinking about how to address mental healing in future healthcare endeavours. This is despite calls from Ugandan psychiatrists and related professionals for more investment in decentralised approaches to mental healthcare (Baingana and Mangen, 2011; Musisi et al., 2021), and the reintroduction of meaningful community participation and accountability in health governance (Mulumba et al., 2021). Health authorities and planners in Uganda need to recognise that most Ugandans, even educated ones, believe that mental illness is caused by supernatural processes, and will consult traditional and religious healers when afflicted with mental ill health (Ovuga et al., 1999; Abbo, 2011).

Consideration of the heritage of psychiatry and mental health in Uganda is particularly important because since independence, Uganda has seen war, political instability, and associated insecurity. This has shaped mortality and morbidity, as well as mental health, especially among conflict-affected populations (Musisi, 2004; Nakimuli-Mpungu et al., 2013). Most studies have focused on investigating PTSD with recent population surveys in northern Uganda estimating that the prevalence of PTSD symptoms may be as high as 54 per cent or even 74 per cent (Vinck et al., 2007; Roberts et al., 2008). Clinical studies in northern Uganda also reveal disproportionately high levels of other psychiatric symptoms, notably depression and anxiety (Okello et al., 2007). These have confirmed fears raised by Ugandan psychiatrists and the Ugandan public since the 1990s about the impact of political violence on the nation's mental health. The *Northern Uganda Psycho-Social Needs Assessment* (NUPSNA) conducted by the Uganda Government and UNICEF in 1998, stressed that war had 'broken down the very fabric of civil society', and that 'traditional customs which brought community people together to discuss problems and implement solutions jointly are no longer followed' (Barton and Mutiti et al., 1998). As such, there was a particular urgency in dealing with the war after-effects, particularly among the Acholi, where so many had witnessed 'psychologically wounding events', and where many children had been abducted and/

or used as combatants with horrendous mental health fallouts (Okello et al., 2007; Amone p'Olak, 2014).

While concerns have been raised about the 'medicalisation' of human responses to war and violence in the wider MHPSS literature, most Ugandan psychiatrists and other mental health workers agree on the need to address the mental health and psychosocial needs of conflict-affected populations in a culturally appropriate manner (Barton and Mutiti et al., 1998). Yet while there has been a proliferation of MHPSS initiatives in recent years, particularly among internally displaced populations and children in northern Uganda (Okello et al., 2007; Betancourt et al., 2009; Ertl et al., 2011), many have lacked sustainability due to piecemeal funding, absence of coordination with Ugandan mental health professionals, and failure of local and government buy-in. Arts-based approaches, including theatre, storytelling, and music represent a key strategy, though such practices tend to be led by religious groups and NGOs, rather than by mental health specialists (Edmondson, 2018; Amone p'Olak, 2014; Opiyo, 2015), and are often tied up with 'particular notions of "productive" citizenship' (Mugishagwe, 2014). What is needed is a national mental health policy that more fully addresses questions of trauma, war, and violence (Muhwezi et al., 2011; Kinyanda et al., 2013; Nakimuli-Mpungu et al., 2013). This will also require that the focus is broadened beyond northern Uganda. Northern Uganda has received disproportionate attention from the international community due to a two-decade long insurgency war (1986–2006), with over a million people displaced in an attempt to escape the violence of the Lord's Resistance Army (LRA) as well as the government's counter-insurgency operations (Okello et al., 2007). It has coincided with the rise of concern about mental health in humanitarian and post-conflict settings more generally, and been a place for experimentation with MHPSS, targeting both civilians and soldiers (particularly child soldiers), often with unintended consequences. This has been at the expense of attempts to address the mental health of those who lived through war and violence elsewhere in Uganda. This has included relations of 'the disappeared' under Idi Amin (in power 1971–1979), those who lived through the Ugandan-Tanzanian war (1978–1979) and the Ugandan Bush War (1981–1986), and survivors of terrorist attacks at the Kichwamba Technical College, Western Uganda (1998) and in Kampala (2010), not to mention the many brutal riot control measures in Ugandan politics (Musisi and Kinyanda, 2020).

Heritage is relevant to understanding mental health and mental healing in Uganda not just because it can be instrumentalised for MHPSS, but because it is a part of health, health seeking, and ultimately healing. Dance and music have served to maintain and facilitate reconciliation and (re)integration among the Acholi in northern Uganda as art forms that work in dialogue with wider peacebuilding and reconciliation processes (Kibirige, 2020). Moreover, the disruption of healing, death, and burial rituals during periods of war and violence represents a form of violence against health and healthcare. It is one that is neglected in calls from international humanitarian organisations for more attention to the effects of, and strategies to protect healthcare from, violence (Elrha and ICRC, 2020), yet its effects can be significant. Indeed, promises of spiritual healing, or cleansing, made from leaders of violent resistance movements such as Alice Lakwena of the Holy Spirit Movement in the wake of the Ugandan Bush War, have been implicated in the perpetuation of war (Allen and Vlassenroot, 2010). More broadly, failure to bury the dead in the appropriate manner in internal displacement camps in northern Uganda has been tied to ongoing concerns about misfortune. Among the Acholi, burial away from home represents 'bones in the wrong soil' and aggrieves the spirits of the dead (Jahn, 2016: 33). Reburial since the end of the conflict has been an important part of attempts to remake lives and honour the dead, yet has been tied up with wider development politics, in which clearing former internal displacement camps has been important for economic objectives (Whyte et al., 2014), and has often proved to be disruptive and expensive for families. In his book, *Healing Invisible Wounds*, Richard Mollica has argued for recognition of cultural and spiritual (religious) rituals and practices in effecting 'paths to hope and recovery in a violent world' (Mollica, 2006).

That anxieties around mourning and death can have physical, as well as psychological effects on the body has long been recognised both by Ugandan psychiatrists, as well as in Uganda's cultural groupings. In Teso, the idea that painful memories can provoke illness is encapsulated in the disease *aomisio* ('too much thinking' or 'overthinking'), which is associated with the growth of 'ulcers' or 'wounds' in the heart and stomach (Wermbter, 2016; Tol et al., 2018). The physical pain caused by such illnesses may never reach the attention of mental health specialists, instead being managed by families, religious or traditional healers, or as physical disease by primary healthcare workers. In the years following the ending of the Ugandan Bush War, for example, traditional healers in the Luwero Triangle reported seeing more cases of *eddalu* (madness, psychosis), *akazoole* (mania/hypomania), *kasiru* (mental retardation), and *akalogojjo* (delirium or any mild/transient form of mental illness characterised by confusion), as well as increases in a wide range of physical illnesses. One prominent exception here has been outbreaks of 'mass hysteria' in girls' boarding schools since the 1980s. An investigation of 'a strange disease' at a primary school in Kitgum District, northern Uganda, in 2009 reported how students had been attacked by 'demons … shouting, running amok, fighting, biting' (Nakalawa et al., 2010). This only stopped when the headteacher 'cut down and burnt the "demonic tree"' from which students claimed demons descended to attack them. In the aftermath, links were drawn to the history of destruction, killings, and violence committed by the LRA on the site of the school grounds, including the nearby presence of two mass graves. Among the responses pursued in the aftermath were traditional cleansing rituals by elders in the community, prayers led by a Christian NGO, psychiatric assessments of schoolchildren, and the construction of a memorial over the mass graves, 'to rest the spirits' (Nakalawa et al., 2010).

The mental health 'benefits' of memorialisation are contested, however, even among Uganda's mental health professionals. They sit uneasily with cultural beliefs and practices around death and dying. In most circumstances, Ugandans do not want to speak openly about the dead, and can consider it painful to be reminded of them. Last funeral rites at the end of the mourning period, for example, include a ceremony to install an heir and are, in a way, aimed at getting 'rid of death' (Ovonji-odida, 2016) or bursting and dispersing death—*okwabya olumbe* and *okusasanya olumbe*. In the 1980s, a brief attempt was made to display the skulls of people killed in the Luwero Triangle. Yet, as one commentator pointed out, this was 'one of the most dastardly and abominable acts of insult to the dead that I have ever seen in my life—it represented callous disrespect, indignation, and violation of the rights of the dead not to leave them in their peace' (Adyanga, 2015). Another researcher also questioned 'the (political) effectiveness of this instrumentalization of fear, as well as the success of the memorial heritage-building to which the Luweero skulls were subjected' (Bernard, 2017). Studies of mass graves in Teso, victims of massacres during a Uganda Peoples' Army (UPA) insurgency that saw a violent crackdown by the government's National Resistance Army (NRA), as well as victims of LRA soldiers, similarly reveal contested politics over reburial and memorialisation. These should serve as a reminder that communities do not have a single way of coming to terms with the violent past, and much of this reflects ongoing political relationships in the country especially in regions distant from Kampala (Wermbter, 2016). It is also indicative of ongoing calls for compensation and reparations—holding symbolic value, as well as having tangible significance—something that the government has made many promises about but has yet to define a coherent policy on. Indeed, memorialisation has been subject to both public and academic debate in Uganda, being regarded both as a Western import, and something that does not adequately address development needs, let alone the mental health needs of communities affected by conflict, violence, and political persecution. A debate hosted by radio station Voice of Teso, about government shortcomings on memorialisation, argued that memorials alone were inadequate while many people still had not been compensated, with some also asking that the government provide something more useful, such as a health centre or a school (Wakabi, 2011). This is part of an ongoing debate on reparations without justice.

There is a need for a wider conversation on heritage and mental health that could be used to guide policy and promote the development of a holistically healthy population. Many physical monuments, for example, are closely tied to colonialism. These span statues, as well as old guns, the names of schools, such as the Sir Samuel Baker Secondary School, Gulu, and towns, such as Fort Portal. Medical students at Makerere University still study in the Sir Albert Cook Medical Library, named after the 'father of modern medicine'. The missionary, Albert Cook, of the Church Missionary Society (CMS) set up the CMS Mengo Hospital in 1897, and even today approximately 20 per cent of Uganda's health and education systems comprises of institutions with missionary roots (Mulumba et al., 2021). Some Afrocentric scholars have argued that the introduction of Western medicine was used as an instrument of entrenching colonialism by the European powers who came to Africa (Mhango, 2015; Musisi, 2021). By contrast, few statues from nationalist movements and independence struggles exist in Uganda, perhaps reflecting the lack of a unified nationalist movement under a single leader. The Baganda Kabaka (king) Sir Edward Mutesa II, Uganda's first president who was exiled by the British in his struggles for Buganda's independence, is a rare exception. There have also only been a few systematic efforts to 'decolonise' by renaming lakes, roads, and mountains. In 1972, Idi Amin declared that colonial names had little meaning or significance, and that renaming sites such as Murchison Falls as Kabelega Falls or Queen's Road as Lumumba Avenue was an appropriate way of 'restoring our cultural heritage, human dignity and respect which has hitherto been denied to us by forces of imperialism and their agents' (Kigambo, 2019; see also Makubuya, 2019). Yet most colonial names were reinstated when Amin was ousted in 1979, with efforts since being directly primarily at removing Ugandan Asian names. What purpose do such monumentalised heritages serve? Certainly not the mental well-being of Ugandans for whom Uganda's Eurocentric history is dominated by European missionaries and the Uganda 'martyrs', a group of Anglican and Roman Catholic converts who historians argue were persecuted by Kabaka Mwanga II (1868–1903). The need to embrace both foreign and traditional heritages is so internalised, it puzzles those Afrocentricists who seek to decolonise the mind and thinking of Ugandans. For the psychiatric profession, it prompts the question: whether such deeply colonised minds can ever be freed of the mental wounds of past colonial tortures. Indeed, there is very little information on the role of colonialism and its accompanying collective transgenerational trauma on the collective mental health and social attitudes of today's postcolonial African societies and how they approach development and well-being.

In recent years, questions of memorialisation, and its implications for mental health and well-being, have been raised in national newspapers, as well as at local government level, though action is not yet a priority. Kampala Capital City Authority (KCCA) has developed *Road Naming Guidelines*, which aims to set out procedures for naming new roads and renaming roads in Kampala in ways that 'act as reminders of local history, culture, and citizens' in 'a fair manner', and which can 'address or replace names which are considered controversial or offensive' (KCCA, 2017). But Uganda has yet to have an open, deep conversation about the past, and in ways that acknowledge longer precolonial histories, too. The modern-day region of Buganda, for example, has a memorial landscape that includes hills, as well as villages and rivers, many given conflict-related names from precolonial wars, including Kiteezi (ambush), Kitagobwa (unconquerable), Lubaga (planning hill), Katalemwa (unassailable), and Namirembe (peace hill). Much of this history—and that of more recent events—has affective power, serving as a link between the past and the present. This was embodied in responses in Buganda in 2010 to the destruction of the Kasubi Tombs, where the bodies of four Baganda kings are interred. Rumours that this was a result of government-backed arson resulted in widespread protest, with thousands participating in spirit possession practices. Yet in doing so, the possessed created a curative space 'during which communities recounted moments in the past when the kingdom of Buganda allayed social anxiety' (Earle, 2020). These events serve as a reminder of the power of heritage, and the ways it can be invoked for symbolic healing, as well as social calm.

Conclusion

The literature on heritage and healing has not yet met up with the literature on MHPSS or global mental health. Yet there are numerous points of intersection, not least the moves to draw on the creative power of communities through arts-based approaches to health, and in the recognition that heritage—broadly conceived—is intimately tied to mental health and well-being practices in the everyday. Further sociocultural analysis of the relationship between heritage and mental health is needed to inform mental health practitioners who have called for more detailed studies of the context in which MHPSS operates. This may also feed into mental health advocacy work in Uganda, particularly around a 'joined up' national mental health policy that more fully considers the legacies of war and conflict and maximises the potential for community responses. Such research is particularly urgent because MHPSS is increasingly instrumentalising heritage, yet, while still lacking an evidence-base for its effectiveness or consequences, it risks causing harm. Further attention to heritage and mental health is also important for heritage researchers and practitioners, because the vague language of 'healing', particularly in post-conflict heritage initiatives, lacks analytical power, and does a disservice to the multiple ways communities navigate their own health and healthcare, as well as the ways heritage is not only continually reshaped and performed, but connected to politics. This requires consideration of the lived experiences of multiple layers of heritage—the heritage of colonialism, as well as of colonial medicine and psychiatry based on Afrocentric thinking. More than just an academic exercise, this can help illuminate the shape of current healthcare policies, as well as mentalities, subjective and embodied experiences, and decisions. It is necessary to fully consider the wider healing environment, and to move towards more holistically healthy societies.

References

Abbo, C. (2011) 'Profiles and outcome of traditional healing practices for severe mental illnesses in two districts of eastern Uganda', *Global Health Action*, 4, pp. 1–15.

Abdi, A.A. (2007) 'Oral societies and colonial experiences: Sub-Saharan Africa and the de-facto power of the written word', *International Education*, 37(1), pp. 42–59.

Abdulla, S. (2016) 'The use of folk media: a contradictory discourse', *Research in Drama Education: The Journal of Applied Theatre and Performance*, 21(4), pp. 459–64.

Adyanga, O.C. (2015) 'A macabre exhibit: Ugandan president Museveni's public display of the Luwero Triangle War's human remains', *Advances in Historical Studies*, 4(5), pp. 389–402.

Ager, A. (1997) 'Tensions in the psychosocial discourse: implications for the planning of interventions with war-affected populations', *Development in Practice*, 7(4), pp. 402–7.

Ahmed, S.J. (2002) 'Wishing for a world without "Theatre for development": demystifying the case of Bangladesh', *Research in Drama Education: The Journal of Applied Theatre and Performance*, 7(2), pp. 207–19.

Allen, T., and Vlassenroot, K. (2010) 'Introduction' in Allen, T. and Vlassenroot, K. (eds) *The Lord's Resistance Army: myth and reality*. London: Zed, pp. 1–24.

Amone p'Olak, K., Stochl J., Ovuga E., Abbot R., Meiser-Stedman, R., Croudace, T.J. and Jones P.B. (2014) 'Post-war environment and Longterm mental health problems in former child soldiers in Northern Uganda: The WAYS study', *Journal of Epidemiology and Community Health*, 68(5), pp. 425–30.

Baingana, F., and Mangen, P.O. (2011) 'Scaling up of mental health and trauma support among war affected communities in northern Uganda: lessons learned', *Intervention*, 9(3), pp. 291–303.

Barton, T., Mutiti, A. and the Assessment Team for Psycho-social Programmes in Northern Uganda (1998), *NUPSNA: northern Uganda psycho-social needs assessment*. Kampala: Republic of Uganda; UNICEF.

Basu, P., and Modest, W. (2014) 'Museums, heritage and international development: a critical conversation' in Modest, W. and Basu, P. (eds) *Museums, heritage and international development*. London: Routledge, pp. 1–32.

Bernard, P. (2017) 'The politics of the Luweero skulls: the making of memorial heritage and post-revolutionary state legitimacy over the Luweero mass graves in Uganda', *Journal of Eastern African Studies*, 11(1), pp. 188–209.

Betancourt, T. S., Speelman, L., Onyango, G. and Bolton, P. (2009). 'A qualitative study of mental health problems among children displaced by war in northern Uganda', *Transcultural Psychiatry*, 46(2), pp. 238–256.

Boardman, J., and Ovuga, E. (1997) 'Rebuilding psychiatry in Uganda', *Psychiatric Bulletin* 21(10), pp. 649–55.

BReaTHe project (2019) 'How virtual reality Is helping refugees in Jordan and beyond', University of Bradford, 18 June. Available at: www.bradford.ac.uk/news/archive/2019/how-virtual-reality-is-helping-refugees-in-jordan-and-beyond.php (Accessed 1 February 2022).

Bubenzer, F., van der Walt, S. and Tankink, M. (2017) *Mapping global practice: healing communities, transforming society. Mental health, psychosocial support and peacebuilding*. Cape Town & Diemen: Institute for Justice and Reconciliation and the War Trauma Foundation.

Bunn, C., Kalinga, C., Mtema, O., Abdulla, S., Dillip, A., Lwanda, J., Mtenga, S.M., Sharp, J., Strachan, Z. and Gray, C.M. (2020) 'Arts-based approaches to promoting health in Sub-Saharan Africa: a scoping review', *BMJ Global Health*, 5(5), pp. 1–15.

Carcelén-Estrada, A. (2018) 'Oral literature' in Washbourne, K. and Van Wyke, B. (eds) *The Routledge Handbook of Literary Translation*. London: Routledge, pp. 131–45.

Caxaj, C. S. (2015). 'Indigenous storytelling and participatory action research: allies toward decolonization? Reflections from the peoples' international health tribunal', *Global Qualitative Nursing Research*, 2, pp. 1–12.

Cheruiyot, R.C. (2018) 'Supportive design model: an approach to promote wellness of psychiatric patients. Case study: Mathari National Hospital, Nairobi County, Kenya', MA Research Project, University of Nairobi.

Chimombo, S. (1987) 'Riddles and the reconstruction of reality', *Africa*, 57(3), pp. 297–320.

Crouch, D. (2015) 'Affect, heritage, feeling' in Waterton, E. and Watson, S. (eds) *The Palgrave handbook of contemporary heritage research*. London: Palgrave Macmillan, pp. 177–90.

Deacon, H.J. (2000), 'Landscapes of exile and healing: climate and gardens on Robben Island', *The South African Archaeological Bulletin*, 55(172), pp. 147–54.

Didier, F., and Rechtman, R. (2009) *The empire of trauma: an inquiry into the condition of victimhood*. Princeton: Princeton University Press.

Disko, S. (2017) 'Indigenous cultural heritage in the implementation of UNESCO's world heritage convention: opportunities, obstacles and challenges' in Xanthaki, A., Valkonen, S., Heinämäki, L. and Nuorgam, P.K. (eds) *Indigenous peoples' cultural heritage*. Nijhoff: Brill, pp. 39–77.

Domínguez, R., Caria, S. and León, M. (2017) '*Buen Vivir*: praise, instrumentalization, and reproductive pathways of good living in Ecuador', *Latin American and Caribbean Ethnic Studies*, 12(2), pp. 133–54.

Duffield, M. (2007) *Development, security and unending war: governing the world of peoples*. Cambridge: Polity Press.

Earle, J.L. (2020) '"*Obuganda Buladde*": power, anxiety, and calm in postcolonial Buganda' in Grant, A.M. and Pringle, Y. (eds) *Anxiety in and about Africa: multidisciplinary perspectives and approaches*. Ohio: Ohio University Press, pp. 217–40.

Edmondson, L. (2018) *Performing trauma in Central Africa: shadows of empire*. Bloomington: Indiana University Press.

Englund, H. (1998) 'Death, trauma and ritual: Mozambican refugees in Malawi', *Social Science & Medicine*, 46(9), pp. 1165–74.

Elrha and ICRC (2020) *Researching violence against health care: gaps and priorities*. Available at: www.elrha.org/wp-content/themes/elrha/pdf/elrha-and-icrc-violence-against-health-care-full-report-010720-digital.pdf (Accessed 18 June 2021).

Ertl, V., Pfeiffer, A., Schauer, E., Elbert, T. and Neuner, F. (2011). 'Community-implemented trauma therapy for former child soldiers in northern Uganda: a randomized controlled trial', *Jama*, 306(5), pp. 503–512.

Fanti, A. (2020) 'Happiness imperialism' in Nehring, D. Madsen, O.J., Cabanas, E., Mills, C. and Kerrigan, D. (eds) *The Routledge international handbook of global therapeutic cultures*. London: Routledge, pp. 55–70.

Giblin, J.D. (2014) 'Post-conflict heritage: symbolic healing and cultural renewal', *International Journal of Heritage Studies*, 20(5), pp. 500–18.

Gilman, L. (2015) 'Demonic or cultural treasure? Local perspectives on Vimbuza, intangible cultural heritage, and UNESCO in Malawi', *Journal of Folklore Research*, 52(2–3), pp. 199–216.

Hafstein, V.T. (2018) *Making intangible heritage*. Bloomington: Indiana University Press.

Helander-Renvall, E., and Markkula, I. (2017) 'On transfer of Sámi traditional knowledge: scientification, traditionalization, secrecy, and equality' in Xanthaki, A., Valkonen, S., Heinämäki, L. and Nuorgam, P.K. (eds) *Indigenous peoples' cultural heritage*. Nijhoff: Brill, pp. 104–29.

Helliwell, J., Layard, R. and Sachs, J. (eds) (2012) *World happiness report*. Geneva: United Nations.

Howell, A. (2011) *Madness in international relations: psychology, security, and the global governance of mental health*. Abingdon: Routledge.

Jackson, L. (2005) *Surfacing up: psychiatry and social order in colonial zimbabwe, 1908–1968*. Ithaca & London: Cornell University Press.

Jahn, I.R. (2016) 'Post-war development and camp-site graves: the politics of reburials in former Pabbo IDP camp, Acholiland', *Journal of Peace and Security Studies*, 2(1), pp. 33–43.

Jeong, T. (2019) 'Sustainable use of cultural heritage in the formation of healing environments: a case study of a healthcare facility on a historic urban site', *Sustainability*, 11(7), pp. 1–19.

Kamlongera, C.F (1982) 'Theatre for development: the case of Malawi', *Theatre Research International*, 7(3), pp. 207–22.

KCCA (2017) *Road naming guidelines*. Available at: www.kcca.co.ug (Accessed 18 June 2021).

Kibirige, R. (2020) 'Dancing reconciliation and re/integration: Lamokowang and dance-musicking in the Oguda- Alel post-war communities of northern Uganda'. PhD thesis, Norwegian University of Science and Technology.

Kigambo, G. (2019) 'Why Makubuya is pushing hard to change names of Kampala streets', *Uganda Monitor*, 2 August 2019. Available at: www.monitor.co.ug/uganda/news/national/why-makubuya-is-pushing-hard-to-change-names-of-kampala-streets-1841026 (Accessed 18 June 2021).

Kigozi, F., Ssebunnya, J., Kizza, D., Cooper, S. and Ndyanabangi, S. (2010) 'An overview of Uganda's mental health care system: results from an assessment using the World Health Organization's Assessment Instrument for Mental Health Systems (WHO-AIMS)', *International Journal of Mental Health Systems*, 4(1), pp. 1–9.

Kilroy-Marac, K. (2019) *An impossible inheritance: postcolonial psychiatry and the work of memory in a West African clinic*. Oakland: University of California Press.

Kinyanda, E., Kizza, R., Abbo, C., Ndyanabangi, S. and Levin, J. (2013). 'Prevalence and risk factors of depression in childhood and adolescence as seen in 4 districts of north-eastern Uganda', *BMC International Health and Human Rights*, 13(1), pp. 1–10.

Klein, E., and Mills, C. (2017) 'Psy-expertise, therapeutic culture and the politics of the personal in development', *Third World Quarterly*, 38(9), pp. 1990–2008.

Kodesh, N. (2007). 'History from the healer's shrine: genre, historical imagination, and early Ganda history', *Comparative Studies in Society and History*, 49(3), pp. 527–552.

Kodesh, N. (2010) *Beyond the royal gaze: clanship and public healing in Buganda*. Charlottesville: University ofVirginia Press.

Lan, D., (1985) *Guns & rain: guerrillas & spirit mediums in Zimbabwe*. Oxford: James Currey.

Liu, X. and Li, M. (2020) 'Safeguarding intangible cultural heritage to promote mental healthcare in China: challenges to maintaining the sustainability of safeguarding efforts', *International Journal of Social Psychiatry*, 66(3), pp. 311–13.

Lwanda, J. (2008) 'Poets, culture and orature: a reappraisal of the Malawi political public sphere, 1953–2006', *Journal of Contemporary African Studies*, 26(1), pp. 71–101.

MacRae, J., Zwi, A.B. and Gilson, L. (1996) 'A triple burden for health sector reform: 'post'-conflict rehabilitation in Uganda', *Social Science and Medicine*, 42(7), pp. 1095–1108.

Mahone, S., and Vaughan, M. (eds) (2007) *Psychiatry and empire*. Basingstoke: Palgrave Macmillan.

Makubuya, A.N. (2019) *Protection, patronage, or plunder? British machinations and (B)uganda's struggle for independence*. Cambridge: Cambridge Scholars Publishing.

Mawere, M., and Awuah-Nyamekye, S. (2015) *Between rhetoric and reality: the state and use of indigenous knowledge in post-colonial Africa*. Bamenda: Langaa RPCIG.

Mawere, M., and Mubaya, T.R. (2016) 'Historic buildings, sustainability and colonial heritage in Zimbabwe' in Mawere, M. and Mubaya, T.R. (eds) *Colonial heritage, memory and sustainability in Africa*. Bamenda: Langaa RPCIG, pp. 55–86.

McGregor, J., and Schumaker, L. (2006) 'Heritage in southern Africa: imagining and marketing public culture and history', *Journal of Southern African Studies*, 32(4), pp. 649–65.

Meskell, L., and Scheermeyer, C. (2008) 'Heritage as therapy: set pieces from the new South Africa', *Journal of Material Culture*, 13(2), pp. 153–73.

Mhango, N. (2015) 'Africa must get rid of colonial debris' in Mawere, M. and Mubaya, T.R. (eds) *Colonial heritage, memory and sustainability in Africa*. Bamenda: Langaa RPCIG, pp. 87–104.

Miller, K.E., and Rasmussen, A. (2010) 'War exposure, daily stressors, and mental health in conflict and post-conflict settings: bridging the divide between trauma-focused and psychosocial frameworks', *Social Science & Medicine*, 70(1), pp. 7–16.

Mills, C. (2018) 'From "invisible problem" to global priority: the inclusion of mental health in the Sustainable Development Goals', *Development and Change*, 49(3), pp. 843–66.

Mills, C., and Fernando, S. (2017) 'Globalising mental health or pathologising the Global South? Mapping the ethics, theory and practice of global mental health', *Disability and the Global South*, 1(2), pp. 188–202.

Mills, C., and Hilberg, E. (2019) '"Built for expansion": the "social life" of the WHO's Mental Health GAP Intervention Guide', *Sociology of Health & Illness*, 41(S1), pp. 162–75.

Mollica R.F. (2006) *Healing invisible wounds – paths to hope and recovery in a violent world*. Nashville, TN: Vanderbilt University Press.

Mugishagwe, A. (2014) 'Music and notions of citizenship in the humanitarian work of two NGOs in Uganda', *African Music: Journal of the International Library of African Music*, 9, pp. 72–90.

Muhwezi, W.W., Kinyanda, E., Mungherera, M., Onyango, P., Ngabirano, E., Muron, J., Kagugube, J. and Kajungu, R. (2011) 'Vulnerability to high risk sexual behaviour (HRSB) following exposure to war trauma as seen in post-conflict communities in eastern Uganda: a qualitative study', *Conflict and Health*, 5(22), pp. 1–15.

Mulumba, M., Ruano, A.L., Perehudoff, K. and Ooms, G. (2021) 'Decolonizing health governance: a Uganda case study on the influence of political history on community participation', *Health and Human Rights*, 23(1), pp. 259–71.

Munjeri, D. (2004) 'Tangible and intangible heritage: from difference to convergence', *Museum International*, 56(1–2), pp. 12–20.

Murray, C.J.L., and Lopez, A.D. (eds) (1994) *Global comparative assessments in the health sector: disease burden, expenditures, and intervention packages: collected reprints from the Bulletin of the World Health Organization*. Geneva: World Health Organization.

Musisi, S. (2004) 'Mass trauma and mental health in Africa', *African Health Sciences*, 4(2), pp. 80–2.

Musisi, S. (2021) 'Afrocentricism and healthcare: the legacy of colonial medicine in Uganda', Afya na Haki Centre of Excellence Inaugural Lecture, delivered 4 November 2021. Available at: www.afyanahaki.org/download/27/publications/2278/grand-launch-keynote-address.pdf (Accessed 1 February 2022).

Musisi, S. and Kinyanda E. (2020) 'Long-term impact of war, civil war, and persecution in civilian populations—conflict and post-traumatic stress in African communities', *Frontiers in Psychiatry*, 11(20), pp. 1–12.

Musisi, S., Muron, J. and Nakku, J. (2021) 'Using mobile mental health clinics to increase access to mental health care in rural Africa: the case of Uganda' in Okpaku, S. (ed.) *Innovations in global mental health*. Berlin: Springer, pp 1–20.

Nakalawa, L, Musisi, S., Kinyanda, E. and Okello, E.S. (2010) 'Demon Attack Disease: a case report of mass hysteria after mass trauma in a primary school in Uganda', *African Journal of Traumatic Stress*, 1(1), pp. 43–48.

Nakimuli-Mpungu, E., Okello, J., Kinyanda, E., Alderman, S., Nakku, J., Alderman, J. S., ... Musisi, S. (2013). 'The impact of group counseling on depression, post-traumatic stress and function outcomes: a prospective comparison study in the Peter C. Alderman trauma clinics in northern Uganda', *Journal of Affective Disorders*, 151(1), pp. 78–84.

Nyombi, C., Kibandama A. and Kaddu, R. (2014) 'A critique of the Uganda Mental Health Treatment Act, 1964', *Mental Health Law and Policy Journal* 3(1), pp. 505–26.

Okello, J., Onen, T.S. and Musisi, S. (2007) 'Psychiatric disorders among war-abducted and non-abducted adolescents in Gulu district, Uganda: a comparative study', *African Journal of Psychiatry*, 10(4), pp. 225–31.

Opiyo, L.M. (2015) 'Music as education, voice, memory, and healing: community views on the roles of music in conflict transformation in northern Uganda', *African Conflict and Peacebuilding Review*, 5(1), pp. 41–65.

Ovonji-odida, P.K. (2016) 'Landscapes of memory: a study of memorialization in northern Uganda', M.Arch dissertation: Dalhousie University.

Ovuga, E., Boardman, J. and Oluka, E.G.A.O. (1999) 'Traditional healers and mental illness in Uganda', *The Psychiatrist*, 23(5), pp. 276–79.

Pham, P.N., Vinck, P. and Weinstein, H.M. (2010) 'Human rights, transitional justice, public health and social reconstruction', *Social Science & Medicine*, 70, pp. 98–105.

Pouw, N., and Gilmore, B. (2012) 'Wellbeing in theory and in practice' in Pouw, N. and Baud, I. (eds) *Local governance and poverty in developing nations*. New York and Abingdon: Routledge, pp. 17–31.

Prince M., Patel V., Saxena S., Maj M., Maselko J., Phillips M.R., Rahman A. (2007) 'No health without mental health', *Lancet* 370(9590), pp. 859–77.

Pringle, Y. (2019) *Psychiatry and decolonisation in Uganda*. Basingstoke: Palgrave Macmillan.

Pupavac, V. (2001) 'Therapeutic governance: psycho-social intervention and trauma risk management', *Disasters* 25(4), pp. 358–72.

Rajpal, S. (2020) *Curing madness?: A social and cultural history of insanity in colonial North India, 1800–1950s*. Oxford: Oxford University Press.

Reynolds, P. (1990) 'Children of tribulation: the need to heal and the means to heal war trauma', *Africa*, 60(1), pp. 1–38.

Roberts, B., Ocaka, K.F., Browne, J., Oyok, T. and Sondorp, E. (2008) 'Factors associated with post-traumatic stress disorder and depression amongst internally displaced persons in northern Uganda', *BMC Psychiatry*, 8(1), pp. 1–9.

Schoenbrun, D.L. (2006) 'Conjuring the modern in Africa: durability and rupture in histories of public healing between the Great Lakes of East Africa', *The American Historical Review*, 111(5), pp. 1403–39.

Ssanyu, R. (2007) 'Mental illness and exclusion: putting mental health on the development agenda in Uganda', Chronic Poverty Research Centre Policy Brief no. 2/2007. Kampala: Development Research and Training.

Stiglitz, J., Sen, A. and Fitoussi, J.-P. (2009) *Report by the Commission on the Measurement of Economic Performance and Social Progress*. CMEPSP.

Tankink, M., Bubenzer, F. and van der Walt, S. (2017) *Achieving sustainable peace through an integrated approach to peacebuilding and mental health and psychosocial support: a review of current theory and practice*. Cape Town & Diemen: Institute for Justice and Reconciliation and the War Trauma Foundation.

Tol, W.A., Barbui, C., Galappatti, A., Silove, D., Betancourt, T.S., Souza, R., Golaz, A. and van Ommeren, M. (2011a) 'Mental health and psychosocial support in humanitarian settings: linking practice and research', *The Lancet*, 378(9802), pp. 1581–91.

Tol, W.A., Ebrecht, B., Aiyo, R., Murray, S.M., Nguyen, A.J., Kohrt, B.A., Ndyanabangi, S., Alderman, S., Musisi, S., and Nakku, J. (2018) 'Maternal mental health priorities, help-seeking behaviors, and resources in post-conflict settings: A qualitative study in Eastern Uganda', *BMC Psychiatry* 18(39), pp. 1–15.

Tol, W.A., Patel, V., Tomlinson, M., Baingana, F., Galappatti, A., Panter-Brick, C., Silove, D., Sondorp, E., Wessells, M. and van Ommeren, M. (2011b) 'Research priorities for mental health and psychosocial support in humanitarian settings', *PLOS Medicine* 8(9), pp. 1–5.

UNESCO (2019) *Promoting culture in emergencies*. Paris: UNESCO.

UNESCO (2020) *Intangible cultural heritage lists*. Available at: https://ich.unesco.org/en/lists. (Accessed 18 June 2021).

Ura, K., Alkire, S., Zangmo, T. and Wangdi, K. (2012) *An extensive analysis of GNH index*. The Centre for Bhutan Studies.

Vanhulst, J., and Beling, A.E. (2014) '*Buen vivir*: emergent discourse within or beyond sustainable development?' *Ecological Economics*, 101, pp. 54–63.

Vaughan, M. (2016) 'Changing the subject? Psychological counselling in Eastern Africa', *Public Culture*, 28(3), pp. 499–517.

Vinck, P., Pham, P.N., Stover, E. and Weinstein, H.M. (2007) 'Exposure to war crimes and implications for peace building in northern Uganda', *JAMA* 298(5), pp. 543–54.

Wakabi, W. (2011) 'Uganda coverage sparks war memorials debate', Institute for War and Peace Reporting, 20 October 2011. Available at: https://iwpr.net/global-voices/uganda-coverage-sparks-war-memorials-debate (Accessed 18 June 2021).

Wanjiru, E., Kaburi, C. and Njogu, Z. (2015) 'Resistance and subversion of traditional social construction of gender in Gikuyu narratives, songs and proverbs', *American International Journal of Contemporary Research*, 5(3), pp. 55–62.

Wanjiru, M.W. and Matsubara, K. (2017). 'Street toponymy and the decolonisation of the urban landscape in post-colonial Nairobi', *Journal of Cultural Geography*, 34(1), pp. 1–23.

Wasamba, P. (2015) *Contemporary oral literature fieldwork: a researcher's guide*. Nairobi: University of Nairobi Press.

Wermbter, A. (2016) 'Ambivalent places of memory: mass graves in Teso', *Journal of Peace and Security Studies*, 2(1), pp. 44–56.

Wessells, M., and van Ommeren, M. (2008) 'Developing inter-agency guidelines on mental health and psychosocial support in emergency settings', *Intervention*, 6(3), pp. 199–218.

WHO (2008) *mhGAP: Mental Health Gap Action Programme: scaling up care for mental, neurological and substance use disorders*. Geneva: World Health Organization.

Whyte, S.R., Babiiha, S., Mukyala, R. and Meinert, L. (2014) 'Urbanisation by subtraction: the afterlife of camps in northern Uganda', *The Journal of Modern African Studies* 52(4), pp. 597–622.

Wigham S., Watts P., Zubala A., Jandial S., Bourne J. and Hackett S. (2020) 'Using arts-based therapies to improve mental health for children and young people with physical health long-term conditions: a systematic review of effectiveness', *Frontiers in Psychiatry* 11(1771), pp. 1–15.

World Bank (1993) *World Development Report 1993: investing in health*. Washington DC: World Bank.

World Bank (2015) *Mind, society, and behaviour*. Washington DC: World Bank.

Wu, H.Y-J. (2021) *Mad by the millions: mental disorders in the age of world citizenship, experts, and technology*. Cambridge, MA: MIT.

10

INDIGENOUS KNOWLEDGE AND HEALING

Traditional Obstetric Care and Global Maternal Health in Southwest Nigeria

Tolulope Esther Fadeyi

Introduction

Maternal health as a critical issue has received wide-ranging attention in global developmental plans. The pervasive effects of maternal mortality on sustainable and economic development and efforts at combatting it have made maternal health an essential preoccupation of international agendas in particular the Millennium Development Goals (MDGs) and subsequent Sustainable Development Goals (SDGs). The focal point within these programmes has typically been on development and maternal health while the relationship between heritage, as tradition, and development has been neglected. Although the potential of heritage for development has begun to be realised more recently, including a growing scholarship on heritage and development in Africa, glaring gaps remain including with regards to maternal health.

With a focus on Nigerian and particularly Yoruba heritage knowledge, this chapter draws from and contributes to existing literature on heritage and development in global studies and brings into discourse the potential roles of Indigenous knowledge in improving maternal health. In postcolonial Nigeria, interest in Indigenous knowledge grew from the critique of globalisation. As in other African communities, in colonial Yorubaland, the region which later became known as Southwest Nigeria, Indigenous heritage was threatened as a result of external domination and marginalisation. Against this backdrop, an analysis of Indigenous knowledge on maternal health in response to global development in the 21st century is vital. Maternal development here refers to global transformative processes that utilise cultural knowledge to enhance female reproductive health. Within precolonial Nigeria, such values, norms, social interaction and religious beliefs of a group of people developed in a pre-literate society to satisfy the social, economic, political, physical and spiritual needs of the people. In this chapter, it is suggested that if such

DOI: 10.4324/9781003107361-13

knowledge is integrated into contemporary global institutions, it will engender maternal health and foster development. Previous studies of traditional Yoruba maternal health practices have focused on the legitimacy of Indigenous knowledge but have failed to translate that into policy and mainstream practice. By contrast, this chapter focuses on the way that reframing traditional health through heritage discourses and practices may present a route to the institutionalisation of these practices – which has relevance far beyond the Nigerian case study.

Maternal health in international development

The 1970s marked a new apogee in the quest for improved female reproductive health. In particular, there has been global interest in fostering maternal health, ending preventable maternal mortality, which are a core integral dimension of primary healthcare. For example, several studies stemming from the World Health Organization (WHO) highlighted the causes of rising maternal mortality rates, focusing on the impact of poor nutritional status on women's reproductive health (WHO, 1991) and suggested that figures were ultimately 'underestimated' (WHO, 2015). However, maternal health is determined by a myriad of sociocultural factors, not just nutrition (Berkman et al., 2000). Consequently, the focus on nutrition in isolation has marginalised other more subjective sociocultural factors in the study of maternal health. Furthermore, the reliance on scientific indicators, such as nutritional status, can be seen as a Western, universalist approach that fails to take into account local contexts, including heritage. For instance, certain taboos may differentially and independently impact the reproductive health of women at different stages of pregnancy, child delivery and post-partum care in Southwest Nigeria. These varying sociocultural factors shape maternal health outcomes and account for the variation of maternal mortality rates in different parts of the globe. To illustrate, the estimate of maternal mortality rate per 100,000 per live births in 2017 highlights South Sudan (1,150), Mali (526), Chad (1,140), Gambia (597), Sierra Leone (1,120), Nigeria (917), Somalia (829) and Cote d'Ivoire (617) (Statista, 2022).

The underlying factors behind the distinction in mortality rates in so-called developing and developed countries have been examined. On one hand, these include adequate access to health services as well as social, economic and medical factors. Alvarez et al. (2009) attributed the direct and indirect causes of maternal mortality in sub-Saharan African regions to poor access to prenatal health service, lack of birth personnel training, lack of access to clean water systems and adult illiteracy, as well as an inefficient annual government budget expenditure on maternal health. Studies have also shown the influence of low educational status of women, poverty, patriarchy, cultural norms, beliefs relating to fertility and value placed on having children on maternal health in Africa (Ajiboye and Adebayo, 2012).

It should be emphasised that in Yorubaland, an appealing motherhood is defined and sustained by the ability to have children in all situations. Yoruba culture places great value on children. It is believed that children are worth far more than the luxuries of life and are essential for sustainable legacies (Aládésanmí and

Ògúnjìnmí, 2019). This cultural and economic framing of maternal health has made maternal mortality a threat not only to female reproductive health and motherhood but also sustainable development. The high rate of maternal mortality has attracted the intervention of global health systems to contain the incidence of birth and child delivery complications. These interventions include addressing complex social and cultural issues that affect the successful implementation of maternal health policies. In this way, maternal health has become a priority goal in global policy, featuring prominently in international health agendas and legal frameworks. OHCHR (2018) noted the commendable recognition of female reproductive rights and the enshrinement of such rights in global and regional treaties such as the International Covenant on Civil and Political Rights (ICCPR); the International Covenant on Economic, Social and Cultural Rights (ICESCR); and the Convention on the Elimination of All Forms of Discrimination against Women. In furtherance of this course, the MDGs and SDGs have made considerable efforts to engender maternal health.

The emergence and growth of non-governmental health advocates and global movements has led to light being shone on the issues of disadvantaged and vulnerable women in sub-Saharan Africa within global development discourse. A major breakthrough was achieved in 1987 with the establishment of the Safe Motherhood Initiative (SMI) to bridge socio-economic inequalities and marginalisation while focusing on international health efforts to engender maternal health in rural communities (Maine and Rosenfield, 1999). In 2005, this global effort was complemented by the establishment of the Partnership for Maternal, Newborn and Child Health (PMNCH) in New Delhi with the aim of achieving MDGs 4 and 5 on maternal and child health (PMNCH, 2009). The unproductive fragmented global health initiatives and the rapid spread of international Public-Private Partnerships (PPPs) that characterised PMNCH has been heavily criticised (Reich, 2002; Harmer, 2011). The core argument is that the growth of private organisations like Bill and Melinda Gates Foundation have undermined the potential service delivery of the WHO and national governments to promote integrated maternal health outcomes. With illustration from cases in malaria and GAVI (the Vaccine Alliance), ethnographers have argued that private organisations limited their focus to safe issues and appropriate the broader policy agenda (Eckl, 2014; Storeng, 2014). Evidence has shown the use of technological devices, such as infusion pumps, electronic foetal monitoring, ultrasonography, blood pressure screening and maternal/foetal pulse oximetry, contribute to reducing risks during pregnancy and eventual incidences of maternal mortality (Miesnik and Stringer, 2002).

Numerous social scientific studies have broached issues relating to frequent friction arising among partners at the local, regional and global levels. The basic argument is that maternal health as a global issue has moved out of the shell of WHO and has witnessed the involvement of relatively new actors such as the Bill and Melinda Gates Foundation and pharmaceutical firms who have shouldered the responsibility of addressing and containing incidences of preventable pregnancy complications and mortality (Ruger and Yach, 2009). In addition are international and local non-governmental organisations including International Women's Health Program, Saving Mothers and AbiyeAfrica Health foundation who work with rural and disadvantaged sub-Saharan Africans to advance the principal goals of global policy on maternal health, such as providing maternity kits, essential medicine, antenatal and postnatal medical care and first aid obstetric services during birth emergencies. Their development programme fashioned along Western expertise and experience is relatively imposed on the Global South with little consideration for Indigenous forms of knowledge. There is still more to be done on the incorporation and training of local traditional midwives who are more integrated into the African soil and understand the social, physical and spiritual maternal needs of the people.

Multidisciplinary approaches to engendering maternal health are key. In addition, the relationship between pregnant women's mental health and foetus development, the prevention of pregnancy complications, including reduced chances of bipolar disorder and panic attack, need to be foregrounded. For example, as argued by the WHO (2008) mental health disorders contribute to maternal mortality and morbidity (Oates, 2003). The varying dimensions of mental health such as– emotional and behavioural – have been well incorporated into the global health agenda and statistical indicators of mental maternal health have been advanced at the global health level (Singh et al., 2021). This perspective constituted the core of Baron et al.'s (2016) analysis of maternal mental health in five districts. The study not only evaluated the varying prevalence of perinatal depression and alcohol consumption by pregnant women but also attested to the fact that analysis of maternal health would not be complete without a mention of mental health.

Engendering maternal health is closely embedded in, and is a precondition for, achieving sustainable development. In general, sociocultural and environmental factors have direct and mediated impact on maternal health. Efforts to address such factors make vital contributions to the understanding of the nexus between heritage and maternal health. It is argued here that this nexus is best understood and accelerated by interventions in heritage projects beyond the maternal health sector, particularly through efforts in awareness, hygiene, nutrition and the environment. The cultural norms, beliefs and values of a particular society shape maternal health outcomes. These intangible heritages are not only complimentary to maternal health but also highly instructive to the overall sustainable development. Both maternal health and sustainable development integrate social, economic, political, environmental and cultural factors to produce meaningful health outcomes. Consequently, sustainable development is not achievable in societies characterised by socio-economic inequalities, shortage of basic amenities and environmental pollution. For example, the Human Rights Council established a legal framework for sustainable development with emphasis on the reduction of maternal mortality and morbidity to the barest minimum taking into consideration adequate respect for human rights obligations and commitments. Efforts at combating the menace of maternal mortality constitute a vital nucleus of the SDG agenda through 2030 (WHO, 2018).

The application of human rights to address preventable causes of maternal mortality and morbidity includes gender empowerment, provision of basic health amenities and the protection of women against structural violence (Yamin, 2013). Fundamental human rights have provided impetus to strategies to engender maternal health in the event of violation of rights. With the shift from addressing maternal mortality and morbidity as a public health concern to as a matter of human rights, international human rights treaties saw the need to safeguard inalienable reproductive rights. In this regard, states were saddled with the responsibilities of providing appropriate resources and eliminating any form of discrimination and inequality that may result in maternal mortality. Championing this course, the Committee on Economic, Social and Cultural Rights (CESCR) in 2018 strongly advocated that states ensure reproductive, maternal and child healthcare. It established that the

> lack of emergency obstetric care services or denial of abortion often leads to maternal mortality and morbidity, which in turn constitutes a violation of the right to life or security, and in certain circumstances can amount to torture or cruel, inhuman or degrading treatment.
>
> *OHCHR, 2018*

Despite the legal mechanism put in place to enforce reproductive health rights, there arise questions on states' compliance with treaty obligations (Cook, 1994). Neglect of and failure to implement female reproductive health rights tends to increase chances of maternal mortality especially in disadvantaged communities (Gebhard and Trimino, 2011).

To enhance reproductive health globally, researchers and health analysts need to gear efforts towards how women in disadvantaged and rural communities integrate themselves into the use of information and communication technologies, in particular internet and mobile phones to access vital pregnancy-related information (Sunday and Wynn, 2015). Information and communications technologies have been decisive in the preservation and dissemination of Indigenous knowledge on birth, pregnancy and reproductive health, hence, Indigenous knowledge systems are embedded within contemporary scientific knowledge. In the context of Southwest Nigeria, Olatokun and Ayanbode (2009) posit that communication among women who possess enormous knowledge on childrearing, birthing practices and production can be enhanced through access to innovative information technology devices. Through this medium, maternal health issues such as changes in body mass, body changes, physical changes, emotional changes and behavioural disorders are deliberated upon. This in turn fosters smooth interaction between pregnant women and health practitioners as well supporting sustainable heritage practices. It will provide avenues for health promotion and enhance effective ways of communicating through such channels, despite overwhelming distance and low levels of infrastructural development. Any attempt to accelerate positive maternal outcomes must include the need to enlighten rural women on access and usage of health communication gadgets. Indeed, this will open a new vista of research to investigate the potentials of cultural heritage and development. Less well analysed is how material and non-material heritage such as water, plant, sacred groves, rituals and incantation can improve maternal health. It is high time that heritage and development researchers, respectively, rise to the task of investigating how the reconstructed African past as heritage can be useful for developmental aims regarding maternal health (Lee, 2004).

Heritage of healing: maternal health in Southwest Nigeria

Indigenous knowledge as a form of cultural heritage is essentially unique and specific to a given culture and society. Local people's knowledge of their health, illnesses and diseases, otherwise known as Indigenous medical knowledge, is decisive to engendering maternal health. The unrelenting efforts of communities in the production and transmission of knowledge reflect their cultural, ecological and socio-economic landscapes (Bruchac, 2014). Furthering this argument, Ellen and Harris (1996) have argued that Indigenous knowledge not only engenders the environment but also fosters global development since the past century. For example, Aderemi et al. (2019) has situated the Yoruba people as major custodians and reservoirs of knowledge on plants and herbs, and shed light on how their medical practices, techniques and application of reproductive ethnomedicine have found considerable expression and interest among scholars of science as essential in promoting sustainable development. By 2007, the recognition of traditional medicine and the conservation of herbal plants without any form of discrimination was refined to a higher state of cultural heritage. As envisaged by WHO, 'some strategies have been put in place to support Member States in developing proactive policies and implementing action plans that will strengthen the role traditional medicine plays in keeping populations healthy' (WHO, 2013). The potential impact of local plants, herbal products, medicinal practices and techniques have been appropriately harnessed to support the health and well-being of the people, and in particular reproductive health. The state recognition of traditional medicine in the prevention and treatment of diseases has brought to the fore the relevance of Indigenous knowledge in the global health service system. Indigenous knowledge plays a very vital role in sustainable development since it is viewed as an institutionalised social responsibility of the whole society (United Nations Department of Economic and Social Affairs Indigenous Peoples, 2007).

Within discussions of Indigenous knowledge as a form of cultural heritage, historians' attention has shifted to the cultural encounter between Africans and Europeans and the impact of colonialism on Indigenous knowledge systems (Olufemi, 1993; Olaore and Drolet, 2017) with a specific focus on medicinal knowledge (Konadu, 2007; Abdullah, 2011; Amusa and Ogidan 2017). Such studies have underscored the negative impact of colonialism on Indigenous medicine. This includes a deliberate undermining of African healers' capacity, healing objects and their skills (Feierman, 1985; Tilley, 2016). In addition, literature has focused on pregnant women's patronage of different health therapies and how the system of local diagnosis and management of diseases shapes the attitude of pregnant women in the utilisation of biomedical facilities. For this reason, Ilesanmi Paul (2018), pointing to the mid-19th century, has highlighted how missionary medicine condemned the use of divinations, which constituted an integral aspect of diagnosing metaphysical orchestrated diseases among the Yoruba. It has also been argued regarding Yorubaland that, although CT scans can provide explanations on the state of a pregnant woman's inflammatory respond to infection, a local herbalist through divination can tell why a particular pregnant woman (and not another) has maternal sepsis at a particular stage of pregnancy (Awolalu, 1979). Such perspectives have added fresh ideas to addressing issues of maternal mortality. However, there is a clarion call for an integrative healthcare system in Southwest Nigeria taking into consideration the interplay of culture and health (Odunlade and Okiki, 2018).

Healing constitutes an integral element of African cultural heritage, which bridges the gap between the past and the future. It transcends beyond the physical heritage and encompasses aesthetic, spiritual, symbolic and other social values. Harriet Deacon (2004) rightly posited that healing as a living heritage includes but is not limited to traditional knowledge, dance, ritual, music, language, oral traditions and cultural spaces. This brings to fore the social and cultural significance of objects and places ascribed to a group of people through heritage developed as a result of complex historical processes aimed at accelerating the physical, social, cultural, medical and economic needs of the people across the globe (Giblin, 2014; Fredheim and Khalaf, 2016; Jones, 2017). In recent times, emphasis has shifted towards the intangible 'cultural values' accrued to heritage rather than tangible physical objects of heritage (Schofield, 2014).

UNESCO's Local and Indigenous Knowledge Systems programme (LINKS) has made considerable effort at promoting Indigenous medical knowledge and its implementation in global maternal health policy. In the spirit of fostering maternal development, UNESCO has advocated for the integration of scientific and local knowledge in the preservation and management of cultural heritage through a series of conventions and legal frameworks (UNESCO, 2003). Such efforts to integrate science and other forms of knowledge by UNESCO include incorporating Indigenous knowledge into global maternal health programmes in various communities, thus reaffirming the significance of cultural heritage in sustainable development. This global effort has fostered multidisciplinary collaboration among scientists, researchers, cultural experts, and scholars of history and heritage to map out methodologies, which will further enhance understandings of maternal health processes, adaptation and implementation. UNESCO's efforts to further enhance the continuous transmission of Indigenous medical knowledge across diverse cultures and generations have been influential in contemporary global policy:

> traditional and local knowledge systems … make and historically have made a valuable contribution to science and technology… there is a need to preserve, protect, research and promote this cultural heritage and empirical knowledge.
>
> *UNESCO LINKS, 2017*

The potential of integrating heritage projects in development health interventions through the use of arts-based methods have been largely explored in literature highlighting the dynamics of a cultural approach to development (Bandarin et. al., 2011:19). Art-based methods, such as images of mothering, photovoice, visual arts, drawings, storytelling, photographs, literary arts, music and song, have been used to communicate health messages to pregnant women and yielded positive maternal outcomes (Fraser and Al Sayah, 2011; Godfrey-Isaacs, 2019). The instrumentalisation of art objects such as music, visual arts, poetry, songs, storytelling and other literary forms were found to be effective in reducing pregnancy induced depression, anxiety and blood pressure levels as well as other complications during childbirth. As Toberna et al., (2020: 214) observe, dance is effective in reducing prolonged labour arising from pregnancy complications. As discussed by Olusegun (2019: 136), the literature remains silent on the impact of medical ethnomusicology on antenatal and postnatal health. For example, engaging in such dance and songs may reduce the duration and intensity of pain during labour and childbirth (Orimogunje, 2003; Taiwo and Salami, 2007; Campbell, 2013). Hence, it is essential that local projects should be initiated within the horizons of cultural relations at larger scales, with due consideration for the recognition of local institutions. Specifically, music has been found to be a culturally appropriate method to enhance pregnancy and maternal mental health. Such approaches have particularly yielded positive outcomes in Southwest Nigeria since expectant and pregnant women engage in musical practices to enhance pregnancy as well as to reduce antenatal and post-partum stress. Although music as a Yoruba heritage influences the normal psyche of the enchanter (expectant mother), analysis of its evolution and production of such knowledge poses a major challenge in appropriating its potentials in fostering sustainable development because it has not been institutionalised. An important question that readily comes to mind is the variations and implications in the responses to maternal depression from one person and region to another. The memories of re-enactment of fertility rituals, sacrifices, incantation, literary verses, usage of herbs and leaves, are now transmitted as historical knowledge. The transmission of such intangible cultural heritage across generations has been dynamic among different cultural groups (Lenzerini, 2011). Attempts to integrate intangible cultural heritage as a health policy initiative poses an imminent threat particularly to the viability of cultural heritage and development and the efforts to safeguard the former, which are crucial to the survival of the local tradition (Mabulla, 2000). Such questions constitute an important discussion in the transmission of intangible heritage from one generation to another. Thus, to a large extent, ability to strengthen and reinforce efforts at safeguarding heritage is key to sustainable development.

More specifically, WHO in their awareness programmes have advocated for an integrated healthcare system that will address female reproductive health problems during pregnancy and child delivery (WHO, 2022). In Britain, access to and interaction with heritage have consistently resulted in the treatment of well-being and mental conditions (Pennington et al., 2019). More precisely, Kay (2018) provided useful explanations on how heritage crafts aid perinatal health of women in the community. Despite the anecdotal and professional experience that characterised the aforementioned examples, they vividly portray interconnectedness between heritage and health in Britain. However, more research still needs to be done on the impact of colonialism on cultural heritage especially in the Global South. With the enactment of colonial witchcraft acts in the Global South, the potentials of promoting cultural heritage diminished. Conversely, the shrouded secrecy that characterised Yoruba traditional medicine counters UNESCO's primary goals of knowledge transmission and 'regeneration' (Maclean, 1971; Ademuwagen, 1979).

Natural and cultural heritage are inseparable with regards to their importance for maternal health. For example, rivers as natural heritage are integral for cultural heritage practices such as rituals, literature, sacrifice, social and religious rites, all of which have been embedded in the instrumentalisation of heritage for health. Similarly, the application of herbs and plants, as natural heritage, have aided holistic psychotherapy during pregnancy and childbirth delivery across many different cultures (Adams et al., 2009; Aiala et al., 2019). This perspective thus calls for approaches that consider 'landscapes of healing' or 'healing environments' for maternal health as a form of holistic healing (Borokini and Lawal, 2014).

Encountering motherhood: understanding Yoruba heritage knowledge

Heritage sites

The Osun Oshogbo sacred grove is good example of the importance of heritage for maternal health in Nigeria. In many places in Africa, groves are believed to be powerful places, possessing sociocultural, transformative capacities, and the ability to enhance communication with ancestors, as well as to contribute towards fertility and healing (Carmichael et al., 1994). This is true in Southwest Nigeria where groves are associated with fertility and healing, with Osun Oshogbo sacred grove being the most important. Yoruba speaking people believe that the Osun grove can act as an antidote to infertility and prevent pregnancy and post-partum complications. As the ultimate source of fertility and healing, through which motherhood and maternal health are engendered, the Osun grove has immense cultural heritage value. In this way, as discussed by Lenzrini (2011), the Osun grove is a form of living heritage as a cultural connecting cord between its creators and their recipients and a reflection of Yoruba cosmological systems and cultural heritage. More importantly, Osun water, used to prepare healing rituals for the revitalisation of maternal bodies among the Yoruba people in Southwest Nigeria, is a veritable intangible heritage (Falokun,1993).

Osun grove has also officially been recognised as a site of national and international importance. In 1977 Nigeria hosted the Second Black and African Festival of Arts and Culture (FESTAC), an event which revisited the roots of African heritage and heralded its uniqueness (Moore, 1977: 20). As a legacy of FESTAC, where it was promoted, Osun Oshogbo sacred grove became known widely as a site of healing, commerce, tourism, fertility, art and festivity in a global setting (Appadurai and Breckenridge, 2002) and latterly became a UNESCO world heritage site in July 2005.

Despite the importance of heritage sites such as Osun Oshogbo sacred grove for heritage and fertility, however, in most cases, attempts at instrumentalising heritage for maternal health have faced challenges stemming from lack of funds, weak health systems, poor governmental structures, dependence of local states on external funding for implementation, inefficient decision-making bodies, distinctive objectives between the various stakeholders involved, political instability and poor relationships between the donors and government (Onyima, 2016).

Traditional healers

Recent research has shifted to the symbiotic relationship between healers and medical doctors in an attempt to engender maternal health in post-independence Nigeria. Ahmed et al. (2005) have observed how in contemporary times maternal health equipment, such as ultrasound scan and foetal stethoscopes, are being

FIGURE 10.1 *Olomowewe iya Osun*. Depiction of Osun as a mother figure with numerous children

Source: Photo taken by author.

employed by traditional healers to diagnosis their patients but within their cultural lens. On the other side, medical personnel have been employing divination to inquire about medical conditions that appear to defy Western treatment. This cooperation has fostered the formal training of traditional birth attendants in the system of Western obstetrics and midwifery, while traditional healers have been successfully integrated into maternal healthcare as counsellors and educators (Matthews et al., 1995). In maternal healthcare, a growing body of literature in Southwest Nigeria shows that healers with adequate knowledge of traditional medicine can be effectively equipped with Western systems of healthcare delivery and can efficiently deliver psychosocial interventions for women with a range of pregnancy and childbirth complications (Oyeneyin et al., 2021). This has shaped the patronage of integrative maternal healthcare system especially among the educated elites. However, research on how Indigenous medical knowledge can be preserved for posterity and developed is scarce.

Integrating Indigenous knowledge into Western medicine thus has the potential to improve health outcomes as well as accelerate effective program interventions. Ultimately, global maternal health policy must consider Indigenous medical knowledge in a bid to equip and prepare medical practitioners for the tasks of successful development health outcomes because local beliefs influence the process of birth, pregnancy, reproduction and motherhood. By so doing, this will expedite the need for collaborative effort in the application of Indigenous medical knowledge to obstetrics and gynaecological practices within changing local settings. This perspective parallels King et al.'s (2012) insightful accounts of how interdisciplinary research in gynaecology and obstetrics practices aid the reduction of global maternal mortality.

The previous two decades of the 20th Century have opened new vistas of research on the dynamics of historical change and the state of Indigenous medical knowledge as a process rather than an archive (Lwanga, 2014). If the significance of herbs, roots and plants in the sustenance of human lives is well appreciated, no doubt, individuals' attitudes and knowledge of preserving herbs will drastically increase. Botanical gardens and biotechnical approaches offer unique roles in improving the yield and potency of medicinal plants and herbs through the development of propagation and cultivation protocols (Chen et al., 2016). The Yoruba of Southwest Nigeria have rich Indigenous knowledge and production techniques on the use of herbs and plants to enhance the birthing process and overall female reproductive health. Plants and roots have served numerous purposes such as traditional medicine and herbal preparations for the treatment of medical conditions during pregnancy and the post-partum period. In this way, the retention of local knowledge on the use of plants will greatly determine sustainable health development outcomes. More importantly, collaborative research with Indigenous communities to keep and sustain such knowledge of traditional herbal medicine should be prioritised. By so doing, new approaches to health management will be opened.

Indigenous knowledge as a form of heritage illuminates understanding of the dynamics of maternal health and healing in Southwest Nigeria. Knowledge of ritual and sacrifice has aided treatment of complications during pregnancy and childbirth. It has fulfilled the traditional, social and cultural mandate of engendering human lives and the society at large. Following encounters with certain leaves and herbs, traditional healers and other custodians of oral tradition were saddled with the responsibility to safeguard the lives of the people. Knowledge was imparted by gods and ancestors to healers, hunters and priests who also established the basic institutions of the medical community. The memories of re-enactment of fertility rituals, sacrifices, incantation, literary verses, usage of herbs and leaves, are now transmitted as historical knowledge. It is expected that such knowledge was transmitted to people to conserve herbs and plants around them for the use of humanity. However, the disruption of healing streams, sacrificial objects, and prenatal rituals during periods of beautification have done more harm (Onyima, 2016).

Conclusion

The literature on maternal health and healing has received considerable analysis in historical scholarship. There have been numerous publications on the impact of heritage on sustainable development, and of interventions of international organisations in engendering maternal health as well as the preservation of art-based knowledge in Southwest Nigeria. However, little attention has been drawn to the interconnectedness between Indigenous knowledge as a form of heritage and global maternal health. Within the rich Yoruba heritage, the cultural potentials of divination, incantation, songs, birthing skills, offering of sacrifice and rituals, appeasement of gods and deities, herbal preparation, treatment of diseases, spirituality, cultural practices, social interactions and healing are clear. More research is needed that explores sociocultural dynamics of Indigenous knowledge and maternal health. Such research is equally important to appreciate the impact of Indigenous knowledge in improving maternal health of communities across the globe.

Researchers, policy makers and experts in sustainable development must take into cognisance the relationship between African heritage knowledge and development. Equally, efforts must be made to integrate such medical knowledge into obstetric practices within the local, national and global community. As envisaged by MHTF (2021), the United Nations' goal of containing maternal mortality rates to less than 70 per 100,000 live births in 2030 will advance female reproductive health. This will accelerate integrative knowledge on maternal health in disadvantaged communities in particular in sub-Saharan Africa where maternal mortality has eaten deep into the normal psyche of vulnerable pregnant women. For sustainable development to be effective, the health of the people must be culturally, economically and environmentally harnessed. Globalisation has eroded the viable potentials of Indigenous knowledge in many African nations and they have been constrained from applying such knowledge to sustainable development in disease management, health, energy, agriculture and biodiversity. To achieve efficient sustainable development, local cultural heritage must be harnessed with global development goals.

References

Abdullah, A.A. (2011) 'Trends and challenges of traditional medicine in Africa', *African Journal of Traditional Complementary and Alternative Medicine* 8(5), pp. 115–123.

Adams, J., Lui, C.W., Sibbritt, D., Broom, A., Wardle, J., Homer, C. and Beck, S. (2009) 'Women's use of complementary and alternative medicine during pregnancy: a critical review of the literature', *Birth*, 36(3), pp. 237–45.

Ahmed, O.A, Odunukwe, N.N., Akinwale, O.P., Raheem, T.Y., Efienemokwu, C.E., Ogedengbe, O. and Salako, L.A. (2005) 'Knowledge and practices of traditional birth attendants in prenatal services in Lagos State, Nigeria', *African Journal of Medicine and Medical Sciences*, 34(1), pp. 55–8.

Aiala, A.S., Sonibare, M.A., Gbadamosi, I.T., Olaleye, S.K., Odeku, O., Adegoke, A.O. and Adejumo, A.G. (2019) 'Validation of Ewé'fá as herbal recipes for reproductive health problems (RHPs) among the Yorùbá of South-Western Nigeria', *Journal of Herbal Medicine Research*, 4(38). Available at: https://escipub.com/Articles/JHMR/JHMR-2019-08-2605.pdf (Accessed 28 March 2022).

Ajiboye, O.E. and Adebayo K.A. (2012) 'Socio-cultural factors affecting pregnancy outcome among the Ogu speaking people of Badagry area of Lagos State, Nigeria', *International Journal of Humanities and Social Science*, 2(4), pp. 133–44.

Aládésanmí, O. and Ògúnjìnmí, I. (2019) 'Yorùbá thoughts and beliefs in child birth and child moral upbringing: a cultural perspective', *Advances in Applied Sociology*, 9, pp. 569–85.

Alvarez, J.L., Gil, R., Hernández, V. and Gil, A. (2009) 'Factors associated with maternal mortality in sub-Saharan Africa: An ecological study', *BMC Public Health* 9, 462. doi: 10.1186/1471-2458-9-462

Amusa, S.B. and Ogidan, C.A. (2017) 'Yoruba indigenous medical knowledge: a study of the nature, dynamisms, and resilience of Yoruba medicine', *Journal of the Knowledge Economy* 8, pp. 977–86.

Appadurai, A. and Breckenridge, C. (2002) 'Museums are good to think: heritage on view in India', in Boswell, D. and Evans, J. (eds) *Representing the nation*. London: Routledge, pp. 404–20.

Awolalu, O. (1979) *Yoruba beliefs and sacrificial rites*. White Plains, NY: Longman.

Bandarin, F., Hosagrahar, J. and Albernaz, F.S. (2011) 'Why development needs culture', *Journal of Cultural Heritage Management and Sustainable Development* 1(1), pp. 15–25.

Baron, E.C., Hanlon, C., Mall, S., Honikman, S., Breuer, E., Kathree, T., Luitel, N.P., Nakku, J., Lund, C., Medhin, G., Patel, V., Petersen, I., Shrivastava, S. and Tomlinson, M. (2016) 'Maternal mental health in primary care in five low- and middle-income countries: a situational analysis', *BMC Health Services Research*, 16(53).

Berkman, L., Glymour, M. and Kawachi, I. (2000) *Social epidemiology*. Oxford: Oxford University Press.

Borokini, T. and Ibrahim, L. (2014) 'Traditional medicine practices among the Yoruba people of Nigeria: a historical perspective', *Journal of Medicinal Plants Studies*, 2(6), pp. 20–33.

Bruchac, M. (2014) 'Indigenous knowledge and traditional knowledge', in Smith, C. (ed.) *Encyclopedia of global archaeology*. New York: Springer, pp. 3814–24.

Campbell, L. (2013) 'Movement and dance: deep medicine for pregnancy, labour and birth', *Essentially MIDIRS*, 4(4), pp. 40–5.

Carmichael, D.L., Hubert, J., Reeves, B. and Schanche, A. (1994) *Sacred sites, sacred places*. London: Routledge.

Chen, S-L., Yu, H., Luo, H-M., Wu, Q., Chun-Fang, L. and Steinmetz, A. (2016) 'Conservation and sustainable use of medicinal plants: problems, progress and prospects', *Chinese Medicine*, 11, p. 37.

Cook, R.J. (1994) *Women's health and human rights: the promotion and protection of women's health through international human rights law*. Geneva: World Health Organization.

Deacon, H. (2004) 'Intangible heritage in conservation management plans: the case of Robben Island', *International Journal of Heritage Studies*, 10(3), pp. 309–19.

Eckl, J. (2014) 'The power of private foundations: Rockefeller and Gates in the struggle against Malaria', *Global Social Policy*, (14), pp. 91–116.

Ellen, R. and Harris, H. (1996) 'Concepts of indigenous environmental knowledge in scientific and development studies literature – a critical assessment', Paper presented at the East-West Environmental Linkages Network Workshop 3. Canterbury UK, 8–10 May 1996.

Falokun, F. (1993) *Osun, Ifa and the spirit of the river*. New York: Original Publications.

Feierman, S. (1985) 'Struggles for control: the social roots of health and healing in modern Africa', *African Studies Review*, 28(2/3), pp. 73–147.

Fraser, K. and Al Sayah, F. (2011) 'Arts-based methods in health research: a systematic review of the literature', *Arts and Health*, 3(2), pp. 110–45.

Fredheim, L.H. and Khalaf, M. (2016) 'The significance of values: heritage value typologies re-examined', *International Journal of Heritage Studies*, 22(6), pp. 466–81.

Gebhard, J. and Trimiño, D. (2012) *Reproductive rights, international regulation*. Oxford: Oxford University Press..

Giblin, J.D. (2014) 'Post-conflict heritage: symbolic healing and cultural renewal', *International Journal of Heritage Studies*, 20(5), pp. 500–18.

Godfrey-Isaacs, L. (2019) 'Maternal journal – championing 'arts in health' initiatives in maternity', *The Practising Midwife*, 22(5), pp. 1–7.

Harmer, A. (2011) 'Understanding change in global health policy: ideas, discourse and networks', *Global Public Health*, 6, pp. 703–18.

Jones, Sian (2017) 'Wrestling with the social value of heritage: problems, dilemmas and opportunities', *Journal of Community Archaeology & Heritage*, 4(1), pp. 21–37.

Kay, J. (2018) *The expressive lives of elders: folklore, art, and aging*. Bloomington: Indiana University Press.

King, T.L., Laros, R.K. and Parer, J.T. (2012) 'Interprofessional collaborative practice in obstetrics and midwifery', *Obstetrics and Gynecology Clinics of North America*, 39(3), pp. 411–22.

Konadu, K. (2007) *Indigenous medicine and knowledge in African society*. New York and London: Routledge.

Lee, A.J. (2004) 'Historians as managers of the nation's cultural heritage', *American Studies International*, 42(2/3), pp. 118–136.

Lenzerini, F. (2011) 'Intangible cultural heritage: the living culture of peoples', *European Journal of International Law*, 22(1), pp. 101–20.

Lwanga, H. (2014) 'Indigenous medicinal knowledge', in Gunstone R. (ed.) *Encyclopedia of science education*. Dordrecht: Springer, pp. 492–493.

Mabulla, A.Z.P. (2000) 'Strategy for cultural heritage management (CHM) in Africa: a case study', *The African Archaeological Review*, 17(4), pp. 211–33.

Maclean, U. (1971) *Magical medicine: a Nigerian case study*. London: Allen Lane.

Maine, D. and Rosenfield, A. (1999) 'The Safe Motherhood Initiative: why has it stalled?', *American Journal of Public Health*, 89, pp. 480–2.

Maternal Health Task Force (MHTF) (2021) *The Sustainable Development Goals and maternal mortality*. Available at: www.mhtf.org/topics/the-sustainable-development-goals-and-maternal-mortality/ (Accessed 18th December 2021).

Matthews, M.K., Walley, R.L., Ward, A., Akpaidem, M., Williams, P. and Umoh, A. (1995) 'Training traditional birth attendants in Nigeria--the pictorial method', *World Health Forum*, 16(4), pp. 409–13.

Miesnik, S. and Stringer, M. (2002) 'Technology in the birthing room', *Nursing Clinics of North America*, 37(4), pp. 781–93.

Moore, S. (1977) *The Afro-Black connection, FESTAC 77: report for the Dutch Ministry of Culture, Recreation and Social Work*. Amsterdam: Royal Tropical Institute.

Oates, M. (2003) 'Perinatal psychiatric disorders: a leading cause of maternal morbidity and mortality', *British Medical Bulletin*, 67, pp. 219–29.

Odunlade, R.O. and Okiki, O.C. (2018) 'Exploring the role of information managers in knowledge transfer and preservation among the "Elewe Omos" (indigenous herbal medicine practitioners) of the Yorubas in Nigeria', *Journal of Information and Knowledge Management*, 9(4), pp. 142–59.

Office of the United Nations High Commissioner for Human Rights (OHCHR) (2018) *Your health, your choice, your rights: international and regional obligations on sexual and reproductive health and rights*. Dagoretti South: Ipas Africa Alliance. Available at: www.ohchr.org/sites/default/files/Documents/Issues/Women/OHCHRFactsheetYourHealth.pdf (Accessed 18th December 2021).

Olaore, A.Y. and Drolet, J. (2017) 'Indigenous knowledge, beliefs, and cultural practices for children and families in Nigeria', *Journal of Ethnic and Cultural Diversity in Social Work*, 26(3), pp. 254–70.

Olatokun, W. and Ayanbode, O. (2009) 'Use of indigenous knowledge by women in a Nigerian rural community', *Indian Journal of Indigenous Knowledge*, 8(2), pp. 287–295.

Olufemi, T. (1993) 'Colonialism and its aftermath: the crisis of knowledge production', *Callaloo*, 16(4), pp. 891–908.

Olusegun, S.T. (2019) 'The roles of Yoruba songs on pregnancy, labour and baby care in antenatal and postnatal clinic in southwestern Nigerian hospitals', *Lwati: A Journal of Contemporary Research*, 4(2), pp. 136–55.

Onyima, B.N. (2016) 'Nigerian cultural heritage: preservation, challenges and prospects', *OGIRISI: A New Journal of African Studies*, 12(1), pp. 273–92.

Orimogunje, O.C. (2003) 'The social context of verbal arts in the Yoruba indigenous healthcare practices', *Folklore (Tartu)*, 24(8), pp. 90–98.

Oyeneyin, L., Osunmakinwa, O. and Olagbuji, Y. (2021) 'Incorporating traditional birth attendants into the mainstream maternal health system in Nigeria – An evaluation of the Ondo State Agbebiye program', *African Journal of Reproductive Health*, 25(4), pp. 82–88.

Paul, I.A. (2018) 'The survival of the Yorùbá healing systems in the modern age', *Yoruba Studies Review*, 2(2), pp. 1–21.

Pennington, A., Jones, R., Begnall, A.-M., South, J. and Corcoran, R. (2019) *Heritage and wellbeing: the impact of historic places and assets on community wellbeing – A scoping review*. London: What Works Centre for Wellbeing.

PMNCH (2009) Partnership Vision: Invest, Deliver, Advance [Online]. https://pmnch.who.int/ (Accessed 6th May 2022).

Reich, M.R. (2002) *Public-private partnerships for public health*. Cambridge, MA: Harvard University Press.

Ruger, J.P. and Yach, D. (2009) 'The global role of the World Health Organization', *Global Health Governance*, 2(2), pp. 1–11.

Schofield, J. (2014) 'Heritage expertise and the everyday: citizens and authority in the Twenty-First Century', in Schofield, J. (ed.) *Who needs experts? Counter-mapping cultural heritage*. Farnham: Ashgate, pp. 1–12.

Singh, M., Stacey, T., Abayomi, J., and Simkhada, P. (2021) 'Maternal mental health and infant and young child undernutrition: protocol for a systematic review', *BMJ Open*, 11, e044989.

Statista (2022) *African countries with the highest maternal mortality rate in 2017 (deaths per 100,000 live births*. Available at: www.statista.com/statistics/1122869/maternal-mortality-rate-in-africa-by-country/ (Accessed 28th February 2022).
Storeng, K.T. (2014) 'The GAVI alliance and the "Gates approach" to health system strengthening', *Global Public Health*, 9(8), pp. 865–79.
Sunday, O.O. and Wynn, R. (2015) 'The use of cell phones and radio communication systems to reduce delays in getting help for pregnant women in low- and middle-income countries: a scoping review', *Global Health Action*, 8(1), 28887.
Taiwo, R. and Salami, F. (2007) 'Discourse acts in antenatal clinic literacy classroom in South-Western Nigeria', *Lingustik online*, 31(2), pp. 1–20.
Tilley, H. (2016) 'Medicine, empires, and ethics in colonial Africa', *AMA Journal of Ethics*, 18(7), pp. 743–53.
Toberna, C.P., Horter, D., Heslin, K., Forgie, M.M., Malloy, E. and Kram, J.J.F. (2020) 'Dancing during labor: social media trend or future practice?' *Journal of Patient-Centered Research and Review*, 7(2), pp. 213–17.
UNESCO (2003) *Convention for the safeguarding of the intangible heritage*. Paris: UNESCO.
UNESCO's Local and Indigenous Knowledge Systems Programme (LINKS) (2017) *Local knowledge, global goals*. Paris: UNESCO. Available at: https://unesdoc.unesco.org/ark:/48223/pf0000259599 (Accessed 24 April 2022).
United Nations Department of Economic and Social Affairs Indigenous Peoples (2007) *United Nations Declaration of the Rights of Indigenous People*. Available at: www.un.org/development/desa/indigenouspeoples/declaration-on-the-rights-of-indigenous-peoples.html (Accessed 11th November 2021).
World Health Organization (WHO) (1991) *Strengthening maternal and child health programs through primary health care: guidelines for countries of the Eastern Mediterranean Region*. WHO Eastern Mediterranean Regional Office Technical Publications Series, 18. Alexandria: World Health Organization Regional Office for the Eastern Mediterranean.
World Health Organization (WHO) (2008) *Millennium Development Goal 5 – Improving Maternal Health*. Available at: www.who.int/news-room/fact-sheets/detail/millennium-development-goals-(mdgs) (Accessed at 6th May 2022).
World Health Organization (WHO) (2013) *Traditional medicine strategy: 2014–2023*. Available at: www.who.int/publications/i/item/9789241506096 (Accessed 26th March 2022).
World Health Organization (WHO) (2015) *Trends in maternal mortality 1990 to 2015: estimates by WHO, UNICEF, UNFPA, World Bank Group and the United Nations Population Division*. Geneva: World Health Organization.
World Health Organization (WHO) (2018) *The Sustainable Development Goals and maternal mortality*. Available at: www.mhtf.org/topics/the-sustainable-development-goals-and-maternal-mortality/ (Accessed 28th February 2022).
Yamin, A.E. (2013) 'From ideals to tools: applying human rights to maternal health', *PLoS Med*, 10(11), e1001456.

PART 4

Heritage, Education and Development

11

SCHOOLS AS SITES OF MEMORY

The Musealization of the Armed Conflict by Students and Teachers in Colombia

Julian D. Bermeo, Julia Paulson and Arturo Charria

Introduction

On the northern side of Colombia, in the Caribbean municipality of Valencia, there is a public school with the name 'Liceo Villanueva'. A commemorative plaque reading '*Fidel Castaño Gil-1988*' catches the visitor's eye at its entrance. The name carved on stone belongs to the founder of the school, who was an influential and well-known paramilitary leader in the region. Through the 1980s and 1990s, Fidel Castaño, in collaboration with his two brothers was responsible for perpetrating multiple crimes, including land dispossession of farmers, forced displacement, massacres and assassinations (Sala Penal de Justicia y Paz del Tribunal Superior de Medellín, 2014).

In 2013, when Liceo Villanueva became a state school, the newly appointed school director had the idea of removing the plaque to symbolize a new beginning for the school. However, this proposal divided Valencia's community. On the one hand, some recognized themselves as direct victims of the Castaños' rule; on the other hand, some felt a sense of gratitude because the Castaño brothers provided the community with quality education when they opened the school. The controversy among the people from Valencia remains unsolved. The commemorative plaque stands in the school. Its presence reminds the members of the school's history, including the material and immaterial traces of the violent past that have the potential to trigger animosities. The stalemate around the plaque makes it difficult for the community to move forward towards a shared peaceful future that overcomes the divisions associated with paramilitary violence.

As this example shows, schools have symbolic power and are enmeshed in the histories of the communities that they serve, including in conflict dynamics and patterns of violence where those communities have experienced armed conflict. Schools have a unique and difficult positioning in sustainable development

DOI: 10.4324/9781003107361-15

processes generally (Tikly, 2020) and even more so when sustainable development possibilities are dependent upon the need to recover from conflict and build sustainable peace – a peace that, beyond the cessation of violence, transforms the social, economic and political causes of conflict (Lederach, 1997; Novelli and Sayed, 2016). Schools carry symbolic power as state institutions and indeed are often the most regular and routine contact that children and families have with the state, a relationship that can be imbued with distrust when state actors have committed direct, structural and cultural violence against groups and individuals (Smith, 2010). They are also seen as vehicles by which to deliver promises of development, sustainable development goals, human rights and peace (e.g., Bengtsson et al., 2018). The history curriculum in particular has been identified as a key space for reform and intervention in order to deliver these promises, despite long-time recognition of the role that history curricula serve in delivering victors' narratives, fomenting division between groups via exclusionary narratives that develop a sense of us and them and excluding historical narratives of minority communities (e.g., Davies, 2016; Sriprakash et al., 2020; Bermudez, 2020).

Research that explores history education and its 'two faces' (Bush and Salterelli, 2011) in promoting peace and conflict (Bentrovato and Schulze, 2016), often focuses at the level of curricular analysis, assuming that schools and teachers operate as top-down institutions that faithfully transmit the historical narratives agreed upon elsewhere and that learners unquestionably ignore this. In our previous work together, we rejected this idea in favour of attention to how school leaders, teachers and students actually navigate and make sense of these processes. They are historical actors positioned in the complex intersections between schools, history, lived experience of conflict and prospects for peace and sustainable development. How do teachers and school leaders navigate the complex ways in which their schools retain and represent the past? How do they understand their schools' role in shaping the ways students engage with the pasts of their community and their nation? How do they respond to the increasing calls upon schools to build peace in the present? Why do they decide to channel historical education through memorial museums? In our previous work together, we have described this way of thinking about schools and history education as understanding 'education as a site of memory' (Paulson et al., 2020), in other words, we see schools as a place where meanings about the past and its importance for the present and the future are actively constructed and contested as a heritage process. This chapter presents one way in which teachers and school communities are navigating the complex terrain of education as a site of memory in Colombia.

The chapter presents what we call the 'musealization' of the armed conflict at Colombian schools as an emergent phenomenon that contributes to making education a site of memory production. The chapter explores connections between understanding education as an active space for constructing and contesting memory and enabling sustainable development goals, including around education and peace. We see musealization happening in the growing phenomenon through which schools create museums of memory, which entails the collection, preservation, documentation and ensemble of exhibited textual, objectual and audio-visual contents connected to the school community and its experiences of armed conflict. In Colombia, principals, teachers and students create school-based museums, mainly but not exclusively, with historical education purposes, putting at the core of the learning processes their experiences related with the country's decades-long violent conflict. Given the emergent character of musealization, the chapter will first situate it within the wider study of education as a site of memory, exploring its connection to heritage, sustainable development and peace, before proposing a conceptual discussion of the historical and cultural nature of musealization. It then describes key instances of school musealization distributed in different regions of Colombia.

After identifying and documenting additional new examples from other regions in Colombia, we make a case for understanding the school museums of memory – and the 'musealization' process they represent – as a feature of the shift from a futurist to a presentist regime of historicity that has changed our relationship with the past. For societies transiting from war to peace, as in the case of Colombia, this move has created an even greater need to find routes to relate to the violent past. Understandings of historical culture – how history is made and engaged with – as a changing and multilevelled process helps to observe the emergence of the school museums of memory, not in isolation, but integrated into major trends of amateur musealization and the fluid exchange between formal and informal history education. Under this frame, we manage to recognize the singularities of the three illustrative examples and identify risks and ambiguities they are exposed to. We conclude by highlighting some research opportunities to continue learning from the school museums of memory and the potentialities of working with education as a site of memory for long-lasting peace.

Memory and the search for routes to the past in Colombia

This search for routes to the past is happening when it is difficult to determine, even for academics, a precise date or a concrete historical event to explain the beginning of the Colombian armed conflict (Fajardo, 2015; Giraldo, 2015; Gutiérrez, 2015; Molano, 2015; Pécaut, 2015; Torrijos, 2015). Something similar has been happening since 2016. After the signature of the Final Agreement to End the Armed Conflict and Build a Stable and Lasting Peace, the term post-conflict was adopted; however, the increased violence and the subsequent reconfiguration of the map of armed actors have cast doubt on the accuracy of such a term to describe the state of affairs of what is going on in Colombia. The terminological issues have been moved to the educative field where teachers experience difficulties finding the correct categories to talk about the war. Despite the long duration of the armed conflict, not until recent years, has the normative production been introduced at the school level. Worth mentioning here is the Basic Competencies in Social Sciences, the curricular space known as *Cátedra de Paz* (Ley 1732 de 2015) and the law that orders the reintroduction of the mandatory teaching of Colombian history (Ley 1874 de 2017).

At first, the Basic Competencies in Social Sciences appeared during the presidency of Alvaro Uribe; however, under his government, the existence of the armed conflict was denied. As a consequence, categories like *victim*, *armed conflict* or *historical memory* were absent from curricular content (Charria, 2015). The Cátedra de Paz and the law that makes Colombian history mandatory were approved during the negotiation and after the peace agreement, including concepts previously neglected (Caharria, 2018). It is true that these legislative outcomes have provided a compulsory framework; but structural problems of educative quality remain: low hourly intensity of social sciences, teaching staff overloaded, lack of teaching training, scarcity of didactic resources developed differentially regarding students' age and the absence of ministerial guidelines for how to curricularize contentious learning content in the field of social sciences. Nevertheless, some teachers have been able to organise, intuitively, thematic content, sequences of learning activities and methodological repertoires. Also, they manage to organize alongside their students a diversity of activities around the memory of the school, whether based on an emblematic case that belongs to the national history or a local event experienced by the school community (Jiménez, et al., 2012). Recently, we have accompanied the experience of some teachers who have successfully modified their curriculums which has provided their historical education practice with a certain level of institutionalization and recognition.[1]

Back to 2013, hundreds of kilometres away from Valencia municipality, in Bogotá, the capital city of Colombia, Arturo Charria, the history teacher at Los Nogales, an elite private secondary school, faced the question of what to do with the material and immaterial traces that the violent past left in the school he worked. As we described in previous work (Paulson et al., 2020), he explicitly addressed this question with his students, encouraging them to identify, through conversations with family members, an object that symbolized their experiences with conflict.

In return, students brought back not commemorative plaques but quotidian objects: the telephone a grandmother answered to receive demands for a bribe, the hammock that was the only refuge of an uncle while he was kidnapped, the invitation to a wedding not attended due to the dangers of travelling. The material objects were accompanied by fragments from interviews that the students conducted with their families. They were collected together and exhibited as display units in the school, creating a museum of memory for the school community (Figure 11.1). Later, Los Nogales students invited their peers from La Giralda, a socio-economically less privileged Bogotá state school, to replicate the experience. Thus, began a memory museum exchange. The resulting exhibitions held poignant objects, each with a story about how the long conflict had differentially but profoundly touched the families in the two school communities.

These two schools are pioneering examples of the emerging phenomenon of musealization in Colombian primary and secondary schools. This type of museum entails collecting, preserving, documenting and exhibiting textual, objectual and audio-visual contents gathered and curated by the school community. When brought together, the different pieces of the museums offer direct and indirect lived

FIGURE 11.1 The School Museum of Memory of Los Nogales School in Bogotá

Source: Photo taken by authors.

experiences of armed conflict from within the school community, which in an educational setting can contribute towards sustainable peace.

Presentism, participatory historical culture and transition in Colombia

Valencia and Bogotá are geographically distinct. Valencia is a rural village and Bogotá an urban capital city. However, the tragic legacies left by violence is a matter of shared concern, in the present, for both localities. In contrast to what happened in Valencia, where the school community still do not know what to do with the controversial plaque, in Bogotá, Los Nogales and La Giralda turned to material objects to explore their meanings with members of the school community (Figure 11.2). Over time, this route to the past originally pursued by Arturo Charria has been taken, with relative independence, in other regions of the country, differently affected by violent conflict dynamics.

The examples we have referred to and the ones we will introduce have a solid local anchoring, revealing how a national-scale phenomenon like the extended and degraded Colombian armed conflict affected each community differently. Still, they followed a similar path in creating a memory museum for dealing with the heavy weight of the violent past. Such a coincidence leads us to believe that these school

FIGURE 11.2 Students visit the School Memory Museum at La Giralda School in Bogotá

Source: Photo taken by authors.

museums of memory are not isolated. On the contrary, we argue they are associated with and part of the global development of 'memorial museums'. In describing these hybrid institutions, Williams (2007) argues that the formal distinctions between memorials and museums fade in order to commemorate mass suffering associated with a particular historical event or series of events.

Colombia's long armed conflict and active efforts to remember its victims and search for peace has resulted in community museums of memory such as the Museo Itinerante de la Memoria y la Identidad de los Montes de María (department of Bolívar), Museo de la Memoria Histórica 'Tras las huellas de El Placer' (department of Putumayo), Monumento – Casa de la Memoria de El Salado (department of Bolívar), Monumento – Casa de la Memoria de El Salado (department of Bolívar), to name just a few examples. Next to the other 24 initiatives, they are organized in what is known since 2015 as Red Colombiana de Lugares de Memoria (RCLM).[2] Most of them have been promoted, developed and sustained by civil society actors from the local population. Meanwhile, a few others have been the result of judicial and governmental decisions. According to Guglielmucci (2018), some of the members of the RCLM have more than 20 years of experience in building memory, truth and peaceful culture within their territories. The same author affirms that a common future of the community organized memorial museums congregated in RCLM is the emphasis they put on the sense of community coexistence, in the present, as a way to stop victimization and reach peace amid the ongoing violent conflict.

Although the Memory School Museums we take as examples in this chapter have not been officially admitted to the RCLM, here we argue they are in continuity with what Grever and Adriaansen (2017) describe as the shift towards a participatory historical culture where ordinary people are more involved in practices related to the past. This includes the popularization and widening of public engagement in developing formal and informal history education and popular history, as well as in academic and popular articulations, narratives and infrastructures. Consequently, we pay special attention to the analysis of historical culture and the integrated multi-level analytical framework of Grever and Adriaansen (2017), which we explore below. We will benefit from this perspective because the concept of historical culture, as these authors suggest, opens an inquiry into how people deal with the past, establishing dynamic interactions between human agency, tradition, the performance of memory, historical representations and their dissemination, including in opening up presumptions about what constitutes history.

As a research concept, the idea of historical culture originated in Germany between the 1970s and 1980s within history didactics as an academic sub-discipline of historiography. It developed as scholars began to pay more attention to the extracurricular sources of historical knowledge that influenced students' historical thinking, like the new popular media (Carretero et al., 2017). Later, the concept achieved more recognition by exploring conflicting representations of the past as provided by historiography and popular TV shows, video games and social media. From the lenses of historical culture, both the narratives provided by historiography and those derived from more popular sources are mutually constitutive parts of historical knowledge.

In order to give more salience to the production, performance and dissemination of memories in communicative interactions between people, groups and institutions, Grever and Adriaansen (2017) suggests a model of analysis for understanding historical culture with three levels of analysis: (1) historical narrative and performance of the past; (2) mnemonic infrastructures; and (3) conceptions of history. The first level refers to the set of acts that may be partly embodied in speech but also in gestures that makes the representations of the past meaningful to its creator and his/her audience. The second level is all those organizations (e.g., schools, museums, among others) that individuals and communities employ to articulate stories about historical experiences and that are anchored in time and space. Last, but not less important, are the underlying conceptions of history that constitute specific interpretations of the relationship between past, present and future.

We draw from this model to argue that school museums of memory emerge from renewed conceptions of history and from the consequent change to the infrastructures that individuals and collectives use to give meaning to the past. With this idea in mind, we deal, first, with conceptions of history and mnemonic infrastructures, while in the next section, we make a brief reference to the narrative and performance strategies followed by the school museums of memory.

The changing relationship of people to the past always presumes a specific idea of history and the underlying relationship between past, present and future. Grever and Adriaansen (2017) point out that history has been mainly articulated in the Western world under three historical conceptions or regimens: (1) pastist, (2) futurist and (3) presentist. Under the first one, in ancient times, the past guided even future-oriented actions. In this sense, tradition operated as a determinant depository of moral lessons to be almost unconditionally followed. Under the second, in modern times, the past no longer provided orientation because all the expectations were put in the future, as evident, for example, in linear assumptions about progress and development which underpin modernity (e.g., Tikly, 2020).

There is an increasing agreement among many social sciences scholars that we are now operating under the third, presentist, relationship to time and history. They argue that something has changed in our way of thinking about the transformation of past phenomena over time (Tamm and Olivier, 2019). Hartog (2015), for example, asserts that a new regime of historicity prevails in the contemporary Western world and in other societies carrying Western influence. While a future-oriented regime ruled the last two centuries, the orientation is shifting with the advent of a presentist regime. This presentist regime of historicity implies that today's present differs from previous conceptions of the present because it is broader and more pervasive than ever compared with the past and the future. Therefore, the past and future are mere extensions of the present. Here and now, a present with no other horizon than itself tries to shape temporality according to its image. In shaping the past and the future, previous futurist confidence in linear progress has been replaced by a concern to safeguard, preserve the past and prevent the repetition of past wrongs in the future (Grever et al., 2012). This combines to result in an obsession with memory, commemoration, patrimony and the present craze for heritagization and musealization (Hartog, 2015) along with the insistence on transitional justice to ensure 'never again' (Bevernage, 2010).

A phenomenon that embodies presentism is the so-called 'memory boom', the ubiquitous use of memory that for the past three decades has swept over both scholarship and civic life (Blight, 2009). Likewise, we see the rise of the 'memory assumption' (Rotondi and Eisikovits, 2015), as the strong and widely shared belief that past political violence must be dealt with in order to deliver social reconstruction, peace and sustainable development (David, 2020). Similarly, Levy (2010) suggests how and what societies around the world remember today falls significantly on a 'memory imperative', a set of political and normative expectations for handling past injustices that came out of the horrors of World War II and, more specifically, the Holocaust. Bickford and Sodaro (2010) commented that the emergence of a new paradigm in remembering and teaching the past had spread worldwide due to the proliferation of new commemorative projects linked to the prevention of violence and atrocity in the future.

The commemorative paradigm mentioned by Bickford and Sodaro (2010) has been influential at the level of mnemonic infrastructures. Grever and Adriaansen (2017) define these as organizations anchored in time and space used to advance historical practice. The extended framework with the underlying precept of knowing what has happened in the past helps us to understand and prevent future violence that has driven societies, mainly but not exclusively transitional ones, to fixate memory in physical sites like memorial museums. As we already mentioned, the memorial museums intended to provide visitors with the freedom to undertake memory work by themselves, as long as they remain faithful to the memory imperative that prays never again.

Alongside official remembering and commemorative projects, community musealization allows individuals and small groups to attempt to explore the past, aiming to access experiential knowledge from it through the display of quotidian objects, ones that hegemonic discourses often fail or refuse to address. Taking, as an example, museums that are dedicated to the German Democratic Republic (GDR) era, Winkler (2015) refers to 'amateur musealization' or 'musealization of the popular'. This trend takes place on the margins of dominant institutions devoted to the scientifically based collection, preservation and documentation of historical value objects. Through community musealization, traditionally privileged representational practices are questioned, as are broader purposes and practices of museums and memorials.

Colombia has not remained detached from the dynamics described here. After decades of continued armed conflict and failed and partial peace negotiations between the national governments and different illegal armed groups, different transitional justice measures have been implemented since the early 2000s. A significant milestone worth mentioning in this matter is the Victims and Land Restitution Law (Law 1448), passed in 2011, through which individual and collective armed conflict victims were officially recognized and at the same time the state's duty to offer material and symbolic reparations was formally stated. Since then, a plethora of memorialization initiatives have been implemented by the national and local governments, with the purpose of fixing armed conflict memories in physical sites like official memorial museums.

The first of this kind of official memorial museum was the House of Memory Museum which as part of a victims' assistance program implemented by Medellin's City Hall, was opened in the same city, in 2006. Simultaneously with the beginning of the peace talks between the National Government of Colombia and the FARC-EP, the Memory Peace and Reconciliation Centre opened its doors in Bogotá in 2012, in compliance with a decision of the city's council. In pursuance of Law 1448, the Memory Museum of Colombia is expected to be opened in 2023. In addition, civil society organizations and local communities carry out armed conflict memorialization and commemoration processes, sometimes in direct response to official projects. As was mentioned before, the RCLM gathers close to 24 non-official and community-based initiatives with the character of memorials, museums or both. Here it is important to notice that there could be more expressions of community memorialization that have not been included in the RCLM and remain unknown. For this reason, it is possible that in Colombia the horizon of memorialization throughout community-based memorial museums could be broader.

No less important are the new developments in schools. Under the presentist regime, people learn about the past through many new ways that fall between formal and informal, opening more opportunities for recent interdisciplinary practices (Bermudez and Epstein, 2020). While in Europe, heritage education has gained attention (Grever et al.,2012), in Colombia, the musealization of the armed conflict by educative communities paves the way for working with education as a site of memory.

The illustration of an emergent phenomenon

This section provides examples of this emergent phenomenon including for instance, popular musealization and the exchanges between more formal academic historiography and popular history infrastructures. In so doing, it highlights the advent of a type of memorial museum in Colombia: the school museums of memory.

The following three examples share a number of common features. First, the creation of all of the school museums of memory was initiated by members of educational communities, such as directors, teachers and students. Second, the creators all recognize and describe their initiatives as school museums of memory. Third, the school museums of memory all refer to the Colombian armed conflict. Finally, they are ongoing initiatives implemented within schools but they involve other members of the wider school community such as parents, human rights defenders and armed-conflict victims.

We conducted in-depth interviews with the creators of these three school museums of memory, which has informed the following discussion. In this chapter, based on previous informed consent, all schools are named with their actual names and teachers are also identified, with their first and sometimes last names. This is an active choice to waive anonymity in order to identify and celebrate the work their schools are doing – part of a brave tradition of memory work in Colombia. Here we use the accounts of the teachers leading the creation of the school museums of memory descriptively to explore aspects such as (1) responsiveness to the local context in which war violence continues; (2) the process of developing the memory museums within the school; (3) the strategies the museums employ to represent the past, including putting at the core their school community's own lived experiences of the armed conflict; and (4) the opportunities and challenges that they face in making the museum sustainable.

School Museum of Memory 'Mnemosyne'

The department of Norte de Santander is located on the northeast side of Colombia. In Cucuta, its capital, there is a neighbourhood called Cundinamarca, well known for its long tradition of handmade shoe manufacture. Here, Jorge teaches philosophy at a school called Julio Pérez Ferrero. In 2018, thanks to previous work with the National Centre of Historical Memory – a national public establishment created in part through the Victims' Law to carry historical memory programs – Jorge's students were invited to a meeting in Bogotá. Once there, they meet students around the country doing memory work. They heard that memorial museums had been a tool for societies to narrate their intense experiences with violence and repression. So, back in Cucuta, being conscious of the violence witnessed on the streets of their neighbourhood, they convinced their teacher, Jorge, to create their memory museum. He saw this idea as an opportunity to let his students exercise their citizenship while applying qualitative research techniques to historical memory reconstruction.

With this purpose in mind, students initiated a research process to recollect and reconstruct testimonies provided by relatives and acquaintances from their neighbourhoods. While doing this, they collected material objects related to the interviews they conducted. Thanks to the team of the Museum House General Santander – an official institution in Cucuta devoted to preserving the heritage of the national republican hero Francisco de Paula Santander – teacher Jorge and his students received training in basic museography and museology, which helped them to arrange an initial gallery.

On the 18th of May, on the occasion of International Museum Day, they presented the first version of the school museum of memory to members of their families, communities and visitors from other schools. They consensually agreed to call the museum 'Mnemosyne', after the name of the Greek goddess of memory. A part of the school's playground was demarcated, using plants and furniture and here they exhibited, for instance, the garments that once belonged to young neighbours who were killed in full daylight by the armed actors who had presence in the surroundings. These clothes were donated by the victims' families to the school museum and were displayed next to cut-outs of local newspapers that had reported the tragic events. Since then, Mnemosyne has safeguarded new conflict-related pieces from nearby visitors.

Because of the pandemic, the students had to put their growing collection in cardboard boxes for more than one year. At the time of writing, they are still waiting for the classes to operate physically again at their school in order to unbox their museum and settle it again in the school's playground. Meanwhile, they have been working, with the help of NGOs, in systematizing the learnings derived from the process of creating the museum.

School Museum of Memory 'Memories of my Wayco'

Samaniego, Nariño is located in Colombia's southeast corner. Martha works as a social sciences teacher at a public school there called Policarpa Salavarrieta. Samaniego has been categorized as a 'red zone' because of the intensity of the clashes between different armed groups for control over territory and drug production and transportation (Garrido et al., 2016). For many years, teacher Martha struggled with the textbooks that she had to use for her lessons, which did not represent the struggles of daily life in Samaniego. As a primary security threat, the armed conflict was only superficially addressed, and mentions of the implications of drug trafficking were absent despite their clear reality on the streets of the town. Complicated questions arise from the classroom when direct violence is perpetrated against students as often happens. A recent case was a massacre perpetrated in August 2020, in the countryside of Samaniego, against a group of eight youths aged between 17 and 24 years, some of them former students of the School Policarpa Salabarrieta (Pardo, 2020).

Being a women's rights advocate and a leader in Samaniego, Martha capitalized on her frustration with conventional teaching resources, participating in a call opened by the National Centre of Historical Memory. The project that Martha submitted was conceived as a participatory action research process whose final product was a museum to share the research findings. In 2017, Martha's project was selected as the winner and thanks to the training, advice and economic resources provided by the National Centre of Historical Memory, she made true the dream of creating a museum from scratch. Martha and students developed every piece contained in the museum together. Together they agreed to call it 'Memories of my Wayco' since in Quecha, a local Indigenous language, Wayco stands for Samaniego.

As the title suggests, this museum was meant to represent Samaniego's history that, in recent times, has been linked to suffering from war as well as to its population's resilience (Andrade, 2018). The museum was placed in one room of the Policarpa Salavarrieta school, covering a wide range of formats and installations. The collection includes timelines, calendars, cartographies, painted murals and a repository of victims' biographies written by the students. My Wayco incorporated interactive strategies too. Teacher Martha mentioned that they delivered postcards at the museum entrance where the visitors could write their thoughts and even share their testimonies. They can deposit them in a mailbox at the end of the tour. Then, if visitors request it, the Wayco team may reconstruct their personal war stories to be added to the school museum of memory's collection.

Since its creation, new projects have been implemented every year, providing new exhibition pieces for the museum. In this sense, the Wayco museum is under permanent expansion while co-research is developed between teachers and students. The next step for Martha and her students is to commemorate the 2020 massacre when the group of eight youths were killed in Samaniego.

School Museum of Memory of the 13th Commune 'MEM-C-13'

Medellín is the capital city of the department of Antioquia. In the outskirts of Medellín, high in the mountain, is Commune number 13. Since the 1980s, it has been an urban stage for different dynamics of armed conflict, drug trafficking and criminality. In 2002, a military operation known as Operation Orion took place there, with a declared purpose to eradicate the armed groups based in the area. However, while military forces were deployed against leftist militias and other criminal groups, paramilitary groups were treated with benevolence (Grupo de Memoria Histórica, 2011). Under the frame of the Orion Operation, with the excuse of regaining control of the territory, military units occupied and used part of the educative infrastructures of the public school Eduardo Santos, which constituted a flagrant breach of international law (Nieto, 2019). Manuel, the principal of Eduardo Santos school registered at least 28 students who lost their lives violently due to the armed conflict from the beginning of Operation Orion to the time of writing.

In 2018, taking advantage of the Victims' Law proclaimed in Colombia years before, Manuel, in discussion with some teachers and students, concluded that Eduardo Santos school, as an educative community, should be recognized as a collective victim of armed conflict. Under this recognition, the school is entitled to a collective reparation. However, being aware that the formal administrative process towards collective reparation would take a long time, they opted for a self-managed process of symbolic reparation. Instead of pursuing a formal collective reparation, they began building a memory museum.

When the question of what they would need for creating a memory museum was raised, the school's answer was that a physical space and a story to be told were enough. Consequently, part of a three-floor building of the Eduardo Santos school was dedicated to the School Museum of Memory of the 13th Commune, which opened on the 16th of October, 2018, during the XVI anniversary of the Orion Operation. The space was designed to offer room for a permanent and a temporary exhibition. The permanent collection comprises large-format murals representing the present and the future of the Eduardo Santos school and the Commune number 13, with the Orion Operation marking the breaking point. A professional artist was invited to execute the murals with the assistance of student volunteers. The temporary spaces are intended for the exhibition of classroom projects and experiential workshops.

One activity is the simulation of what can be experienced when a school is attacked during armed clashes, resembling what the members of the school went through during the most critical moments of the armed confrontations in Commune number 13. As part of this interactive simulation of a real-life situation, visitors are locked in a small classroom where they are asked to hide under the school desks while simultaneously hearing the sounds of bullets, explosions and screams. As it was described to us, the experience provided by this simulation triggers visitors' emotions, with the risk of causing them emotional distress, potentially causing harm and revictimization. Therefore, it has demanded not only pedagogical but ethical consideration.

After creating the Commune number 13 School Museum of Memory, the Eduardo Santos school readjusted its curriculum so that students from primary to secondary could have permanent access to the museum content and activities. Since this museum has gained recognition, mediators received training to conduct guided visits. Despite the Covid-19 pandemic, in 2021, Medellin's government awarded the museum a prize for its contributions to local peace and reconciliation. They are taking advantage of this recognition to gain support in adopting the 16th of October as Medellin's official date for commemorating Orion Operation's victims.

Understanding school museums of memory

We have visited three different examples of musealization in schools, with the brief descriptions above offering a glimpse of each example. Here we discuss some cross-cutting issues.

Musealization of armed conflict experiences

Similar to the museums devoted to life in the GDR, which have been created by amateur individuals and small groups working outside of hegemonic heritage institutions to represent the quotidian East German past (Winkler, 2015), the school museums of memory point to the existing democratization of traditionally privileged practices and spaces of heritage representation. Although the school museums of memory rely on the collection and display of objects, they transcend a strategy that is simply expository. Our three examples are inherently related to pedagogic and research practices, epistemologically aligned with the recognition that there are knowledges of the past grounded in the local context and distributed among the local people.

Such knowledge is embodied mainly, though not exclusively, in the figure of the survivor-victims who directly suffered or witnessed the horrors of the armed conflict and who are among the members of the educational communities. Not surprisingly, from the 1980s, with the memory boom, there has been a simultaneous rise of notions of victimhood. In Hartog's (2015) view, the presentist historical regime has provided victims with an authentic authority concerning the past (Lorenz, 2019). Hence, the testimonial accounts of the victims become the cornerstone of the exhibits' contents, materialized in products like murals, timelines, calendars and exhibition objects. Next to the educational workshops and the guided tours, interactive simulations are offered to intensify and expand the visitors' experience.

The relevance of testimonial accounts and visitors' interaction within the exhibits leads us to think that the school museums of memory have adopted specific discourse models. According to Asensio and Pol (2017), museums can be comparatively analysed under the frame of the discourses they mobilize. The four discourse models suggested by Asensio and Pol are descriptive, explanatory, narrative and participatory. Although this classification may be the subject of extensive discussion, we see school museums of memory mainly drawing on narrative and participative models, without prejudice towards excluding the other two. More conventional discursive models are focused on the transfer of knowledge as the ultimate goal of an exhibition, acting in subordination to a discipline of reference, under the premise that the more information the better. Distinctly, Asensio and Pol (2017) explain that the narrative models rely on the centrality of narration for the human mind. The same model provides a sustainable communication tool where museology and museography support the exhibition narrative. In addition to the narrative model, for Asensio and Pol (2017), a vital function of the participatory discourse model is to gather testimonies to create exhibitions to honour the memory of recent historical events. Participation is also enhanced by way of a dynamic, sensory aspect to what the museums display where visitors are encouraged to touch, speak, hear and even feel emotions like fear as in the case of the interactive simulation offered in the School Museum of Memory of 13th Commune.

The deployment of narrative and participatory strategies is not free of practical difficulties and ethical dilemmas. In terms of the practicalities, the school museums of memory are part of schools. Therefore, they must adapt to the schools' limited spaces, times, resources and constraining relationships and regulations. It was typical for the three examples that, during the Covid-19 pandemic, the installations of the schools were closed for health reasons. Therefore, the school museums of memory experienced a temporary cessation of activity. Similar to academic classes, the activities related to the museum moved from physical to virtual spaces. For this reason, they were forced to implement adaptive strategies, potentializing social media as alternative channels through which they offer, for instance, guided video tours.

Among the most significant challenges teachers and students face are the environments under which the school museums of memory operate. Despite the signing of the 2016 Peace Agreement, the armed conflict remains active in Colombia and around the schools, which poses threats to the lives, safety and integrity of their creators and visitors due to the sensitive matters addressed in the museums. Such circumstances intensify the contradictions of making memories of the violent past when the violence is an experience in present times (Bermeo, 2017).

In gathering and exhibiting testimonies of war suffering, the content presented in the school museums of memory carries a tremendous amount of trauma and horror. In this regard, teachers talked about how far they could go with the vivid representation of the past. For this reason, this type of school musealization requires group-care strategies, in addition to the narrative and participatory ones. As was mentioned earlier, the use of some interactive devices may have the potential to harm students and visitors and to cause the re-victimization of the victims. An aim of the creation of the Memory School Museums is the development of a sense of respect, empathy and caring for the feelings of others, as well as one's own; however, it does not necessarily guarantee that school communities have enough psychosocial skills to manage unexpected crises.

We see that the musealization of the armed conflict by students and teachers in Colombia benefits from trends like popular musealization and its interactions with formal and informal approaches to historical knowledge, operating under a broad presentist historical regime. This kind of amateur musealization is not limited to the decontextualized exhibition of material objects. It incorporates supportive narrative and immersive strategies, putting testimonies and the interactive simulation of real-life situations at the core of experience offered by the school museums of memory. Nevertheless, musealization involves difficulties and risks that the leading creators must face to preserve their projects. For Asensio and Pol (2017), musealization is a bet on the future, meaning that its practice is driven by a desire for transmission of its interpretations of the past over time. This idea converges with the motivation for creating the School Museums of Memory as a way of understanding, transforming and overcoming the root causes of the armed conflict and to promote sustainable peace and development, not only in the future but in the present.

Heritage cultures and creation of a public sense of the past from below

Regarding patrimony, Asensio and Pol (2017) point out that citizens produce it, enjoy it and eventually contribute to its preservation and thus heritage should be considered from citizen perspectives. For the case of the school museums of memory, this assertion is particularly true. The participatory practices that have involved school communities and have resulted in the creation of school-based museums contribute to the expansion of the concept of heritage. As Simon (2010) highlights, when people can actively participate with cultural institutions, those places become central to culture and community life. However, as Preciado (2019) critically asserts, a renewed approach to heritage institutions like museums should not be reduced to the inclusion and diversification of different publics. Instead it should focus on the epistemological rationale from which the museum as a political and social institution has been built.

Often school communities (including teachers and students) are excluded from the possibility of preserving, creating and representing historical narratives and are merely treated as potential audiences of heritage (Bazalgette and Buckingham, 1995; Johanson and Glow, 2012; Tzibazi, 2013). However, in the examples shared here local school communities are not only representing the stories of their lives, but they are, from below, making contributions to (re)writing and (re)presenting local history. This contrasts with academic historiography and museography, which, with some exceptions, has dictated a centralized national narrative and image where small populations like those from the Cundinamarca neighbourhood in Cucuta, the Commune number 13 in Medellín and Samaniego in Nariño have no proper place. In addition, with the content they exhibited, the school museums of memory are doing something to counter the hegemonic narratives circulating in mass media that frame their communities purely as territories of danger or simply red zones. Their interventions and memories of the past present their communities through lenses of survival and resilience.

Education as a site of memory and ambiguities contesting state narratives

It is commonly assumed that as the formal systems of schooling carry the imprimatur of the state, the historical practices within it consequently serve political purposes defined from the top, reaffirming the political establishment and its power (Freedman, et al., 2008; Wang, 2008; Novelli et al., 2017). These assumptions pale when confronted with the realities of the schools showcased in this chapter, who are aware of their symbolic positions and are making demands on the state as memory actors. Contrary to the idea that the schools are mere automaton reproducers of discourses from above, the examples illustrate an active approach to working with education as a site of memory. In part, it occurs thanks to the crucial agency of educators and young people involved in attempts to stabilize or transform memories and make them meaningful in the present and for the future. With this, we question the unproblematic way education's role is confined to simply and effectively transmitting 'official' narratives of the past.

Jelin (2007) notes that where settling accounts with the past remains an issue, the production of 'official' memories through state institutions can be disputed by various societal forces. Consequently, at first glance, School Museums of Memory display stories and objects that hegemonic discourses and institutions fail or refuse to address. However, there is an ambiguity concerning the contestation of state narratives in education since the three schools explored here are state-funded; hence they are state institutions. Although teaching and learning remain subject to government policies that dictate the curricular content and pedagogic practices, the interviewed teachers expressed that even though they followed national policies and standards, they held a high degree of flexibility in determining what their students learn about, even if it implies contradicting official memories. Moreover, in practice, the school museums of memory do not exist in full contradiction with state institutions. On the contrary, they coexist, even sometimes complementing one another. While benefiting from material resources, training and advice, school museums of memory may collaborate to advance other institutions' mandates without seriously compromising their independence, allowing them to be critical of official narratives. Ultimately, what we saw looked more like a collaborative and dynamic memory landscape between school museums of memory and other heritage, memorial and commemorative institutions.

Conclusion: working with education as a site of memory and the potential of school musealization

After having visited three different examples of school musealization from three regions in Colombia, we have recognized singularities and common elements of what was noted at the beginning of the chapter as an emergent phenomenon. With the purpose of better understanding the school museums of memory, we turned to the concept of historical culture. Although it has been helpful, we know that the analysis is still incomplete. According to Grever and Adriaansen (2017), historical culture is the outer side of learning about the past. Every historical culture entails a historical consciousness that is, in contrast, the inner side. Historical culture refers to the ways in which relationships to the past are established in a dynamic interaction between the narration and the performance of memory; historical representations and their dissemination through infrastructures fixed in time and space; and, presumptions about what constitutes history. Meanwhile, historical consciousness is the awareness of the historicity of everything such as present human behaviour, knowledge, institutions, events and developments in society, including one's own historical position (Gadamer, 1987; Seixas, 2017; Grever and Adriaansen, 2017). Consequently, the latter must be included if we want a comprehensive view of the 'coin' from both sides. So, historical culture and historical consciousness should be worked with side by side, especially in the complex contexts discussed in this chapter (Grever and Adriaansen, 2017).

In previous work, we have suggested that history education can play a fundamental role in sustainable peacebuilding (Paulson et al., 2020). But if school musealization by teachers and students is helpful to meet different demands of the present such as peace and sustainable development, evidence is needed to substantiate its contributions. Therefore, we agree with Bermudez and Epstein (2020) when they call for further research to elucidate what features of museum narratives and experiences enhance students' critical-historical understanding. Also, they noted that more research is required on the impact of museum visits on students' knowledge of the violent past. Therefore, in adherence to the research agenda for working with education as a site of memory (Paulson et al., 2020), more study is needed on how the creation of and participation in School Museums of Memory transforms people's historical consciousness and how it may contribute to processes such as building sustainable peace. Importantly, consideration must be given to the perspective of school communities, taking their knowledge as a legitimate starting point for analysing how they manage to find historical orientations to overcome, in the present, the challenges imposed by the repetition of armed conflict violence.

Acknowledgements

This project has received funding from the European Union's Horizon 2020 Research and Innovation Programme under the Marie Skłodowska-Curie grant agreement No. 847624. In addition, a number of institutions back and co-finance this project. This chapter reflects only the authors' views and the Agency is not responsible for any use that may be made of the information it contains.

Notes

1 Some of these experiences have been gathered and published by us in the book *Diez propuestas para el estudio de la historia reciente de Colombia con énfasis en el Conflicto armado* (2022).

2 For more information on the RCLM, visit https://redmemoriacolombia.org/.

References

Andrade, M. (2018) 'Museos Escolares' in *Centro Nacional de Memoria Histórica's Recorridos de la memoria histórica en la escuela. Aportes de maestras y maestros en Colombia*, Bogotá: CNMH, pp. 27–29.

Asensio, M. and Pol, E. (2017) 'The Never-ending Story About Heritage and Museums: Four Discursive Models' in Carretero M., Berger, S. and Grever, M.(eds) *The Palgrave Handbook of Research in Historical Culture Education.* London: Palgrave Macmillan, pp. 755–80.

Bazalgette, C. and Buckingham, D. (1995) 'The Invisible Audience', in Bazalgette, C. and Buckingham, D. (eds) *Front of the Children: Screen Entertainment and Young Audiences*. London: British Film Institute, pp. 1–14.

Bengtsson, S.E.L., Barakat, B. and Muttarak, R. (2018) *The Role of Education in Enabling Sustainable Development*. London: Routledge.

Bentrovato, D., and Schulze, M. (2016) 'Teaching about a Violent Past: Revisiting the Role of History Education in Conflict and Peace', in Bentrovato, D., Korostelina, K. and Schulze, M. (eds) History Can Bite. *History Education in Divided and Postwar Societies*. Göttingen: V & R Academic, pp. 15–28.

Bermeo, J. (2017) 'Reenmarcando la producción social de memoria: la experiencia de docentes y estudiantes en dos colegios de Bogotá', *Revista colombiana de sociología*, 40(1), pp. 65–82.

Bermudez, A. (2020) 'Narrative Justice? Ten Tools do Deconstruct Narratives About Violent Past', in Keynes, M., Elmersjö, H., Lindmark, D. and Norlin, B. (eds) *Historical Justice and History Education*. Basingstoke: Palgrave Macmillan, pp. 269–90.

Bermudez, A. and Epstein, T (2020) 'Representations of Violent Pasts in Memorial Museums. Ethical Reflection and History Education', *Journal for the Study of Education and Development*, 43(3), pp. 503–43.

Bevernage, B. (2010) 'Writing the past out of the present: History and the politics of time in transitional justice', *History Workshop Journal*, 69(1), pp. 111–31.

Bickford, L., and Sodaro, A. (2010) 'Remembering Yesterday to Protect Tomorrow: The Internationalisation of a New Commemorative Paradigm', in Gutman, Y., Brown, A. and Sodaro, A. (eds) *Memory and the Future Transnational Politics, Ethics and Society*. London: Palgrave MacMillan, pp. 66–88.

Blight, D. (2009) 'The Memory Boom: Why and Why Now', in Boyer, P. and Wertsch, J. (eds) *Memory in Mind and Culture*. New York: Cambridge University Press, pp. 238–51.

Bush, K., and Saltarelli, D. (2011) *The Two Faces of Education in Ethnic Conflict: Towards a Peacebuilding Education for Children*. Florence: Unicef Innocenti Research Centre.

Carretero, M., Berger, S. and Grever, M. (2017) 'Introduction: Historical Cultures and Education in Transition', in Carretero M., Berger, S. and Grever, M. (eds) *The Palgrave Handbook of Research in Historical Culture Education*. London: Palgrave Macmillan, pp. 1–35.

Charria, A. (2015) '¿Qué es la Cátedra de la paz?', *El Espectador.* Available at: Retrieved from: www.elespectador.com/opinion/columnistas/arturo-charria/que-es-la-catedra-de-la-paz-column-615893/ (Accessed 16 April 2022).

Charria, A. (2018) Los micos en la historia de la educación en Colombia. *Palabra Maestra*. Available at: www.compartirpalabramaestra.org/actualidad/columnas/los-micos-en-la-historia-de-la-educacion-en-colombia (Accessed 16 April 2022).

David, L. (2020) *The Past Can't Heal Us: The Danger of Mandating Memory in the Name of Human Rights*. Cambridge: Cambridge University Press.

Davies, L. (2016) 'The Politics of Peace Education in Post-Conflict Countries', in Langer, A. and Brown, G. (eds) *Building Sustainable Peace: Timing and Sequencing of Post-Conflict Reconstruction and Peacebuilding*. Oxford: Oxford University Press, pp. 181–99.

Dean, D. (2013) Museums as Sites for Historical Understanding, Peace, and Social Justice: Views from Canada. *Peace and Conflict Journal of Peace and Psychology*, 19(4), pp. 325–37.

Fajardo, D. (2015) 'Estudio sobre el origen del conflicto social armado, razones de su presencia y sus efectos más profundos en la sociedad colombiana', in *Contribución al entendimiento del conflicto armado en Colombia*. Bogotá: Ediciones Desde Abajo, pp. 361–422.

Freedman, S., Weinstein, H., Murphy, K. and Longman, T. (2008) 'Teaching History after identity-based Conflicts: The Rwanda Experience', *Comparative Education Review*, 52(4), pp. 663–90.

Gaedamer, H. (1987) 'The Problem of Historical Consciousness', in Rabinow, P and Gadamer, H (eds) *Interpretative Social Sciences: A Second Look*. Berkeley: University of California Press, pp. 82–114.

Garrido, M., Mouly, C. and Adler, A. (2016) 'Jiu-jitsu en context de conflicto aramdo: el poder de la resistencia no violenta', *Ciudad paz-ando*, 9(2), pp. 155–67.

Giraldo, J. (2015) 'Aportes sobre el origen del conflicto armado en Colombia, su persistencia y sus impactos', in *Contribución al entendimiento del conflicto armado en Colombia*. Bogotá: Ediciones Desde Abajo, pp. 423–70.

Grever, M. and Adriaansen, R. (2017) 'Historical Culture: A Concept Revisited', in Carretero M., Berger, S. and Grever, M. (eds) *The Palgrave Handbook of Research in Historical Culture Education*. London: Palgrave Macmillan, pp. 73–89.

Grever, M., de Bruijn, P. and van Boxtel, C. (2012) 'Negotiating Historical Distance: Or, How to Deal with the Past as a Foreign Country in Heritage Education', *Paedagogica Historica*, 48(6), pp. 873–87.

Grupo de Memoria Histórica (2011) *Desplazamiento Forzado en la Comuna 13: La Huella Invisible de la Guerra*. Ediciones Semana.

Guglielmucci, A. (2018) 'Pensar y actuar en red: los lugares de memoria en Colombia', *Aletheia*, 8(16), pp. 1–3.

Gutiérrez, F. (2015) '¿Una historia simple?', in *Contribución al entendimiento del conflicto armado en Colombia*. Bogotá: Ediciones Desde Abajo, pp. 521–64.

Hartog, F. (2015) *Regimes of Historicity: Presentism and Experiences of Time*. New York: Columbia University Press.

Jelin, E. (2007) 'Memorialisation in Perspective: Truth, Justice and Memory of Past Repression in the Southern Cone of South America', *International Journal of Transitional Justice*, 1(1), pp. 138–56.

Johanson, K., and Glow, H. (2012) 'It's Not Enough for the Work of Art to Be Great: Children and Young People as Museum Visitors', Journal of Audience and Reception Studies, 9(1), pp. 26–42.

Lederach, J.P. (1997) *Building Peace: Sustainable Reconciliation in Divided Societies*. Washington, D.C.: United States Institute for Peace.

Levy, D. (2010) 'Changing Temporalities and the Internationalisation of Memory Cultures' in Gutman, Y., Brown, A. and Sodaro, A. (eds) *Memory and the Future. Transnational Politics, Ethics and Society*. London: Palgrave Macmillan, pp. 15–30.

Lorenz, C. (2019) 'Out of Time? Some Critical Reflections on Francois Hartog's Presentism', in Tamm, T. and Oliver, L. (eds) *Rethinking Historical Time. New Approaches to Presentism*. London: Bloomsbury, pp. 23–42.

Molano, A. (2015) 'Fragmentos de la historia del conflicto armado (1920-2010)', in *Contribución al entendimiento del conflicto armado en Colombia*. Bogotá: Ediciones Desde Abajo, pp. 565–626.

Nieto, J. (2019) 'Tras 17 años, víctimas de Orión esperan que la verdad salga a la luz. *El Tiempo*'. Available at: www.eltiempo.com/colombia/medellin/se-cumplen-17-anos-de-la-operacion-orion-en-medellin-423672 (Accessed 16 April 2022).

Novelli, M., Lopes Cardozo, M.T.A. and Smith, A. (2017) 'The 4Rs Framework: Analysing Education's Contribution to Sustainable Peacebuilding with Social Justice in Conflict Affected Contexts', *Journal on Education in Emergencies*, 3(1), pp. 14–43.

Novelli, M. and Sayed, S. (2016) 'Teachers as Agents of Sustainable Peace, Social Cohesion and Development: Theory, Practice and Evidence', *Education as Change*, 20(3), pp. 15–37.

Pardo, D. (2020) 'Masacre de Samaniego: una nueva matanza de jóvenes deja en evidencia el recrudecimiento de la violencia en Colombia', *BBC News*. Available at: www.bbc.com/mundo/noticias-america-latina-53801935 (Accessed 19 April 2022).

Paulson, J., Abiti, N., Bermeo, J., Charria, C., Keo, D., Manning, P., Milligan, L., Moles, K., Pennell, K., Salih, S., and Shanks, K. (2020) 'Education as Site of Memory: Developing a Research Agenda', *International Studies in Sociology of Education*, 29(4), pp. 429–51.

Pécaut, D. (2015) 'Una lucha armada al servicio del statu quo social y político', in *Contribución al entendimiento del conflicto armado en Colombia*. Bogotá: Ediciones Desde Abajo, pp. 627–78.

Preciado, P. (2019) 'Cuando los subalternos entran en el museo: desobediencia epistémica y crítica institucional', in Pizarro, B. (ed) *Exponer o exponerse: la educación en museos como producción cultural crítica*. Madrid: Alcantara, pp. 15–26.

Rotondi, J., and Eisikovits, N. (2015) 'Forgetting After War: A Qualified Defense', in Corradetti, C., Eisikovits, N. and Rotondi, J. (eds) *Theorizing Transitional JusticeDorchester*. Dorchester: Ashgate, pp. 15–28.

Sala Penal de Justicia y Paz del Tribunal Superior de Medellín (2014) *Jesús Ignacio Roldán Pérez, nº de radicado: 110016000253-2006-82611*. Available at: www.ramajudicial.gov.co/documents/6342975/6634902/09-12-2014-sentencia-bloque-calima-de-las-auc-jesus-ignacio-roldan-perez-monoleche.pdf/d69ba9ab-92bc-4b83-ab80-5e398721af69 (Accessed 16 April 2022).

Seixas, P. (2017) 'Historical Consciousness and Historical Thinking', in Carretero M., Berger, S. and Grever, M. (eds) *The Palgrave Handbook of Research in Historical Culture Education*. London: Palgrave Macmillan, pp. 59–72.

Simon, N. (2010) *The Participatory Museum*. Santa Cruz: Museum 2.0.

Smith, A. (2010) *The Influence of Education on Conflict and Peace Building. Background Paper for EFA Global Monitoring Report 2011*. UNESCO.

Sriprakash, A., Nally, D., Meyers, K. and Ramos-Pinto, P. (2020) '*Learning with the Past: Racism, Education and Reparative Futures. Background Paper for the Futures of Education Initiative*', UNESCO: 374045eng.pdf (edu.ro).

Tamm, M. and Olivier, L. (2019) 'Introduction: Rethinking Historical Time', in Tamm, M. and Olivier, L. (eds) *Rethinking Historical Time. New Approaches to Presentism*. London: Bloomsbury, pp. 1–22.

Torrijos, V. (2015) 'Cartografía del conflicto: Pautas interpretativas sobre la evolución del conflicto irregular colombiano' in *Contribución al entendimiento del conflicto armado en Colombia*. Bogotá: Ediciones Desde Abajo, pp. 628–79.

Tikly, L. (2020) *Education for Sustainable Development in the Postcolonial World*. Abingdon: Routledge.

Tzibazi, V. (2013) 'Participatory Action Research with young people in museums', *Museum Management and Curatorship*, 28(2), pp. 153–71.

Wang, Z. (2008) 'National Humiliation, History Education, and the Politics of Historical Memory: Patriotic Education Campaign in China', *International Studies Quarterly*. 52(4), pp. 783–806.

Williams, P. (2007) *Memorial Museums: The Global Rush to Commemorate Atrocities*. Oxford and New York: Berg.

Winkler, A. (2015) 'Remembering and Historicising Socialism: The Private and Amateur Musealization of East Germany's Everyday Life' in McIsaac, P. and Mueller, G. (eds) *Exhibiting the German Past: Museums, Film, and Musealization*. Toronto: University of Toronto, pp. 100–22.

12

HERITAGE AND EDUCATION

Mobile Approaches to Peacebuilding

Abiti Nelson Adebo, Lizzi O. Milligan, Nono Francis, and Kate Moles

Introduction

This chapter explores the potential of heritage as a developmental resource within mobile education settings with specific reference to peacebuilding. While there has been a big increase in the attention paid to peace education within education studies, heritage as a site, means, or process of informal education is often neglected within these considerations. From an education perspective on peacebuilding, where heritage has been included, it has been framed only as a resource for education through memory work at formal heritage sites for example at museums and public memorials, separate from the formal school curriculum (Bellino et al., 2017). In this way, just as formal education settings have been neglected as sites of memory (see Paulson et al., 2020), heritage has similarly been sidelined in discussions of teaching and learning about the violent past, such as in history and peace education. Heritage is often positioned as a supplement or an add-on to formal education curriculums, rather than a site of education in and of itself.

In terms of peacebuilding, this practical reality contrasts sharply with the United Nations (UN) Sustainable Development Goals (SDGs). For example, under SDG 4: Quality Education, SDG 4.7 calls for all learners to acquire the skills needed to promote sustainable development through education for amongst other things a culture of peace and non-violence, appreciation of cultural diversity and of culture's contribution to sustainable development. Implicit to SDG 4.7 then, it could be argued, is a perceived role for heritage, as a past-looking aspect of culture, to contribute to sustainable, peaceful societies through informal education. In this chapter, as scholars and practitioners from education, sociology, and heritage studies, we seek to explore that relationship from a variety of approaches before drawing out some of our observations through a research case study of mobile informal education workshops in northern Uganda.

DOI: 10.4324/9781003107361-16

Museums, transitional justice, and education

Museums have frequently been cited as having a role to play in peacebuilding by collecting and exhibiting violence as a way of educating the population about past conflicts. For example, UNESCO has promoted the role of museums in attaining social cohesion through educational policies (UNESCO Report on Museums, 2015). The role of museums in education is attributed to the relationship between teachers, parents, learners, textbooks, and object interactions between home and school (van den Dungen and Yamen, 2015). The focus of these claims is typically the perceived potential of museums as spaces where dialogue and memory work about difficult pasts can take place, which is essential for transitional justice underpinned by ideas of truth and reconciliation. Within this context, formal heritage sites such as museums and public memorials may thus be viewed as valuable informal education sites for peacebuilding. As spaces where alternative narratives can be accommodated, questions posed, and interest provoked, they offer ways for different generations to come together and learn about difficult pasts. However, the possibilities for these aims to be achieved need scrutinizing because there are many examples in the literature that demonstrate the challenges in aligning the aims, processes, and outcomes of peace education, for example, in enacting critical and intergenerational dialogue (see for example, Bekerman and Zembylas, 2011; Salomon, 2011).

It is also clear that the formal space of many museums in the Global South and North may also be considered sites of violence due to their colonial histories and the persistence of colonial power structures into the present. For example, most national museums in Africa were established under colonial rule and are implicated in past violence against Indigenous communities (see Peterson et al., 2015), and continue to promote colonial thinking in their representation of African history. The marginalization of Indigenous knowledge within these museums, we argue, acts against the effective use of museums as sites of education as populations, and especially the youth, remain disconnected from the representations within them. The buildings themselves, the histories they represent, the forms of exhibition and the stories that are often told are often very different to the lived experiences of those who visit, and as such lack relevance to the ways the visitors make sense of their lives and the challenges they face in the present.

Formal schooling has similarly been critiqued for being a space where epistemic violence is perpetrated, for example, when it promotes exclusive group identities, silences cultures and experiences, or legitimizes conflict and injustice (Cole and Barsalou, 2006; Bellino, 2016; Davies, 2017). School curricula also often fail to include difficult issues or only partially deal with them (van den Dungen and Yamane, 2015). Few formal curricula give space for opportunities to discuss ways of preventing and resolving conflicts or for children and young people to engage critically with difficult pasts and question received singular narratives. In turn, peace education can often be minimised to issues of personal conflict resolution or as part of a broader curriculum of human rights and/or citizenship. Consequently, curricula often limit opportunities for students to develop knowledge and understanding of the specific historical, cultural, political, and economic roots of the conflicts and violence that affect them, much less the skills to transform these conflicts and contribute to peaceful futures (Paulson, 2015).

It is also important to note the important scholarship that problematizes research about teaching and learning about the violent past for its focus predominantly on policy decisions about curricular content. As Sobe (2014: 313) argues, schools are not neutral spaces where top-down messages are passively transmitted, rather they are 'sites of contestation, negotiation, and cultural production'. Here, it is important to consider both how teachers contest and negotiate content in their teaching practices and the crucial role that learners themselves play in what they choose to accept, confront and question. Furthermore, these processes of teaching and learning cannot be separated from teachers and learners' experiences and understandings of the past and how they interpret these in the present and for their futures (Paulson et al., 2020).

In response, some authors have suggested the potential for travelling and co-constructed exhibitions to respond to the challenges that formal education and heritage spaces represent and so provide alternative, informal education venues for peace and reconciliation. Gachanga and Walters (2015) have highlighted how a travelling exhibition on African cultures in Kenya created spaces for dialogue and provided symbols as a starting point for interfaith and intergroup discussion. Another example of such dialogue can be seen in the exhibitions in the District Six Museum, Cape Town, South Africa where Rassool (2006) (see also Julius, 2008) engaged the community through exhibitions to discuss the past violence of the apartheid regime with the aim of promoting transitional justice and restitution following the forced removal of District Six communities. Similarly, Romero-Amaya (2019: 104) has shown how an exhibition of *Silencios* – a photography series by the Colombian artist Juan Manuel Echavarría of 120 photographs of abandoned schools due to armed conflict in Los Montes de María, Colombia – sought to 'ignite multiple narratives and counterhegemonic memories' as a 'an educational opportunity to stimulate reflection and resistance.' What comes through strongly in this literature is the importance of dialogue, here prompted by objects, and the space for multiple narratives, both of which are principal tenets of critical peace education (Bajaj, 2019).

There exist deliberate moves by museums in the Global South to more formally support educational policies to actively engage young learners to build confidence in the management and prevention of conflicts and the maintenance of peace. It is clear that while museums, heritage sites, and exhibitions are recognized as important sites of learning, formal heritage and formal education remain separate entities, with heritage presented as an alternative to, not a constituent part of, formal educational practices and content. As van den Dungen and Yamane (2015: 213) have observed, 'museums are typically seen as representing a complementary, largely informal venue for education, offering different ways of learning and experiences from that available in the classroom'.

However, what this informal education looks like and how it contributes to broader educational and social outcomes is ill-defined. In our work, we have particularly highlighted the potential for multigenerational education settings where parents, grandparents, teachers, and the young can engage in peace education from different perspectives. This has meant reimagining the spaces of heritage themselves, as well as the ways in which people are enrolled into the narratives. By attending to the ways that heritage can be seen as part of the everyday lives of people, connected to lived experiences and meaningful within understandings of self, society, and relations between both, we can enable reflective and reparative practices through engagement with the past to build peaceful futures.

Informal heritage spaces and education

While the importance of museums and other formal heritage sites as learning spaces continues to be cited, there remains remarkably little evidence about the outcomes of such learning and their potential impact for sustainable peace, or about the potential for heritage to be harnessed for education outside of formal heritage spaces. Salomon (2002) usefully summarizes some of the outcomes that may be harnessed through peace education initiatives, although cautions that not all programmes 'are created equal'. Possible outcomes outlined include changing mindsets – such as promoting understanding, respect and tolerance, cultivating a set of behaviours, acquiring a non-violent disposition, and the promotion of human rights. From a critical peace education perspective, there are further considerations of the ways that education can be transformative and enable young people to be 'change agents' (see Bajaj, 2019) and contribute to 'positive' peace, beyond simply the absence of violence (Cremin and Bevington 2017). This perspective is particularly important given the emphasis placed on localised understandings and experiences of peace and the ways that voices not normally included in formal mechanisms of teaching the past can be included.

To explore the potential learning outcomes and impact for sustainable peace, we formed a research collaboration, funded by the UK's Global Challenges Research Fund (GCRF), which focused on identifying indicators for informal learning through a mobile heritage network of conflict-affected communities in Uganda. The following case study focuses on that project and in so doing highlights some of the ways that learning about peace and reconciliation can happen through a travelling exhibition, including key learning that participants identified. Through this, the example promotes informal peacebuilding education through formal heritage practices, an exhibition, in informal heritage spaces.

Post-conflict memory practices

In Uganda, national memorialization of 20th- and 21st-century wars has failed to promote teaching about the history of past conflicts nor has it built strong pillars for peaceful negotiations. Against this backdrop, community memorialization has become the basis for remembering the pains of war in post-conflict contexts, for example, in northern Uganda in the aftermath of a civil war that devastated the region between 1986 and 2006. The hostilities in northern Uganda saw Ugandan government soldiers on one side and the Lord's Resistance Army (LRA) rebels led by Joseph Kony on the other. The prolonged civil war caused death, displacement, and the abduction of children. More than two million people were forced to seek refuge in congested Internally Displaced Peoples (IDPs) camps (Mwenda, 2010). The conflict also changed the landscape in northern Uganda as well as people's mindsets, it required a process of resettlement in addition to reconstruction programs, including ones that engaged with issues of community cultural memory.

To push for reconstruction, the government and international development aid partners focused on economic and social well-being without considering the potential of cultural heritage. This may not seem surprising but is contrary to the Constitution of Uganda (1995) (see principle and objective XXIV), which stipulates the fundamental role and value of culture in promoting human rights, freedoms, human dignity, and democracy. Instead, the promotion of heritage in peacebuilding was left to elders who initiated peace talks in 2000 and 2006 and advocated for the inclusion of culture in the reconstruction process, arguing that 'cultural reconstruction is as important as infrastructural reconstruction' (Abiti, 2018: 83–88).

To deliver on this aim it was first essential for the communities that had been impacted by the war to define for themselves what cultural heritage resources were of value for peace and development. Within this context, community memorialization emerged as a bottom-up approach to remember the pains of war in a post-conflict situation. Despite a history of conflict in 20th- and 21st-century Uganda, many communities remain resilient and wish to engage in questions of reconciliation and peacebuilding as part of post-conflict reconstruction efforts. Memorialization also presented an alternative way of generating reliable information about the history of the conflict, which was lacking (Hopwood, 2011). In this context memorialization offered a means to interrogate claims of injustice and stories of conflict from community perspectives. The acknowledgment of violence is a key factor in addressing the wrongs of violence, and practices of memorialization offer a way to acknowledge the violence and its victims and the importance to remember both.

Mato-oput is an example of how local people in northern Uganda adopted alternatives to standard transitional justice practices. *Mato-oput* refers to a traditional Acholi healing and reconciliation ritual that historically was used as a way of reintegrating offending individuals into communities. Within the context of the so-called Northern War, it was employed as a form of reconciliation to reintegrate former members of the LRA who were responsible for killings. In most cases of *Mato-oput*, reconciliation happens after a burial or funeral ceremony to allow the spirits of the dead to rest at peace. The process of *Mato-oput* begins with a family approaching an elder. As mediator, the elder discusses the matter in confidence with each of the family members, or the clan groups, to assess their acceptance of the situation (Afako, 2002: 67). After this, representatives of the clans engage in shuttle diplomacy to collect confessions and establish the truth. When families have agreed, the offending family is asked to pay compensation for the loss of the life in the form of either cattle or cash. Some families of the victims also request an apology from the offender. During this process, the representatives or the affected persons will go to the victim's family and community members are invited to participate as witnesses. The elders instruct representatives of the two clans or families to bend on their knees to drink the bitter juice of oput from a calabash. The Acholi believe that the oput root juice symbolizes blood and washes away impurities and therefore it helps to restore relations between the offended clans. It is a 'cooling off' of the bitterness (Anyeko et al., 2012: 111). Once the offender acknowledges their guilt and the victim's family accepts the forgiveness, the mediator organizes a public ceremony of *Mato-oput*. The elders of the two families or representatives of the clan bring in their spears and stand on the roadside where they bend them as a sign of ending the conflict. The ritual chief brings branches of olwedo leaves to bless the clans and members of the family and exhorts them to lead a peaceful life.

Mato-oput reconciliation was critical for Acholi communities because as described by Okot P'Bitek (1971: 155), a Ugandan writer, blood feuds (*kwor*) must be settled otherwise the ghost of the deceased will bring much trouble to your people (see also Onyango-Ku-Odongo and Webster 1976: 61–65). The reintroduction of *Mato-oput*, as a traditional justice system, also challenged the simplistic definition of community members into categories of either perpetrators, victims, or bystanders, for example, by recognizing that in many cases perpetrators could also be victims and vice versa. As discussed by Veale and Stavrou (2007: 290), many Acholi people recognize that former LRA child soldiers were forcibly recruited and were themselves victims of the conflict. However, after returning to their communities a sense of guilt for the children and their families could persist and grow and the children would often remain isolated. In this context, bottom-up memorialization combined with *Mato-oput* reconciliation practices provided mechanisms through which unresolved differences could be processed as a form of community healing and reintegration for former child soldiers.

Mobile exhibitions and peace education

As a response to this context our research funded memory work through mobile exhibitions that sought to go beyond fixed narratives of past violence, to promote reconciliation, peace, and healing. Mobile exhibitions meant that peacebuilding education could be located in the heart of the communities as an alternative model of learning, involving divergent views and experiences that reworked contested spaces (Abiti, 2018: 83–96). This work was premised on the belief that the loss of intangible memory could lead to behavioural problems in young people and in turn incite violence and a sense of hopelessness.

The project was called 'Indicators for Informal Learning: A Mobile Heritage Network for Conflict' and was funded by a UK-AHRC 2018 grant on the theme of Education in Conflict and Protracted Crisis. We assessed the mobile exhibition projects that were developed by Uganda National Museum and other civil society organizations in northern Uganda, including the National Memory and Peace Documentation Centre of the Refugee Law project and the Justice for Reconciliation Initiatives. Over the past three years, mobile exhibitions were shown at four locations, Mucwini in Kitgum, Barlonyo in Lira, Lukodi and Patiko in then Gulu district. Each exhibition was tailored to the location, including their specific experiences of the conflict and its legacies. For example, at Barlonyo and Lukodi, where there had been massacres, and issues of community conflict and accountability persisted, the exhibitions focused on reconciliation and transitional justice respectively.

Over three months, exhibition workshops were held at each location over the course of two to three days, for two to three hours per day, between 7 and 12 participants at each one. For example, at Kitgum Memorial Centre, the workshops included male and female elders, ex-soldiers, and victims. At times, to support productive conversations, participants were separated into particular groups. For example, in Kitgum, women preferred to have a separate conversation, while youths and elders had discussions separately and then joined together to share their perspectives on peace and reconciliation. In Lukodi, we focused on youths' and children's stories about the conflict and their learning about peace.

In summary, our project showed that museum objects have great educational potential when they are activated within communities rather than behind the walls of museums. For example, our research highlighted how combining oral histories with artefacts was more effective at promoting traditional forms of conflict resolution and thus bringing about reconciliation in the present. During a demonstration of a reconciliation ceremony in Mucwini as part of one of our mobile exhibition workshops, the representatives of two conflicting families performed a forgiveness ceremony by sharing spears and bending them to signify the absence of violence (Figure 12.1).

> Once bended then they interchange: one from the killer would be handed over to the victim while the victim's will be given to the killer. That signifies that me and you will no longer fight each other again; we have already bended the blades of the spears.
>
> *Mucwini workshop participant*

Other participants reflected on how learning could be seen through compassion and empathy in relation to one of the exhibition themes – others' experiences of the conflict. Children's stories in the exhibition about everyday objects such as a blanket or bicycle as symbols of war were especially effective at eliciting empathetic responses. Broader learning was suggested through, for example, increasing degrees of willingness from different clans to participate in cultural festivals and different dances, to send their children to the same schools and to accept their young people taking part in the same football matches. Clearly it is difficult to make one-to-one associations between these changes and the exhibition in isolation from other

FIGURE 12.1 A community member showing a bended spear in Kitgum

Source: Photo taken by author (Abiti).

potential causal factors, however, community members did highlight the exhibition as one mechanism that was supporting community-based learning about peace and education leading to these broader behavioural changes. In this way, learning happening in the exhibition cannot be separated from broader informal learning processes and the outcomes.

Some of the participants highlighted the important role of exhibitions in learning about the history of conflict and being able to demonstrate an understanding of that history. However, it was felt that this was not shared across all participant groups. While the elder participants focused on narrating the history of the conflicts, most children and young people focused on traditional knowledge associated with the objects rather than the conflict narrative. This led the elders to question how much children understand about the history of the conflict, with some suggesting that children may take part in post-conflict traditional activities such as dance, but they may just be observing and reproducing what their parents perform rather than gaining a deeper understanding as intended. Thus, due to a potential lack of awareness and engagement, the elders expressed a concern that the perspectives of young people may not be taken into account in peacebuilding dialogues. Therefore, a holistic approach that includes songs and dances of reconciliation as well as engagement with the history of conflict is required. The exhibition workshops also found that children living with parents who directly experienced the war were more likely to be taught about peace more than those whose parents did not have direct experience of the violence. This again highlighted the need for educational spaces, such as mobile exhibitions, for critical dialogue about the historical causes of conflict as well as contemporary peacebuilding practices (Figure 12.2).

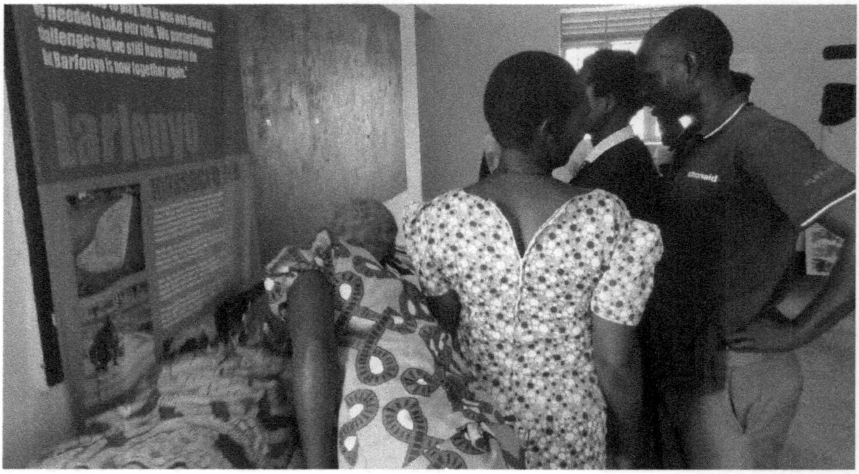

FIGURE 12.2 Mobile exhibition being reviewed by a women's focus group at Barlonyo memorial site

Source: Photo taken by author (Abiti).

Mobile exhibitions can bring heritage learning into the heart of the community, socially situating and embedding that learning within the community and thus potentially making it more effective. While the formal school curriculum may in some situations silence alternative histories (Paulson, 2015; Bellino, 2016; although see Bermeo et al., this volume for an exception), the discursive and reflexive nature of the exhibition and workshops provided space for the emergence and negotiation of alternative narratives. Elsewhere, we have argued that such a participatory approach allows for

> the production and acceptance of narratives of the past within communities, rather than in spaces dislocated from those who have experienced injustices and live with the affects … [allowing] epistemic injustices to be disrupted, which in turn can facilitate a more sustained transitional justice.
>
> *Abiti et al., 2021*

Despite the successes of this approach, however, the potential to use artefacts for peacebuilding is yet to have been realised by policy makers.

Travelling exhibitions can, thus, offer a different context for peace education, outside of conventional museums that traditionally have collected and presented cultural objects in ways that have presented communities as 'out of time and out of politics' (Butler, 2000: 79). In terms of critical, urgent, contemporary perspectives on heritage, mobile exhibitions have the potential to recontextualize museum objects through community participation that presents 'problems not solutions', leaving space for dialogue and negotiation. For example, as Konare (1983) has argued, in most cases of museum collection, local populations were not consulted, nor did they want their objects turned into public goods, taken away to be stripped of their values and displayed in locations that are inaccessible to their creators. While others, such as Karp and Kratz (2014) through their 'interrogative museum', have highlighted how curators working in collaboration with communities need to exhibit problems not solutions. It is with these aspirations in mind that we undertook our mobile exhibition and peacebuilding research in northern Uganda.

Conclusion

Education has the potential to play a major role in transforming society. Peace education is an element of peacebuilding and is a field of scholarship and practice that utilizes teaching and learning not only to dismantle all forms of violence, but also to create structures that build and sustain a just and equitable peace' (Bajaj, 2019: 65). However, processes of education and peacebuilding are consistently seen to be limited by the formal structures associated with governance of peace education where narratives are refocused, reinvented, and reconstructed in line with state powers. We see this clearly in both the formal institution of the school and museum. For example, the tools used to transmit peace education in formal classrooms limit the development of peace at community level, where social cohesion is nurtured and established. Peace education in post-conflict situations is, therefore, often limited by challenges of disconnect, denial and contextual approaches to dialogues, and reinterpretation of the past violence (Paulson et al., 2020).

While a critical development agenda has highlighted the post-conflict significance of cultural heritage, this has tended to focus on the roles of museums and other formal heritage sites in peacebuilding, where the past can be reconstructed or renegotiated to promote new seemingly more inclusive and reconciliatory narratives (see Giblin et al. this volume). In this chapter, we have argued for the potential of mobile heritage, in the form of travelling exhibitions, as alternative spaces for learning about violent pasts and for sustainable peaceful futures.

We acknowledge that, all memories of past violence are not equal due to the experiences of ethnic differences, the traumas, and structural approaches of reconciliation that are being redeveloped along side the heritage projects as exemplified in Rwanda, Kenya, Uganda, and Sierra Leone. The community memorial process outlined in this chapter has pointed to one possible way that heritage spaces could provide critical peace education but how these are developed and implemented will depend on understanding the processes of memory-making in a local community, including how people's participation in a museum project might define its future outcome.

Further research is required to see how some of the possible learning outcomes identified in our study – such as potential for changing behaviours – could be more broadly assessed. However, what is clear is that mobile heritage education as a form of participatory, sustainable, and informal learning practice can play an important role in peacebuilding through its provision of community access to tangible heritage objects and intangible heritage practices, strengthening local action, and enabling people, especially young people, to learn from the past and look towards the future.

References

Abiti, A. N. (2018) 'The Road to Reconciliation. Museum Practice, Community Memorials and Collaborations in Uganda', in Laely, T., Meyer, M., and Schwere, R. (eds) *Museum Cooperation between Africa and Europe: A New Field for Museum Studies*. Bielefeld: Transcript Verlag, pp. 83–96.

Abiti, A. N., Nono, F., Moles, K. and Milligan, L. O. (2021) 'Participatory Curatorship: Negotiating Heritage, Memory and Justice in Northern Uganda', in Cin, M. and Mkwananzi, F. (eds) *Post-conflict Participatory Arts: Socially engaged development*. Abingdon: Routledge, pp. 54–70.

Afako, B. (2002). Reconciliation and justice: 'Mato oput' and the Amnesty Act. *Accord: An International Review of Peace Initiatives*, 11, 64–67..

Anyeko, K., Baines, E., Komakech, E., Ojok, B., Owor Ogora, L. and Victor, L. (2012) 'The Cooling of Hearts': Community Truth-Telling in Northern Uganda', *Human Rights Review*, 13(1), pp. 107–124.

Bajaj, M. (2019) 'Conceptualising critical peace education for conflict settings', *Education and Conflict Review*, 2, pp. 65–69.

Bekerman, Z. and Zembylas, M. (2011). *Teaching contested narratives: Identity, memory and reconciliation in peace education and beyond*. Cambridge: Cambridge University Press.

Bellino, M. J. (2016) 'So that we do not fall again: History education and citizenship in "postwar" Guatemala', *Comparative Education Review*, 60(1), pp. 58–79.

Bellino, M. J., Paulson, J. and Anderson Worden, E. (2017) 'Working through difficult pasts: Toward thick democracy and transitional justice in education', *Comparative Education*, 53(3), pp. 313–332.

Butler, S. R. (2000) 'The politics of exhibiting culture: Legacies and possibilities', *Museum Anthropology*, 23(3), pp. 74–92.

Cole, E. A. and Barsalou, J. (2006) 'Unite or Divide', in *The Challenges of Teaching History in Societies Emerging from Violent Conflict*. Special Report. US Institute of Peace.

Constitution of Uganda (1995) Available at: www.constituteproject.org/constitution/Uganda_2017.pdf?lang=en (Accessed 30 April 2022).

Cremin, H. and Bevington, T. (2017) *Positive Peace in Schools: Tackling Conflict and Creating a Culture of Peace in the Classroom*. Abingdon: Routledge.

Davies, L. (2017) 'Justice-sensitive education: The implications of transitional justice mechanisms for teaching and learning', *Comparative Education*, 53(3), pp. 333–350. doi:10.1080/03050068.2017.1317999

Gachanga, T. and Walters, D. (2015) 'Journeys of peace: Exhibitions, objects, and creative dialogue', *African Conflict and Peacebuilding Review*, 5(1), pp. 123–135. doi:10.2979/africonfpeacrevi.5.1.123

Hopwood, J. (2011). *We Can't Be Sure Who Killed Us*. International Centre for Transitional Justice and Reconciliation Centre Project.

Julius, C. (2008) ''Digging [D] eeper than the eye approves': oral histories and their use in the Digging Deeper exhibition of the district Six Museum', *Kronos*, 34(1), pp. 106–138.

Karp, I., and Kratz, C. A. (2014) 'Collecting, exhibiting, and interpreting: Museums as mediators and midwives of meaning', *Museum Anthropology*, 37(1), pp. 51–65.

Konaré, A. O. (1983) 'Towards a new type of 'ethnographic' museum in Africa', *Museum International*, 35(3), pp. 146–151.

Mwenda, A. (2010) 'Uganda's politics of foreign aid and violent conflict: the political uses of the LRA rebellion,' in Allen, T. and Vlassenroot, K. (eds) *The Lord's Resistance Army: Myth and Reality*. London: Zed Books, pp. 45–58.

Onyango-Ku-Odongo, J. M., and Webster, J. B. (1976) *The Central Lwo during the Aconya*. Nairobi: East African Literature Bureau.

Paulson, J. (2015) '"Whether and how?" History education about recent and ongoing conflict: a review of research', *Journal on Education in Emergencies*, 1(1), pp. 7–39.

Paulson, J., Abiti, N., Bermeo Osorio, J., Charria Hernández, C. A., Keo, D., Manning, P., Milligan, L. O., Moles, K., Pennell, C., Salih, S. and Shanks, K. (2020) 'Education as site of memory: developing a research agenda', *International Studies in Sociology of Education*, 29(4), pp. 429–451.

P'Bitek, O. (1971) *Religion of the Central Luo*. Nairobi: East African Literature Bureau.

Peterson, D. R., Gavua, K. and Rasool, C. (2015) *The Politics of Heritage in Africa: Economies, Histories, and Infrastructures*. Cambridge: Cambridge University Press.

Rassool, C. (2006) 'Community Museums, Memory Politics, and Social Transformation in South Africa: Histories, Possibilities, and Limits,' in Rasool, C. and Kirshenblatt-Gimblett, B. (eds) *Museum Frictions: Public Cultures/Global Transformation*. Durham, North Carolina: Duke University Press, pp. 286–321.

Romero-Amaya, D. (2019) 'Empty schools and Silencios: Pedagogical openings for memory-making in Colombia', *Journal of Peace Education*, 16(1), pp. 104–125. doi: 10.1080/17400201.2018.1492373

Salomon, G. (2002) 'The nature of peace education: Not all programs are created equal', in Saloman, G. and Nevo, B. (eds) *Peace education: The concept, principles, and practices around the world*, East Sussex, UK: Psychology Press, pp. 3–13.

Salomon, G. (2011). 'Four major challenges facing peace education in regions of intractable conflict', *Peace and conflict*, 17(1), pp. 46–59.

Sobe, N.W. (2014) 'Textbooks, schools, memory, and the technologies of national imaginaries', in Williams, J. H. (ed) *(Re)Constructing Memory: School textbooks and the imagination of the nation*. Rotterdam: Sense Publications, pp. 311–18.

UNESCO (2015) 'Recommendation concerning the Protection and Promotion of Collections and Museums, their diversity and their role in the society', Available at: http://umac.icom.museum/wp-content/uploads/2018/08/246331m.pdf (Accessed 30 April 2022).

van den Dungen, P., and Yamane, K. (2015) 'Peace education through peace museums', *Journal of Peace Education*, 12(3), pp. 213–222. doi:10.1080/17400201.2015.1103393

Veale, A. and Stavrou, A. (2007) 'Former Lord's Resistance Army child soldier abductees: Explorations of identity in reintegration and reconciliation', *Peace and Conflict: Journal of Peace Psychology*, 13(3), pp. 273–292.

PART 5

Heritage, Peace, Security and Development

13

HYBRIDITY, HERITAGE AND THE GOVERNANCE OF SECURITY

Community Policing in Tanzania

Charlotte Cross

Introduction

This chapter explores attempts to instrumentalise heritage in addressing contemporary security challenges through analysis of 'hybrid governance' approaches within international development. Interest in hybridity has emerged from critiques of state-centric assumptions in development programming and increased understanding of the diversity of institutions that exercise public authority and are involved in the provision of public goods and services, including security and policing. This might include a range of 'traditional' authorities, or other institutions that embed practices, values and meanings derived from or legitimated in relation to the past. It is suggested that hybrid models, which combine such institutions with some attributes of 'modern' statehood can engender more effective and locally acceptable forms of development. However, attempts to instrumentalise hybridity pay insufficient attention to how appeals to both the past and the future are implicated in power relations and their contestation and, thus, how hybrid arrangements evolve over time and between places. Rather than assuming that the existence of 'local' security provision arrangements implies they are legitimate and effective, this chapter argues that these questions should be interrogated from the perspective of those who rely on such services for their safety.

Hybrid governance for development

For much of the 1990s and early 21st century, dominant ideas within international development policy and practice were predicated upon the assumption that improving governance in aid-recipient countries entailed promoting institutional forms derived from elsewhere. The pursuit of 'good governance', conceptualised in terms of 'Western' democratic institutions and civil society and a free market,

DOI: 10.4324/9781003107361-18

however, has attracted increasing criticism. Not only are such approaches based on the questionable assumption that democracy is a necessary precondition for development, which does not reflect historical experience in today's wealthy industrialised countries, they in any case often fail to achieve their stated objectives of making governance more effective and accountable (Andrews, 2013; Booth and Cammack, 2013).

A growing body of scholarship and practice instead urges a focus on the 'function not the form of institutions' (Unsworth, 2010: 8). Advocates of going or working with 'the grain' in supporting governance for development, argue that the starting point of developmental reform should be those governance arrangements that are already in place, rather than promotion of 'best practice' solutions derived from elsewhere (Booth and Cammack, 2013; Levy, 2014). Although not often explicitly articulated in terms of heritage, ideas about what 'the grain' is are informed by understandings of culture and of historically durable ideas, values and practices that influence ideas of moral obligation, accountability and how power is exercised (Kelsall, 2008; Booth, 2011). The grain is often assumed to be manifest in a range of 'traditional' or 'customary' authorities and practices (e.g., Boege et al., 2009). It is thus proposed that the past be reconceptualised as an asset and used to bring about contemporary development.

Parallel trends are evident in fields specifically focused on governing peace and security, where criticism has grown of initiatives premised on the assumption of the desirability and feasibility of developing a Weberian-ideal type state with liberal democratic institutions in aid-recipient countries. Within peacebuilding, promotion of the 'liberal peace' has given way to a 'local turn', which privileges local agency over prescriptions for peace based on international models based on liberal assumptions about statehood (Mac Ginty and Richmond, 2013). Critiques of 'statebuilding' interventions have seen a range of 'informal' institutions, previously pathologised as indications of 'state failure', recast as potentially effective and desirable modes of governance (Meagher, 2012). Debates about security sector reform and policing interventions are similarly characterised by increased recognition of the role and potential of alternatives to the state police such that, by 2012 Hills (2012: 2) identified, 'an emergent policy orthodoxy that policing is a multi-layered activity requiring police to co-operate with informal providers'. The World Development Report for 2011, for example, which focused on conflict, security and development, argued for a 'best fit' approach that might involve 'combinations of state, private sector, faith-based, traditional, and community structures for service delivery' (World Bank, 2011: 106). The OECD's Development Assistance Committee has similarly advocated a 'multi-layered' approach to security sector reform which would divide international assistance between the state as a regulator, but only a minority provider, of security, and non-state justice and security service providers, 'given their position as the primary purveyors of day-to-day service delivery' (OECD, 2007: 7), and major bilateral aid donors have also engaged with what are variously termed 'informal', 'customary', 'traditional' or 'non-state' security providers (DFID, 2004; DANIDA, 2010).

In addition to recognising the existence of alternative security providers, interest has emerged in provision of security and other public goods through arrangements that entail integration of locally existing institutions and those of the state, the latter being assumed to conform to different standards more consistent with international norms. Booth and Cammack (2013: 112), for example, writing specifically about Africa advocate 'practical hybrids', referring to 'modern state structures that have been adapted to, or infused with, contemporary cultural preferences'. This appears to offer a potential compromise between the strengths and weaknesses of both kinds of provision. Bruce Baker (2010: 609), one of the most influential advocates of increasing attention to non-state and hybrid solutions within security provision in aid-recipient countries, describes a hypothetical 'win-win linkage', whereby state institutions better meet local needs and non-state practices are brought closer in line with international standards in areas such as appropriate punishment and gender equality.

Although much support for security and justice sector reform remains state-centric (Denney, 2014), development organisations have sought to co-opt or capitalise upon 'traditional' institutions for security in diverse contexts including Afghanistan, Solomon Islands, Timor-Leste and Nigeria (e.g., Schmeidl and Karokhail, 2009; Allen et al., 2013; Arnot, 2015; Wallis et al., 2016). The OECD's Development Assistance Committee even positions doing so as one of the key challenges of supporting governance in the Global South, noting that: 'the challenge is to understand how traditional and formal systems interact in any given context and to look for ways of constructively combining them' (OECD, 2011: 25).

It is not only 'external' development actors who have pursued hybrid approaches. Somaliland and Botswana are among nations often cited as having successfully incorporated modes of customary authority into state governance structures and practices (Boege et al., 2009; Giblin, Ntagwabira and Mugabowagahunde, this volume). Governments of diverse countries including Ethiopia, Mexico, Nigeria and Peru have undertaken some form of recognition and incorporation of 'community-based' police that draw on traditional, religious or cultural authority (Baker, 2013; Gitlitz, 2013; Merino and Colarado, 2013; Ogbozor, 2016). Tanzania's *sungusungu*, discussed in this chapter, as well as variations developed in neighbouring Kenya, have become one of the most frequently cited examples of state-sponsorship of traditional policing, and are often positioned as a 'successful' attempt at hybridity (Boege et al., 2009).

There are pragmatic reasons for supporting hybrid governance solutions in so-called 'fragile' or conflict-affected contexts. Firstly, where the state is not in any case the only or even the main provider of security, there is an argument for considering which institutions *are* involved in keeping people safe, rather than which *should* be (Albrecht and Kyed, 2011). This may present a cheaper option than rebuilding state institutions, particularly following conflict (Baker, 2010). Hybrid models are also sometimes envisaged as offering a way of improving efficiency, by capitalising on an existing 'cultural repertoire' that enables cooperation, rather than incurring the costs of trying to set up imported solutions (Booth, 2011: 7). New forms of public authority may benefit from being able to 'piggy-back' on locally familiar frameworks (Lund, 2006: 692). Thus practices, forms of authority and ideas drawn from the past are reframed not as obstacles to development, but as 'assets and sources of solutions' (Boege et al., 2009: 20) to contemporary challenges. The perceived utility of traditional practices may also reflect more explicit political calculations, as in Ethiopia where the government's incorporation of customary institutions within policing provision aimed to capitalise on their ability to provide an effective service, while also seeking to assert greater control over their activities (Baker, 2013).

While rejecting normative assumptions about the primacy of the state in security provision, other normative assumptions about the attributes of 'local' institutions often do inform arguments for hybrid governance. One of the 'assets' frequently attributed to alternative providers is greater legitimacy and popularity due to their origins in local 'tradition' and culture and compatibility with local norms (Bagayoko et al., 2016). Such 'organic grounded legitimacy' has been framed as a 'resource' upon which external actors can draw to enhance processes of state formation and peacebuilding (Clements, 2014: 15).

A move away from discourses of 'failed states' and 'good governance' to greater recognition of the diversity of institutions that exercise public authority and the complex connections between them, is welcome. However, recognition of the utility of hybridity as an analytical lens does not imply it is something that can be prescribed, instrumentalised or manufactured with guaranteed outcomes (Mallet, 2010; Mac Ginty and Sanghera, 2012). Important questions arise regarding how such processes are mediated by power at different scales, and, the ways in which appeals to the past, as well as to the future, are themselves implicated in such processes. Attempts to promote hybridity as a policy solution thus risk privileging particular articulations of both heritage and development and the connections between them, which benefit some more than others. Such questions are especially pressing in discussion of security governance. While security can be seen in terms of an entitlement of citizens to protection, security also entails 'creation and maintenance of authoritative social orders' (Luckham and Kirk, 2013: 339). Thus, security is something for which there is a demand and which is integral to achieving other development goals, but it is also something that is enacted upon some individuals or groups, often violently, to protect the interests of others.

Community policing in Tanzania

The rest of this chapter reviews some key challenges with attempts to instrumentalise heritage within development initiatives illustrated through discussion of community policing in Tanzania. It draws on research conducted between 2009 and 2018 in the city of Mwanza. Of particular interest here is the promotion of citizen participation in neighbourhood watch schemes. This can be understood as a hybrid form of security governance, which draws on 'traditional' precolonial modes of governance known as *sungusungu* vigilantism but is intended to operate in collaboration with state institutions and in accordance with state law.

Sungusungu emerged in the early 1980s in response to a wave of violent crime, including high rates of cattle theft in rural areas. Villagers in central Tanzania developed local defence groups called *sungusungu*[1] to retrieve stolen cattle and identify and punish suspected offenders, which they appeared to do much more effectively than the state police, as well as performing local dispute resolution. All village residents contributed funds to support subsistence for the *sungusungu* and were also involved collectively in implementing punishments of ostracism on village residents accused of wrongdoing. By 1987 such institutions were widespread across areas of central and northern Tanzania occupied by the Sukuma and Nyamwezi ethnic groups (Abrahams, 1987).

Sungusungu reflected village-level forms of collective organisation among the Sukuma and Nyamwezi, which have co-existed, in various relationship to institutions of chieftaincy and the state, since at least the mid- to late-nineteenth century (Abrahams, 1989). The authority of *sungusungu* leadership was linked to expertise in medicine and divination, used to protect *sungusungu* and in identification of suspects and determination of punishment (Bukurura, 1994). Initiation ceremonies incorporated historical oathing practices and *sungusungu* reproduced the nomenclature of Sukuma chieftainship, which had been abolished alongside other customary authorities in Tanzania by the post-independence government. *Sungusungu* also reflected wider generational roles and power relations in Sukuma and Nyamwezi society, with leadership roles occupied mainly by senior men while the young were mobilised to provide labour for collective endeavours, much as was the case for forms of agricultural labour (Abrahams, 1987). Gender norms also informed its operation and in addition to retrieving stolen cattle, *sungusungu* also sometimes returned women who had left their husbands or eloped to their families and tried and punished elderly women suspected of witchcraft (Bukurura, 1994; Mesaki, 2009). In preventing and addressing criminality, *sungusungu* operated in accordance with local norms and understandings of justice rather than state law, using violence to extract confessions and punish suspected offenders. Writing about *sungusungu* at the time, Abrahams observed that Sukuma and Nyamwezi heritage had 'provided a continuing model and a source of practical experience for villagers who wish to organize their own affairs' (Abrahams, 1987: 193–4).

The state police and judiciary initially opposed *sungusungu* and many participants were arrested. However, Tanzania's ruling party, *Chama Cha Mapinduzi* (CCM), under the leadership of President Nyerere was quick to endorse *sungusungu* for pragmatic and normative reasons. In addition to being a cheap and effective crime prevention strategy, this village-led initiative was consistent with Nyerere's ideas of grassroots socialism, which emphasised self-reliance alongside respect for 'traditional' African values (Heald, 2002). In this period Tanzania was a de jure one party state and CCM and the administration were closely entwined. Party and thus administrative support protected *sungusungu* from prosecution and groups took on additional duties on behalf of the government, such as collecting development taxes, enforcing participation in development activities, policing public meetings and attending district security committees (Grawert, 2009; Shivji, 1990; Heald, 2002).

As *sungusungu* was incorporated to some extent into the administration and extended outside of its heartland, some 'traditional' Sukuma and Nyamwezi practices such as divination became less important and groups were often organised on a co-ethnic basis (Heald, 2002; Cleaver et al., 2013).

From the late 1980s, formation of *sungusungu* groups was promoted across the country, with participation in night patrols compelled by the local administration and CCM's network of local leaders (Kakoti, 1998). This state-sponsored version of *sungusungu* often became highly unpopular, experienced as an 'instrument of state coercion' (Heald, 2006: 273). In the early 1990s a multiparty system was reintroduced in Tanzania and where *sungusungu* was strongly associated with CCM compulsion it largely ceased operating. In parts of the country, *sungusungu* endured, but continued to evolve in locally specific ways, informed by existing local practices and beliefs, and the relationship between local institutions and the state (Cleaver, 2002; Heald, 2006).

Since the 1990s a range of a range of non- and intergovernmental development organisations have sought to reinvigorate *sungusungu* in the interests of meeting contemporary challenges, including wildlife and forest conservation, provision of security in refugee camps and reduction of urban crime 'in accordance with local traditions' (Assiago, n.d.: 6). Contemporary community policing initiatives introduced by the Tanzania Police Force (TPF) in 2006 also echo *sungusungu*.

Although community policing is officially distinct from *sungusungu*, and is legitimated in policy documents in terms of its contribution to 'democratic' policing rather than consistency with grassroots socialism, there are many similarities in terms of practices and organisation. The involvement of all local young men (and sometimes women) in patrolling on a shift basis, the use of whistles for communication, collection of contributions from other community members to provide equipment and subsistence and the division of labour envisaged between elders, who assume leadership roles, and the young who perform physical labour, all draw strongly on the *sungusungu* model. The tools available to today's community police are also largely the same as those used by *sungusungu*, such as machetes, sticks, clubs and sometimes bows and arrows and spears. They are described as '*silaha za jadi*' (traditional weapons) to differentiate them from 'modern' automatic weapons.

Senior police described *sungusungu* as the genesis of the Tanzanian approach to community policing, which represented 'our tradition' (interview, 2011). One senior officer described how the 'loophole of *sungusungu*' meant that it had been straightforward to inform people about community policing and encourage them to initiate it. In Mwanza, the expertise of former leaders of *sungusungu* was recognised and they were often selected for key roles in organising or advising community police. In some areas of the city, the name *sungusungu* was retained alongside titles for leadership posts derived from institutions of Sukuma chieftaincy. For many residents, there was no clear distinction between *sungusungu* and community policing. In the words of one local CCM leader: 'It's not that *sungusungu* has died. Its name has changed. Now we call it *ulinzi shirikishi*, but its origin is *sungusungu* … there's no difference' (interview, 2011).

In reviving *sungusungu*, however, the stated intention of police reformers is to increase links between community initiatives and the state police, for example in terms of delivery of criminal suspects to a police station, and to ensure community police adhered to the law. Much as envisaged by proponents of hybrid security governance, the police described their objective as reviving historic practices, but providing additional education about human rights (interview, 2011). Alongside former leaders of *sungusungu*, retired police officers and soldiers and recipients of state militia training were all among community policing leaders interviewed in Mwanza. Community policing is also organised through local government institutions, which receive no regular funding from central government and can vary considerably in terms of the activities they undertake but are composed of volunteers elected on a party-political basis. Community policing operates in the same way as many other local development activities in Tanzania, through the selection of committee members, requirements for community 'participation', entailing contributions of funds or labour, and discussion in public meetings organised by the local government. Community policing might thus be understood as a form of hybrid security governance, deriving practices and claims to authority from ideas of tradition, as well as links to the state and claims to represent the 'community'.

Where it had been initiated and sustained, community policing was widely considered to have contributed to preventing and addressing crime and improved neighbourhood safety. State police patrols in Mwanza are largely confined to the city centre and the larger tarmac roads and the police are widely perceived to be corrupt and ineffective, thus for residents of informal settlements and peri-urban areas, community policing provided a local service that was largely considered to have been previously absent. However, this case study also illustrates some key challenges affecting attempts to instrumentalise heritage for contemporary security.

Firstly, there is a danger of assuming that 'the grain' comprises the kind of governance people actually desire. Hybridity may equally imply a pragmatic compromise that formalises 'second-best' solutions to fill gaps in service delivery. As Meagher (2012: 1078) notes, this raises questions about whether such forms are intrinsically more desirable or comprise instead a form of 'bargain basement governance', informed by the same logics as neoliberal privatisation. The labour and costs entailed in bringing about local development have been extensively discussed in the critical literature on 'community-based' and participatory development projects, which often rely on unrealistic assumptions about local capacity and can be experienced as a burden, rather than an opportunity for 'empowerment' (Ribot, 1995; White, 1996). However, this is rarely recognised in enthusiasm for heritage-informed initiatives.

As outlined above, the fact that *sungusungu* was recognised as part of Tanzanian heritage provided a kind of cognitive shortcut that police and local government attempting to promote community policing could capitalise on, or to put it another way community policing could 'piggy-back' (Lund 2006: 262) on the memory of *sungusungu*. However, this did not mean that this represented the kind of local policing people wanted. Indeed, many expressed a desire for local policing to have more 'modern' and 'state-like' characteristics, rather than to be closer to *sungusungu* as practised in the past. This reflected a desire for protection from abuses of power, and greater access to resources required to sustain local security provision.

Like other hybrid governance solutions, community policing appears to offer a cost-effective solution to shortages of state capacity. For the police, it represents 'a way of reducing crime at a low cost' (observation of training event, 2011). However, carrying out local policing entails considerable costs for 'communities', which are unequally distributed within them. Participants are required to patrol at night at a risk to their own personal safety. The relatively wealthy can avoid potentially dangerous patrols by paying an additional fee, whereas for others any required contributions can be difficult to afford. In wealthy areas of the city, residents have gated houses and a private security guard. Thus, traditional policing is something that is reserved for the poor. The deprivation indicated by designation as traditional is also evident in discussion of the weapons and equipment available to the community police, which are positioned as 'only traditional' and offering little protection against the automatic weapons available to police and armed criminals.

Although community policing is supposed to strengthen linkages between community initiatives and the state, these are not typically well-institutionalised. Community police receive no regular financial support from the government or formal training and participants lacked confidence that they would receive a timely response from the police if they needed to call for support in an emergency. Indeed, it could feel like 'it's not community policing, it's just the community' (interview, Mwanza resident, 2011).

Although today's community police do not use violence as systematically as *sungusungu* did, police sponsorship has not prevented violent neighbourhood policing including the imposition of punishments without due process specified in law. This may to some extent be consistent with local cultural norms in Tanzania, where killings of suspected criminals by groups of citizens are not uncommon (LHRC, 2021). However, this does not mean that violence is not keenly opposed by many, particularly those who are most vulnerable to being policed in this way, and that how and against whom violence is used is not contested. Indeed, Heald's (2002: 9) analysis of earlier promotion of *sungusungu* by CCM highlights the ways in which designating forms of policing as 'traditional' can remove protections available to citizens and constrain accountability:

> it allows the administration to give them credence on the grounds of their supposedly traditional form but at the same time to dissociate themselves both from a direct role within such organisations and from any abuses that they might perpetrate.

Residents' suggestions for how community policing could be improved frequently referred to closer links to the state, particularly provision of equipment and allowances for participants and assistance from police with patrolling, and for community police to display more 'state-like' attributes and to be more, not less, consistent with state law rather than local norms. Suggested necessary reforms included that community police should have uniforms and carry identification, should take oaths of service like the police, and should have formal training and better knowledge of the law. Community policing groups sometimes adopted symbols and practices associated with state policing, such as performing drills like those conducted by the state police and wearing uniforms, in order to bolster their authority and seek external recognition. Thus, whilst the rationale underpinning promotion of hybrid forms of policing rests upon the assumption that non-state policing is closer to what communities desire and has greater local legitimacy, the pursuit of additional state support and state-like characteristics by community police and residents in Mwanza, suggests that this should not be taken for granted. Indeed, while designating practices as 'traditional' enables state administrations to distance themselves from any wrongdoing, it can also entail the disavowal of responsibility for meeting material needs.

Secondly, attempts to repurpose past practices to meet contemporary challenges often neglect the extent to which both heritage and development are fluid and contested. Treating heritage like an asset upon which people can draw to bring about development neglects the extent to which making claims about a valued past and a desirable future are ways in which individuals and groups negotiate their own interests, informed by prevailing power relations and their contestation. While ostensibly concerned with the importance of specific context – 'the grain' that should inform policy – such calls are also in tension with a desire to develop standardised policy solutions for the production of 'successful' hybrid models. Many attempts to draw on past practices are surprisingly ahistorical, neglecting to consider how institutions evolve over time, and indeed how they may be reshaped by interventions aimed at achieving particular visions of 'development'. Thus, those 'successful' exemplars, such as *sungusungu*, which reoccur in discussions of heritage and security, are often discussed as static, with reference to an example drawn from one place and time, and are compared to other similarly reified cases.

A critical institutionalist perspective is useful in illuminating these challenges. Critical institutionalism raises questions about the possibility of 'crafting' institutional solutions to engender development. It urges attention to how institutions evolve over time, emphasising the role of power in shaping and reshaping institutions, and locating these processes within broader social relations that inform to what extent new arrangements become meaningful and legitimate (Cleaver and Whaley, 2018). Frances Cleaver developed the idea of institutional bricolage, to explain how institutions emerge and evolve as people respond to challenges. Bricolage in this sense refers to,

> the processes in which people (consciously and non-consciously) draw on existing social formulae and arrangements (rules, traditions, norms, roles, and relationships) to patch together institutions in response to changing situations. Such innovations and adaptations are legitimised by reference to tradition, socially acceptable ways of doing things, and existing relations of

> authority. The institutions so produced are dynamic hybrids of the modern and traditional, the formal and informal.
>
> *Cleaver et al., 2013: 168*

These ideas are useful in explaining the relationship between heritage and development. Rather than discussing heritage as a kind of 'cultural repertoire', and something to be instrumentalised to bring about 'good change', considering the mobilisation of practices and meanings derived from the past as part of processes of bricolage draws attention to hybridity as a 'dynamic and uneven process', which does not in itself have inherently positive or negative connotations (Cleaver et al., 2013: 168). Such processes are closely informed by power relations. There are winners and losers, and 'the room for maneuver is less for some actors than for others' (ibid.: 169).

The dangers of assuming 'communities' subject to development interventions to be homogenous and harmonious have long been identified in critical development studies literature, which highlights the way in which social, economic and political inequalities mediate how development is defined and pursued and who benefits from its outcomes (Mosse, 1995; Gujit and Shah, 1997; Cooke and Kothari, 2001). Development is a nebulous and malleable concept, amenable to competing and contradictory framings and definitions articulated in terms of collective goals, but also understood in relation to individual objectives. As Green (2014: 13) observes, in Tanzania the idea of development as a national project co-exists with that of development as a 'personal project of self-improvement'. Participating in development efforts, might sometimes be better understood as 'an individual strategy for gaining access to social status and material resources' (Mercer, 2002: 104). Attempts to institutionalise heritage for development from 'above' also impact on these politics, as they offer opportunities to renegotiate or entrench power hierarchies (Mosse, 1995). Thus 'local' projects should be understood within power relations at wider scales, with important implications for the accountability and legitimacy of local institutions (Mohan and Stokke, 2000; Meagher, 2012). Although *sungusungu* is often celebrated as an exemplar of successful hybrid security governance, analysis of its evolution over time illustrates the challenges in positioning cultural heritage as a resource to be deployed for development, and the dangers of equating apparent social embeddedness, in terms of consistency with local norms or symbolic references to tradition, with legitimacy (Meagher, 2012).

The case of *sungusungu* illustrates how the meanings and values attached to the past may change over time, influenced by its articulation in the service of different political and economic interests. Claims to authority based on heritage are often contentious and can be vulnerable, much like those based on a promised future. In many parts of Tanzania, the co-optation of *sungusungu* by the ruling party indeed contributed to its decline in the early 1990s amid a return to multipartyism. Today, community policing continues to be associated with CCM. UN Habitat's efforts to reintroduce *sungusungu* neighbourhood watch in 2000 were impeded by refusal of opposition party members to participate in something that was called *sungusungu* (UN HABITAT, 2000) and today attempts to introduce community policing may be opposed when viewed as an attempt by locally elected leaders to boost their party's electoral prospects by bringing 'development' to their constituents (Cross, 2014). Although in some regions, local adaptations of *sungusungu* have been seen as bolstering community autonomy in relation to the state (Heald, 2006), elsewhere *sungusungu* and subsequently community policing have come to operate like many other forms of development predicated upon community participation in Tanzania. Thus, rather than reflecting an expression of valued heritage or the pursuit of local development objectives, participation is often experienced as coercion to provide resources or labour following directives from above, and as something that serves only the interests of leaders.

In addition to party politics, *sungusungu* has historically been shaped by unequal gendered and generational relations as outlined above. The hybrid model of community policing did entail some attempts to address gendered inequalities by incorporating 'modern' principles associated with the state police. Some community police, for example, stated that they emulated police regulations stipulating that a woman must only be searched by a female officer. However, generational divisions of labour remained similar to those underpinning *sungusungu*, whereby those holding leadership positions were largely senior residents and those required to provide labour under their direction were the relatively young. Controlling young people's activities and mobility was a key focus of community policing, sometimes to the extent of colluding with the police to frame youth who were perceived to behave badly but might not have broken the law.

Community police were operating under severe resource constraints and potentially at a cost to their own lives and livelihoods. Thus, they did seek opportunities to cover costs and to provide a small allowance where possible, for example through collecting money for items such as torch batteries from other residents. In some cases, community police adopted attributes of commercial security providers, initiating more easily excludable services for which they could levy a charge, such as guarding parked vehicles or providing security for weddings or funerals. Some residents reported they were no longer able to afford to report crime to the community police, and fees and contributions were often described as 'corruption'. In one sub-ward, the leaders sought to position themselves for other opportunities in the 'market' for local development contractors (Green, 2014: 119) by registering as a 'community-based organisation' which would enable fundraising from international development organisations. The often porous boundaries between 'traditional', 'community-based' and commercial forms of security governance also have implications for the assumed legitimacy of hybrid security governance. Perceptions that security providers have only pecuniary motives are firmly implicated in negotiations over how legitimate authority is exercised and by whom (Buur and Jensen, 2004).

Conclusion

This chapter has argued that rather than something that is amenable to instrumentalisation, hybridity is a ubiquitous characteristic of institutional arrangements, and is better understood as a set of complex processes of negotiation generating norms and practices, which can be intensified by interventions aimed at producing development (MacGinty and Sanghera, 2012). Analysing such processes in terms of bricolage demonstrates the importance of understanding the confluence of heritage and development as comprised of dynamic, contingent and often contested processes, which individuals and groups have differential capacities to shape. Here, heritage is not something that is easily capitalised upon as an asset of communities or nations, but is fluid and malleable, and the legitimacy of past-looking solutions to contemporary challenges may vary over time. Although the transformation of *sungusungu* into community policing is frequently heralded as a success story, analysis of its evolution over time more convincingly demonstrates the difficulty of instrumentalising ideas and practices drawn from the past. The views of those affected by these initiatives and required to participate in them paint a much more ambiguous picture, revealing the dangers of assuming what kind of pasts or futures people value.

Note

1 The term *basalama* was historically used among the Sukuma and Nyamwezi, but the name *sungusungu* is now more commonly used across Tanzania.

References

Abrahams, R. (1987) 'Sungusungu: village vigilante groups in Tanzania', *African Affairs*, 86(343), pp. 179–96.

Abrahams, R. (1989) 'Law and order and the state in the Nyamwezi and Sukuma area of Tanzania', *Africa*, 59(3), pp. 356–70.

Albrecht, P. and Kyed, H.M. (2011) 'Non-state and customary actors in development programs', in Albrecht, P., Kyed, H.M., Isser, D. and Harper, E. (eds) *Perspectives on involving non-state and customary actors in justice and security reform*. Rome: International Development Law Organization, pp. 3–22.

Allen, M., Dinnen, S., Evans, D. and Monson, R. (2013) *Justice delivered locally: systems, challenges and innovations in Solomon Islands.* J4P Research Report. World Bank. Available at: https://openknowledge.worldbank.org/handle/10986/16678 (Accessed 23 February 2022).

Andrews, M. (2013) *The limits of institutional reform in development: changing rules for realistic solutions*. Cambridge: Cambridge University Press.

Arnot, B. (2015) 'How traditional justice in Nigeria is changing', *British Council*, 24 February. Available at: www.britishcouncil.org/voices-magazine/how-traditional-justice-nigeria-changing (Accessed 23 February 2022).

Assiago, J. (n.d.), 'Promoting urban crime prevention strategies in Africa', undated paper written for UN HABITAT. Available at: ww2.unhabitat.org/programmes/safercities/documents/Urban_Crime_Preve ntion.PDF (Accessed 20 September 2021).

Bagayoko, N., Hutchful, E. and Luckham, R. (2016) 'Hybrid security governance in Africa: rethinking the foundations of security, justice and legitimate public authority', *Conflict, Security and Development*, 16(1), pp. 1–32.

Baker, B. (2010) 'Linking state and non-state security and justice', *Development Policy Review*, 28(5), pp. 597–616.

Baker, B. (2013) 'Hybridity in policing: the case of Ethiopia', *The Journal of Legal Pluralism and Unofficial Law*, 45(3), pp. 296–313.
Boege, V., Brown, M.A. and Clements, K.P. (2009) 'Hybrid political orders, not fragile states', *Peace Review: A Journal of Social Justice*, 21(1), pp. 13–21.
Booth, D. (2011) 'Introduction: working with the grain? The African Power and Politics Programme', *IDS Bulletin*, 42(2), pp. 1–10.
Booth, D. and Cammack, D. (2013) *Governance for development in Africa: solving collective action problems*. London: Zed Books.
Bukurura, S.H. (1994) 'The maintenance of order in rural Tanzania: the case of sungusungu', *Journal of Legal Pluralism*, 34, pp. 1–29.
Burr, L. and Jensen, S. (2004) 'Introduction: vigilantism and the policing of everyday life in South Africa', *African Studies*, 63(2), pp. 139–52.
Cleaver, F. (2002) 'Reinventing institutions: bricolage and the social embeddedness of natural resource management', *The European Journal of Development Research*, 14(2), pp. 11–30.
Cleaver, F., Franks, T., Maganga, F. and Hall, K. (2013) 'Institutions, security, and pastoralism: exploring the limits of hybridity', *African Studies Review*, 56(3), pp. 165–89.
Cleaver, F. and Whaley, L. (2018) 'Understanding process, power, and meaning in adaptive governance: a critical institutional reading', *Ecology and Society* 23(2), 49. doi:/10.5751/ES-10212-230249
Clements, K.P. (2014) 'What is legitimacy and why does it matter for peace?' *Accord: an international review of peace initiatives*, 25, pp. 12–16.
Cooke, B. and Kothari, U. (eds) (2001) *Participation: the new tyranny?* London: Zed Books.
Cross, C. (2014) 'Community policing and the politics of local development in Tanzania', *Journal of Modern African Studies*, 52(4), pp. 517 – 40.
DANIDA (2010) *How to note: informal justice systems*. Available at: www.netpublikationer.dk/um/10459/pdf/informal_justice_systems.pdf
Denney, L. (2014) 'Overcoming the state/non-state divide: an end user approach to security and justice reform', *International Peacekeeping*, 21(2), pp. 251–68.
Department for International Development (DFID) (2004) 'Non-state security and justice systems', DFID Briefing, May 2004. Available at: www.gsdrc.org/docs/open/ssaj101.pdf
Gitlitz, J.S. (2013) 'Peru', in Nalla, M.K. and Newman, G.R. (eds) *Community policing in indigenous communities*. Boca Raton, FL: CRC Press, pp. 117–122.
Grawert, E. (2009) *Departures from post-colonial authoritarianism*. Frankfurt: Peter Lang.
Green, M. (2014) *The development state: aid, culture and civil society in Tanzania*. Woodbridge and Rochester, NY: James Currey.
Gujit, I. and Shah, M.K. (eds) (1997) *The myth of community: gender issues in participatory development*. London: Intermediate Technology Publications.
Heald, S. (2002) 'Domesticating Leviathan: *sungusungu* groups in Tanzania', Crisis States Research Centre Working Paper 16. London School of Economics.
Heald, S. (2006) 'State law and vigilantism in northern Tanzania', *African Affairs* 105 (419): 265–83.
Hills, A. (2012) 'Partnership policing: is it relevant in Kano, Nigeria?', *Criminology & Criminal Justice* [online]. doi: 10.1177/1748895812454860
Kakoti, G.R. (1998) 'Community crime prevention in Africa: a study of Sungusungu citizen patrols in Tanzania'. Unpublished MA thesis. Indiana University.
Kelsall, T. (2008) 'Going with the grain in African development?', African Power and Politics Programme Discussion Paper No. 1. Available at: https://assets.publishing.service.gov.uk/media/57a08ba4ed915d3cfd000e56/APPP_Discussion_Paper_1_Kelsall.pdf (Accessed 18 February 2022).

Legal and Human Rights Centre (LHRC) (2021) *Tanzania Human Rights Report 2020: human rights protection and the threat posed by COVID19 in Tanzania*. Dar es Salaam: LHRC.

Levy, B. (2014) *Working with the grain: integrating governance and growth in development strategies*. Oxford: Oxford University Press.

Luckham, R. and Kirk, T. (2013) 'Understanding security in the vernacular in hybrid political contexts: a critical survey', *Conflict, Security and Development*, 13 (3), pp. 339–59.

Lund, C. (2006) 'Twilight institutions: public authority and local politics in Africa', *Development and Change*, 37(4), pp. 685–705.

Mac Ginty, R. and Richmond, O.P. (2013) 'The local turn in peace building: a critical agenda for peace', *Third World Quarterly*, 34(5), pp. 763–83.

Mac Ginty, R. and Sanghera, G. (2012) 'Hybridity in peacebuilding and development: an introduction', *Journal of Peacebuilding and development*, 7(2), pp. 3–8.

Mallett, R. (2010) 'Beyond failed states and ungoverned spaces: hybrid political orders in the post-conflict landscape', *eSharp*, 15, pp. 65–91.

Meagher, K. (2012) 'The strength of weak states? Non-state security forces and hybrid governance in Africa', *Development and Change*, 43(5), pp. 1073–1101.

Mercer, C. (2002) 'The discourse of maendeleo and the politics of women's participation on Mount Kilimanjaro', *Development and Change*, 33(1), pp. 101–27.

Merino, M. and Colorado, J.H. (2013) 'La Policía Communitaria: self-defense groups in Mexico: the aftermath of a poorly designed policy', *Georgetown Journal of International Affairs*, 14(2), pp. 147–55.

Mesaki, S. (2009) 'The tragedy of ageing: witchcraft killings and poor governance among the Sukuma', in Haram, L. & Yamba, C.B. (eds) *Dealing with uncertainty in contemporary African lives*. Uppsala: Nordiska Afrikainstitutet, pp. 72–90.

Mohan, G. and Stokke, K. (2000) 'Participatory development and empowerment: the dangers of localism', *Third World Quarterly*, 21(2), pp. 247 – 68.

Mosse, D. (1995) 'Authorty, gender and knowledge: theoretical reflections on participatory rural appraisal', *Economic and Political Weekly*, 30(11), pp. 569 – 71 and 573 – 78.

OECD (2007) *Enhancing the delivery of justice and security: governance, peace and security*. Paris: OECD.

OECD (2011) 'Supporting statebuilding in situations of conflict and fragility: policy guidance'. DAC Guidelines and Reference Series.

Ogbozor, E. (2016) 'Understanding the informal security sector in Nigeria'. Special report of the United States Institute of Peace. Available at: www.usip.org/sites/default/files/SR391-Understanding-the-Informal-Security-Sector-in-Nigeria.pdf (Accessed 18 June 2021).

Ribot, J. (1995) 'From exclusion to participation: turning Senegal's forestry policy around?' *World Development*, 23(9), pp. 1587–99.

Schmeidl, S. and Karokhail, M. (2009) 'The role of non-state actors in "community-based policing" – an exploration of the Arbakai (tribal police) in south-eastern Afghanistan', *Contemporary Security Policy*, 30(2), pp. 318–42.

Shivji, I. (1990) *State coercion and freedom in tanzania*. Roma: National University of Lesotho.

UN HABITAT (2000) *Crime and policing issues in Dar es Salaam Tanzania focusing on: community neighbourhood watch groups – "sungusungu"*. Presentation at the 1st Sub Saharan Executive Policing Conference International Association of Chiefs of Police, Durban, South Africa, 27–30 August. Available at: https://mirror.unhabitat.org/downloads/docs/1825_12883_sungusungu.pdf (Accessed 20 June 2021).

Unsworth, S. (2010) *An upside down view of governance*. Brighton: Institute of Development Studies.

Wallis, J., Jeffery, R. and Kent, L. (2016) 'Political reconciliation in Timor Leste, Solomon Islands and Bougainville: the dark side of hybridity', *Australian Journal of International Affairs*, 70(2), pp. 159–78.

White, S. (1996) 'Depoliticising development: the uses and abuses of participation', *Development in Practice*, 6(1), pp. 6–15.

World Bank (2011) *World Development Report 2011: conflict, security and development*. Washington DC: World Bank.

14

HERITAGE AND POST-CONFLICT DEVELOPMENT

International Discourse, Authorised Heritage and the Institutionalisation of Precolonial Customs and Traditions

John D. Giblin, Maurice Mugabowagahunde and André Ntagwabira

Introduction

The turn to heritage is a common response in the aftermath of violent conflict when the past can be both a problem to be selectively remembered, and by extension forgotten, and a resource within which solutions might be found for future peace, security and other forms of development (Winter, 2007; De Jong and Rowlands, 2008; Giblin, 2014; Kisić, 2020). This chapter discusses these issues in two ways. The first way is through a summary of the well-rehearsed post-conflict role of mostly tangible, formal notions of authorised heritage (c.f. Smith, 2006) as promoted by international organisations and managed by national heritage agencies. This is a role that has been well explored in critical heritage studies and well stated in international and national heritage policies but is more peripheral to international development discussions. For example, in heritage studies, museums and memorials are understood to contribute towards the construction of national identities through the definition and communication of collective memories as well as being potential resources for reconciliation and social cohesion (Giblin, 2014; McDowell, 2016). However, development is rarely the explicit, initial aim of the post-conflict establishment of memorial and museum sites.

The second way that this chapter explores the post-conflict developmental role of heritage is through a summary of the post-conflict institutionalisation of precolonial traditions and customary practices, particularly in the areas of transitional justice, conflict resolution and reconciliation. By contrast with museums and memorials, the institutionalisation of precolonial traditions and customary practices is frequently discussed in development debates but is rarely labelled heritage nor included within post-conflict critical heritage studies. In response, this chapter argues that formalised heritage and the institutionalisation of tradition and

DOI: 10.4324/9781003107361-19

customary practice are both aspects of a post-conflict developmental heritage complex, which state parties and other development actors selectively adapt and adopt in each new post-conflict context. Thus, despite not being directly linked to economic development, international development debates should include museums and memorials, as much as post-conflict heritage debates should include the institutionalisation of tradition and customary practice.

Normative heritage

Internationalisation

The potential of formal or normative notions of heritage, such as architectural and archaeological sites, memorials and museums, to contribute towards post-conflict development has been recognised by major international organisations, such as the World Bank, the European Commission and most notably UNESCO (for a discussion of the international post-conflict heritage discourse and its contradictions see Giblin, 2014). The World Bank (Kreimer et al., 1998: 32) was one of the earliest international developmental organisations to cite the potential of heritage to 'inspire hope and to remind people of their creativity' in post-conflict contexts, specifically Bosnia and Herzegovina, Rwanda, Uganda, Cambodia, El Salvador, Eritrea, Haiti, Lebanon and Sri Lanka. Similarly, the Council of Europe (2011) published *The Role of Culture and Cultural Heritage in Conflict Prevention, Transformation, Resolution and Post-Conflict Action*, which identified the post-conflict role of heritage in collective identity building.

Due to its remit as the United Nations' (UN) organisation with responsibility for the world's tangible and intangible heritage, UNESCO has offered the most consistent international position on the post-conflict role of heritage. In the 2008–2013 Medium-Term report UNESCO highlighted the role that culture can play 'in situations of conflict or post-conflict as a "vehicle" for reconciliation through cultural heritage' and how the preservation of heritage would have positive 'effects on development, social cohesion and peace' (UNESCO, 2008: 27). In the 2014–2021 Medium-Term report, UNESCO claimed it would

> harness the power of heritage as a positive and unifying force that can help prevent conflicts and facilitate peace-building as well as recovery and reconciliation. This effort will be part of a global strategy to fight impunity for cultural heritage destruction and to build the power of culture for resilience, social inclusion, national reconciliation, and peace-building
>
> *UNESCO, 2014: 24*

The UN Sustainable Development Goals (SDGs) do not mention culture and heritage in relation to peace and security. However, UNESCO has made this connection in their interpretation of the SDGs. Hosagrahar (2017), writing as Director of the Division for Creativity in the Culture Sector at UNESCO, highlighted how Target 4.7 (SDG 4), calls for 'education to promote a culture of peace and non-violence, an appreciation of cultural diversity and of culture's contribution to sustainable development'. Hosagrahar (2017) has also made a connection between SDG 16 (Peace, Justice and Strong Institutions) and the potential for cultural diversity to facilitate cultural understanding and peace, prevent conflict and protect the rights of marginalised people. In addition, when UN Resolution 2437 was adopted in March 2017, the UNESCO Director-General Irina Bokova explained, '[w]eapons are not enough to defeat violent extremism. Building peace requires culture also; it requires education, prevention, and the transmission of heritage. This is the message of this historic resolution.' Although Resolution 2437 aims only to protect cultural heritage from conflict, the Director-General made explicit why UNESCO believes it to be worth protecting beyond its potential economic tourism benefits, i.e., a peacebuilding purpose for heritage.

There thus exists an international discourse about the importance of culture and heritage for post-conflict development centered on positive, singular, inherently good, unifying imaginings of the usable past. What is missing from this discourse, however, is an understanding of heritage as something that is multiple, dynamic, divergent, potentially subversive, always dissonant and a potential cause of conflict (Giblin, 2014; see also Cross and Giblin, Chapter 1, this volume). The discourse leaves many questions unanswered, for example, should all heritages be protected and preserved, or only those deemed to be unifying, and who decides? Is there such a thing as a collective heritage in heterogeneous societies? Can reconciliation, as it is normatively understood, i.e., as two or more sides resolving their differences, be achieved if the victor authorises what can be considered heritage? Or can all sides' heritage be equally valued without causing conflict? What of the conflict itself as heritage? And does the preservation of sites of conflict or memorials prolong post-conflict trauma?

National

The international 'heritage for post-conflict development' discourse is relatively new compared to the much longer political use of the past in the aftermath of violence at national scales. Museums and memorials, for example, have long been used to construct and maintain a sense of collective memory as a form of post-conflict nation building. Although these sites are rarely understood in terms of international development, they often serve post-conflict governments through the presentation of legitimating versions of the past with the intention of fostering peace and security and eventually national cohesion. In this understanding, national cohesion 'requires a sense of collective awareness and identity endorsed through common historical experience' (McDowell, 2016: 41). The heterogeneity of society, and consequent plurality of the past, therefore has the potential to act against national cohesion when memories conflict. In response, the repeated performance and consumption of national narratives at memorials and museums, including by generations who did not experience the specific historical events, foster a sense of collective memory.

War memorials have long been put to political use to celebrate or mourn national versions of conflict. For example, after the First and Second World Wars thousands of individual memorials were installed in European countries and their colonial territories to acknowledge the dead, in addition to mass grave memorials located at the sites of the worst atrocities, such as Auschwitz. In contrast to earlier more celebratory forms of war memorialisation, the new memorial landscape in Europe extended into cities, towns and villages and reflected a radical democratisation of the memorial process away from the metropolitan elite. However, despite this democratisation, these monuments and associated annual memorial events have always promoted state-sanctioned views of the past emanating from European capitals, with the purpose of maintaining authorised collective post-conflict remembering (Niven, 2007).

The wide distribution of memorial structures in the aftermath of the First and Second World Wars provided a physical template for many proceeding conflicts and the construction of memorials across conflict landscapes continues today. For example, although the detail of memorialisation is based on Rwandan traditions, since 1995 the post-genocide Rwandan government has created an extensive mass grave memorial hierarchical landscape consisting of hundreds of district level structures and a small number of national memorials located at the sites of some of the worst atrocities. In addition, since 2012, four of these sites (Nyamata, Murambi, Kigali Genocide Memorial Centre and Bisesero) have been nominated for inscription on UNESCO's World Heritage List. As well as providing locales for mourning and emotional healing, some authors have suggested that memorials also serve other developmental functions, for example: as places that promote education about genocide in terms of 'never again' (KGMC, 2021); as places that support forms of reconciliation (Giblin, 2014) and peacebuilding (King, 2010); as locations for high level diplomatic visits to acknowledge the genocide perpetrated against the Tutsi in 1994 and to offer explicit or implicit apologies for the international failure to prevent it (Giblin, 2017); and public spaces for national narratives explaining the causes of the genocide (Jessee, 2017).

Similar functions can also be observed in national museums where legitimating and ostensibly unifying national narratives may also be disseminated. For example, since the end of the genocide, Rwanda has constructed seven new national museums, including the Rwandan Art Museum at the site of the former Presidential Palace, the Kandt House Museum, the Museum of Environment, Rwesero Kwigira Museum, King's Palace Museum, the National Liberation Museum Park and the Campaign Against Genocide Museum. Although only two of these museums have names that link them directly to the preceding conflict and genocide, the content of others also indicates post-conflict aims. For example: the Rwandan Art Museum is largely populated by works that depict aspects of the genocide or symbols of peace, and in the grounds of the Museum, visitors can view the remains of the plane carrying the presidents of Rwanda and Burundi that was shot down during the civil war; the Rwesero Kwigira Museum holds an exhibition about Home Grown Solutions (HGS), a post-conflict developmental programme (discussed in detail later in this chapter); while the Ethnographic Museum, which was established shortly before the civil war and genocide, has since had ethnic labels removed from its displays because they promoted divisive colonial ethnic ideas instead of a sense of post-genocide national unity.

In addition, heritage may also be activated in post-conflict eras to support economic development through tourism. However, although tourism often forms around post-conflict national memorials and museums (see Seaton, 1996; Lennon and Foley, 2000; Stone, 2006; Skinner, 2012), it is rarely the primary reason for the post-conflict establishment of these sites. Instead, to drive tourism, post-conflict governments more frequently invest in the establishment of rural or urban heritage sites or areas that are not defined by or do not refer to preceding conflicts (for a Rwandan example see Giblin et al., 2017). In so doing, these initiatives are comparable to the common economic potential of heritage for tourism (discussed elsewhere in this volume in chapters by Katapidi and Robinson; and Huong and Bushell) and are less directly related to post-conflict contexts.

The critique of national attempts to use memorials and museums for non-economic post-conflict development focus on the observation that, even when laudable unifying aims may be genuine, there is an unsurprising tendency for singular, official, legitimating narratives to be promoted at the expense of plurality and conflicting versions of the past. The response to that critique from national agencies is often that there is only one correct version of the past and that the presentation of contested and competing pasts may lead to future conflict, but the critique exists nevertheless. There are also questions about who is encountering and consuming these pasts. For example, national heritage narratives may eventually reach large parts of a population through school visits to museums, supporting similar national narratives in school syllabi and national memorial events. However, it is questionable whether all demographics will access memorials and museums equally.

Local

Formal heritage work may also be desired and undertaken for local-level development in the aftermath of violence as a grassroots or bottom-up initiative but in ways that are nevertheless entangled with international and national development agencies. For example, grassroots' demand for memorialisation in Uganda in the absence of national memorialisation has been cited as a reason for a rise in Pentecostalism (Quinn, 2004; Tankink, 2007; see also Pringle and Musisi, this volume), while successive population-based surveys of attitudes regarding peace and justice in northern Uganda undertaken in the aftermath of the so-called Northern War (c. 1986 to 2006) have demonstrated grassroots' desire for memorialisation (Pham and Vinck 2010). In response, a series of community memorial projects were created in Northern Uganda, which are managed by community heritage committees and are framed in post-conflict development terms as sites for emotional healing, education, economic development through tourism and as places with symbolic potential for transitional justice acts. Despite their community scale and the absence of external support today, however, they were initially created as part of a post-conflict heritage landscape project supported by a grant from the Norwegian Directorate for Cultural Heritage working in partnership with the National Museum of Uganda (Giblin, 2014).

The Community Peace Museums (CPMs) in Kenya are another example of the local being entangled with the international and national. Today the CPMs operate as a network of community centres organised under the Community Peace Museums Heritage Foundation, which promote local-level peacebuilding activities by engaging with histories of violence. However, they were established in the 1990s by a senior curator at the National Museums of Kenya who was influenced by a USAID program to promote peacemaking and peacebuilding in the region and by a Mennonite peace project (Coombes and Hughes, 2014; Giblin, 2018).

Local post-conflict heritage initiatives are often promoted as grassroots, bottom-up initiatives and thus inherently more authentic, plural, democratic and appropriate in contrast to top-down, official, national heritage programmes. However, as heritage work moves from individual and personal to collective levels it is invariably co-opted by local powerholders through committees and other political structures and subject to their political maneuverings. Furthermore, as illustrated by the above examples, rarely are local post-conflict heritage initiatives distinct from international and national developmental contexts and so they may be liable for elements of the same critique (see Cross and Giblin, Chapter 1, this volume).

Pre-colonial customs and traditions for post-conflict development

This chapter has outlined how an international discourse promotes heritage as a force for post-conflict development and how formalised heritage has been created and employed on the ground at national and local scales in post-conflict contexts for developmental ends. By contrast, this section focuses on the post-conflict institutionalisation of precolonial traditions and customary practices for post-conflict development based on the premise of being more culturally authentic and unifying compared to divisive colonial or neocolonial policies. This is not unique to post-conflict contexts. For example, the use of tradition and customary practice in governance in the Global South has been mapped through precolonial, colonial and postcolonial eras (e.g., Verweijen and Van Bockhaven, 2020). In addition, it sits within a more recent history of international developmental debates about the role of Indigenous knowledge (Briggs, 2005), participation (Cross, 2016) and the pluriversal approach, or decolonisation, of development (Rutazibwa and Ndushabandi, 2019). For example, as a decolonial alternative to standard ideas of development, and without reference to an immediately preceding conflict, Bolivia and Ecuador incorporated participatory precolonial Indigenous philosophies, Buen Vivir, into their constitutions in 2007 and 2008 (Walsh, 2010). Nevertheless, the institutionalisation of precolonial traditions and customary practices frequently takes place in conflict related or post-conflict contexts, specifically in areas of transitional justice, conflict resolution and reconciliation.

This topic is receiving renewed attention in development discussions (Verweijen and Van Bockhaven, 2020). However, the institutionalisation of tradition and customary practices have received less attention from the heritage field. This may be because, despite fulfilling a contemporary definition of heritage, i.e., the use of the past in the present (c.f. Smith, 2006; Harrison, 2012), it is not labelled as heritage or managed by heritage agencies and professionals. This academic disconnect is problematic for both development and heritage studies if our joint aim is to generate a more comprehensive understanding of how the past is employed to generate peace and security following violence.

Rwanda's HGS, which have been incorporated into Article 11 of the Rwandan Constitution, are a prominent example of the post-conflict revival of precolonial customary practices. Since the 1994 genocide committed against the Tutsi, the Rwandan government has introduced practices based on precolonial customs, which have since been packaged together as HGS, as explained by the Rwanda Government Board (RGB):

> Home Grown Solutions (HGS) are Rwanda's 'trade mark' solutions developed by the Rwandan citizens based on local opportunities, cultural values and history to fast track their development.
>
> As stipulated by the Constitution of the Republic of Rwanda of 2003 amended in 2015, Rwandans, based on their values, initiate home-grown mechanisms to deal with matters that concern them in order to build the nation, promote national culture, and restore dignity. Being locally created, HGS are appropriate to the local development context and have been the bedrock to the Rwandan reconstruction and transformation journey after 1994 Genocide against Tutsi. They have significantly enabled Rwanda to lift millions of its population out of extreme poverty and become one of the fast growing economy on the continent. Furthermore, HGS have been the key drivers in helping Rwanda to achieve the target of global initiatives like MDGs and they expected to continuously support the country to meets SDGs targets and other national, regional, continental and global commitments to spur socioeconomic development.
>
> *RGB, 2014, 2022*

Rwanda's HGS are classified into four main categories: Governance, Social, Economic and Justice. Some HGS, such as Gacaca and Iteroro (described below), are more directly articulated by the RGB as post-conflict developmental practices compared to others, such as Girinka which is more directly framed as a pro-poor developmental practice. Whether referred to in explicitly post-conflict terms, however, the RGB (2014) explains that all HGS' contribute towards reconciliation, unity and development, and thus they can all be considered post-conflict development policies. Seven of the most prominent precolonial linked HGS are summarised here based on the RGB (2022) website.

Governance

- **Imihigo**, to vow to deliver, is based on a precolonial practice when an individual would agree to complete a target or goal within an allotted time. Since 2006 it has referred to the agreement of performance contracts.
- **Itorero** is claimed to date to AD 1312 and King Ruganzu I Bwimba when Rwandans went to a cultural school to learn about their language, their history, social relations, sports, dancing, songs, patriotism and national defence. It was revived in 2007 and now refers to the practice of sending certain groups to academies to educate them about 'civic education exercises, cultural values, patriotism and social political development'. Itorero was banned during colonial rule from 1924 to 1994 and it is suggested by the RGB that its absence led to the distortion and breakdown of Rwandan culture contributing towards the genocide.

Social

- **Ubudehe** refers to mutual assistance and is currently employed to achieve socio-economic development, for example, through a community credit scheme that was launched in 2001. It has been linked with precolonial practices of collective responsibility for community problems and their resolution.
- **Girinka** is a programme introduced in 2006 to give one cow to every poor family. It was reportedly inspired by the c. AD 1660 King Mibambwe II Gisanura decree that 'no Rwandan child was ever to lack daily milk again while others had plenty' (RGB, 2018).

Economic

- **Umuganda**, reintroduced in 1998 and formalised in 2007 and 2009, is based on precolonial ideas of self-help and coming together, translated as 'coming together in common purpose to achieve an outcome' (RGB, 2017: 1). As an HGS, it refers to compulsory communal work on the morning of the last Saturday of each month, for example, fixing rural roads or planting trees.

Justice

- **Gacaca**, in Kinyarwanda, means 'justice on the grass' and was a precolonial, community-led, negotiated form of conflict resolution. As an HGS, it refers to a form of mandatory, community, grassroots justice used to try genocide suspects. The new form of gacaca was created in 2001 and rolled out in 2002

and 2005 to manage a backlog of cases that reportedly might have taken the courts up to 200 years to process. Gacaca officially came to an end in 2012.
- **Abunzi**, or 'those who reconcile', are mediation committees introduced in 2004 to resolve disputes and lesser criminal offences through a mixture of precolonial and modern methods of conflict resolution (RGB, 2019).

Rwanda is not alone in the post-conflict institutionalisation of precolonial practices. Like Gacaca and Abunzi, traditional conflict resolution and reconciliatory practices are an increasingly common element of conflict transformation and post-conflict recovery in other countries. Whereas in Rwanda it was the government that revived and institutionalised precolonial customary practices, elsewhere existing or revived traditions and customs have more frequently first been practised at grassroots levels before being co-opted by governments or non-governmental organisations (NGOs). Somaliland is one prominent example where the existing clan structure has been institutionalised with the intention of contributing towards conflict resolution, governance and law and justice (Richards, 2020). In 1991, the Somali National Movement (SNM) defeated Siad Barre's forces in Somaliland. After their victory the SNM continued to utilise the clan system as they had during the war to create a hybrid system of government combining modern and traditional approaches through the elected House of Representatives and the House of Elders whose members are nominated by respective clans (Richards, 2020: 1070). In explicitly post-conflict terms, clan elders historically played important peacemaking roles in Somali society and this is a role that they continue to play today both within and outside of government. As described by Richards (2020: 1074), '[a]lthough undeniably altered through its political institutionalisation, the Somaliland House of Elders is a powerful symbolic reminder of these traditional councils as well as a practical inclusion of clan governance in the central government.'

The Somaliland approach can be compared to post-conflict South Africa when, following the end of Apartheid and the introduction of democratic rule, the ruling African National Congress incorporated existing forms of traditional leadership (chieftaincies) into national governance and local development (Beall and Ngonyama, 2009). Although the place and success of traditional leadership in South Africa remains contested, its institutionalisation has been articulated in terms of post-conflict development. For example, as quoted by Beall and Ngonyama (2009: 10), the foreword to the draft White Paper on Traditional Leadership and Governance (Department of Provincial and Local Government, 2002: 4) stated that,

> the institution has a place in our democracy, and has a potential to transform and contribute enormously towards the restoration of the moral fibre of our society and in the reconstruction and development of the country, especially in rural areas.

Traditional forms of conflict resolution were also revived towards the end of the war between the Lord's Resistance Army (LRA) and the Uganda Peoples Defence

Force in Northern Uganda. Of these, the Acholi practice of *mato-oput* (drinking the bitter herb or root) has received the most attention. *Mato-oput* is a tradition linked to homicide conflict resolution between families or clans, which can involve a long process of truth-telling confessions and compensation at the end of which both parties drink 'sheep's blood and roots from the bitter oput plant, symbolizing the washing away of bitterness between the clans' (Anyeko et al., 2012: 111). Following overseas peace conferences in the late 1990s, traditional community approaches to conflict resolution were promoted to support the return and reincorporation of the tens of thousands of children that the LRA abducted to fight for them or become their 'wives' (Allen, 2006). In the early 2000s the prospects for such an approach were investigated by the Agency for Cooperation and Research in Development (Acord) and by research funded by international governments. Allen (2006) has described how, despite the highly critical findings of this research, the potential for traditional justice remained popular amongst religious groups and Ugandan and international NGOs (iNGOs), including USAID's Northern Ugandan Peace Initiative, who facilitated these approaches, and that by mid-2005 dozens of *mato-oput* ceremonies were being undertaken. Of interest for this discussion is the way in which iNGOs, NGOs and others encouraged the national institutionalisation of these practices, but the government of Uganda kept them at arm's length. For example, although the 2000 Amnesty Act, which supported the return and reintegration of former combatants, approved the use of traditional conflict resolution measures, *mato-oput* and other traditional or customary practices were not referred to specifically. By contrast, *mato-oput* and other traditions and customs were mentioned specifically in the 2007 Agreement on Accountability and Reconciliation between the LRA and Ugandan government (Government of Uganda, 2007):

> 3.1 Traditional justice mechanisms, such as Culo Kwor, Mato Oput, Kayo Cuk, Ailuc and Tonu ci Koka and others as practiced in the communities affected by the conflict, shall be promoted, with necessary modifications, as a central part of the framework for accountability and reconciliation.

However, government support for these remained focused on the north and national institutionalisation was not undertaken (Allen, 2006).

Calls for the institutionalisation of similar precolonial traditions and customary practices for conflict transformation and post-conflict development continue to grow, as recently reported in South Sudan (Bedigen, 2020), alongside the 'Western' academic critique of these hybridisations, typically in terms of authenticity, relevance and effectiveness. The authenticity critique alleges that the co-opted traditions and customs are either invented or have undergone significant modification in their institutionalisation, which brings into question their relevance. Proponents of this critique typically cite Hobsbawm and Ranger's (1983) *The Invention of Tradition* volume, which identified how some traditions that are claimed to have great antiquity are more recent, having either been formally and deliberately invented or come about accidently (e.g., see Allen, 2006 and Branch,

2008 for a discussion of *mato-oput* as an 'invented tradition' (cited in Anyeko et al., 2012: 111)). Once traditions and customs are shown to be inauthentic then a key part of their justification, i.e., local relevance, is undermined. Relevance is also an issue if precolonial traditions and customs are applied nationally when previously they would only have applied to segments of society, such as specific ethnicities, regions or social strata. Finally, issues over authenticity and relevance are connected to concerns over effectiveness, as precolonial traditions and customs, which were supposedly successful because they were voluntary, negotiated and or locally specific, become imposed, compulsory and static as they are institutionalised and applied nationally.

Discussion and conclusion

This chapter has summarised how the use of the past for post-conflict development is a common practice happening across and between scales of governance and has argued for thinking about these different uses as part of the same phenomenon, as a post-conflict developmental heritage complex. In this discussion, the chapter raises some theoretical and empirical questions to consider when appraising the relationship between heritage and post-conflict development, including: the problematic centrality of authenticity, relevance and effectiveness in current post-conflict heritage debates, the social construction of authority and legitimacy as a function of post-conflict heritage, the sharing and standardising of a post-conflict heritage complex and finally the symbolic appeal of post-conflict heritage.

Questions of authenticity, relevance and effectiveness remain central to discussions about the institutionalisation of precolonial traditions and customary practices as they also do for discussions about formalised post-conflict heritage. However, as argued from separate historical (Verweijen and Van Bockhaven, 2020) and heritage (Giblin, 2014) perspectives, focusing on these aspects in isolation distracts from developing understanding of the agency and symbolic functions of these actions. In their discussion of customary authority in Central and East Africa, for example, Verweijen and Van Bockhaven (2020) highlighted how traditions and customary practices have consistently been adapted and manipulated in precolonial, colonial and postcolonial eras, an observation which brings into question what authenticity and relevance means in a contemporary context. Authenticity has also long been debated in critical heritage studies where it is similarly understood that traditions and customary practices regularly undergo modification and that no heritage is ever pristine (c.f. Silverman, 2015). Therefore, although the adaption of customary practices and traditions over time is of historical interest, it is less important for a discussion of their contemporary institutionalisation. In addition, when heritage is understood as a common cultural production process that is intensified after violence, as societies look to the past to reconstruct the present, questions about effectiveness are also decentred while ones about function and meaning emerge (Giblin, 2014).

To approach the function and meaning of authorised post-conflict heritage, it is useful to consider issues of authority and legitimacy. For example, Verweijen and Van Bockhaven (2020) have emphasised the agency of various actors in the social construction of customary authority through the symbolic negotiation of the past in precolonial, colonial and postcolonial eras. Following this line of thought, if the construction of authority and legitimacy is intensified following conflict when new regimes need to establish themselves, then there may be a parallel intensification of the negotiation of the past. Thinking about post-conflict heritage in terms of the social construction of authority and legitimacy, thus, provides an answer to the overarching function of top-down heritage initiatives and suggests that it will manifest differently in each national context based on separate historical trajectories.

However, while authorised post-conflict narratives will be distinct, post-conflict nations do not exist in isolation and increasingly they are sharing post-conflict heritage modes as parts of a post-conflict developmental heritage complex. The examples in this chapter have demonstrated how memorials and museums, alongside school history syllabi, are commonly used to deliver national post-conflict narratives, while the institutionalisation of precolonial tradition and customary practice are increasingly providing authority and legitimacy for transitional justice, reconciliation and conflict resolution policies. The sharing of post-conflict heritage practices takes places in multiple ways, but we have observed it specifically at professional and political levels. For example, a delegation of community members and heritage professionals who were developing plans for the northern Ugandan memorials first visited the Rwandan genocide memorials to help inform their work, while later a political delegation from Central African Republic (CAR) visited the memorials in northern Uganda to inform approaches in CAR. Rwandan Peacekeepers have also introduced Umuganda in CAR and Haiti and there have been many international delegations to the Kigali Genocide Memorial Centre to learn from that approach. In addition, visiting delegations exist against a backdrop of international museum professional training in post-Apartheid South Africa at sites such as Robben Island, and attendance and participation at international peace conferences, for example, in post-genocide Cambodia. (This is a limited account from our perspectives as heritage professionals, however, it is hoped that future ethnographic studies may fruitfully map the movement of ideas about the use of the past between post-conflict nations).

The social construction of authority and legitimacy may provide an overarching function for the top-down appeal of post-conflict heritage at various scales of national, regional and local governance. However, it is also necessary to consider its wider appeal for post-conflict societies. In this context, heritage as therapy is a useful way to approach this topic (c.f. Meskell and Scheermeyer, 2008). For example, there is a long history of public healing related to authority and legitimacy in central and eastern Africa (Schoenbrun, 2006; Giblin, 2014; Verweijen and Van Bockhaven, 2020). 'Social problems like poverty, war, and famines were perceived as an illness of society stemming from disturbed relations with the spiritual world' which were to be addressed through 'healing institutions.' Thus, 'in the pre-colonial era, leaders had continuously tried to control these healing phenomena by being healers themselves or by tying ritual specialists to their courts' (Verweijen and Van Bockhaven, 2020: 9). There is thus a historical connection between authority, legitimacy, public healing and the negotiation of the past in central and eastern Africa where many of the examples presented in this chapter come from. In addition, the healing metaphor is common in post-conflict heritage academic and professional discourses, and members of post-conflict communities in Uganda and Rwanda repeated it when interviewed about the post-conflict role of heritage (Giblin, 2014). Drawing on these observations and Hall's (1992) concept of heritage encoding and decoding through 'sign-vehicles', Giblin (2014) has argued that post-conflict developmental heritage can be considered a form of symbolic healing that is actively desired by post-conflict societies seeking emotional, social, political and economic renewal. This argument has direct relevance for central and eastern Africa in terms of the historical precedents presented here. However, it may also be applicable to other post-conflict contexts where the ills of the past and present are symbolically and literally negotiated through reference to the past either through formal heritage sites and performances or through acts that are not labelled as heritage but nevertheless use the past for post-conflict development.

References

Allen, T. (2006) *Trial justice: the International Criminal Court and the Lord's Resistance Army*. London: Zed Books.

Anyeko, K., Baines, E., Komakech, E., Ojok, B., Ogora, L. O., and Victor, L. (2012) '"The cooling of hearts": community truth-telling in Northern Uganda', *Human Rights Review*, *13*(1), pp. 107–124.

Beall, J. and Ngonyama, M. (2009) *Indigenous institutions, traditional leaders and elite coalitions for development: the case of Greater Durban, South Africa*. London: London School of Economics.

Bedigen, W. (2020) 'Significance of societal customs in the South Sudan civil war resolution', *Journal of Peacebuilding and Development*, 15(1), pp. 3–17.

Branch, A. (2008) 'Ethnojustice: the theory and practice of traditional justice in northern Uganda', paper presented at the Annual American Political Science Association (APSA). Available at: https://onlinelibrary.wiley.com/doi/10.1111/dech.12094 (Accessed 29 January 2022).

Briggs, J. (2005) 'The use of indigenous knowledge in development: problems and challenges', *Progress in development studies*, 5(2), pp. 99–114.

Coombes, A. E. and Hughes, L. (2014) *Managing heritage, making peace: history, identity and memory in contemporary Kenya*. London: Bloomsbury Publishing.

Cross, C. (2016) 'Ulinzi shirikishi: popular experiences of hybrid security governance in Tanzania', *Development and Change*, 47(5), pp. 1102–1124.

De Jong, F. and Rowlands, M. (2008) 'Postconflict heritage', *Journal of Material Culture* 13(2), pp. 131–134.

Department of Provincial and Local Government (2002) *White Paper on Traditional Leadership and Governance*. Available at: www.gov.za/sites/default/files/gcis_document/201409/239841.pdf (Accessed 29 January 2022).

Giblin, J. D. (2014) 'Post-conflict heritage: symbolic healing and cultural renewal' *International Journal of Heritage Studies*, 20(5), pp. 500–518.
Giblin, J. D. (2017) 'The performance of international diplomacy at Kigali Memorial Centre, Rwanda', *Journal of African Cultural Heritage Studies*, 1(1), pp. 49–67.
Giblin, J. D. (2018) 'Heritage and the use of the past in East Africa' in Spear, T. (ed) *Oxford research encyclopedia of African history*. New York: Oxford University Press. doi: 10.1093/acrefore/9780190277734.013.135
Giblin, J. D., Mugabowagahunde, M. and Ntagwabira, A. (2017) 'International heritage tourism in Rwanda: paving over the past at the Musanze Caves', *Conservation and Management of Archaeological Sites*, 19(2), pp. 126–140.
Government of Uganda (2007) *Agreement on accountability and reconciliation between the LRA and Ugandan government*. Available at: https://peacemaker.un.org/uganda-accountability-reconciliation2007 (Accessed 29 January 2022).
Hall, S. (1992) 'Encoding/decoding' in Hall, S. (ed) *Culture, media, language: working papers in cultural studies, 1972, 1979*. London: Routledge, pp. 107–116.
Harrison, R. (2012) *Heritage: critical approaches*. Abingdon: Routledge.
Hobsbawm, E. and Ranger, T. (eds) (2012) *The invention of tradition*. Cambridge: Cambridge University Press.
Hosagrahar, J. (2017) *Culture at the heart of the SDGs*. Available at: https://en.unesco.org/courier/april-june-2017/culture-heart-sdgs (Accessed 29 January 2022).
Jessee, E. (2017) 'The danger of a single story: iconic stories in the aftermath of the 1994 Rwandan genocide', *Memory Studies*, 10(2), pp. 144–163.
KGMC (2021) *Education*. Available at: https://kgm.rw/education (Accessed 29 January 2022).
King, E. (2010) 'Memory controversies in post-genocide Rwanda: implications for peacebuilding', *Genocide Studies and Prevention*, 5(3), pp. 293–309.
Kisić, V. (2020) 'Reconciliation through cultural heritage in the post-Yugoslav space: an political endeavor', in Labadi, S. (ed) *The cultural turn in international aid: impacts and challenges for heritage and the creative industries*. Abingdon: Routledge, pp 173–191.
Kreimer, A., Eriksson, J., Muscat, R., Arnold, M. and Scott, C. (1998) *The World Bank's experience with post-conflict reconstruction*. Washington, DC: The World Bank.
Lennon, J. and Foley, M. (2000) *Dark tourism – the attraction of death and disaster* (2nd Edition). London: Continuum.
McDowell, S. (2016) 'Heritage, memory and identity' in Graham, B. and Howard, P. (eds) *The Ashgate research companion to heritage and identity*. Abingdon: Routledge, pp. 37–53.
Meskell, L. and Scheermeyer, C. (2008) 'Heritage as therapy: set pieces from the new South Africa', *Journal of Material Culture*, 13(2), pp. 153–173.
Niven, B. (2007) 'War memorials at the intersection of politics, culture and memory', *Journal of War and Culture Studies*, 1(1), pp. 39–45.
Pham, P. and Vinck, P. (2010) *Transitioning to peace: a population-based survey on attitudes about peace, justice, and social reconstruction in Northern Uganda*. Berkeley: International Center for Transitional Justice and the Human Rights Center, University of California.
Quinn, J. (2004) 'Constraints: the un-doing of the Ugandan Truth Commission', *Human Rights Quarterly*, 26(2), pp. 401–427.
RGB (2014) *The assessment of the impact of Home Grown Initiatives*. Kigali: RGB.
RGB (2017) *Impact assessment of Umuganda 2007–2016*. Kigali: RGB.
RGB (2018) *Assessing Girinka Programme (2006–2016): citizen perspectives*. Kigali: RGB.
RGB (2019) *Impact assessment of Abunzi committees 2004–2018*. Kigali: RGB.
RGB (2022) *About Home Grown Solutions*. Available at: http://rgb.rw/home-grown-solutions/about-home-grown-solutions (Accessed 29 January 2022).

Richards, R. (2020) 'Fragility within stability: the state, the clan and political resilience in Somaliland', *Third World Quarterly*, 41(6), pp. 1067–1083.

Rutazibwa, O.U. and Ndushabandi, E.N.S. (2019) 'Agaciro: re-centering dignity in development', in Kothari, A., Salleh, A., Escobar, A., Demaria, F. and Acosta, A. (eds) *Pluriverse: a post-development dictionary*. New Delhi: Tulika Books, pp. 79–81.

Schoenbrun, D.L. (2006) 'Conjuring the modern in Africa: durability and rupture in histories of public healing between the Great Lakes of East Africa', *African Historical Review*, 111, pp. 1403–1439.

Seaton, A.V. (1996) 'Guided by the Dark; from Thanatopsis to Thanatourism', *International Journal of Heritage Studies*, 2(4), pp. 234–244, Intellect.

Silverman, H. (2015) 'Heritage and authenticity', in Waterton, E. and Watson, S. (eds) *The Palgrave handbook of contemporary heritage research*. London: Palgrave Macmillan, pp. 69–88.

Skinner, J. (2012) *Writing the dark side of travel*. London: Berghahn Books.

Smith, L. (2006) *Uses of heritage*. New York: Routledge.

Stone, R. (2006) 'A dark tourism spectrum: towards a typology of death and macabre related tourist sites, attractions and exhibitions', *Tourism: An International Interdisciplinary Journal*, 54(2), pp. 145–160.

Tankink, M. (2007) '"The moment I became born-again the pain disappeared": the healing of devastating war memories in born-again churches in Mbarara District, Southwest Uganda', *Transcultural Psychiatry*, 44(2), pp. 203–231.

The Council of Europe (2011) *The role of culture and cultural heritage in conflict prevention, transformation, resolution and post-conflict action. The Council of Europe approach*. Available at: www.coe.int/t/dg4/cultureheritage/News/CultureReconciliation_en.pdf (Accessed 29 January 2022).

UNESCO (2008) *Medium-term strategy for 2008–2013*. Available at: http://unesdoc.unesco.org/images/0014/001499/149999e.pdf (Accessed 29 January 2022).

UNESCO (2014) *Medium-Term Strategy for 2014–2021*. Available at: www.unesco.org/new/en/bureau-of-strategic-planning/resources/medium-termstrategy-c4/ (Accessed 29 January 2022).

Verweijen, J. and Van Bockhaven, V. (2020) 'Revisiting colonial legacies in knowledge production on customary authority in Central and East Africa', *Journal of Eastern African Studies*, 14(1), pp. 1–23.

Walsh, C. (2010) 'Development as buen vivir: institutional arrangements and (de) colonial entanglements', *Development*, 53(1), pp. 15–21.

Winter, T. (2007) *Post conflict heritage, post colonial tourism*. Abingdon: Routledge.

PART 6

Epilogue and Conclusion

A Role for Heritage in Development?

15

A ROLE FOR HERITAGE IN DEVELOPMENT?

Rodney Harrison

It is now a well-established cliché that heritage and culture are an integral part of sustainable development, conflict resolution and post-conflict development. While advocates for the role of heritage in development point to a few well-known examples of instances in which heritage is said to have helped to broker peace and (re)build lives, cultures and economies in developing and post-conflict states, critical studies of the role of heritage and culture in conflict and development have for a long time taken precisely the opposite view – that culture and cultural heritage are often employed to emphasise difference and can be triggers for conflict, and in this way produce impediments to the development of peaceful and prosperous societies. As such, questions regarding the precise circumstances under which heritage could be said to build peace and contribute to sustainable development, the ways in which it does so, and the political, social, economic and ecological consequences of its deployment in such a manner are, to my mind, some of the key questions of the new millennium, and ones which emerge even more strongly from various crises which have marked the early 2020s, including the climate and extinction emergencies, Black Lives Matter protests and the coronavirus pandemic. As the introduction to this volume indicates, the question of how 'progress' and development are defined is integral to, and instrumental in, how the relationship between culture and development is defined and understood.

The chapters in the present volume make significant headway in exploring these questions critically. Drawing on my own work, I would reflect on two issues which I think more or less implicitly underpin many of the perspectives brought by the authors represented here. These relate on the one hand to the integral and co-definitional relationship between the concepts of 'culture' and 'progress', and to related questions of power and expertise on the other. Here I draw particularly on work undertaken with colleagues Tony Bennett, Fiona Cameron, Nélia Dias, Ben Dibley, Ira Jacknis and Conal McCarthy regarding the history of different

DOI: 10.4324/9781003107361-21

forms of early to mid-20th century anthropological collecting practices and their relationship with practices of social government (see Bennett et al., 2017). One of the concerns which drove this collaborative investigation was to consider the various transactional realities which have been established in the relations between specific anthropological collecting practices, the associated rationales for ordering population which emerged from these anthropological collecting practices and the particular modes of governing which these rationales for ordering population have facilitated.

We take the concept of transactional realities from Michel Foucault's *The Birth of Biopolitics* (2010) in which he notes that:

> Civil society is not a historical-natural given…it is not a primary or immediate reality; it is something which forms part of a modern governmental technology…Civil society is, like madness and sexuality, what I call transactional realities. That is to say those transactional and transitional figures we call civil society, madness, and so on, which, although they have not always existed are nonetheless real, are born precisely from the interplay of relations of power and everything which constantly eludes them, at the interface, so to speak, of governors and governed.
>
> *2010: 297*

Bennett (2013: 44–45; 2014) has suggested that one of the important roles of 20th century anthropology in this respect has been in producing what he terms 'working surfaces on the social', that is, in producing transactional realities which provide distinctive discursive and technical means by which populations might be differentiated and by which specific forms of action on those differentiated populations might be mediated as a function of the relations between governors and governed. In this regard, 'culture' can be seen as a 'reformer's science' (Bennett, 1998), as both a potential impediment to development to be overcome as well as a potential instrument for liberal social governance, as what other scholars might refer to as a form of 'soft power'. But culture can only work in this way through related notions of 'progress' and civilisation, which manifest in this context in hierarchies of development which themselves establish and define various forms of culture which they are each associated with.

I write this piece on my return from the UNFCCC International Climate Change Conference, COP26, where I have co-curated an exhibition – Reimagining Museums for Climate Action – which aims to inspire radical change in the museum sector to address the climate emergency (Harrison and Sterling, 2021; McGhie, 2021). The exhibition developed out of an international design and ideas competition which asked the public how museums would need to be reimagined to facilitate them taking the forms of climate action they wished to take. What emerged from working with competition entrants and engaging with publics at COP26 itself was that museums (and I would suggest heritage and development related organisations more generally) need to fundamentally reorient how they see their roles in society – not as experts but as facilitators for radical change for the publics they serve. Many have been arguing for some time for such a radical reorientation of authority and the notions of expertise which would have to underpin it for the museum and heritage sector (e.g., see Harrison, 2013; Harrison, Byrne and Clarke, 2013). This would also require fundamental reforms to the ways in which notions of progress, development, culture and cultural heritage are understood and operationalised. It is only through such fundamental reforms that the role of heritage in development might become something more than a form of soft power and truly develop the potential to be transformative for 'developing' and post-conflict societies.

References

Bennett, T. (1998) *Culture: a reformer's science*. London: Sage.

Bennett, T. (2013) *Making culture, changing society*. Abingdon: Routledge.

Bennett, T. (2014) 'Liberal government and the practical history of anthropology', *History and Anthropology*, 25(2), pp. 50–70.

Bennett, T., Cameron, F., Dias, N., Dibley, B., Harrison, R. and Jacknis, I. (2017) *Collecting, ordering, governing: anthropology, museums, and liberal government*. Durham. Duke University Press.

Foucault, M. (2010) *The birth of biopolitics: lectures at the Collège de France, 1978–1979*. New York: Picador.

Harrison, R. (2013) *Heritage: critical approaches*. Abingdon: Routledge.

Harrison, R., Byrne, S. and Clarke, A. (eds) (2013) *Reassembling the collection: ethnographic museums and indigenous Agency*. Santa Fe: School for Advanced Research Press.

Harrison, R. and Sterling, C. (eds) (2021) *Reimagining museums for climate action*. London: Museums for Climate Action. Available at: www.museumsforclimateaction.org/mobilise/book (Accessed 8 February 2022).

McGhie, H. (2021) *Mobilising museums for climate action: tools, frameworks and opportunities to accelerate climate action in and with museums*. London: Museums for Climate Action. Available at: www.museumsforclimateaction.org/mobilise/toolkit (Accessed 8 February 2022).

16

TOWARDS DECOLONISING DEVELOPMENT

A Role for Heritage

Uma Kothari

Global protests against injustice, inequality and racism, and calls to decolonise public spaces, histories and knowledges, have recently gained momentum. These calls to decolonise compel a fundamental rethinking of development discourse and practice and the need to situate it within its historical legacy and more specifically, its colonial inheritance. The imperative to address past injustices that continue to persist has never been more urgent, timely and salient. In this short epilogue, I consider the contribution that rethinking heritage in development can make to the wider project of decoloniality and how it can enable the field of development to move beyond its complicity with imperialism. One of the most high-profile manifestations of these surging global campaigns challenges the contemporary practices of retaining public statues that reflect slavery and colonialism. Here, I focus on another controversy in the campaigns that seek to restore appropriated artefacts to their original people and locations from the museums that now house them. I consider how development can forge decolonial solidarities through the repatriation of these stolen objects.

An examination of the role of heritage in the project to decolonise development is particularly challenging given that the development discourse is fraught with partial histories. To date, mainstream histories of development have concealed its colonial genealogy, failing to acknowledge the ongoing relationship between colonialism and the workings of the post-independence development industry. One of the reasons for this abbreviated, uncritical version of the emergence of development has been an unwillingness to acknowledge its uncomfortable imperial past and to distance development thought and practice from the contemporary negativity that surrounds Western imperial history. Accordingly, the dominant version of development effectively conceals its colonial genealogy, obscuring long histories of exploitation and dispossession.

DOI: 10.4324/9781003107361-22

Importantly, this abridged historical analysis reveals the largely unreflexive nature of the field, partly engendered by the imperative to achieve development goals and targets and push towards the future. While some development scholars (see Crush, 1995; Cowen and Shenton, 1995) attempt to take a longer historical perspective and provide alternative readings of the origins and evolution of development, 'narratives of speed and of contingency privilege future orientations and instantiations while there is much less that forces us to take account of the past' (Raghuram et al., 2009: 10). This linear, future-oriented outlook closes off options to deal with the past and past injustices.

As Melber (2019: 278) writes, we will continue to reproduce colonial forms of power and control 'as long as the historically rooted animosities and structural legacies as well as internalized value systems and behavioral patterns prevail'. Tronto (2003) agrees, arguing that conceiving of the past as irrelevant except insofar as it shapes our present and future options has devastating consequences for justice. Furthermore, Matthes (2019: 180) contends, 'if we construe heritage as necessarily positive, then negative aspects of the past, such as historical injustice, will be excluded from counting as part of one's heritage'. Thus, the privileging of the future over the past creates problems for thinking about justice for historical wrongdoing and leaves no room for remedying past injustices or for moving towards a responsible accountability (Tronto, 2003). Importantly then, we need to begin not with how the past can inform better futures but by interrogating how the past is being constructed in the present. In reaching towards this goal, it is critical to identify whose versions of heritage dominate; as Said (1978: 28) argues, 'the unrepresented narratives of the formerly colonised are essential in order to confront their entanglement in a process through which they have become defined and confined'.

Consequently, understanding the role of heritage in development must involve decentring authoritative historical narratives while remaining vigilant to those historical relations that remain hidden, unrecognisable or have mutated. This critically involves the painstaking construction or reconstruction of knowledge. Tronto (2003: 133) judiciously summarises this:

> the solution to these problems, then, is not to wish for a brave new world, to recommend that we should consider only the future. Instead, we need to return to the painful, ugly and yet perhaps redeemable excesses and injustices of the past … Only if we are willing to give the past its due will we have any firm ground to stand upon and pursue hope for the future.

Moreover, this reconfiguration of development's heritage requires moving beyond a simple recognition of Indigenous and non-Western voices and perspectives in also acknowledging that development is an ongoing site of contestation and of oppression (Quijano, 2000; Mignolo, 2011).

In this context, a critical engagement with understandings of heritage might generate a more progressive development, instil solidaristic principles and forge practices of care. This involves a shift in focus towards how formerly colonised people and places continue to be represented through a Western imagination in museums, through curation and artefacts. Drawing on the work of decolonial scholars who have questioned the role of museums and the histories and cultures of collections, I focus here on the potential impacts of the repatriation of objects pilfered by colonialists. There is increasing recognition that museums in former centres of colonial power reflect the preoccupations, politics, obsessions, values, and violence of their historical era and therefore, as Basu and Modest (2014: 21) contend, typically carry 'a colonial baggage'. Attempts to decolonise thus require unearthing the deep historical and cultural contexts in which these artefacts have been gathered. Critical heritage studies offer valuable insights that could usefully contribute to a rethinking of the heritage of development. An exploration of contemporary relationships between people, heritage, and power is particularly relevant in the context of development as it acknowledges that heritage is 'produced through socio-political processes reflecting society's power structures' (Logan and Wijesuriya, 2015: 569).

As explorers and colonialists encountered and 'discovered' other places, they often envisaged them as landscapes without people, *terra nullius*. In settler colonialism in Australia, land was legally deemed to be unoccupied or uninhabited justifying its acquisition by British occupation without treaty or payment. This effectively denied the prior occupation of Indigenous peoples and their connection to the land (Coulthard, 2014). The extermination and elimination of Indigenous people was violent (Reynolds, 1996) and attempts to change subjectivities, behaviours, beliefs, and values through the assimilation of Indigenous people also played a role in the theft of their possessions. Return of sacred and historically significant objects would offer one way of acknowledging these and other such past injustices.

In many European national collections, objects from colonised places have been used to construct 'celebratory national narratives' (Smith, 2006: 17). This exemplifies a particular example of Harrison's understanding of heritage (2013: 2):

> [h]eritage is not a passive process of simply preserving things from the past that remain, but an active process of assembling a series of objects, places and practices that we choose to hold up as a mirror to the present, associated with a particular set of values that we wish to take with us into the future.

In continuously owning and showcasing stolen objects, national, colonial narratives can be sustained, while simultaneously, they are a powerful reminder for the formerly colonised of their painful dispossession. Indeed, the embodied, sensuous, agential, and affective notions of heritage (Tolia-Kelly et al., 2016) retained by these formerly colonised subjects are intimately connected to these material objects, offering a point of reconnection to the past.

Accordingly, their repatriation can potentially foster new solidaristic connections. Objects hold stories that have affective and political power. Also, as Thomas writes (2009), objects embody social relations, they have a cultural biography, articulating a place and culture, carrying a trace of where they came from, but these social relations shift, dissipate, and are reforged as the meanings of objects changes. Through listening to the diverse, often overlooked stories about objects that continuously emerge, we can begin to address the problem of a forgetful past. As Tynan (2021) reminds us, stories are held in the land and in memory and through the repatriation of objects, the past can be pushed 'unfinished into the present' (Gibson 2002: 107).

In November 2019, Manchester Museum, in partnership with the Australian Institute of Aboriginal and Torres Strait Islander Studies (AIATSIS), established 'The Return of Cultural Heritage Project' and began returning sacred artefacts to Indigenous aboriginal communities in Australia. It was acknowledged that these items were taken by force under processes of colonisation and would never have been given over willingly. The Curator of Manchester Museum, Stephen Welsh, acknowledged that:

> Western processes and protocols established to catalogue, preserve and analyse objects and specimens in isolation from traditional owners, countries of origin and diaspora communities, continues to inflict loss, trauma and exclusion on those people most closely connected with collections.
>
> *Ward, 2019*

This was recognised by the CEO of AIATSIS, who stated that the repatriation of objects 'fosters truth telling about our Nation's history'. A representative of a Native Title Aboriginal Corporation added that the 'repatriation of our sacred cultural heritage items is a fundamental part of the healing process' as 'locked deep within these items is our lore; our histories, our traditions and our stories'. At the repatriation ceremony powerful themes of global solidarity emerged, articulated by the Museum's director, Esme Ward, who emphasised that a museum's duty is to foster 'thinking about our common humanity'. This was affirmed by Mangubadijarri Yanner, one of the Traditional Owners, who said 'we share a dark history – but it's moments like this, when we come together as one, united by our desire to do better, to be better and to right the wrongs of the past, that we start to heal spiritual hurts and the intergenerational trauma that still exists today (Ward, 2019).

Returning these stolen objects constituted a progressive, transformational, decolonial approach to heritage from which development might learn. Importantly, if development is concerned with addressing inequalities, there is a need to reconsider relations between the so-called Global South and Global North. This necessitates interrogating the West's own heritage and shifting the development gaze and interventions to how it reproduces the very inequalities it purportedly attempts to address. This compels the adoption of an expanded, creative and productive, notion of heritage (see Harrison et al., 2016), one that is based on solidaristic principles that can not only confront past injustices but represents a move towards shifting the structures that continue to create them. This more solidaristic approach requires forging practices of care for others that are based on revealing those historical relations that continue to be hidden. Because, as Mbembe (2016: 30) put it, it is only through memory and remembering, that we can 'put history to rest'.

References

Basu, P. and Modest, W. (eds.) (2014) *Museums, heritage and international development*. London: Routledge.

Coulthard, G. S. (2014) *Red skin, white masks: rejecting the colonial politics of recognition*. Minneapolis: University of Minnesota Press.

Cowen, M. and Shenton R. W. (1995) 'The invention of development', in Crush, J. (ed.) *Power of development*. London: Routledge, pp. 27–43.

Crush, J. (ed.) (1995) *Power of development*. London: Routledge.

Gibson, R. (2002) *Seven versions of an Australian Badland*. Indooroopilly: University of Queensland Press.

Harrison, R. (2013) *Heritage: critical approaches*. New York: Routledge.

Harrison, R., Bartolini, N., DeSilvey, C., Holtorf, C., Lyons, A., Macdonald, S., May, S., Morgan, J. and Penrose, S. (2016) 'Heritage futures', *Archaeology International*, 19, pp. 68–72.

Logan, W. and Wijesuriya, G. (2015) 'The new heritage studies and education, training, and capacity-building', in Logan, W., Craith, M. N. and Kocke, U. (eds.) *A companion to heritage studies*. Malden, MA: Wiley, pp. 557–573.

Matthes, E. H. (2019) 'Environmental heritage and the ruins of the future', in Bicknell, J., Judkins, J. and Korsmeyer, C. (eds.) *Philosophical perspectives on ruins, monuments, and memorials*. London: Routledge, pp. 175–186.

Mbembe, J. A. (2016) 'Decolonizing the university: new directions', *Arts and Humanities in Higher Education*, 15(1), pp. 29–45.

Melber, H (2019) 'Knowledge production, ownership and the power of definition: perspectives on and from sub-Saharan Africa', in Baud, I., Basile, E., Kontinen, T. and von Itter, S. (eds.) *Building development studies for the new millennium*. London: Palgrave Macmillan, pp. 265–287.

Mignolo, W. D. (2011) 'Geopolitics of sensing and knowing: on (de) coloniality, border thinking and epistemic disobedience', *Postcolonial Studies*, 14(3), pp. 273–283.

Quijano, A. (2000) 'Coloniality of power and Eurocentrism in Latin America', *International Sociology*, 15(2), pp. 215–232.

Raghuram, P., Madge, C. and Noxolo, P. (2009) 'Rethinking responsibility and care for a postcolonial world', *Geoforum*, 40(1), pp. 5–13.

Reynolds, H. (1996) *Dispossession: black Australians and white invaders*. Sydney: Allen & Unwin.

Said, E. (1978) *Orientalism*. New York: Pantheon Books.

Smith, L. (2006) *Uses of heritage*. London: Routledge.

Thomas, N. (2009) *Entangled objects: exchange, material culture, and colonialism in the Pacific*. Cambridge, MA: Harvard University Press.

Tolia-Kelly, D. P., Waterton, E. and Watson, S. (2016) *Heritage, affect and emotion*. London: Routledge.

Tronto, J. (2003) 'Time's place', *Feminist Theory*, 4(2), pp. 119–138.

Tynan, L. (2021) 'What is relationality? Indigenous knowledges, practices and responsibilities with kin', *Cultural Geographies*, 28(4), pp. 597–610.

Ward, E. (2019) *The tide of change: open letter from our director Esme Ward*. Manchester Museum. Available at: www.museum.manchester.ac.uk/about/thetideofchange/ (Accessed 24 February 2022).

17

DECOLONISING HERITAGE FOR DEVELOPMENT

Why Positionality and Perspective Matters

Shadreck Chirikure

Introduction

In various forms, some contradictory, but others mutually reinforcing, heritage has been touted as a central pivot in pursuit of development, whatever the term means to whoever is defining it. From the position of the Global South, especially that of the former colonies, development is wrapped up in colonial and neocolonial meanings (Chirikure et al., 2010, 2016; Ndlovu-Gatsheni, 2020). Genealogically, development is tied to notions of progress coming out of the European Enlightenment and was further thrust to the fore of international agendas after the Second World War and achievement of independence by many African countries, especially after 1950 (see Cross and Giblin, this volume). This often resulted in the mobilisation of powerful international agents such as the World Bank and International Monetary Fund (IMF) advocating for concepts of development favourable to the Global North but unfavourable to the Global South (Ndlovu-Gatsheni, 2021). But that is development from the point of view of Western modernity. In my native Shona, development translates into *budiriro*, a holistic concept that deals with many things such as improvement in material and non-material situations, ability to help others, and a change in individual and collective circumstances (Ndoro and Pwiti, 2001; Chirikure, 2021; Sinamai, 2020). One can use the heritage – or *nhaka* – comprising skill, knowledge, and practices, some acquired from years bygone, but others continuously created. Heritage or *nhaka* does not belong to a period; it brings together everything from different times and is contradictory. Heritage is life – *nhaka youpenyu*. Development therefore is a consequence of heritage and heritage making, and it takes place at personal and interpersonal levels, within a community and nearly everywhere (Chirikure, 2021).

This is just but one perspective from one position. How do we develop new understandings of development and heritage that are meaningful at global and

DOI: 10.4324/9781003107361-23

cross-cultural levels? Is that even possible? One of the critical themes running through the contributions to this volume is the way that ideas about heritage for development are generally derived from dominant positions and perspectives associated with powerful nations, powerful institutions, powerful writers, and powerful places. In contrast, examples from the less powerful are often positioned in relation to dominant understandings such as those of UNESCO or the World Bank. If we can identify an authorised discourse around heritage for development (see Giblin et al., this volume), does this call for insurgent scholarship (see Ndlovu-Gatsheni, 2021) to provincialise dominant understandings? In the very brief remarks that follow, I make a case for a bold stand to decolonise notions of heritage for development to learn from the marginalised and the subaltern.

Decolonising heritage and decolonising development

Who defines development, and from what position and from what intellectual perspective? There is an alertness in this volume to the different ways in which development and heritage can be defined and how both as dominant practices today have their roots in a Western genealogy emerging from the European Enlightenment and the post-Second World War responses (Cross and Giblin, this volume). These are supported by very influential UNESCO perspectives. Some of the positions are based on the notions of progress where some areas are backward and require guidance, international aid, and patronage from the Global North (Ndoro., 2017, 2021). The main problem is that this is wrapped up in the colonial matrices of power, where international finance and skill flows are controlled by the former colonial metropoles (Ndlovu-Gatsheni, 2021). Definitions of development based on that are therefore not inclusive and certainly international aid has caused more harm than good in Africa, Asia, and Latin America. For example, most African, Asian, and Latin American countries are suffering from the legacies of the World Bank and IMF-sponsored economic Structural Adjustment Programs (SAPs) (Ndlovu-Gatsheni, 2020). The SAPs were implemented by experts from the Global North and were hardly associated with meaningful transfer of skills. Similarly, the international views that have shaped notions of what heritage is are Western centred (Munjeri, 2004; Sinamai, 2020). The Venice Charter and its emphasis on monumentality influenced the 1972 UNESCO Convention and for a very long time defined what World Heritage was and was not (Taruvinga, 2019). Efforts were made to be inclusive for example through the Nara Declaration on Authenticity and through the UNESCO Convention on Intangible Heritage, but other heritages are not well emphasised (Munjeri, 2004).

Indeed, international finance and skills have resulted in the construction of large-scale infrastructure projects such as dams (Ndoro, 2017). However, most heritage impact assessments associated with such projects are done by specialists from the Global North. Therefore, Global North and Chinese finance work in cahoots with Global North and Chinese skills often ensuring that no sustainable skills are left post the life of projects. Consequently, Global South regions continue to be dependent on the Global North for capital, skills, and even for notions of what is and what is not heritage. As shown by Cross (this volume) and others, an incorporation of concepts from ancient Africa is one way of alleviating the situation. Of course traditions can be invented, not just in Rwanda (Giblin et al., this volume), but also even in Euro-America where development is a tool for perpetuating influence in the former colonies (Ndlovu-Gatsheni, 2020, 2021).

Development requires decolonisation to make it relevant to local needs. The African Union Agenda 2063: The Africa We Want proposes to use heritage as a lever for sustainable development and silencing the guns to promote peace and resilience (Taruvinga, 2019; Ndoro, 2021). Along the same lines, various African scholars too have written on heritage and development, defining what these might mean. Marginalising such perspectives risks reinforcing the coloniality associated with understanding heritage and development from the Global North point of view. More fundamentally, borrowing from Dipesh Chakrabarty, can we provincialise Western-centred understandings of development and heritage by defining these in our own languages? If we do so in Hindu, Maori, Swahili, or Shona and using philosophical frameworks such as ubuntu, we might derive new positions and perspectives for assessing opportunities associated with using heritage for development. As suggested earlier, using the Shona concept of *nhaka*, heritage is part of everyday innovation and encompasses everything from the built to the non-built, the tangible and intangible, and the terrestrial and celestial. Heritage is not just about monuments, or sacred groves, or landscapes – it combines the tangible and intangible (Chirikure et al., 2016). Development is a holistic response to the need to fulfil biological, material, and spiritual needs making it multifaceted.

In undertaking this decolonisation project, it will be necessary to draw theoretical insights and flavours from multiple disciplines, including history, heritage studies, anthropology, archaeology, philosophy, and economics. Part of this endeavour must inevitably involve developing joined up thinking to bring together different specialisations to offer multifocal perspectives on what is development and what is heritage and the points at which they intersect. Indeed, there is no need to repeat the current imbalances and power structures that privilege some notions but not others. Heritage for development, in our multiple languages, remains a very helpful concept.

Conclusion

The different perspectives that inform understandings of what is heritage and what is development also speak to positionality, power, and structures that constrain or promote the two. Heritage for development can empower some, but it can disadvantage, or even exploit others. International capital flows with its skills, concepts, and power to the extent that the Global South remains marginalised. Heritage for development is neither neutral nor value free. This calls for decolonisation to provincialize dominant understandings to bring equitable and just planetary futures.

References

Chirikure, S. (2021) *Great Zimbabwe: reclaiming a confiscated past*. London: Routledge.

Chirikure, S., Manyanga, M., Ndoro, W. and Pwiti, G. (2010) 'Unfulfilled promises? Heritage management and community participation at some of Africa's cultural heritage sites', *International Journal of Heritage Studies*, 16, pp. 30–44.

Chirikure, S., Mukwende, T. and Taruvinga, P. (2016) 'Post-colonial heritage conservation in Africa: perspectives from drystone wall restorations at Khami World Heritage site, Zimbabwe', *International Journal of Heritage Studies*, 22, pp. 165–178.

Munjeri, D. (2004) 'Tangible and intangible heritage: from difference to convergence', *Museum International*, 56, pp. 12–20.

Ndlovu-Gatsheni, S. J. (2020) *Decolonization, development and knowledge in Africa: turning over a new leaf*. London: Routledge.

Ndlovu-Gatsheni, S. J. (2021) 'Insurgent decolonisation: Ndlovu-Gatsheni on the sins of colonialism', *Review of African Political Economy*, 2 March. Available at: https://roape.net/2021/03/02/insurgent-decolonisation-ndlovu-gatsheni-on-the-sins-of-colonialism/ (Accessed 12 February 2022).

Ndoro, W. (2017) 'World Heritage and development in Sub-Saharan Africa', *American Anthropologist,* 119, pp. 129–131.

Ndoro, W. (2021) Heritage and/or development—which way for Africa?. In: Baillie B., Sørensen M. L. S. (eds) *African heritage challenges. globalization, urbanization and development in Africa*. Singapore: Palgrave Macmillan. https://doi.org/10.1007/978-981-15-4366-1_4

Ndoro, W., Chirikure, S. and Deacon, J. (2017) *Managing heritage in Africa: who cares?* London: Routledge.

Ndoro, W. and Pwiti, G. (2001) 'Heritage management in southern Africa: local, national and international discourse', *Public Archaeology*, 2, pp. 21–34.

Sinamai, A. (2020) '"We are still here": African heritage, diversity and the global heritage knowledge templates', *Archaeologies*, 16, pp. 57–71.

Taruvinga, P. (2019) *Stakeholders, conservation and socio-economic development: the case of Mapungubwe Cultural Landscape World Heritage Site, South Africa*, unpublished PhD thesis, University of Cape Town. Available at: https://open.uct.ac.za/bitstream/handle/11427/30542/thesis_sci_2019_taruvinga_pascall.pdf?sequence=1&isAllowed=y (Accessed 12 February 2022).

18

A ROLE FOR HERITAGE IN DEVELOPMENT?

Sophia Labadi

The edited volume 'Critical Approaches to Heritage for Development' represents an essential contribution to the field. Of importance is its wide consideration of the multifarious contributions of heritage to different aspects of sustainable development, including to food security, peace, governance, women's rights, economic development, health, biodiversity, and education. These foci are in line with other recent publications (e.g. Labadi et al., 2021; Labadi, 2022) that advocate for a greater role to be played by heritage in the sustainable development debate, beyond considering its mere conservation and management. What also clearly emerges from this edited volume is the impossibility of considering sustainable development issues in their diversity and complexity when heritage is compartmentalised as being either culture or nature, tangible or intangible. Heritage needs to be understood holistically, as this volume clearly demonstrates, transcending these narrow categories.

Various chapters in this publication have highlighted the essential and enabling dimension of UN organisations, primarily UNESCO, both in clarifying the role of heritage for different aspects of sustainable development, and in funding and implementing different projects, including on economic development (see chapters in Part 1); heritage and health (see chapters in Part 3); and peace and security (see chapters in Part 5). Some of these chapters, in particular, have provided insightful reflections on key principles of the UNESCO 2015 Policy on Heritage and Sustainable Development (UNESCO, 2015; for discussion on this policy see Labadi, 2019). These discussions focus on equitable economic development that generates decent employment and income for local communities (see chapter by Huong and Bushell); the strengthening of educational programmes and capacity-building initiatives for all (see chapters by Bermeo et al. and by Abiti et al.); the protection and enhancement of biological and cultural diversity, as well as ecosystem services and benefits for people that contribute to environmental sustainability (see chapter

DOI: 10.4324/9781003107361-24

by Lane and Sulas); respect for gender equality and the careful consideration of the social and economic contributions of women (see chapter by Hazareesingh); and the potential of heritage properties to prevent conflicts through celebrating shared histories and to contribute to post-conflict reconstruction through including heritage in appropriate programmes and policies involving multiple stakeholders (see chapters by Cross and by Giblin et al.).

Most chapters also clearly detail the issues facing the key principles of the 2015 UNESCO Policy. The introduction by Cross and Giblin is particularly forceful in denouncing the unequal power relations that have marred various heritage for development projects. Funded by international aid, these projects aim to promote the expertise, vision, and interests of donor countries. As a result, aid-funded heritage for development projects become a means for Western countries to impose their views and ways of functioning onto the Global South (see also Labadi, 2020 for similar discussions). To quote the introduction to this volume: 'the West is positioned as the location of authorised knowledge about how to "do" heritage for development best'. Aid-funded projects tend to pay for international consultants or consultants from donor countries, with only a small portion of the funding reaching targeted populations, often with limited impacts. Considering these continuing unequal power relations, it is important for donor countries to change their practices. One suggestion is for project evaluations to be gathered from locals themselves, to gain a better understanding of the potentials and limitations of heritage for development projects (see Labadi, 2021: 13).

In addition, chapters in this volume question the widely held assumption that tourism can be the solution for economic growth and poverty reduction. Current tourism models mainly benefit international and foreign companies and individuals, with the core tools of air travel, hotels, and e-commerce concentrated in the Global North, while locals tend to remain in low level and precarious jobs such as tour guiding or selling souvenirs. As a result, any tourism initiative that aims to address local needs must tackle established hierarchies and existing power relations between locals and players from the Global North (see also Labadi, 2021 and Labadi, 2022). The 2015 UNESCO Policy itself warns against heritage projects focusing solely on tourism; instead, this document calls for economic diversification between tourism and non-tourism activities. It also requests that local needs are addressed, including through the strengthening of capacity-building, innovation, and local entrepreneurship for diversified initiatives.

Finally, this edited volume will be useful in understanding the fundamental roles played by women in addressing the sustainable development goals, including, but not limited to, food security. The gap between international understandings of women's roles and the reality on the ground, often leading to missed opportunities for their effective support, is clearly detailed here. In such a context, it is important to reiterate the need for local organisations working on women's empowerment to participate in any project on gender equality, thereby moving away from the imposition of Western concepts and understandings. Such an approach is all the more important considering that women have been disproportionately affected by the Covid-19 pandemic, facing increased caring and household responsibilities, and fewer opportunities for employment.

Overall, this edited volume fills a significant gap through its comprehensive, critical, and innovative approaches towards the challenges of heritage for development.

But is there a role for heritage in development? The conclusions of my latest (2022) book on the topic highlight seven prerequisites that would ensure that there is a role of heritage in development (Labadi, 2022). These prerequisites include the need to consider heritage as dynamic and not as static and 'authentic'. Locals need to stop being considered as being stuck in the past, and to be understood as changing and as able to contribute to key challenges. The negative aspects of heritage need also to be taken fully into account, to ensure that it can really be a force for good. Finally, actors need to change the logic of international aid and ensure that it is better aligned with the reality of the Global South.

References

Labadi, S. (2019) 'Re-examining world heritage and sustainable development', in Bharne, V. and Sandmeier, T. (eds) *Routledge companion of global heritage conservation*. London: Routledge, pp. 15–26.

Labadi, S. (ed.) (2020) *The cultural turn in international aid: impacts and challenges for heritage and the creative industries*. Abingdon: Routledge.

Labadi, S. (2021) *Policy briefs and recommendations. Rethinking heritage for development*. The University of Kent. Available at: https://blogs.kent.ac.uk/heritagefordevelopment/files/2021/08/POLICY-BRIEFS-FINAL-version_web.pdf (Accessed 24 February 2022).

Labadi, S. (2022) *Rethinking heritage for sustainable development*. London: UCL Press.

Labadi, S., Giliberto, F., Rosetti, I., Shebati, L., and Yildirim, E. (2021) *Heritage and the sustainable development goals. Policy guidance for heritage and development actors*. Paris: ICOMOS. Available at: www.icomos.org/images/DOCUMENTS/Secretariat/2021/SDG/ICOMOS_SDGs_Policy_Guidance_2021.pdf (Accessed 5 February 2022).

UNESCO (2015) *Policy document for the integration of a sustainable development perspective into the processes of the world heritage convention*. Available at: https://whc.unesco.org/en/sustainabledevelopment/ (Accessed 24 February 2022).

19

CONCLUSION

Heritage for Development: Decolonisation, Expertise, Ownership, and Agency

Charlotte Cross and John D. Giblin

In its discussion of heritage for development, this volume has explored diverse articulations of valued pasts in relation to desired futures and includes many different voices and viewpoints. In this conclusion we briefly take stock of the approaches to understanding heritage for development and its implications seen here, from our introduction, to the individual chapters, to the perspectives of our epilogue contributors, in order to suggest some common threads and emerging questions.

We began this volume with a critique of the presentation of dominant and formalised notions of heritage as having straightforward and unproblematic applications in international development. We questioned the assumption, prevalent in development-led approaches to using the past, that heritage constitutes a shared objective reality and a public good, is something about which incontestable and universal truths can be claimed, and which can be instrumentalised to do development better. Similarly, we also questioned heritage's rush to align itself with unproblematised notions of development as a set of universal values and aspirations, for example, by aggressively and uncritically co-opting the United Nations' Sustainable Development Goals for heritage ends. In so doing, we observed how established critical perspectives, which understand both heritage and development as political and contested practices, were often side-lined when it came to heritage being instrumentalised for development. We argued that, heritage and international development's uncritical enthusiasm for one another has occurred because the pursuit of development provides new purpose and funding routes for formalised heritage, and because heritage provides a culturally contextual, ostensibly sustainable response to former critiques of the universalism of development. We paid particular attention to the Enlightenment, colonial and ultimately Western roots of the dominant discourses of heritage and development, and thus heritage for development, and the ways in which contemporary attempts to foster heritage and development in the Global South can serve to reproduce and perpetuate colonial power

DOI: 10.4324/9781003107361-25

relations. Rather than reject a role for heritage in development, however, we called for greater understanding of heritage and development as closely related, contested, and political, cultural-production processes, and for exploration of how heritage for development is articulated and practised outside of formalised and often Western-led frameworks, and the resultant potentials and problems alike.

It is notable that, despite taking critical positions on some aspects of heritage for development, all of the chapters in the volume highlight a potentially positive role for heritage in development, whether economically through direct benefits from tourism (e.g. Katapidi and Robinson; Huong and Bushell) or establishing intellectual property rights (Waelde et al.), or indirectly by harnessing funding to support community cohesion or through tailoring interventions to make them better suited to local desires and needs (e.g. Pringle and Musisi; Bermeo et al.; Abiti et al.; Cross), by looking to the past to find strategies for responding to future challenges (Hazareesingh; Lane and Sulas; Lamont), or by co-opting heritage discourses and practices to bring Indigenous knowledge into mainstream development practice (Fadeyi). More broadly, contributors highlight the potential for negotiation of the relationship between the past and desired futures to generate a rethinking of how heritage and development, individually and as they intersect, are understood, practised, and experienced (e.g. Melhuish; Giblin et al.; Harrison; Kothari; Chirikure; Labadi). Across the volume four key, overlapping themes emerge that we will engage with here: the coloniality of heritage for development and calls for decolonisation, and related questions of expertise, ownership, and agency.

As outlined above, the introduction to this volume described the colonial histories of both heritage and development and identified problematic colonial continuities in the way heritage is practiced for development today, themes with which many of the contributions engaged. Some highlighted how colonial laws criminalised and repressed expressions of cultural heritage (Pringle and Musisi; Fadeyi), and how development policies have challenged and disrupted cultural practices linked to livelihoods, subsistence, and the relationships between people and the environments in which they live (Melhuish; Hazareesingh; Lane and Sulas; Lamont). However, some chapters also show how engagement with the past as heritage might contribute to identifying and dismantling the influence of colonial power relations in knowledge production in and about development, and the material and institutional legacies of colonialism that characterise it. Heritage for development thus emerges as a way of reclaiming and reframing spaces, symbols and practices associated with progress, to better support well-being in locally meaningful ways (Pringle and Musisi) and may lead to forms of repatriation, restitution and reparation, and potentially decolonial relationships of solidarity (Kothari).

One way in which power relations are reproduced and maintained in the professionalised heritage and development sectors is through the monopolisation of expertise, and power over knowledge production, by the Global North. Contributions show the extent to which this can be replicated in heritage *for* development, whereby northern 'experts' continue to shape the versions of progress for which heritage is mobilised in formerly colonised countries (Huong and Bushell; Melhuish; Chirikure; Labadi). Despite the proclaimed advantages of incorporating heritage into development including better fit to local context, standardised approaches that can be transferred between countries problematically continue to hold considerable appeal (Huong and Bushell; Cross). However, chapters also demonstrated how appeals to heritage can disrupt the established politics of knowledge production in global development, offering a way of decentring dominant understandings of what a good life is by recognising alternative knowledge about valued pasts and futures (Chirikure). Reimagining the role of development and heritage organisations as 'facilitators', rather than experts, may thus enable contributions to meaningful transformation (Harrison).

Questions of power and expertise, and their implication within the coloniality of development are central to the fundamental question of ownership, and whose development and whose heritage is at stake in heritage for development. Contributions to this volume provide many examples of the instrumentalisation and co-optation of heritage for development as determined 'from above', by political parties (Cross), national and local government (Melhuish; Hazareesingh; Giblin et al.), non-governmental and inter-governmental organisations (Katapidi and Robinson; Huong and Bushell; Pringle and Musisi), and private businesses (Waelde et al.). Such approaches have implications for the kind of 'development' that can be achieved, often resulting in unsustainable, exclusive processes, which do not reflect 'local' priorities and are often contested by ostensible 'beneficiaries'. Who is able to benefit from the use of heritage for development, and who defines how it is operationalised, is often shaped by existing hierarchies and divisions, whether those between international tourists and local communities (Katapidi and Robinson; Huong and Bushell), socio-economic divisions within neighbourhoods (Cross), or gender relations at different scales (Hazareesingh; Lamont; Labadi).

However, the contributions also remind us of the agency of 'communities' or groups in contesting and renegotiating their own heritage and development, often destabilising the relationships between power and expertise outlined above, whether by instrumentalising authorised discourses for individual and group gains (Katapidi and Robinson), drawing on legal tools to protect ownership of their intellectual property (Waelde et al.), or creating alternative post-conflict narratives (Bermeo et al.; Abiti et al.). Indeed, the contributions demonstrate the vitality of heritage for development as a dynamic, negotiated and contested cultural production process, something that is very much part of people's everyday lives. In seeking appropriate healthcare (Pringle and Musisi; Fadeyi), trying to keep their neighbourhoods safe (Cross), or preparing food to eat that tastes good (Hazareesingh), people draw on what they value about the past to address challenges and pursue opportunities.

These accounts demonstrate the limitations of a binary construction of heritage as focused on the past, and development as concerned with the future. Instead, they illustrate the extent to which heritage and development are mutually constitutive (Harrison), something which we can better understand through learning from alternative perspectives on the meanings of the concepts and their relationship to each other (Chirikure). However, we are also reminded that the past does not only matter insofar as it shapes desired futures. The separate histories of development and heritage, as scholarly disciplines and bodies of practice and discourse, are inseparable from colonialism. A solidaristic approach to heritage, which acknowledges, explores, and seeks to provide redress for pasts often euphemised as 'difficult', might inform development that seeks meaningful transformation and challenges the relationships, practices, and knowledges that sustain historical injustices today (Kothari). These contributions offer some hopeful possibilities for how this could occur but remind us of the many challenges ahead.

INDEX

Note: Figures are indicated by *italics*. Endnotes are indicated by the page number followed by "n" and the endnote number e.g., 86n9 refers to endnote 9 on page 86.

For Product Safety Concerns and Information please contact our EU
representative GPSR@taylorandfrancis.com
Taylor & Francis Verlag GmbH, Kaufingerstraße 24, 80331 München, Germany

www.ingramcontent.com/pod-product-compliance
Ingram Content Group UK Ltd.
Pitfield, Milton Keynes, MK11 3LW, UK
UKHW020316270926
475702UK00050B/916